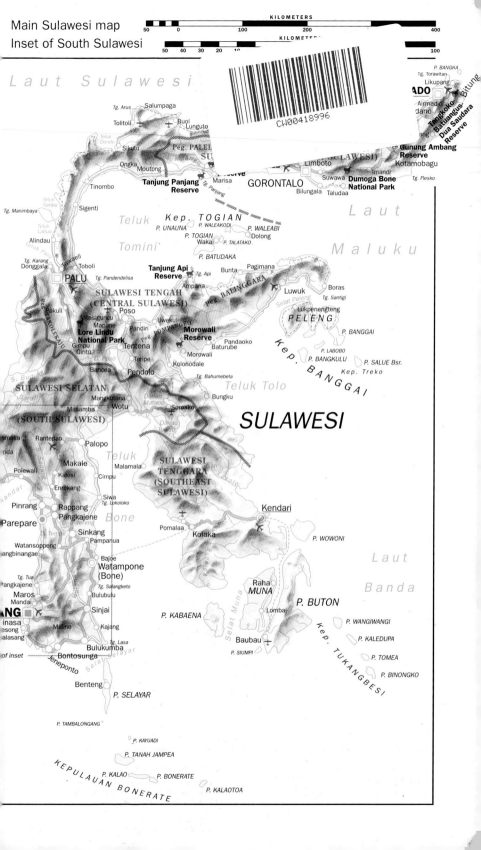

Main Sulawesi map
Inset of South Sulawesi

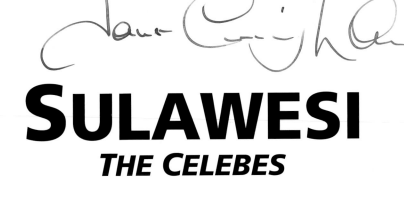

SULAWESI
THE CELEBES

Revised by
Kal Muller

First edition edited by
Toby Alice Volkman, Ian Caldwell
and Eric Oey

PERIPLUS
EDITIONS

Sulawesi

- South Sulawesi
- Tana Toraja
- Central Sulawesi
- North Sulawesi
- Southeast Sulawesi

ISBN 962-593-005-1
Publisher: Eric Oey
Editors, 2nd edition: David Pickell, Mike Cooper
Design: Peter Ivey
Marketing Director: Julian Sale
Cartography: Periplus (S) Pte. Ltd.

INTERNATIONAL DISTRIBUTORS:
Australia *Northern Territory*: Channon Enterprises, 8 Davies Street, Jingili NT 0810; *Victoria & South Australia*: Ken Pryse & Associates, 156 Collins Street, Melbourne 3000; *Queensland*: Queensland Book & Maps, First Floor, 37 Tully Street, South Townsville 4810; *S. Queensland*: Robert Brown & Associates, 67 Holdsworth Street, Coorparoo 4151; *W. Aust.*: Edwards Book Agencies, Unit 4, 48 May Street, Bayswater 6053
Benelux Countries Nilsson & Lamm bv, Postbus 195, 1380 AD Weesp, The Netherlands
France Éditions Sedag, 15 rue de Prony, 92600 Asnières
Germany ILH GeoCenter, Postfach 800830, 7000 Stuttgart 80
Hong Kong and Taiwan Asia Publishers Services Ltd., 16/F Wing Fat Commercial Building, 218 Aberdeen Main Road, Aberdeen, Hong Kong
Indonesia C.V. Java Books, Cempaka Putih Permai C-26, Jakarta 10510
Japan Charles E. Tuttle Inc., 21-13, Seki 1-Chome, Tamaku, Kawasaki, Kanagawa 214
Scandinavia Platypus Förlag, Inspektörsgatan 4, 252 27 Helsingborg, Sweden
Singapore and Malaysia Berkeley Books Pte. Ltd., 2A Paterson Hill, Singapore 0923
Thailand Asia Books Co. Ltd., 5 Sukhumvit Road Soi 61, Bangkok 10110
U. K. GeoCenter U.K. Ltd., The Viables Center, Harrow Way, Basingstoke, Hampshire RG22 4BJ
U.S.A. NTC Publishing Group (Passport Guides), 4255 W. Touhy Avenue, Lincolnwood, Illinois 60646-1975

The Periplus Adventure Guides Series

BALI
JAVA
SUMATRA
KALIMANTAN *Indonesian Borneo*
SULAWESI *The Celebes*
EAST OF BALI *From Lombok to Timor*
MALUKU *Indonesia's Spice Islands*
IRIAN JAYA *Indonesian New Guinea*
UNDERWATER INDONESIA
A Guide to the World's Greatest Diving
SURFING INDONESIA *(end 1995)*
BIRDING INDONESIA *(1996)*
WILDLIFE INDONESIA *(1996)*
A Guide to Nature and National Parks
WEST MALAYSIA *and Singapore*
SABAH & SARAWAK *with Brunei Darussalam*

CAPTIONS:
Cover: A Bugis girl dressed in her traditional best. Photo by Kal Muller.
Pages 4–5: Toraja children outside the highland village of Paken. Photo by Deborah Hill.
Frontispiece: Toraja man at a funeral ceremony. His necklace is made of boars' tusks. Photo by Kal Muller.

Contents

Part I: Introducing Sulawesi

INTRODUCTION   15
Toby Alice Volkman

GEOGRAPHY   16
Oddly Shaped Island of
Contrasts
Tony Whitten

   Map: Formation of Sulawesi   16

FLORA AND FAUNA   20
Straddling Wallace's Line
Tony Whitten

PREHISTORY   24
Hunters, Gatherers and
Navigators
Peter Bellwood

EARLY HISTORY   28
Ancient Kingdoms of the South
Ian Caldwell

DUTCH HEGEMONY   32
The Fall of Mighty Makassar
Anthony Reid

INDEPENDENCE   36
The Rocky Road to Nationhood
Anthony Reid

ECONOMY   38
Fisheries, Farms and Forests
Tim Babcock

PEOPLES   42
An Island of Great Ethnic
Diversity
Kal Muller and Toby Alice Volkman

   Map: Language Groups   43

LANGUAGE & LITERATURE   48
A Wealth of Idiom and Ideology
Roger Tol

ARCHITECTURE   50
Pile Dwellings and Saddle Roofs
Roxana Waterson

SHIPS   52
Sulawesi's Archipelagic Fleet
Horst Liebner

ARTS AND CRAFTS   54
Silk, Iron, Bamboo and Gold
Toby Alice Volkman

FOOD   56
Spicy Rat and Buffalo Cheese
Tim Babcock

Part II: South Sulawesi

INTRODUCTION   61
Toby Alice Volkman

PEOPLES OF THE SOUTH   62
Seafarers, Traders and
Christians
Ian Caldwell

OLD MAKASSAR   66
Cosmopolitan Kingdom
by the Sea
Anthony Reid

UJUNG PANDANG   68
The Gateway to Eastern
Indonesia
Anthony Reid

   Map: Ujung Pandang   69

UJUNG PANDANG AREA   74
Coral Islands, Caves and
Waterfalls
Kal Muller and Anthony Reid

HISTORICAL SITES   80
Reminders of a Royal Past
Ian Caldwell and Anthony Reid

   Map: Old Gowa   80
   Map: Historical Sites   81

WEST COAST   86
The Road North to Parepare
Anthony Reid

   Map: Parepare   86

MANDAR DISTRICT   88
Ship Builders of the Northwest
Charles Zerner

SOUTH COAST   90
Maritime Makassarese
Homeland
Anthony Reid

Map: South Coast   91

TANA BERU   96
Craftsmen on the Brink of Change
Horst Liebner

SELAYAR ISLAND   98
Beaches and an Ancient Drum
Anthony Reid

Map: Selayar Island   99

BONE AND SOPPENG   100
Vanished Bugis Kingdoms
Anthony Reid

LUWU DISTRICT   104
*Land Where the Gods
Descended*
Anthony Reid

Map: Luwu   105

Part III: Tana Toraja

INTRODUCTION   111
Roxana Waterson

HISTORY   112
*Establishing a New
Ethnic Identity*
Toby Alice Volkman and Roxana Waterson

TONGKONAN   116
Elaborate 'Houses of Origin'
Roxana Waterson

RELIGION   120
Aluk: The Way of the Ancestors
Toby Alice Volkman

TAU TAU   126
*Effigies for the
Spirits of the Dead*
Toby Alice Volkman

ROAD TO RANTEPAO   130
*Ascent to the Tana Toraja
Highlands*
Kathleen Adams and Ian Caldwell

MAKALE AND RANTEPAO   132
*The Growing 'Downtowns'
of Tana Toraja*
Kathleen Adams and Nancy Caldwell

Map: Rantepao   133

VISITING TORAJA   134
*Lush Valleys, Tongkonan
and Gravesites*
Kathleen Adams

TREKS   140
*Finding the Hidden Hamlets
of Tana Toraja*
Nancy Caldwell and Kal Muller

Map: Tana Toraja   141

TO MAMASA   142
*Trekking into the Remote
Highlands*
Kal Muller

AROUND MAMASA   145
*New Frontiers in Western
Tana Toraja*
Kal Muller

Part IV: Central Sulawesi

INTRODUCTION   151
Greg Acciaioli

BARKCLOTH   152
*Rare 'Paper' Cloth of the
Highlands*
Lorraine V. Aragon

PALU   154
The Bustling Capital of Sulteng
Greg Acciaioli

Map: Palu City   155

DONGGALA & THE NORTH   156
Old Port and the 'Northern Neck'
Greg Acciaioli and Kal Muller

Map: Palu Area   156

LORE LINDU   159
Exploring the Western Highlands
Greg Acciaioli

Map: Lore Lindu   161

BADA VALLEY   163
*Remote and Rugged
Land of Megaliths*
Kal Muller

POSO AND TENTENA   167
*A Huge and Enchanting
Highland Lake*
Greg Acciaioli and Kal Muller

Map: Poso and Tentena   169

EASTERN PENINSULA   171
'Fire Cape' and Other Rarities
Greg Acciaioli and Kal Muller

Map: Eastern Peninsula   171

Part V: North Sulawesi

INTRODUCTION 179
Tim Babcock

   Map: North Sulawesi 180–181

HISTORY 182
Colonial Stronghold in the North
Tim Babcock

PEOPLES OF THE NORTH 184
Lively, Fun-Loving and
Extroverted
Tim Babcock

MANADO AND BUNAKEN 186
Thriving City and World-Class
Diving
Kal Muller

EXPLORING MINAHASA 190
Extraordinary Day Trips
from Manado
Kal Muller

   Map: Minahasa Area 193

GORONTALO 197
Scenic Drive, Old Forts
and Lake Limboto
Kal Muller

NATIONAL PARKS 199
Visiting the Nature reserves
Kal Muller

MALEO BIRD 203
Sulawesi's Endangered
Megapode
René Dekker

SANGIHE–TALAUD 204
Seascapes and Isolated Islands
Kal Muller

Part VI: Southeast Sulawesi

INTRODUCTION 209
Dinah Bergink

   Map: Southeast Sulawesi 208

KENDARI AND KOLAKA 210
Major Towns of the Southeast
Dinah Bergink, Ian Caldwell and Kal Muller

BUTON 212
Palace of a Powerful Sultanate
Dinah Bergink and Kal Muller

MUNA 214
Stallion Fights and Cave
Paintings
Kal Muller

Travel Primer

INDONESIA AT A GLANCE 218

   Map: Indonesia 218

TRAVEL ADVISORY 219

INDONESIAN LANGUAGE PRIMER 231

TRANSPORTATION 233

   Map: Merpati Routes 234–235

   Map: Pelni Routes 236–237

Area Practicalities

UJUNG PANDANG 242
Ian Caldwell and Kal Muller

SOUTH SULAWESI 248
Ian Caldwell and Kal Muller

TANA TORAJA 252
Ian Caldwell, Nancy Caldwell and Kal Muller

CENTRAL SULAWESI 258
Ian Caldwell and Kal Muller

   Map: Bada Valley Megaliths 264

NORTH SULAWESI 268
Sheridan Angerilli, Kal Muller and Mary
Thorne

   Map: Manado 271

   Map: Sangihe–Talaud 276

SOUTHEAST SULAWESI 279
Ian Caldwell and Kal Muller

FURTHER READING 282
Compiled by Marijke Romeijn

ABOUT THE AUTHORS 283

INDEX 284

PART I

Introducing Sulawesi

Like the petals of a windblown orchid, the unruly peninsulas of Sulawesi reach out into the Celebes, Molucca, Banda, and Flores seas. Within its odd, dancing outlines—the product of the collision of ancient continents—are found extraordinary landscapes. Rugged mist-covered mountains, primal tropical jungle, emerald-green rice terraces and deep, mysterious lakes dominate the interior. Along the coast, dazzling coral reefs encircle dormant volcanoes that jut dramatically out of the sea. Stretches of white sandy beach fringed with coconut trees and scattered fishing villages are flanked by rugged limestone outcroppings that might have stepped out of a Chinese painting.

Sulawesi—once known as the Celebes—is home to an amazing variety of peoples. Fishermen inhabit its coasts, catching flying fish, shark, tuna, mackerel, and squid, as well as scores of fish. Sailing and trading peoples, in particular the Bugis, Makassar and Mandar peoples of the south, are renowned for their remarkable wooden sailing crafts and their voyages to destinations as distant as Singapore and Australia.

There are lowland-dwelling peoples who farm wet and dry rice, maize and manioc, sago and vegetables, coffee, cacao, and cloves. Numerous small groups of upland peoples practice slash-and-burn agriculture in the interior. Dispersed along the coasts are the boat-dwelling Bajau, many of whom are now settled on land.

Sulawesi is home to Muslims, Christians, Buddhists, Hindus and Confucians, as well as followers of indigenous religions whose names are unknown. There are dancers, singers, and drummers; weavers of silk sarongs and exuberant *ikat*; pounders of bark cloth; forgers of iron; master architects of houses and sailing vessels.

With its tremendous expanse of coastline, Sulawesi has never been isolated from the outside world. For centuries, its skilled seafarers linked the island to extensive trading networks that brought not just goods but also ideas, practices and people from India, China, the Middle East, and Europe.

In the 1970s the colorful ritual life of Sulawesi's Toraja people was "discovered" by foreign tourists. But this remarkable culture constitutes only a part, albeit a stunning part, of the complex, ever-changing tapestry of the island. From the mysterious megaliths of the Bada Valley to the superb coral gardens near Manado, the island of Sulawesi offers a visual and cultural feast for the traveler with sufficient time and a sense of adventure.

We have divided this book into five parts. Although Sulawesi consists officially of four provinces, a separate chapter has been devoted to Tana Toraja (part of the province of South Sulawesi), in part because it is the area most frequently visited by travelers to Sulawesi, and in part because of the striking cultural differences between the Toraja and other groups in the south. But while Tana Toraja is the area most frequently visited by travelers to Sulawesi, the other regions of the island are equally as fascinating.

We have sought to provide all the practical information a traveler needs to know, while at the same time offering a view of what the island is about: its history, its people, its social and cultural life, its contemporary struggles. The writers of this book, many of whom are experts in their fields, have attempted to convey their enthusiasm for Sulawesi along with a basic understanding of what has happened—and is still happening—on this remarkable island.

—*Toby Alice Volkman*

Overleaf: *The beautiful Toraja highlands. Photo by Deborah Hill.* **Opposite:** *A Bugis girl dressed in her traditional best. Her transparent outer garment is made of silk. In her hands she carries an old and rare* sirih *set made of Ming porcelain pieces held together by gold. Photo by Kal Muller.*

GEOGRAPHY

Oddly Shaped Island of Contrasts

Quite likely the world's most strangely shaped island, Sulawesi with its gangling appendages evokes the image of a drunken spider, or perhaps a scarecrow in a hurricane. The island is composed of a group of elongate land masses thrust together by geological shifts whose repercussions continue to this day. The island's flora and fauna have been greatly influenced by the island's proximity to the Philippines, the Lesser Sundas and the Moluccas, though not to any marked degree by its closest neighbor, Borneo. Yet its natural history is not totally Asian—Australian links can be seen in eucalyptus trees and possums or phalangers.

The total land area of Sulawesi and its adjacent islands is 227,000 square kilometers (87,645 mi), a little smaller than The United Kingdom. The distance from the northernmost island, Miangas (just 90 kilometers or 55 miles south of the Philippine island of Mindanao), to the southernmost, Satengar, is equivalent to a trip from Amsterdam to Moscow—nearly 2,000 kilometers (1,200 miles).

Sulawesi is divided into four provinces of unequal size. South and Central Sulawesi are the largest, at 83,000 sq km (32,000 sq mi) and 68,000 sq km (26,000 sq mi), respectively. Southeast Sulawesi is 36,000 sq km (14,000 sq mi). North Sulawesi, while extending over the greatest linear distance, is so narrow that it occupies only 25,000 sq km (10,000 sq mi), or just 13 percent of the island's surface area.

Turbulent beginnings

About 250 million years ago, the earth comprised two great continents: Laurasia (including present-day North America, Europe and much of Asia) and Gondwanaland (present-day South America, Africa, India, Australia, Antarctica and the rest of Asia). Up until the last decade, the widely accepted view of the geological history of Indonesia and surrounding regions was that the Malay Peninsula, Sumatra, Java, Borneo and western Sulawesi had been part of Laurasia, separate until just recently (geologically speaking) from eastern Sulawesi, Timor, Seram and other islands which had been part of more southerly Gondwanaland.

This picture has changed with the results of new geological work. It now appears that

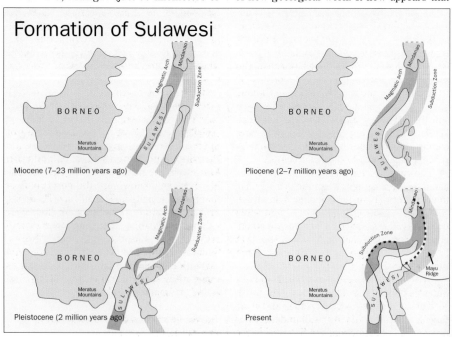

Formation of Sulawesi

Miocene (7–23 million years ago)

Pliocene (2–7 million years ago)

Pleistocene (2 million years ago)

Present

southern Tibet, Burma, Thailand, the Malay Peninsula and Sumatra were actually part of Gondwanaland, and that they rifted from the margin of the Australia-New Guinea part of the continent some 200 million years ago. Western Sulawesi, together with Sumatra, Borneo and other islands, is thought to have separated from Gondwanaland about 180 million years ago. Some 90 million years later, eastern Sulawesi, together with New Guinea, the Moluccas and Australia, broke away from Antarctica, and galloped northward at 10 centimeters (4 inches) a year.

About 15 million years ago, what is now eastern Sulawesi separated from New Guinea and collided with land that is now western Sulawesi, hitting it like a spearhead and causing the southwest peninsula to rotate counter-clockwise. The Gulf of Bone was created between South and Southeast Sulawesi, and the north-pointing northern peninsula pivoted about its tip, rotating clockwise 90 degrees (see map).

It has been suggested that three million years ago western Sulawesi collided with eastern Borneo, closing the Makassar Strait. Hard evidence to support this theory is lacking, but along the northern and deeper parts of the strait, the submarine contours of eastern Borneo do fit neatly into western Sulawesi. Thick sediments in the Makassar Strait indicate, however, that the straits have been open for at least 25 million years.

Sea levels have risen and fallen considerably during the last 10 million years in coordination with the waxing and waning of the Ice Ages. During times when the sea level was low, islands surfaced, particularly in the south. When sea levels were 100 meters (330 ft) lower than today, an almost continuous sheet of land would have stretched between southeast Borneo and southwest Sulawesi. When seas were high, Sulawesi would have comprised a number of islands dissected by straits near Gorontalo and Lake Tempe.

The most recent peak in sea level was about 4,000 years ago, when the sea was five to six meters (16 to 19 ft) higher than at present. Sulawesians tell stories of a time when travelers did not have to sail round the southern tip of Sulawesi, but could take a short cut from the Gulf of Bone to the Makassar Strait through the then brackish Lake Tempe.

Still-active fault lines stretch across Sulawesi—near Gorontalo, from Palu south to Koro, through Lake Matana, and near Luwuk. The main island is still undergoing a process of fragmentation, and Sulawesi in the

distant future could become a cluster of islands separated by narrow straits, like the Philippine archipelago today.

Coasts and reefs

With its several long and narrow peninsulas, Sulawesi has more coastline relative to its land area than any other Indonesian island. No point on the mainland is more than 90 km (56 m.) away from the sea, and most are within 50 km (30 mi). In addition, the four provinces include more than 110 offshore islands with land areas in excess of 1.5 sq km (1 sq mi).

Coral reefs occur around most of Sulawesi's shores. The most accessible (and therefore disturbed) are the 16,000 sq km (6,180 sq mi) of reef in the Sangkarang or Spermonde archipelago. The reefs around Bunaken and neighboring islands off Manado in the north are also quite accessible. Less well-known are the coral reefs of the Togian Islands in Tomini Bay. These are unique in Indonesia because all the major reef environments—fringing, barrier and atoll—can be found around their shores. Sulawesi also boasts some very remote and little-disturbed reefs and shoals, such as those at the extreme end of the Tukang Besi Islands in Southeast Sulawesi.

Above: *The thick canopy of a North Sulawesi forest almost shuts out the day.*

ALAIN COMPOST

Volcanoes and rock formations

Sulawesi is largely mountainous. Most of the island lies above 500 meters (1,650 ft), and fully one-fifth lies above the 1,000-meter mark (3,300 ft). The highest peaks are found in Central and northern South Sulawesi; the island's highest point is on Mt. Rantemario, north of Enrekang, at 3,450 meters (11,200 ft). The climb to the summit is strenuous and very cold. The mountain can be reached from the south, with two nights spent on the slopes.

In South Sulawesi there are several dead volcanoes whose debris has contributed, as in Java, to the fertility of the surrounding plains. The most prominent of these is Lompobatang ("swollen belly"), southeast of Ujung Pandang.

Northern Sulawesi's volcanoes are far from dead. In 1983 a mighty eruption sent a plume of ash 15 km (9 mi) into the sky, with some falling 900 km (560 mi) away in southeast Kalimantan. The explosion blew apart the small island of Una Una in Tomini Bay: fortunately, the Vulcanology Service had predicted a major eruption and all the island's inhabitants were safely evacuated. In 1991 Mount Lokon volcano blew up, killing a Swiss doctor who went up for a close look.

Sulawesi has 11 active volcanoes (Java has 17 and Sumatra 10) and many fumaroles (crevices through which hot vapors issue) and volcanic springs. The majority are in the Minahasa region of North Sulawesi. In the last decade the most troublesome volcanoes have been Soputan-Aeseput, Lokon-Empung, and Gunung Api Siau on the island of Siau, between the mainland and Sangihe Island. Sangihe Island's volcano, Awu, erupted in 1966, claiming more than 7,300 lives.

These volcanoes are active because the seabed north of Tolitoli and east of Minahasa and the Sangihe arc is moving toward the northern arm of Sulawesi. Instead of piling up in a crumpled heap, the seabed is forced under the island at an angle of some 60 degrees. The enormous forces and friction involved produces earthquakes and heat so intense that the rocks melt. The molten stone generally cools down way beneath the earth's surface. But on occasion it is forced up through a weakness in the crust, and the volcano above it erupts.

Parts of Sulawesi (in the south and southeast) have the greatest extent of ultrabasic rocks in the world. These rocks yield notoriously infertile soils, due to high levels of magnesium and heavy metals. The distribution of ultrabasic rock is marked by the boundary between uncultivated and cultivated land (except where overambitious resettlement or agricultural schemes have tried to cultivate land farmers would never touch).

Mineral wealth

Sulawesi is blessed with considerable mineral deposits. Parts of the north are currently experiencing a gold rush, with individuals and small companies using traditional methods of extracting the metal. At the upper end of the scale, joint ventures between Indonesian and foreign companies conduct detailed surveys and state-of-the-art mining.

Petroleum fields have been discovered, but none has yet been exploited commercially. Oil has been found south of the eastern arm of Sulawesi near Luwuk; this area may become a production field in the not-too-distant future. Large reserves of natural gas exist near Lake Tempe. Buton Island off Southeast Sulawesi holds Asia's largest deposits of natural asphalt.

The island's largest mine, at Soroako on the shores of Lake Matana, is situated on a huge deposit of low-grade nickel. Inco, a Canadian-based company, began to construct

Above: *A cascading waterfall in North Sulawesi. The island has no long rivers, but waterfalls are common in the island's limestone hills.*
Opposite: *Mount Lokon near Tomohon in North Sulawesi. The lake here has since evaporated.*

its massive processing facilities here in 1968. The ores in this ultrabasic rock have transformed life in a former village of shifting cultivators, and the once dense green jungle that was their source of livelihood has been razed.

Lakes and rivers

Sulawesi has 13 lakes of more than 5 sq km surface area, including Towuti and Poso, the second and third largest lakes in Indonesia. In the wet season, Lake Tempe rivals Lake Poso in size: surrounded by low-lying land, it can more than treble in area from 10,000 to 35,000 hectares (25,000 to 86,5000 acres). Some lakes, like Tondano and Moat in North Sulawesi, occupy the craters of old volcanoes, while others have been formed by tectonic activity. Some are extremely deep, such as Lake Matana. The bottom of Lake Matana, 540 meters (1,755 ft) from the surface, lies 160 meters (520 ft) below sea level.

The shape of Sulawesi precludes the development of any large rivers such as those found on Sumatra or Kalimantan. The longest river in Sulawesi, the Lariang which flows into the Makassar Strait below Palu, is barely 200 km (120 mi) long.

Climate

Starting in September, cool northwesterly winds pick up moisture while crossing the South China Sea, and arrive in North Sulawesi via the Sulawesi Sea in about November. Similar winds arrive on the west coast of South Sulawesi via the Java Sea in late November or early December. The west coast of central Sulawesi is sheltered from the effects of these winds by the close presence of Borneo, and so is relatively drier.

By April, variable humid southeasterly winds blow toward eastern Sulawesi. Rainfall peaks on the southeast coast occur between then and June, and on the northeast coast sometime later. Southeasterly winds from the now dry and wintery Australian land mass become stronger and drier, influencing Sulawesi's southern tips. Jeneponto in the southwestern peninsula has a long dry season between April and November, while Manado on the northern peninsula experiences a short dry season from August to October.

Areas on the west coast of Sulawesi tend to have their highest rainfall in December, whereas those on the east coast have their wettest month around May. There are areas between these with two dry seasons. Valleys oriented in a north-south direction are in a rain shadow for virtually the whole year. The sheltered nature of the central part of the west coast results in the Palu Valley being one of the driest areas in Indonesia, with yearly rainfall of less than 600 mm (24 in). Here, and on the dry tip of the southwest peninsula, the thriving prickly pear cactus testifies to the severity of the climate.

— Tony Whitten

FLORA AND FAUNA

Straddling Wallace's Line

The great 19th-century naturalist Alfred Russel Wallace was the first to observe that the Indonesian archipelago is inhabited by two distinct sets of wildlife. "Wallace's Line," as this boundary is still known, is drawn between Bali and Lombok and between Borneo and Sulawesi. The birds and mammals of Borneo and Sulawesi are strikingly different, although the islands are not separated by any significant physical barrier. For botanists, the line is less apparent: Sulawesi's plants appear to be most closely related to those of other dry parts of the archipelago.

What little is known of the island's prehistoric wildlife comes from fossils excavated in river sediments in South Sulawesi. Among the finds are an enormous tortoise with a shell two meters (6.5 ft) long, a pygmy elephant and a giant pig. There are also two stegodonts, similar to modern elephants but with curved tusks growing closely together. It is believed that these animals probably swam north to Sulawesi from the Lesser Sunda Islands.

These beasts became extinct thousands of years ago, but even today Sulawesi is noted for its peculiar fauna. Of 127 native mammal species, 62 percent (79 species) are found only on Sulawesi, a figure which rises to an astounding 98 percent if 62 species of bats are excluded. By comparison, only 18 percent of Borneo's mammalian species are endemic. Sulawesi's birds are a bit less distinctive, but still exceptional: 34 percent of the non-migratory species are found nowhere else, the highest figure in Asia except for the island of New Guinea.

Extraordinary mammals

The largest Sulawesi mammal is the dwarf buffalo, or *anoa*. There are two species: one in the mountains with smooth conical horns, and the rough-horned lowland *anoa*. Captive *anoa* sometimes may be seen in villages, but no attempt should be made to approach them. Although they look like small versions of placid water buffalo, they are unpredictable and aggressive, and sensibly feared by locals. *Anoa* are generally solitary but will share a single water spring. They are sometimes shot (illegally) by hunters who know the spots and wait in nearby blinds.

Perhaps the strangest of Sulawesi's mam-

mals is the enigmatic *babirusa,* or "pig deer." The male's upper canine teeth, while initially growing normally, turn upwards so that they pierce the skin and curl around toward (though not quite into) the skull. These tusks appear to be used in fighting, to jab other males. If a *babirusa* can hook his curved upper tusk over an adversary's lower one, the latter is rendered useless and the advantaged male can stab his opponent's throat or face.

Babirusa were kept by early rulers and may have been given as gifts to visiting emissaries. It is likely that some were brought by Bugis traders to Bali, where they may have inspired demonic *raksasa* masks. Interestingly, the *babirusa,* whose hoof is uncloven, is considered *halal* (permitted, or "kosher") by local Muslims.

Tailless monkeys

Sulawesi is home to four species of black or brown tailless macaques, whose ancestors may have arrived from Borneo. All four species live in forests in groups of 15 to 30. They may be seen at the splendid Tangkoko-Batuangas–Dua Saudara Reserve on the northern tip of North Sulawesi.

The tarsier, another local native, is among the world's smallest primates, with head and body length of just 10 cm (4 in), a tail twice as long, enormous eyes, and a weight of just 100 grams. Tarsiers live in family groups consisting of an adult pair and their offspring. Just

before dawn, when they cease their nocturnal perambulations, the entire family sings a complicated territorial call of squeeks and squeals. After the song, the group retires to its nest hole in a tree, a thicket, or in tangles of roots and vines. Tarsiers live in a wide range of habitats including secondary scrub and even urban areas (though humans may not be aware of their presence).

The only other medium-sized mammals in the canopies of Sulawesi's forests are two cuscuses. The slow-moving, dark-brown bear cuscus can be seen during the day feeding on leaves. The dwarf cuscus is nocturnal (hence rarely seen), and feeds on fruit. Both species have a prehensile tail which they use as a fifth limb when climbing from tree to tree.

Dazzling birds

Most remarkable among the 88 bird species found only on Sulawesi are the dark green purple-bearded bee-eater, the brightly colored red-knobbed hornbill, the crowned mynah, the long-tailed white-necked mynah, the black and white piping crow, and the finch-billed starling which nests in hundreds of holes pecked out of dead trees. Several bird species are rare, and the caerulean paradise flycatcher of the Sangihe Islands may

Opposite: *The bear cuscus, a shy and slow-moving leaf-eater.* **Below:** *The rare* anoa, *a dog-sized buffalo, is unique to Sulawesi.*

ALAIN COMPOST

have recently become extinct, its forest habitat having been almost entirely converted to coconut plantations. Sulawesi's most unusual bird is surely the maleo (see "The Maleo Bird," page 203), which incubates its 250-gram eggs in mounds of soil warmed by sunlight, hot springs, or volcanic vents.

Endangered fish

Some of the most remarkable animals in Sulawesi are the residents of the high lakes, such as Matana, Towuti, Mahalona, and Wawontoa. Of the 60 species of crustaceans, snails, and fish unique to those lakes, only one—a shrimp—is found in all four. Each lake appears to have evolved its own fauna. Two other large lakes, Poso and Lindu, share

ALAIN COMPOST

members of a group of fish unknown outside Sulawesi. Unfortunately, species from elsewhere in Indonesia have been introduced for fisheries without regard to the native animals, and some of the latter have become rare, perhaps even extinct, due to competition or newly introduced parasites.

Cave life

Sulwaesi has large areas of limestone around Bantimurung (near Maros), between Lakes Matana and Towuti, and southeast of Lake Towuti. The majority of these areas are rich in caves, some of them among the longest in Indonesia, and most can be explored for some distance without specialized equipment. Commonly encountered residents of

the grottos are swiftlets (small echo-locating relatives of the common swifts) and a variety of bats; there are also scuttling cockroaches, nightmarish spiders, grotesque whip-scorpions and crickets with huge antennae. A hitherto unknown species of blind shrimp was recently found in one of the Bantimurung caves, indicating that it has been there long enough to adapt to total darknesss.

Coconut crabs and giant turtles

The sandy beaches of Sulawesi are used as nesting sites by four species of sea turtle. The largest of these is the enormous leatherback turtle, or *Dermochelys coriacea*, which has a dark brown, ridged carapace (upper shell) up to 2.5 meters (8 ft) long and can weigh up to a ton. It is one of the curiosities of nature that this species feeds solely on jellyfish. It is a strong swimmer and can maintain a body temperature 18 degrees above sea temperature. Individuals migrate over long distances, and though generally limited to the tropics they have been found as far away as the Arctic Circle.

No description of Sulawesi's exotica would be complete without mentioning the famous coconut crab. Once widely distributed throughout the western Pacific and eastern Indian oceans, in Sulawesi the coconut crab is now restricted to small islands, preferably those unblemished by man. What makes this crab stand out in a crowd is his fabled ingenuity and skill in gathering his food. According to legend, the crab scurries up the trunk of a coconut palm, snips off a juicy pod, then dashes it to the ground to crack it open, after which he rips into it with his powerful pincers.While the crabs do actually use their claws to open coconuts, accounts of the tree-climbing bit are not reliable, usually third-hand or second-hand at best. If you catch one in the act, let us know.

Sulawesi is also the home of the world's largest snake, the 10-meter-long reticulated python, which has been known to eat people. Estuarine crocodiles used to be common around the coasts of Sulawesi, as well as in its rivers and some lakes. Not many decades ago, riverside villages had to be protected by sturdy fences to prevent crocodiles from entering at night. In local lore, crocodiles are often associated with the ancestors and are treated with respect.

— *Tony Whitten*

Above: *Sulawesi's endemic Celebes macaque.*
Opposite: *The unique* babirusa *or "pig-deer."*

PREHISTORY

Hunters, Gatherers and Navigators

From the viewpoint of early human history, just as early animal history, the single most important observation about Sulawesi is that it lies within Wallacea, the region of deep water and islands separating the continental shelves of Australasia and Asia. Thus, unlike what was the case for Java, Sumatra, and Borneo, no land bridge connected Sulawesi to the Asian continent during the last ice age

In Java are found remains of Homo erectus as old as around 1,000,000 BC; whereas Australia and New Guinea were not clearly settled until around 40,000 years ago. And although geography suggests that these settlers first came by sea from Asia via Sulawesi and the Lesser Sunda Islands, direct evidence of human occupation in Sulawesi only begins at around 30,000 BC.

This archeological evidence comes from a single cave in the limestone hills near Maros, northeast of Ujung Pandang. Here, some 30,000 years ago, families were collecting riverine shellfish and making fine flakes and blades of chert. Pebble tools and flakes which might be older have been collected from river terraces in the Walanae Valley between Soppeng and Sengkang, together with the bones of extinct giant pigs and elephants, including the important genus *Stegodon*. The age of the Walanae tools is uncertain—the stone tools and animal bones could have been washed together from different sources by river action—and though cruder than those from Maros, they are not necessarily older.

Beginning of the Holocene Period

About 10,000 years ago the present interglacial period—the Holocene—began. In the cave at Ulu Leang in the limestone hills of Maros, deposits dating between 10,000 and 7,000 years have produced thick chunky stone flakes and cores of chert, characteristic of both Indonesia and Australia at this time. The inhabitants of Ulu Leang lived by hunting and gathering. Few traces of their plant foods have survived, but a mound of shells at Paso, on the shores of Lake Tondano in Minahasa, was built up over several centuries from the shells of edible gastropods from the nearby lake. Both sites have produced the bones of wild pigs, together with smaller numbers of bones of *anoa*, monkeys, rodents, birds, tortoises and snakes. Pigs do not appear to have been domesticated until the beginnings of settled agriculture, perhaps as late as four thousand years ago.

Maros points and microliths

About 8,000 years ago, the stone tool industries of the southwestern peninsula of Sulawesi underwent major changes. Small blade tools and microliths made a sudden appearance in the southwest peninsula, as they did at similar dates in the Philippines, Australia, and parts of Java. It is difficult to explain these changes. At present there is no evidence to suggest settlement by a new population in Sulawesi—neither is there any evidence that such tools were made elsewhere in Sulawesi—though possibly improved techniques of stone tool-making, especially for arrowheads and spearheads, were introduced from some unknown outside region.

The Toalean stone-tool industry of South Sulawesi is the most elaborate of these new industries discovered anywhere in Southeast Asia. (The Swiss Sarasin cousins who discovered it in 1902 supposed the Toale people, who still lived in the forests and caves of Camba, to be the physical descendents of the prehistoric stone toolmakers.) Toalean sites occur in caves, rock shelters, and in open locations on slightly raised alluvial deposits near rivers. The best sequence comes from the higher levels of the shelter of Ulu Leang, where small elongated or trapezoidal-shaped microliths appeared about 8,000 years ago and distinctive hollow-based and serrated projectile points ("Maros points") at about 6,000 years.

Other artefacts found in Toalian levels include flakes with an edge gloss that may have resulted from mat or basket manufacture, bone points, and possible bivalve shell scrapers. Like their predecessors, the Toalians also hunted native Sulawesi mammals—tree-dwelling marsupials, macaque monkeys, civet cats, *anoa*, and pigs (both *Sus*

Opposite: *The exquisitely crafted* nekara, *the famous Dongson drum of Selayar, cast in bronze in what is now Vietnam around 200 BC.*

celebensis and the unique Sulawesi *babirusa*).

Paintings of pigs and "hand stencils" (outlines of human hands made by blowing red haematite pigment over a hand placed flat onto a surface) are found in some Toalean caves. The hand paintings are paralleled in the rock art of Australia, and while the Maros examples cannot be dated, they could well belong to the pre-agricultural era marked by the Toalian tools.

The Austronesians

The present inhabitants of Sulawesi speak Austronesian languages introduced to the island from the north, via Taiwan and the Philippines, about 4,000 years ago. The modern population of Sulawesi is part of the southern Mongoloid grouping which today occupies most of Southeast Asia. The current explanation for this major period of human expansion, which affected all the islands of Southeast Asia, is that it was linked to population growth and a need to clear new coastal lands for cultivation, though trade may also have been a factor. Early Austronesian-speakers are known to have been adept canoe builders and navigators—many of them settled the far-flung islands of Polynesia.

The hunters and gatherers who occupied Sulawesi until about 4,000 years ago, and whose archaeological remains have just been described, are presumed to have been of generalized Australo-Melanesian physical appearance, according to the rather slight skeletal evidence which has survived in other parts of Indonesia. We will never be able to trace the languages spoken by these groups, even though some of these populations might still have existed as isolated groups until recent centuries. Many of their genes undoubtedly live on today in the modern inland populations of the island.

The early agricultural pioneers of Sulawesi were few in number, and probably restricted to the coastal regions. The equatorial rain forests and wet climates of interior Sulawesi would not have been favorable to stone-using rice cultivators. Settlement of these areas may not have occurred until well within the last 2,000 years, by which time iron tools were widely available, but rice may have arrived in the island as early as 2,000 BC, since it is known to have been grown in Borneo at this time.

The most important Neolithic site discovered to date on Sulawesi lies close to the Karama River at Kalumpang, inland from Mamuju in the west-central part of the island. Kalumpang has produced a remarkable range of stone adzes, slate spearheads, a stone bark cloth beater (bark cloth was used before loom-woven cloth in Indonesia), and fascinating pottery with fine and detailed geometric ornamentation. Although the Kalumpang find is undatable, similar pottery found in Sabah in East Malaysia is as old as

3,000 years. The Kalumpang assemblage as a whole may be related to that carried by the first Austronesian-speaking settlers of the Pacific islands, bearers of the so-called Lapita culture.

The Bronze and Iron Ages

By about 2,000 years ago the peoples of Sulawesi had learned how to cast bronze and smelt iron. By this time, they would have found themselves on the edge of the zone of Indian influence which was to be so important for Bali and Java. Sulawesi was never "Indianized" to any major extent, and even its coastal cultures may be considered fundamentally Austronesian until the spread of Islam in the sixteenth and seventeenth centuries. However glass, carnelian, and agate beads of Indian inspiration, and in some instances even of Indian manufacture, were imported into the island and are found in the majority of Metal Age sites.

Metal Age artifacts and sites are known from many parts of the island, although these do not so far include any specimens of the massive Vietnamese Dong Son bronze drums which were widely distributed across southern Indonesia from about 2,000 years ago. The closest example in geographical terms is the splendid drum from Selayar Island, with its characteristic friezes of birds and feathered warriors (the latter highly schematic, shown around the middle of the mantle), and its more naturalistic and unique elephants and peacocks. It may have been manufactured in Vietnam in about AD 200; elephants and peacock are unlikely to have been introduced into Sulawesi as early as this.

Another famous bronze object, the large "flask" purchased in Ujung Pandang and now on display in the Jakarta Museum, has stylistic features, including a face mask, which relate it to the massive bronze drum from Pejeng in Bali. Both of these items are probably of local Indonesian rather than Vietnamese manufacture, but whether the flask was actually made in Sulawesi we may never know.

During the first millennium AD the inhabitants of Sulawesi appear to have adopted the custom, common at this time in the Philippines and parts of Borneo, of burying the bones of the dead in pottery jars in caves. Several assemblages of this type are known from the Maros caves in the southwest, but the best-documented one comes from a cave called Leang Buidane in the Talaud Islands northeast of Manado. The mortal remains of the Leang Buidane people were placed in large jars and pottery boxes on the cave floor, and were accompanied into the afterlife by small and finely decorated pots, carnelian and agate beads from India, bronze axes and iron tools, and shell and glass bracelets. These artifacts probably date to some time during the first millennium AD. Sites with

almost identical assemblages have been discovered in coastal portions of Borneo and the Philippines around the Sulawesi Sea, attesting to considerable inter-island trade and contact at this time.

Burial jars and statues

Other well-known archaeological features of Sulawesi include the remarkable *kalamba,* stone burial jars with carved lids which are located in the Lore Lindu National Park in the mountains west of Lake Poso, in the central part of the island. Some of the jars near Besoa and Bada recently investigated by Indonesian archaeologists have yielded pottery and items of iron, and the general context suggests a first-millennium AD date. Near the jars, there are a number of large stone statues up to four meters (13 ft) high, with carved features including headbands, carved flat nipples, and clearly delineated genitalia of both sexes. (See "Bada Valley," page 163.)

When this ancient culture first became known to scholars shortly before the First World War, the megaliths were ascribed to an Aryan, Mediterranean people, who had supposedly wandered through the archipelago searching for gold and pearls. This strange hypothetical people was thought to have brought the art of constructing irrigated terraced paddy fields, of carving in stone, of washing gold and working metals. Today the megaliths are recognised as part of the general Austronesian culture which spread across Indonesia and the Pacific starting 5,000 years ago.

Other large stone monuments of Sulawesi—the circles and rows of standing stone memorial pillars which are found throughout the Toraja region around Rantepao, together with the *waruga,* stone burial jars of Minahasa—are most probably of fairly recent date, although none of these monuments have yet been thoroughly investigated by archaeologists. The *waruga* are generally believed to be associated with Chinese pottery, which was probably not imported into Sulawesi until around AD 1400. The so-called "megalithic" tradition that pervades many Sulawesi cultures is not, however, an easy subject for archaeological investigation, mainly because the structures rarely exist in undisputed association with datable artifacts, as they are not usually buried underground. Nonetheless, the use of upright stones, sometimes carved in human form, is so widespread in the Austronesian world that it is undoubtedly a tradition of great antiquity.

—Peter Bellwood

Opposite: *A stone figure of unknown origin in the Bada Valley stares across the millennia.*
Above: *"Hand stencils" on cave walls near Maros in South Sulawesi, produced by blowing haematite over a hand, may be very old.*

EARLY HISTORY

Ancient Kingdoms of the South

May my mouth be torn open, may my tongue be torn out, may my head be split open should I cause offense. Now he who was called Simpurusia descended into the world and she who was called Patiajala arose also from the foam of the wave; she married Simpurusia, may I not swell…

Thus begins the Chronicle of Luwu, the oldest, and for several centuries the most powerful kingdom in Sulawesi. Simpurusia's name is a corruption of Sanskrit *sinhapurusa*, "lion-man," while his wife's name—also Sanskrit—means "she who trapped her lord in the snares of a net." But Indian influence was slight: unlike Java or Bali, Sulawesi has no great temples or stone inscriptions, and the Indian epics, the *Ramayana* and *Mahabharata*, are completely unknown.

Simpurusia and Patiajala are probably composite figures, the distant memories of ancient rulers, perhaps dating back to the first millenium AD, for Luwu's origins are shadowy. Most historians place its early capital on the Cerekang River, about halfway between Wotu and the sleepy village of Ussu. Here, according to the epic Bugis poem *I La Galigo*, the gods descended to earth to establish the first kingdom in South Sulawesi. The son of the second ruler, Sawerigading, is a great seafarer, and the places he visited are mentioned: Taranate (Ternate in the Moluccas), Gima (Bima on Sumbawa), Jawa Rilau and Jawa Ritengga (East and Central Java). After many adventures he marries Wé Cudai, a princess of Cina, a prehistoric kingdom recently discovered near the mouth of the Cenrana River. And if we accept Luwu's location in the Wotu-Ussu region, awaiting discovery somewhere along the Cerekang River lies her ruined capital, Ware.

Makassar chronicles

The early history of Sulawesi is, in effect, the history of South Sulawesi. There are no known chronicles from the other three provinces dating back to pre-Islamic times. Bugis, Makassar and (as yet unexamined) Mandarese chronicles form our only real sources before the arrival of Dutch traders in the early 17th century. From these chronicles, we learn that 15th century Luwu dominated the entire east and south coast, and the west coast as far as Makassar. Her economy was based on trade. Valuable resins and alluvial gold—and perhaps also slaves—were brought down the pass leading from Rantepao to Palopo (a much more likely location for Luwu's capital) in exchange for fish, salt and weapons. Nickel and iron ore dug from mines near Malili was exported to Java, where even today, a certain type of laminated nickel in the Javanese *keris* is called *pamor* (damascene) *Luwu*.

The origins of the kingdoms of South Sulawesi can be traced to the 13th-14th centuries. This is the limit of the written sources, as the Bugis-Makassar script (probably based on a South Sumatran script) was invented around the year 1400. A recent archaeological survey of the landlocked kingdom of Soppeng has revealed a large kingdom dominating much of the central Walanae Valley as early as AD 1200. The capital of this kingdom, called West Soppeng, was on a hilltop seven kilometers (4.2 mi) north of Watasoppeng. More than 2,000 pieces of broken Chinese, Vietnamese and Thai stoneware and porcelain sherds were collected from the site, many dating back to the 12th or 13th century. Away from the wooden palaces and warehouses, at the far end of the hill, lay the graves of her 15th- and 16th-century rulers, some still containing pieces of the blue-and-white Ming jars in which their cremated remains were once placed.

Chiefdoms and conflict

What was Sulawesi like before the arrival of Europeans in the 16th and 17th centuries? The southern peninsula was divided into several large kingdoms, occupying roughly the same areas as the modern *kabupaten* (regencies) which today bear their names. These kingdoms consisted of a number of chiefdoms—28 in the case of Soppeng—each with its own ruler and territory, loosely united round a central "king." The king ruled direct-

Opposite: *18th-century representation of a king of Makassar touring his realm by boat. Europeans at this time would have seen a Sulawesi virtually unchanged for several centuries.*

ly only his own chiefdom; the rest of the territory was administered by his chiefs, an arrangement which at times must have severely limited his power.

Islam did not become an official religion until the 17th century. Sulawesians may have worshipped the sun and moon, as early Moslem graves are oriented east-west rather than north-south as is the Islamic custom. The ruler, seen as the source of fertility, took part in elaborate rituals assisted by his transvestite *bissu* priests, who appear to have originally been, or included, women.

Ruling power was limited to a small hereditary elite, believed to belong to the line of the *tomanurung*, heaven-descended founders of the kingdoms. Purity of descent was jealously guarded, and careful records were kept of the royal families and their marriages. Marriage of a woman to a man of lower status was strictly forbidden under pain of death.

Both women and men could rule. The first historical individual about whom we have any real information is a queen of Soppeng who ruled around the year 1400. A powerful monarch (the chronicle of Soppeng states that she "broke the long and split the broad"), her reign is remembered as a time of prosperity and good harvests. She directed the expansion of wet-rice agriculture along the southern edge of Lake Tempe, to which settlers flocked "as ants to sugar."

The 15th century saw an important shift from trade to wet-rice agriculture as the basis of political power. Several rulers are remembered as having "taken an interest in agriculture." Luwu, which had little agricultural land (her staple food was sago) was challenged by Bone, situated on a large and fertile plain. Three times in the 16th century the armies of Luwu and Bone clashed. On the third occasion, Luwu was defeated: her royal umbrella was captured and the ruler of Luwu allowed to flee—on the express orders of the king of Bone—with just 20 of his men.

The rise of Gowa

Bone's great rival was Gowa, 17th-century Sulawesi's most prosperous and powerful kingdom. Gowa's rise was also rapid: in the early 16th century, it was just one of a number of small chiefdoms located on the southwest coastal plain. Through a series of conquests and alliances, by 1600 Gowa (allied with neighboring Tallo) had wrested control of most of the western and southern coasts of the peninsula. A palace coup in 1593 brought Karaeng Matoaya, an ambitious and capable Tallo prince, to the seat of power. Around 1605 he embraced Islam, then proceded to forcefully Islamize the major Bugis kingdoms (with the exception of Luwu, which had accepted Islam in 1603) in a series of battles through which Gowa established itself as the preeminent power on the peninsula.

—Ian Caldwell

De verovering van
MACKASSER

1. Het slaen van d'Elf scheepen tegen d'Stadt Makasser
2. Het Conincklijcke Hooft-Casteel Samboupe
3. dese scheepen maecken met haer Canon d'Straudt-scheou onder welck Favier d'nederlanders Landen
4. menighte van sloepen en boets daer d'nederlanders mede sijn gelandt
5. poort waer ver d'vijandt is geslagen en d'Hollanders sijn ingedrongen
6. een Casteel van macasser
7. d'z op straudt gejaeghde portugesen scheepen
8. Het portugees quartier met menichte van batteryen versien
9. battery van macasser
10. een Schoone rivier die door macasser loopt
11. Scheeps Timmerwerven

Het Noorder Fordt
IOUPANDAN

DEN
o'o Zean

Het Casteel
PANNAKOKE

c. decker. fe.

DUTCH HEGEMONY

The Fall of Mighty Makassar

The Dutch arrived in Asia in 1596 with the aim of seizing Portugal's trade in pepper and spices. Allying themselves with Ternate, the strongest of the spice-island "clove sultanates," the Dutch quickly found themselves leading a predominantly Islamic coalition against both the Portuguese and the Spanish, who had bases in the Philippines.

Within fifty years, this conflict had spread to northern and eastern Sulawesi. In 1617 the Spaniards established a small fort at Manado, which supplied rice to their garrisons in the Moluccas. Attempts to establish the Catholic faith in the populous rice-growing Minahasan area around Lake Tondano met with resistance, and in 1643 local chiefs invited the (Protestant) Dutch to their aid. By 1657 the Dutch had the upper hand in North Sulawesi, as well as in the Moluccas, and had established a permanent base at Manado.

CORNELIS SPEELMAN
Gouverneur Generaal van Nederlands Indien.

The Battle of Makassar

In the southern area of the island, Makassar's importance as a trans-shipment point in the international spice trade had been growing steadily throughout the 16th century. Makassar received an added boost when Portuguese Malacca surrendered to the Dutch in 1641. English, Portuguese, Danish and Gujarati factors had headquarters in Makassar, buying and re-shipping the valuable spices that poured into Makassar from the eastern spice islands.

The Dutch East India Company knew it had to break Makassar if it was to make its attempted monopoly of Moluccan cloves and nutmeg effective, but it might never have succeeded in doing so without the help of neighboring Bone, smarting since 1644 from the humiliation of defeat and subjugation by Gowa. Encouraged by the Dutch Admiral Speelman, Aru Palakka, an outstanding Bugis warrior with a particular grievance against Sultan Hasanuddin of Makassar, gathered a large Bugis army, and in 1666 the joint war against Makassar began. Makassar was defeated at Buton, then Bantaeng, and finally at Galesong and Barombong just south of the capital. In November 1667 the Treaty of Bungaya effectively hamstrung Makassar, banning European traders from the city and transferring the fort at Ujung Pandang to the Dutch. In June 1669, fighting broke out again, this time resulting in the total destruction of old Makassar.

The proud aristocracy of Makassar could not reconcile itself to defeat, and time and again attempts were made to reverse it. Many Makassarese fled Sulawesi to fight the Dutch again with the troops of Trunojoyo in East Java or of Banten in the west. Some fled to Siam, where in 1688 they met their demise in the courageous "Revolt of the Makassars" against the growing French colonial presence. In Sulawesi, the first rebel to succeed in uniting the country behind him was Karaeng Bontolangkasa, who seized the throne of Gowa and besieged the Dutch in their fort in 1739. His eventual defeat brought fresh humiliation and destruction. A new rebellion, and a new devastation of the Gowa capital, took place in 1778. This long and bitter series of confrontations not only

Overleaf: The conquest of Makassar by combined Dutch and Bugis forces. **Left**: Admiral Speelman, commander of the Dutch fleet. **Opposite**: 19th-century view of Fort Rotterdam in Ujung Pandang.

destroyed all physical trace of old Makassar, but also served to reinforce the conservative aspects of Makassar society. Having been the most ardent borrowers of Western ideas in Indonesia, they were now obliged to identify such ideas with the enemy.

The Bugis diaspora

Initially it was Bone which profited from the new situation. The Dutch were not interested in ruling South Sulawesi, only in preventing their ejection from their Makassar foothold. Bone, which enjoyed the advantage of distance, dominated South Sulawesi until Aru Palakka's death in 1696, bringing fire and sword to districts such as Wajo and Mandar which had remained loyal to Gowa. Even the Toraja, well protected in the fastness of their mountain domains, remember Aru Palakka as the threat which united their villages into a defensive federation.

The people of Wajo, with perhaps the keenest sense of local autonomy of any in pre-colonial Sulawesi, had become active sailors and traders in the last decades of their alliance with Makassar. When Makassar and then Wajo itself were destroyed, many of these traders left the island to seek their fortune in eastern Kalimantan, Malaya, Sumatra or even further afield. Many royal dynasties, like those of Kutai (Kalimantan), Johor and Selangor (Malaya), and Aceh, originated with these late 17th-century emigrants. The Bugis diaspora also provided the basis for reviving Wajo itself. Arung Sengkang La Ma'dukelleng (1700-65), a Wajo aristocrat who had made himself raja of Kutai in Kalimantan, returned in 1737 to liberate Wajo from the Bone yoke. For a century and a half thereafter Wajo was left in freedom to pursue its extensive trade throughout the archipelago. Many of the Bugis now living in Malaya are descendents of Wajo traders. Wajo also acquired a reputation as having the most democratic institutions in the archipelago.

Minahasa and the Dutch

In 1667, the Bungaya Treaty had designated most of Makassar's South Sulawesi dependencies as Bone territory. Makassar's further-flung and more tenuous tributary states were allotted to another Dutch ally, Ternate. (Banggai and Tobungku in eastern Sulawesi remained nominally under the sovereignty of Ternate until 1900, and sent an annual tribute of their fine steel swords.) In 1693, however, Ternate was forced by the Dutch Company to relinquish its slender claims to North Sulawesi.

To make the Dutch presence effective, Robert Padtbrugge, the Dutch governor of Ternate, traveled throughout North Sulawesi in 1677-79. Fort Amsterdam was established in Manado as the main Dutch base, and the Sangir-Talaud islands were conquered. Gorontalo and its twin-state Limbotto made

an agreement with Padtbrugge in 1677, but had to be chastised by a Dutch-Ternate fleet in 1681 for their independent spirit.

Padtbrugge was more successful with the tiny *walaks* (domains) which would later comprise the Minahasa, persuading 24 of them to sign a treaty with the Dutch Company in 1679. These states were obliged by the agreement to send annual deliveries of foodstuffs to the Dutch posts at Manado and Ternate. These eventually became the basis for the Dutch system of forced coffee cultivation in Indonesia in the 19th century.

The rise of colonial power

In the late 18th century, the sway of the Dutch Company had weakened throughout its colony. In the south, Bone became such a threat that it virtually took over the Noorderdistricten (northern administrative region) of Maros and Pangkajene, which the Dutch had attempted to rule since the Bungaya Treaty. Between 1811 and 1816 the British occupied Makassar, Manado and other Dutch possessions including Selayar, Bantaeng and Bira. The British also took arms against those they had earlier encouraged to rebel against the Dutch (Holland was from 1808 an ally of Napoleonic France), as in the case of Bone in the Maros area.

With the Dutch restoration, stability gradually returned. From 1817 Minahasa was firmly part of the Dutch Indies, and one of the few directly-ruled areas outside Java. Its effective conversion to Protestant Christianity was the work of two German Pietist missionaries, Johan Riedel and Johannes Schwarz. During the 19th century, the Netherlands Missionary Society (NZG) also developed an effective education system in the region, using the Malay language as the medium of instruction.

In the south, Dutch control was less secure even in the areas near Makassar which it ruled directly. Only after Dutch troops attacked Bone itself, in 1824-25, was Bone influence eliminated from the Noorderdistricten around Maros, which provided the rice for Makassar.

During the 19th century, improved communications, along with the spread of Singapore-based trade to small ports, made the Dutch increasingly uneasy about the effective independence enjoyed by Gorontalo, Tolitoli, and all the Bugis states. The British adventurer James Brooke, who established his own *raj*, or kingdom (albeit in distant Sarawak), underscored the weakness of the Dutch hold. Through the second and third wars against Bone (1858-60) the Dutch established their sovereignty on Sulawesi, though they still actually ruled only its two opposite extremities.

Dutch rule

Not until the first decade of this century did the Dutch resolve to attempt subjugation of the entire island of Sulawesi, and to make contact with the little-known people of the highlands. Under the aggressive military policy of Governor-General van Heutsz, small mobile military units were sent all over the island, pursuing even the remotest chiefs who refused to submit to the new order. By 1906 all the rulers were obliged to sign a Korte Verklaring (Short Declaration) agreeing to accept all instructions from the Netherlands Indies Government. This victory for the Dutch, however, was achieved at the cost of great bloodshed.

Armed opposition had to be overcome in Donggala, Tolitoli, Gorontalo, Kulawi, and Banggai. Much the heaviest fighting, however, was against the proud and populous Bugis and Makassar states. The Dutch expeditionary force first attacked Bone in July 1905, hoping that its defeat would provoke a general submission. The Bone capital was taken after a bitter fight thought to have cost more than 1,000 lives.

After the city's capitulation, the raja, La Pawawoi was pursued and finally captured in four months of guerrilla warfare. On other fronts, the main Dutch force had moved against Gowa in October 1905, forcing the sultan to flee northwards with his closest followers. The sultan of Gowa made his most important resistance efforts at Sawitto (Pinrang), in alliance with the bellicose La Sinrang, son of the raja of Pinrang. Sultan Husen of Gowa died in December 1906, still in flight from Dutch troops.

Subsequent Bugis resistance was short-lived. A number of leading Luwu aristocrats died in a short but desperate stand on the beach at Palopo in 1906. From Palopo, Dutch columns fanned out in several directions, encountering their stiffest resistance in northern Toraja. There Pong Tiku had established an unprecedented degree of power by wresting control of the newly established trade in coffee and slaves—obtaining in exchange rifles, salt, and foreign produce from the Bugis of Palopo and Sidenreng. The Dutch attacked his base at Pangalla in April 1906, but did not finally capture him until a

year of difficult guerrilla warfare later. He was executed in Rantepao in July 1907. In this manner, many of Sulawesi's hitherto impregnable mountain areas which had withstood all previous assaults from outside were eventually brought within the suzerainty of the Netherlands Indies.

Scholars and missionaries

The success of the Dutch "pacification" campaign made it possible for ethnographers such as the Swiss cousins Sarasin to explore the center of the island, and for Christian missionaries to work among peoples who had been scarcely touched by the Islam which dominated the coasts. Dutch Protestant missionaries entered the Poso area in 1892, and began making converts following the Dutch subjugation of the area. In the Sa'dan Toraja area (modern Tana Toraja), more Dutch missionaries began their holy struggle in 1913, though their efforts did not bear fruit for nearly twenty years .

The 35 years of effective Dutch rule were probably the longest period of peace in Sulawesi's history. The population was mobilized to build the present network of roads and irrigation works. A centralized administration was established. The Governor in Makassar presided over Assistant-Residents in Parepare, Palopo, Watampone (Bone), Majene, Bantaeng and Baubau (Buton), while the Resident in Manado was responsible for Gorontalo, Donggala, and Poso.

Among the directly ruled areas of Sulawesi, Minahasa held a special place. Its people were overwhelmingly Christian in number and better educated than other groups in Netherlands India. Hence they were extensively used as teachers and clerks throughout the colony.

In 1919 Minahasa was rewarded with a part-elected representative council—the *Minahasaraad*. Because of their generally advanced social standing, the Minahasans were later also better represented in the nationalist movement than any of the other peoples of Sulawesi.

Most of Sulawesi was, in theory, indirectly governed using Dutch contracts with coastal rajas as the pretext for controlling the interior—even if most hill people had little more than a trading relationship with the coast. Financial control was firmly in the hands of the Dutch, and the two most powerful thrones in Sulawesi, Bone and Gowa, were left empty. Only in 1931 was it deemed safe to place the son of the last Gowa sultan, Andi Mappanyuki, on the Bone throne. Five years later, the Gowa dynasty was restored to a faded grandeur in Sungguminasa.

—*Anthony Reid*

Above: *Dutch soldiers look on as La Pawawoi, the last Bugis ruler of Bone, is carried to the sedan chair which will take him into exile (1905).*

INDEPENDENCE

The Rocky Road to Nationhood

Even if the modern (and largely Western-educated) Indonesian nationalist movement was little developed outside the two major cities of Sulawesi, the spirit of resistance towards Dutch rule remained strong in many areas. When the lightning Japanese advance on Indonesia began in January 1942, Indonesians in several parts of the island pre-empted them by taking action against Dutch authority. In Gorontalo a committee led by Nani Wartabone seized power several weeks before the Japanese arrival, imprisoning the Dutch community in the local jail. Similar events followed in Luwuk, Tolitoli, and Bone. These independence committees, however, were soon swept aside by the Japanese tide, and the red-and-white Indonesian flag they had proudly raised was banned.

A leading Minahasan nationalist intellectual educated in Zurich, Dr. Sam Ratulangie (1890-1949), was brought from Java to head the propaganda organization Sudara and to "advise" the military in Sulawesi. Following the declaration of independence in August 1945, Ratulangie was appointed by Sukarno as the first Republican Governor of Sulawesi.

The return of the Dutch

Australians troops arrived in Makassar to accept the Japanese surrender on September 21, and in Manado on October 2. They were received enthusiastically by Indonesians, including even the fledgling Republican movement. The efforts of young activists were directed primarily against the Dutch presence, and only when the Australians handed control back to Dutch administration in January 1946 did serious fighting begin. Young nationalists attacked the Dutch units in Palopo (South Sulawesi) and held the town for two days, suffering hundreds of casualties against the better-armed Dutch.

Even in Minahasa, where the Dutch had rapidly set about recruiting new soldiers for the colonial army, there was strong resentment against the unexpected return of colonial attitudes with the returning Dutch. Minahasan units of KNIL (the Netherlands Indian Army) revolted in support of independence on February 14, 1946. The rebels held much of the Manado-Minahasa area for a month, though a settlement was eventually arranged peaceably with the Dutch.

In the south there was very little support for the Dutch return except among Christian and other minorities and a few Bugis aristocrats. After a number of skirmishes with patriotic youth forces, the Dutch arrested Ratulangie, his six principal lieutenants, and the rajas of Bone and Luwu in April 1946. Most of the youth resistance then moved to Java, to return at the end of 1946 with better arms and military training. They were able to launch a very effective guerrilla movement, to which the Dutch responded by embarking upon the harshest campaign of terror anywhere in Indonesia. Between December 1946 and March 1947, at least 3,000 people were killed in the province by the notorious Captain "Turk" Westerling's "special troops."

The struggle for power

In an attempt to compete with the popularity of the revolutionary Republic of Indonesia, the Dutch in December 1946 initiated a federal "State of East Indonesia" (NIT), with its capital in Makassar. The state's first prime minister was the ambitious Makassarese Nadjamoeddin, who tried in vain to get a hearing for the state at the United Nations. He was indicted for corruption in September 1947, having fallen foul of his companions.

Faced with increasing popular opposition, the federal state was dissolved into the unitary Republic of Indonesia on August 17, 1950. In addition to finishing off the Dutch as colonial masters in Indonesia, the victory of the Republic also presaged the end for the rajas who had dominated Sulawesi for centuries. They were so powerful in many areas, however, that initially the government could not do without them.

The most serious conflicts of the period from 1950 to 1965 were inside the military itself. The end of the Indonesian revolution saw a struggle for power within the new army by various groups who had fought the Dutch in Java or in the jungles of Sulawesi. The leader of the discontents in South Sulawesi was Kahar Muzakkar, a Bugis teacher who had been prominent in organizing Sulawesi armed youth in Java. In July 1950 he abandoned his position in the

Indonesian army (TNI) and began a rebellion, periodically interrupted by negotiations. Increasingly it took on both an Islamic and a "locals-first" flavor, and eventually it joined the West Java-based *Darul Islam*, nominally fighting for an Islamic state. In South Sulawesi during the 1950s the government had firm control only over the main cities and the districts of Tana Toraja and Selayar.

Rebellion in the north

North Sulawesi's discontent was more economic than political, centering on the flourishing copra trade and the inefficient efforts of the central government to control and regulate it. The whole of Sulawesi shared the general discontents of the period, partly comprised of regionalism, partly of impatience with the weakness of the government in Jakarta, partly of the excessive expectations the revolution had aroused. On March 2, 1957, 50 leading military and civilian figures in Makassar signed the Permesta Proclamation, the name being an acronym for *Piagam Perjuangan Semesta Alam*—Charter of Inclusive Struggle. At the same time, martial law was proclaimed throughout Eastern Indonesia, on the authority of the Minahasan military commander Ventje Sumual. These prominent signatories denied they were rebels, but sought fundamental changes in the way regional affairs were run.

Within three months, Jakarta had undermined military support for the Permesta movement in the south by creating a military command for South and Southeast Sulawesi under Bugis-Makassar control. Lt. Col. Sumual, the last of a succession of North Sulawesi officers who had dominated military affairs in the island, withdrew to Manado in June. Henceforth Permesta's only secure base was in North Sulawesi. In February 1958 it threw in its lot with the more overt rebellion known as the PRRI, based in Sumatra. Their aim was not only to protect regional interests against Jakarta, but even more to reverse what was seen as a drift toward a more authoritarian communist-influenced government under Sukarno's personal control. It sought and obtained clandestine arms and air support from the United States.

The central government responded with full force. Manado was bombed on February 22, but the government thereafter was busy quelling the Sumatra rebels until May. The TNI invaded North Sulawesi, taking Manado on June 26, though failing to capture the rebel headquarters at Kotamobagu until

more than a year later, in September 1959. Resistance did not finally end until 1961.

In the south, the restoration of government authority was largely the work of Colonel Andi Mohammad Jusuf, a Bugis soldier who had received professional training first at Bandung and then at Fort Benning in the U.S. Appointed local commander in 1959, he made the army both more disciplined and more local in composition. He became a cabinet minister in 1965, and later Minister of Defense. The other factor in the defeat of Kahar Muzakkar was the Siliwangi Division, brought from Java in 1963 to pursue the rebels. Kahar was finally killed in 1965.

Only after peace was restored could the work of development go ahead. Sulawesi got off to a slow start in restoring communications, rebuilding the national infrastructure, and opening the country up to tourism and investment. The development-oriented New Order government of President Suharto, which began in 1966, coincided with the first period of peace in Sulawesi since 1941. Progress in Sulawesi has been rapid since 1970, as evidenced by the new roads and buildings which are being built across the island.

—*Anthony Reid*

Above: *Captain Raymond "Turk" Westerling, whose notorious "special troops" brought terror to the villages of South Sulawesi. His campaign was part of the Dutch "pacification" program.*

ECONOMY

Fisheries, Farms and Forests

Most of the inhabitants of Sulawesi derive their living from the land, the forests, and the sea. Within the region, however, there is much variation in patterns of livelihood, depending to a great extent on geography. North and South Sulawesi are more fertile and wealthier than the Central and Southeast provinces, due to their rich volcanic soils.

Agriculture

The cultivation of food crops—rice, corn, cassava, vegetables and fruits—probably employs more people in Sulawesi than any other occupation. Rice is grown mainly in paddies (rain-fed or irrigated fields), though in some areas dry rice is grown. Rice cultivation is concentrated in the fertile, irrigated southern peninsula, whence a large surplus is exported to other parts of Indonesia.

North Sulawesi also grows much of its own food, but its major agricultural wealth derives from tree crops, in particular coconuts and cloves, but also nutmeg. Veritable fortunes continue to be made from cloves, used largely to flavor Indonesian *kretek* cigarettes, especially in Minahasa. North Sulawesi accounts for some 30 percent of Indonesian clove production, but "clove fever" has been spreading throughout Sulawesi over the last two decades, as even a few trees in one's backyard can provide substantial cash .

Commercial crops, such as coffee in South Sulawesi and cacao in western Southeast Sulawesi, are becoming increasingly important, along with secondary food crops such as soybeans.

Agricultural production in Sulawesi is small-scale, and commercial estates are rare. Most farming is done by individual smallholders on family-owned plots, growing a variety of crops. Livestock is important—South Sulawesi is the third largest cattle-producing province in the country—but breeding and rearing are also small-scale, with only one or two ranch-style operations.

Fish, lumber and mines

Fishing provides a livelihood for a large number of Sulawesi's inhabitants. Much of the coastal fishing is carried out using "traditional" boats and techniques, but modern fisheries and processing facilities are also being established. The most dramatic developments have been the establishment or expansion of coastal (brackish-water) fish and shrimp ponds, particularly in the south. Large fortunes are to be made in freezing shrimp for export to Japan.

Other important natural resources are forestry and mining. With its valuable hardwoods, Central Sulawesi derives important revenues from forestry, while Southeast Sulawesi is a producer of teak. Rattan is another a valuable source of revenue. In the past, logs and rattan were exported unprocessed, but recent government regulations have banned the export of logs and other unprocessed forest products.

Mining is dominated by the Inco nickel mines at Soroako in South Sulawesi, where low-grade ore is partially processed for export; only recently has the operation managed to break even. Nickel ore is also mined at Pomalaa in Southeast Sulawesi, and bitumen for asphalt on the island of Buton. In recent years, gold fever has swept Indonesia and has encouraged a small-scale search for gold, notably in the Bolaang-Mongondow district of North Sulawesi. Deposits of copper in North Sulawesi and a few other minerals offer future prospects of developments.

Limited manufacturing

Despite the area's wealth of important natural resources, manufacturing has contributed only in limited ways to economic development. Small-scale processing of agricultural products and manufacture of foodstuffs is fairly widespread. A large flour mill (using imported wheat) operates in Ujung Pandang, while several factories turning out coconut products—in particular cooking oil—are found in North Sulawesi. Several cement factories and limestone quarries in South Sulawesi take advantage of widespread demand, while a paper mill is found in Gowa to the south of Ujung Pandang. Sugar mills

Opposite: *P.T. Inco's nickel smelting plant at Soroako near Malili on the Gulf of Bone. The Canadian-run mine is one of the world's largest producers of low-grade nickel.*

have recently been constructed in the district of Bone in South Sulawesi.

Sulawesi in general, however, suffers because of its distance from important domestic markets. It has a small local population and high labor costs compared with densely populated Java, the site of most Indonesian manufacturing.

Service industries such as transportation and tourism are becoming more important. With improvements and expansion in the road system, land transport is now light-years ahead of its status in the early 1960s. Air services linking provincial capitals and some of the smaller centers are also well developed.

For centuries Sulawesi has been famous for its sea transport, and the armada of South and Southeast Sulawesi sailboats, most now motorized, still accounts for a substantial proportion of inter-island and local shipping. Tourism is a much more recent industry, for which the government has high hopes. To date, however, tourism has had an impact only in South, and to a lesser extent in North Sulawesi, the only two provinces with any real tourism infrastructure.

The economic future

What does the economic future hold for Sulawesi? To a great extent this will be determined by world commodity prices, as well as by government policy and practice. In the past, the government's role was extremely influential, and development seemed to be synonymous with government initiative.

After a long period of stagnation during the regional rebellions of the 1950s and 1960s, initial emphasis was placed on infrastructure, in particular roads and irrigation systems. Rice cultivation received much attention, since Indonesia was determined to regain, and maintain, self-sufficiency in rice and other food crops. Only since the early 1980s, however, has much attention been given to secondary food crops (cassava, corn, pulses), which are far more suitable than rice in many areas of Sulawesi.

As Sulawesi continues on the fifth of Indonesia's five-year plans, people throughout the country, as well as the government, are beginning to pay greater attention to environmental conservation and sustainable development.

Increased global consciousness is playing a role here, but equally important are the obvious long-term consequences of greedy or technologically inappropriate exploitation. Declining revenue from oil exports means that the prominence of government in economic development will decline, while the private sector—small and medium-sized firms, but mainly the hundreds of thousands of small-holder families—will play a leading role.

—Tim Babcock

PEOPLE

An Island of Great Ethnic Diversity

The extraordinary variety of Sulawesi's landscapes is matched only by the island's great ethnic, cultural and religious diversity. Over half of the 11.5 million Sulawesians counted in the 1985 census inhabit the fertile plains and valleys of the south, while another million cluster around Manado and the adjacent Minahasa district on the island's northeastern tip. Ujung Pandang, the largest city in Sulawesi, is a polyglot of peoples and cultures.

Best known are the coastal and lowland peoples of the south: the Bugis (about 3.5 million), the Makassarese (1.5 million), the Mandarese (half a million), and the highland Toraja (330,000). There are scores of lesser-known groups: the Wana, Mori, Kaili, Taijo, Pendau, Lauje, Kahumamoan, and others of the rugged center; and the Tolaki of the Southeast. In the north, the Minahasans are a large and well-known group, but there are

also the Sangirese, the Bolaang Mongondow, and the Gorontalo peoples.

Names alone do not convey the richness and complexity of the island's cultural life. While each of these groups have both shared and distinctive social forms and expressive arts, there is also great variation. Take language, for example. The Minahasans of the north, who number nearly a million, have a strong sense of ethnic identity, and yet speak half a dozen different (though related) languages. The Mandarese, who live primarily from fishing and trade, and who are often casually grouped with their Bugis neighbors to the south, actually speak several languages (primarily Mandarese and Campalagian). The term "Toraja" (from the Bugis *to riaja*, "highland people") was formerly applied to most non-Islamic peoples of the highlands. But the southern (Sa'dan) Toraja speak a language closer to their Mandarese and Bugis neighbors than to the either the eastern or western Torajan languages. While the Luwurese speak a language closely related to those of their Torajan neighbors, they are considered "Bugis" because of their shared Islamic culture. The "Toraja," for their part, have stressed their Toraja identity in recent years both as a way of countering Islam, and as a means of enhancing their attractiveness for the tourist market.

Outside of urban and official contexts, where *Bahasa Indonesia* is spoken, the traveler is more likely to hear the lively local languages of the island. Many people speak several local languages as well as Indonesian. And if they are ritual specialists, they may even speak some of their "high" poetic forms, rich in metaphor and allusion.

Many of these ancient literary and ritual forms, however, are fast disappearing. Within the last ten years, transcriptions and translations (into Indonesian) of poetic forms of speech have appeared in small books published in Sulawesi (and in a number of anthropology dissertations). Similarly waning is the ability to read the old manuscripts, on which the histories of kingdoms in the south were chronicled in the indigenous script.

A great crossroads

Like so much of Southeast Asia, island Sulawesi has always been open to new ideas

KAL MULLER

Overleaf: *A Toraja displays aristocratic dress and a proud demeanor at a death feast. By Kal Muller.*
Left: *Young Bugis girl at a wedding, wearing distinctive traditional clothing.*

Language Groups

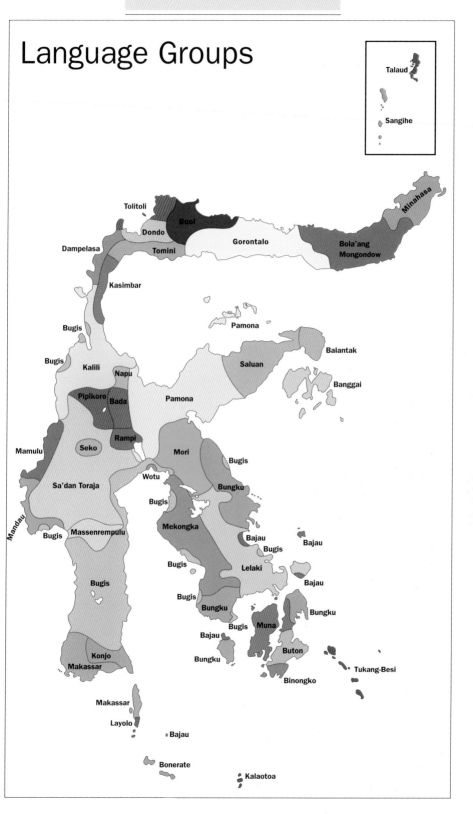

Talaud

Sangihe

Tolitoli

Buol

Dondo

Tomini

Gorontalo

Minahasa

Bola'ang Mongondow

Dampelasa

Kasimbar

Bugis

Pamona

Balantak

Bugis

Kalili

Napu

Saluan

Banggai

Pipikoro

Bada

Pamona

Mamulu

Seko

Rampi

Mori

Bugis

Sa'dan Toraja

Wotu

Bungku

Bugis

Mandau

Bugis

Massenrempulu

Mekongka

Bajau

Bajau

Bugis

Bugis

Lelaki

Bajau

Bugis

Bugis

Bungku

Bungku

Bugis

Muna

Bajau

Buton

Konjo

Bungku

Makassar

Tukang-Besi

Binongko

Makassar

Layolo

Bajau

Bonerate

Kalaotoa

from distant worlds across the sea. This has been true from the time of the ancient Austronesian-speaking agriculturalists and navigators who arrived perhaps as early as 4,000 years ago from the north via Taiwan and the Philippines. In the great age of commerce, the *Pabicara Butta* (prime minister) of Makassar, Karaeng Matoaya, kept a library of European books and studied the latest developments in mathematics and optics. Outside influences were strongest on or near the coasts, and in urban ports and centers, penetrating less directly into the deep forests and high mountains where so many Sulawesian peoples have maintained their distinctive character even unto the present.

As elsewhere in Indonesia, the Chinese in

Sulawesi live mostly in the major cities. There have been Chinese in Makassar and Manado since the 17th century, and today about one percent of the population is Chinese. Although most are now Indonesian citizens, a few thousand were still registered as Chinese nationals (or as stateless) in 1990. Many are Christians, though there are substantial numbers of Buddhists and Confucians as well.

In recent years Sulawesi has also become home to Javanese and Balinese transmigrants, people moved by the government from their overcrowded islands to more sparsely populated and (it is hoped) potentially productive land. Balinese have been migrating to certain parts of Sulawesi since

the early 20th century, and probably account for most of the 47,000 Hindus recorded in the 1980 census. Nearly 54,000 Javanese have settled on the island since 1962.

One large and particulary successful community of Javanese is in Wonomulyo, along the western coast north of Parepare. Some Javanese ply their trades in non-Javanese communities: in Mandar, women sellers of *jamu* (herbal remedies) do a brisk business providing drinks to the fishwives who line the shore each morning, awaiting the day's catch from incoming ships.

Islam, Christianity and *adat*

Although today the majority of Sulawesi's population is Muslim, in the 16th century Portuguese and Spanish spice traders—and their Catholic priests—had extensive dealings with states on the west coast and in the north. In the second half of that century, a number of local rulers in Siang (on the west coast of South Sulawesi), Siau, Manado, and Kaidipan were baptised along with thousands of their followers. In most areas, such conversions were short-lived, particularly after the Portuguese captain of Ternate (in the neighboring Moluccas) murdered the sultan there in 1570. The anti-Portuguese crusade launched by the sultan's son led Gorontalo, Buton, Banggai, and other parts of Sulawesi to convert to Islam.

According to legend, Islam was first brought to South Sulawesi in 1603 by three holy men from the Minangkabau area of Sumatra. They went first to Luwu, then to Makassar (the twin state of Gowa and Tallo). Having converted the ruling elite, they continued on to the southern Bugis kingdoms, including Bone. By 1611 they had persuaded rulers throughout the whole of South Sulawesi, except for the Toraja highlands, to accept Islam.

In fact, Islam (as well as Christianity) had been known in the south long before these dramatic conversions. Malay Muslim traders lived in the south as early as the 15th century, though by the mid-16th century South Sulawesi was one of few important nodes on the inter-island trading network where Islam had *not* yet been officially embraced.

The Islamic conversions of the early 17th century were sweeping but not always smooth. One account describes the inauguration of the first royal mosque in South Sulawesi: On the eve of the Friday prayer (the holiest time of the week), a prince of Gowa slaughtered pigs inside the mosque and smeared their blood across its walls. This act of desecration—the ultimate befoulment in Islamic terms—was ironically carried out by drawing on pre-Islamic sacralization rites of touching pig's blood to persons and places. In Bone and Soppeng there was strong opposition to the new religion from the nobility, and Islam finally entered Gowa only on the edge of a sword.

Today Islam is embraced by 80 percent of the population of Sulawesi. It is Islam of the Sunni tradition with some Shi'ite vestiges, such as festivities to celebrate Maulud, the Prophet's birthday. Throughout the Bugis, Makassarese and Mandarese areas of the south, Kaili, Donggala, Palu, and Tolitoli on the west coast, Gorontalo in the north and Buton in the southeast, the domes of mosques are visible in town and countryside, and the droning call to prayer (now taped and sounded over loudspeakers even in remote villages) awakens villager and visitor alike before dawn each day.

Islam in Sulawesi has been, and continues to be, remarkably flexible. This is not to say that it is not extremely serious, or that its followers are not devout: even the rebellion which began in the 1950s was later cast in ardently Islamic terms. But Sulawesi's Muslims have long found ways of joining their Islamic devotion with local practices associated with ancestors and with spirits of earth, rice and sea. One sees such conjunctions in all kinds of acts: from boat-blessings or healing rites to the esoteric chants of transvestite *bissu* priests; from the magical potency of Thursday night (*malam jum'at*) for spells and charms, to the practice of requesting favors at graves of Muslim saints or ancestors.

Church spires

A visitor to Sulawesi will see not only mosque minarets but church spires. The island's substantial Christian population (17 percent Protestant, 2 percent Catholic) is concentrated in the north (Minahasa and the Sangir-Talaud islands), in the Poso district of the center, and in the southern highlands of Tana Toraja, where a rapid process of conversion has taken place just since Indonesian independence. There are Christian minorities as well in most towns and cities.

In the north, where European presence has a long history—the Portuguese arrived from Ternate in the mid-1500s with priest, and the Spanish followed—the area came under full Dutch control only after 1800, when massive conversions to Protestant

Christianity took place. This conversion was enhanced by the spread of schools: by the turn of the century, there was one school for every 1,000 people in Minahasa, compared to one per 50,000 people in Java. Though the Protestant Church (descended, as in Toraja, from the Dutch Reformed Church) is dominant, scores of other sects and churches are found today. But not all the north is Christian: the Gorontalo and Mongondow people are almost entirely Muslim, the latter having accepted Islam only in the 19th century.

Missionaries of many sorts, including institutions ranging from the Dutch Reformed Church to the Salvation Army, have been active in Central Sulawesi since the late 19th century. Christianity came

KAL MULLER

slightly later to Tana Toraja, where the first Dutch Reformed missionary was killed in 1917 (his successors took a more conciliatory attitude toward traditional ritual). Today, while ritual continues to flourish and draw the public eye, Protestant, Catholic and Pentecostal churches in Toraja still engage in sometimes tense debates about their relationship to local belief and practices.

Nomads of the sea

One of Sulawesi's most interesting groups

Opposite: A Toraja man wearing a boars' tusk necklace during a nobleman's funeral.
Above: A woman from the Bada Valley in Central Sulawesi.

are the Bajau, formerly known as "Sea Gypsies," who for centuries have followed a nomadic way of life aboard their small, broad-beamed boats. The Bajau are actually one of several related groups who have established themselves across the Riau and Lingga archipelagos, around coastal Borneo, and on the east coast of Sumatra.

The provenance of this seaborne people remains conjectural. Since the times of recorded history in Sulawesi, the Bajau have been peripherally connected to Makassarese and Bugis centers of power. The name of the Bajau (pronounced "Bojo" in the Bugis tongue) most likely derives from Wajo, one of the semi-independent Bugis states around bone and Luwu.

Expert sailors and skilled collectors of marine products—notably trepang and tortoise shells—the Bajau supplied much of Sulawesi's export material for the China trade, through Makassarese and Bugis middlemen. They traditionally spent their entire lives upon their boats, disdaining the settled existence of the shorebound peoples with whom they traded to obtain foodstuffs, cloth and a few other basic necessities.

As with most of the world's formerly nomadic peoples, the Bajau have today been tamed by governmental policies, competition from big industry, and international fishing laws. Many of them have been absorbed into the land populations, though groups remain in the Banggai Islands and elsewhere such as the thousand or so who are moored off of the islands outside of Kendari Bay in Southeast Sulawesi. Fishing and gathering are still the source of sustenance for these last semi-nomadic Bajau families. Their handsome craft ride just offshore, ready to weigh anchor for a *trepang* hunt.

Ritual and the spirit world

Sulawesi is probably best known for the tiny percentage of its population which does not count itself as part of a "world" (or officially sanctioned) religion, but continues to practice some form of "animism," a term coined by 19th-century anthropologists. In animist beliefs, the universe is considered to be suffused with and animated by a kind of cosmic energy or life-force.

This energy or potency pervades the world, but it often has nodes in specific places in the landscape—rocks, trees, mountaintops, streams or rainbows—or in the realm of human technology—house rafters, boat navels, ancestral cloths or swords. Power and well-being depend on tapping this energy, drawing it to both the community and individuals through various means including trance-possession, spirit and healing cults, meditation, and a great many other ritual practices, large and small.

Ritual in Sulawesi, as elsewhere in the archipelago, is not only a rich component of a

complex social fabric, but also the means by which health, wealth, and fertility are called forth, assured and displayed. It is also the arena for struggles over power—in the family, the kin group, the community; in the kingdom (now the state) and in the cosmos.

The best-known rituals of Sulawesi are the death rites of the Toraja. These, however, represent just a fraction of Sulawesi's abundant ceremonial life. A ritual may be as simple as an offering bowl of rice and incense placed by a Mandarese fisherman's wife at the house "navel" post, when her husband goes to sea. It may be as dramatic as the launching of a flying-fish boat in the same village, with a profusion of offerings, Islamic prayers, raucous children, and the night-time torching of the *prahu* on the beach. Throughout the island, there is great variation: lavish Bugis, Makassarese, and Mandarese weddings and circumcisions sparkle in brilliantly colored silks; neither of these occasions, however, is ritually elaborated in Toraja.

Rituals in Sulawesi are partly about establishing status. The Toraja funeral is perhaps the most dramatic example, as participants compete to bring the most splendid water buffalo, or to host the greatest number of followers from afar. But status and links with spiritual potency are actually inseparable. The Toraja *maro* ritual, for example, simultaneously demonstrates a family's rank and creates an open field for trance and spirit possession. Even the drummings and summonings of a Wana shaman in the hills of Central Sulawesi are intended not merely to call a spirit and heal a patient but also to create an audience, and thereby enhance the authority of a shaman.

Witnessing traditional rituals

One of the great pleasures of traveling in Sulawesi is the opportunity to be present at rituals—though one of the perpetual frustrations is not understanding what is going on. Nonetheless, just being at a ceremony conducted as an integral, essential part of social life, is a privilege which few Westerners are able to enjoy in their own society. We cannot simply join in a stranger's, or even a neighbor's, wedding on the streets of Manhattan, Paris or London.

Beyond the fascination of access to a world defined by the West as private, the rituals of Sulawesi seem to offer a glimpse of a social world more whole than our own, a world in which rituals do have meaning, in which there is a community larger than the

individuals who comprise it, and in which the sacred is not lost but is heightened.

While in a way all this is true, travelers should remember that too romantic a view of "otherness" may cause one to forget that Sulawesians, like everyone else on this planet, live in the late 20th century. They too are caught up in the crises of this era, in questioning and contesting the meaning of their rituals, the rifts within their communities, the nature of spiritual potency and political power. A Toraja funeral is not simply an unchanged ancestral act—it may well be a hotly debated demonstration of a particular family's claim to status, or a drama highlighting tensions between animists and Christians, or a great performance that will find its way to television screens in Europe and America, and in the process assert the significance of Toraja identity in a vast multi-cultural state.

A traveler's experience in Sulawesi will be considerably enriched by understanding that one is witnessing, maybe even participating in, not endless replays of unchanging perfect rituals, but contemporary dramas which are both personal and political, in which the outcome may be uncertain.

—*Toby Alice Volkman and Kal Muller*

Opposite: *A Konjo horseman equipped with a lariat for catching deer.* **Above:** *Women preparing to pray at a mosque in South Sulawesi.*

A Wealth of Idiom and Ideology

Linguistically, Sulawesi is very complex compared with other parts of Indonesia. No less than 80 separate languages are spoken; Java, by contrast, has just five. Sulawesi's languages all belong to the huge Austronesian language family which stretches in a great island arc more than halfway round the world, from Madagascar on the African coast, to Easter Island in the remote Pacific.

The largest language groups are found in the most densely populated province, South Sulawesi. Five related but distinct languages are spoken here: Makassarese (with 1.5 million speakers in the South, on the island of Selayar and on several smaller islands), Mandarese (300,000 speakers in the northeast region), Sa'dan Toraja (spoken by half a million people in the Toraja highlands), Massenrempulu (200,000 speakers between the Mandar and Sa'dan area) and Bugis, whose 3.5 million speakers make it the largest linguistic group in Sulawesi.

As in other parts of Indonesia, these local languages are gradually being displaced by *Bahasa Indonesia*, the national language of modern Indonesia. Most inhabitants of Sulawesi have at least some knowledge of Indonesian, while a growing number of young people—due to a strict language policy in favor of Indonesian carried out at all levels of education—have Indonesian as their mother tongue. Malay—the ancestor of modern Indonesian—for centuries played a major role in Sulawesi as the language of trade, commerce and religion. Important Malay dialects, including Manado Malay and Makassar Malay, are still spoken in Manado and Ujung Pandang.

The literature of Sulawesi

Written traditions exist only in South Sulawesi and on the southeast island of Buton. Little is known of the latter, written in the Wolio language and consisting mainly of poetry and religious works. Makassarese and Bugis literature (and to some extent Mandarese) have been studied more extensively.

All three reveal a rich literary heritage, written in a syllable-based script which derives from an Indic system. Similar scripts, called *ka-ga-nga*, after their first three characters, were once used as far away as Sumatra and the Philippines, but Bugis, Makassarese

GREG ACCIAIOLI

and Mandarese used the script long after other peoples had switched to Arabic or Roman writing systems. The syllabary, has 23 letters, representing consonants with the inherent vowel *a*, altered by adding dots or dashes. Manuscripts written in this script were originally on leaves of the *lontara'* (papyrus or fan) palm; surviving texts today are mostly on paper.

Writing appears to have developed around 1400, probably based on a South Sumatran script. At least two scripts—the ancestor of the modern South Sulawesi script and the Old Makassarese script—were in use up to the late 17th century.

The first use to which writing was put appears to have been the recording of genealogies. Entries were made in a single line of text on a continuous strip of palm leaf; the strips were then glued or stitched together and rolled into spools which were set in simple wooden frames.

Because of unfavorable climatic conditions, manuscripts of more than one century old are rare. Fire and rats also took their toll. Most of the surviving older manuscripts are preserved in European libraries and the majority of these are copies made for European scholars from borrowed originals. One Scottish administrator, however, who was posted to Makassar in 1810, appears to have made off with a borrowed manuscript of the Bugis romance *I La Padoma*: both the copy he had commissioned and the original were sold to the British Museum in 1846.

Forms of Bugis literature

Makassar and Bugis literature is extremely varied, but can be divided into two basic categories: metric and non-metric. Metric texts include long heroic poems (*tolo'*) in meters of eight syllables. Non-metric texts include myths, histories, king lists, law books, tracts, diaries, genealogies, and wise sayings. There are also a number of prose translations and adaptations from Malay and Arabic literature, and many Islamic legends and tracts.

Both the Makassarese and the Bugis are well known for their tradition of history writing. Every kingdom, big or small, had its own state history, which related the origin of the state, its successive rulers and the events of their reign. These histories are chronologically ordered and unusually reliable. Most of them date from the 17th century, but are based on earlier sources. Supernatural events are rare and reasoned explanations prevail. In the History of Wajo, for example, the

chronicler carefully distances himself from an account of the sale of a tortoise said to excrete gold, and relates with wry humor the disappointment of the buyer who did not get what he expected. Also unusual are the state diaries, daily registers kept by a high official and sometimes by the king himself. In these registers all matters of importance are scrupulously noted down, with the dates often given in both the Muslim lunar and the Julian calendars.

I La Galigo

Few are aware that probably the longest literary work in the world is found in South Sulawesi. This is a vast epic cycle written in Bugis, known as *I La Galigo*. Its size is estimated at approximately 6,000 folio-pages. Set in a meter of five and occasionally four syllables, it relates events from pre-Islamic, 14th century Luwu, the cradle of Bugis culture.

Consisting of dozens of different episodes, each with its own protagonists, and covering several generations, using a wide range of literary conventions such as flashback and foreshadowing, the epic tells the story of the arrival on earth of the gods and the adventures of their descendants. The main protagonist of the story is Sawerigading, the great Bugis culture hero, who travels to remote places and falls deeply in love with his twin sister. This incestuous love is strictly prohibited and Sawerigading ultimately marries another woman. In the end the whole divine family gathers in Luwu and all the gods depart from the earth, having lived there for seven generations.

—*Roger Tol*

Opposite: *Man reciting prayers near Lore Lindu. He is probably requesting help for a healing or recovery of a lost article, or offering thanks for a the resolution of such a problem.* **Above:** *A 19th-century copy of the* Tragedy of La Padoma, *a Bugis romance, somewhat rat-worn.*

ARCHITECTURE

Pile Dwellings and Saddle Roofs

Traditional styles of architecture in Sulawesi share some ancient features found in other parts of the archipelago. Pile buildings with saddle-shaped roofs and outward-sloping gable ends, and gable finials in the shape of crossed horns, are widespread throughout island Southeast Asia. The dramatic forms of the Toraja house, for example, with their impressive bamboo roofs sweeping up to high, arching points, are clearly related to the structures of the Toba Batak and the Minangkabau of Sumatra.

Engravings on bronze-age Dong Son drums (ca. 500 BC—AD 100), made on the Southeast Asian mainland and in Indonesia, show similar pile dwellings with saddle roofs. These are the earliest-known representations of such buildings to have survived, but the style is probably much older. The Dong Son drums were mostly made in what is now Vietnam, and were traded far afield throughout the Indonesian islands. But the influence of Dong Son culture, formerly made much of by archaeologists, was probably too fragmentary and diffuse to account for the spread of a style of architectural construction.

The same style of building can be found even farther away in Micronesia, an area not touched by Dong Son Bronze Age influences. In New Guinea, too, the saddle roof has undergone some amazing elaborations in the forms of men's ceremonial houses. All this points to the conclusion that this unique style of house construction originated with the early Austronesian settlers, whose migrations through the Indonesia and Pacific islands from somewhere on the Southeast Asian mainland began at least 6,000 years ago.

Pile dwellings

Pile building is to be found almost everywhere in Indonesia: carvings from 8th-century Borobudur show houses on piles, although in Java and Bali a shortage of wood in subsequent centuries led to houses being built directly on the ground. In Sulawesi, however, it remains the favored form of building, though Javanese-style brick houses are beginning to appear.

Pile dwellings are remarkably cool, having excellent under-floor ventilation, and offer protection from heavy rains and mud. But a second type of foundation structure, made of heavy logs crossing each other at the corners (much like a log cabin) was typical of Central Sulawesi, as well as in an older and now almost vanished style of Sa'dan Toraja house. This style also appears to be ancient: it is depicted on a bronze age drum from South China, which shows people storing grain in two crossed-log granaries.

The Bugis house

Little survives of older Bugis architectural styles, largely because of the destruction of houses during the troubled 1950s, when older buildings were often linked by Muslim fundamentalists with pagan ways. Formerly, there were at least three house styles, each with a different type of roof line: straight, convex, or saddle-shaped. Today, the typical Bugis house has a straight ridge line, often ending in gable horns at each end. These may be simple extensions of the rafters, or sometimes are more elaborately carved.

Like most traditional houses of Indonesia, the house is symbolically divided into three levels: the undercroft, where animals are sometimes tethered and waste is thrown down from the kitchen; the floor level, inhabited by humans; and the roof space, the most sacred part where heirlooms are stored. These correspond to the underworld, the earth, and the upperworld of traditional Austronesian cosmologies.

Houses are treated as if they were in some sense living entities; the "spirit" of the house is attached at the central pillar, the *posi' bola* ("navel of the house"). It is sometimes spoken of as an abstract force, and sometimes as a personified guardian spirit. Such ideas fit within an indigenous pre-Islamic world view in which everything is considered to be imbued with its own share of a cosmic vital force.

Communal houses of the north

Numerous peoples of Sulawesi formerly lived in enormous houses accomodating several nuclear families. These were built on massive

Opposite: *An old-style pile-built Toraja house with thatched roof.*

piles seven to nine feet high, and had steep roofs to facilitate the run-off of rain water.

Typically, the communal house consisted of a large central room with anywhere from two to five apartments giving off each side. As many as ten nuclear households could occupy one structure, each maintaining its own hearth and rice bins. This type of house has long vanished, however, and the style which is today regarded as "traditional" in Minahasa is actually one which developed in the 19th century.

The Toraja house

In highland South Sulawesi, some of the peoples living north of Tana Toraja also built multi-family houses. Today the To Maki still do. In Central Sulawesi in the early decades of this century, several styles existed, mostly featuring very steeply pitched shingled roofs with carved gable horns.

In the region east of Poso, various types of temple (*lobo*) associated with the traditional religion were formerly to be found. Great changes have been wrought in this area since the turn of the century by Salvation Army missionaries, however, and none of these structures survive.

The most vigorous and spectacular architectural tradition still flourishing in Sulawesi is undoubtably that of the Sa'dan Toraja, whose nobility continue to construct their magnificent saddle-roofed houses, covered with carved and painted panels in red, black, yellow, and white. Some stylistic changes can be noticed in newer houses, namely a preference for ever greater extension of the ridgeline, the eaves ending in a sharper point. This style, now general, was formerly typical only of the Rantepao area, and is actually a recent development.

Surviving older houses have much blunter, shorter eaves than their predecessors, and only a slight curve to the roof; the older houses also tended to be much smaller. Today, house carpenters have increasingly become centralized in Rantepao, and this has also led to some standardization in the execution of the carved patterns which decorate the wall panels.

Economic growth in Tana Toraja since the late 1960s seems to have reversed a trend towards the extinction of these buildings, which today are still regarded as an important index of a family's social standing, and as essential sites for the performance of ceremonies. New wealth has begun to erode traditional social hierarchies, and people who in the past would have been prohibited from building large, carved houses may now, in defiance of the old rules, build themselves much grander houses. Much of the money for rebuilding houses comes from successful migrants who use this as a means of enhancing their family's prestige.

—Roxana Waterson

DEBORAH HILL

SHIPS

Sulawesi's Archipelagic Fleet

Until recently perhaps the world's most impressive fleet of sailing wooden trade vessels were the Bugis *prahus* of Indonesia. Today there are an estimated 800 of these craft engaged in the timber trade from Kalimantan to Java, ranging in size from 120 to 200 or more tons. As many as 200 large *pinisi* may be seen in the port of Sunda Kelapa in Jakarta, while Ujung Pandang's Paotere harbor is lined with smaller boats: copra-carrying *lambo* cutters of Buton; single-masted *pinisi* unloading Kalimantan timber; motor boats from nearby islands laden with passengers and vegetables; and lateen-rigged boats from islands far off in the straits, carrying dried fish to be exchanged for household wares and daily articles.

Gone are the days when large sailing schooners carried trade throughout the Indonesian archipelago, visiting even the small ports in remote islands. Most of today's large *pinisi* ply the waterways between Kalimantan and Java, carrying timber. It is still possible to see a few of them, though, trading among the outer islands, carrying kerosine, cement and household pots and pans. All but a few are motorized: the last of the true *prahu pinisi* of Surabaya, driven by sails alone, sank in 1987.

The age of trade

When Western explorers and traders first came into contact with the archipelago in the 16th century, *prahus* from South Sulawesi were sailing as far as Malacca on the coast of West Malaysia. The Portuguese apothecary Tome Pires, writing during a voyage in Malacca in 1515, recorded that Bugis-Makassar traders "come in their large well-built pangajavas [*pajalas*] with merchandise. They bring many foodstuffs: very white rice; they bring some gold. They take [home] cloths from Cambay and black benzoin in great quantities, and incense."

Local 18th and 19th-century sea charts show routes reaching to the coasts of Indochina and Burma. Sailing regulations and maritime laws of various South Sulawesi kingdoms dating from the early 18th century give fixed costs and schedules for cargo and passengers carried to Malaka in the west, Cambodia in the north, and as far east as Papua New Guinea.

In 1792, the English country-trader Captain Forrest stated: "I have seen, 25 years ago, 15 Prows at a time at Bencoolen [on the west coast of Sumatra], loaded with a mixt cargo of spices, wax, cassia, sandle wood ... and the cloths of Celebes called cambays." Early European settlers on the north coast of Australia were astonished to find Bugis and Makassarese *prahus* collecting *trepang* (sea cucumber, an expensive ingredient in Chinese cuisine) around the coasts of Australia, usually with the help of hardy Bajau "Sea Gypsies." The goods were then sold to Chinese traders in Makassar. Even today, every year some 30 vessels are caught in Australian waters, fishing without licenses, their crews asserting a centuries-old tradition of working the seas on Australia's coastal shelf.

In the 19th century a fleet of 800 *prahu padewakeng* sailed from as far east as Dobu in the Aru Islands to Singapore, bringing back a wealth of goods including cotton cloths, gold dust, birds' nests, tortoise shells, bird-of-paradise feathers, *trepang*, sandalwood, coffee and rice. In his journals, the future rajah of Sarawak, James Brooke, noted: "It is on the return cargo that the Bugis usually make their profits; it consists chiefly of arms, gunpowder, opium and cotton."

The trade routes of past centuries were fixed by the monsoons. With the end of the rainy season in March, ships used the slackening westerlies to sail to the eastern islands of the archipelago, where they collected local products. When the east monsoon started up in April, these goods were exchanged for other commodities along the coasts of Java, Kalimantan, and Sumatra. With the return of the west monsoon in September, sailors returned homeward to dock and refit their vessels during the stormy months of December and January.

Motorization and change

Today's elegant three-masted, eight-sailed Bugis *pinisi* is modeled on the 19th-century

Opposite: *Schooner docked at Paotere Harbor in Ujung Pandang.*

European schooner, which had a carrying capacity of 100-200 tons. If the winds were good, it could sail from Ujung Pandang to Surabaya in three days. Today, they are outfitted with diesel engines.

Motorization has brought considerable changes to the *prahu pinisi*: modern hulls are stronger and much larger, sometimes of up to 500 tons carrying capacity, and the mizzen mast and bowsprits have been shortened. Purists lament the passing of the earlier vessels, which were unquestionably more elegant than the huge "timber tankers" which have replaced them.

Motorization has also brought great changes to the dozen or so traditional centers of trade and shipbuilding in Sulawesi: Bira on the southern coast has been a village of sailors and shipowners for centuries. During the 1930s, some 4,000 men were employed on 300 Bira schooners. Today the harbor is virtually empty, with only a handful of small vessels docking at its shores. Many of today's *pinisi* crews are either Javanese or Madurese, or perhaps Bugis living in the port cities of Surabaya and Jakarta.

The last of the real sailors

The decline of sailing has meant a decline in seamanship, as engines strong enough to hold a fixed course with less fear of the hazards of wind and sea have replaced much of the knowledge formerly indispensable for long voyages. Knowledge of weather and winds, splicing and working ropes, and the maintenance of rigging and sails is no longer taught to youngsters who in former times followed their fathers out to sea as cooks and deckhands at the age of twelve. The ship's course, once set by knowledge of stars, sights, waves, and clouds, is today fixed by compass and chart.

There are still occasional sailors who follow their trade in real sailing ships. Small vessels still go as far abroad as Singapore, where they may illegally exchange birds from Irian Jaya and the Moluccas for consumer goods. Their crews still sail over the whole of Indonesia with two charts only—one for the western part, one for the east—and still rely more upon the stars than upon the small compasses they carry for navigation.

This dying breed of "real" sailors in Sulawesi still retain the traditional knowledge of uncharted reefs off forgotten islands, or of currents between dangerous straits far from the regular trading routes. On board the ships, one experiences the unchanging essence of a millennia-old way of life—lying becalmed on an oily sea before a storm, running with a good wind to an island never visited by anything other than these sailing boats, and gliding with a rising evening breeze into a sunset on the open sea.

—Horst H. Liebner

ARTS AND CRAFTS

Silk, Iron, Bamboo and Gold

From huge wooden boats evocative of Noah's ark, to tiny filigree earrings found on Makassar's street of gold; from boldly patterned *ikat* cloths of Kalumpang to the simple plaiting of a reed rice pouch in Toraja—Sulawesi's arts are almost entirely creations of the hand. As elsewhere in Indonesia, cloth, metal, wood and bamboo are the main resources.

Sulawesi is famous for two dramatically different types of cloth: the delicate checked silks of the south—some so fine that you can draw them through a gold ring—and the magnificent, massive, zig-zag *ikats* of Rongkong and Kalumpang.

Silk has been woven into sarongs by women of South Sulawesi for centuries. Today Soppeng is the center of Sulawesian sericulture, thanks to a project initiated in the mid-1970s with Japanese assistance. Much of the finest silk thread used by Sulawesi's weavers, however, is still imported.

The brilliant colors of modern Bugis silks at once catch the eye: startling juxtapositions (mostly in plaids) of multiple shades of magentas, blues, greens, purples, yellows, indeed every imaginable (and some unimaginable) color combination. Occasionally one finds an exceptionally subtle silk: ivory-colored squares laced, for example, with thin stripes of violet and silver.

In Mandar, home of the most refined silks in the archipelago, typical patterns are small checks, and colors tend to be more somber than the work of the Bugis: dark reds, browns, and indigos. As among the Bugis, natural dyes have been replaced by aniline colors, which are far simpler to prepare.

In both Bugis and Mandar society, silk sarongs are not merely treasured garments for both men and women, but are signs of wealth and status. In the past, certain patterns were restricted to the nobility. This is no longer true, but people still remember pattern-names and ranks.

Silk is not the stuff of everyday life, and silk sarongs are usually worn only at weddings, on Islamic holidays, and sometimes for Friday mosque prayers. It is not unusual in South Sulawesi to see a well-dressed couple zooming by on motorcyle, clad in stunning silks that somehow seem impervious to the dusty road.

All cloth in Sulawesi is made by women, using a backstrap or body-tension loom. The process is complex (spinning, dying, threading the warp, and eventually weaving), and the work is laborious. On the other hand, weaving can be carried out at home, and, if necessary may be stopped at any moment, the loom quickly rolled up and stored.

Traveling through South Sulawesi, it is not uncommon to see women weaving in the shade beneath their house, or on the front porch. In parts of Mandar, every woman wove both silk and cotton a century ago. Now weaving is becoming increasingly rare: other work (fish-trading, for example) is more lucrative. And, as throughout Indonesia, ready-made clothing is now easily available and more popular.

Exuberant *ikats*

Unlike silk, which was and still is produced primarily for clothing, the cotton *ikat* textiles of Central Sulawesi were woven not as garments, but as ceremonial hangings and shrouds. *Ikat*, "to tie," entails tying the pattern into the threads before they are dyed. The knotted sections are covered with a fiber that resists the dye, the design emerging in the woven cloth.

The magnificent *ikats* from the Rongkong and Kalumpang river valleys were originally funeral shrouds. They were also traded to other parts of Sulawesi, and in southern Toraja, they were used as funeral banners.

Both Rongkong and Kalumpang were destroyed in the guerrilla war that raged from 1951-64, but many of the cloths produced there survived in other areas. Today such cloths appear in shops in Rantepao and Ujung Pandang, as local people, encouraged by high prices, sell once-precious family heirlooms. A few spectacular examples of 19th-century cloths survive: these textiles "radiate power" through their monumental vision, precise execution, and their "warm orange glow, like embers in a forge."

Right: *Weavings in the remote Rongkong Valley in Tana Toraja. In the background are handsome Toraja rice barns.*

KAL MULLER

Metalwork

A pairing of cloth and metal is often found in Indonesian ritual, the cloth associated with female, metal with male. In the past, brass and copper ornaments, amulets, and small statues were produced in Central Sulawesi by the "lost wax" (*cire perdue*) casting method. Today this art is no longer known, but metalworking survives in Tana Toraja where a number of iron-forgers still practice the trade using the traditional "Malay bellows."

A unit of paired bamboo pipes is fired from below; the forger sitting above and pumping the bellows with a pair of pistons tipped with chicken feathers. On an anvil, long knives are fashioned from automobile springs and other scrap iron, to be used for purposes both sacred and mundane. Iron has a tremendous historical significance in this region: it is likely that the source of nickel-rich iron ore in Malili was a basis for the greatness of the ancient kingdom of Luwu.

Elegant 18th and 19th-century silver *sirih* (betel nut) sets and the delicate silver *caping* worn by young girls can still be purchased in silver and gold shops along Jl. Somba Opu in Ujung Pandang. The workmanship is exquisite: bold, flower-shaped spittoons, delicately beaten *sirih* servers and silver bowls with embossed floral patterns compete for the eye.

Of all metals, gold is the most highly prized, and in poetry is referred to as the highest good. Village women keep and wear gold if at all possible; in the past only the nobility could do so. In earlier times the gold was often mixed with silver in equal proportions. Modern copies of silver filigree-work from Kendari are also sold along Jl. Somba Opu. Delicately fashioned earrings and pendants, hair pins and bracelets can be purchased either in silver or gold. In some shops, the goldsmiths are working in the back, and you may ask to watch.

Bamboo and basket-weaving

Bamboo containers are used everywhere for transport and storage. These range from a freshly cut green bamboo stem full of frothing *tuak* to a smoke-blackened tobacco container, decorated with fine plaited bamboo strips and a carved wooden lid.

Baskets are woven throughout the island, but the finest examples come from Tana Toraja. The classic Toraja basket, the bamboo *baka,* is carried by a woven tump line across a woman's forehead, the basket supported on her back.

Another classic item which has changed only slightly from earlier times is the conical bamboo hat worn by Toraja women. These hats have an extraordinarily delicate weave. Often sold to tourists, they are still an indispensable possession for every village woman.

—*Toby Alice Volkman*

FOOD

Spicy Rat and Buffalo Cheese

Chances are the visitor will arrive in Sulawesi at Ujung Pandang, the capital of South Sulawesi and a city renowned all over Indonesia for its seafood. Crabs, shrimp, squid, and lobster are prepared here by roasting over charcoal, then served with rice and fresh chili sauce. *Bandeng* (milkfish) or *baronang* (rabbitfish)—popular with foreigners because it has relatively few bones—freshly grilled and dipped in a piquant-sweet sauce, is a truly memorable dish. Poached fish, called *pallumara* in Makassarese, is another tasty method of preparing seafood.

Ujung Pandang is also famous for a dish called *coto Mankasara*—a spicy stew of chopped buffalo innards flavored with a dash of fresh lime and chili sauce. It is normally served in the morning with rice cakes steamed in woven leaf containers.

A unique specialty of the Duri-speaking area of the Enrekang district is *dangke,* a cheese made from buffalo milk, which is sometimes eaten fried. East and Southeast Asian cultures in general traditionally make little use of milk or dairy products; the buffalo-milk cheese of this part of South Sulawesi is a rare exception.

Chili rat

The largely Christian Minahasans of north Sulawesi seem to consider almost no dish to be palatable without a generous addition of *cabe* or chili peppers. Any dish with the words *rica-rica* in its name is likely to be plastered with a *sambal* mixture of hot peppers, tomatoes, onions, garlic and ginger. A further local distinction is a predilection for unkosher dishes including wild rats, bats, and of course pork. *RW* (pronounced "airway," and meaning "fine-haired") is a euphemism for dog.

But fear not: there is food too for the faint of heart. Try delicious charcoal-grilled Manadonese pork *sate*, or fried carp (*ikan mas*), eaten with a hot chili, onion, tomato and lime dip known locally as *dabu-dabu*. Even better (though strangely uncommon in restaurants) is local smoked tuna (*cakalang fufu*) fried or cooked in coconut milk.

Another popular Manadonese dish is *tinutuan* or *bubur Manado,* a thick savory rice porridge mixed with various greens and eaten with bits of fried salt fish. *Milu,* a won-

derfully clear, slightly sour soup made with kernels of young corn, small shrimp, chilis, lime, and other seasoning, is native to the Gorontalo district in western Manado.

An Eden of tropical fruit

Bananas come in all shapes and sizes in Sulawesi, ranging from the tiny *pisang lilin* (candle banana) to the huge *pisang tanduk* (horn banana). Eat them raw, fried in batter, cooked in a sweet, coconut cream stew (*kolak*), or fried in little chips.

Citrus fruits here are also of an abundance unknown in the West: sweet *jeruk siompu* from Buton in Southeast Sulawesi and *limung cina* from Manado are excellent. Mixed with boiling water and plenty of sugar, *jeruk panas* (variously called *air jeruk, jeruk peres,* or *jeruk nipis*) is a marvelous drink, even on a hot day. *Markisa* or passion fruit juice—available in bottles—is great with gin.

Other local specialties include the reddish-purple mangosteen (*manggis*) the huge rough-skinned jackfruit (*nangka*), and the hairy red-skinned *rambutan* (related to the lychee). Exotic creatures like the palmyra fruit (*lontar*), the *salak* or snakefruit, along with papayas, mangos, starfruits, guavas and soursop, round out this cornucopia of tropical delicacies. And then there is the durian.

If you are fortunate enough to be in in Sulawesi during April—the peak of the durian season—you will see stalls piled high with the huge spiky fruit set up along the sides of roads. The smell and the appearance are unmistakable. Approach the durian with an open mind and persist beyond the first attempt at friendship; it is, as they say, "an acquired taste."

Drinks and sweet confections

Sulawesi produces some of the finest *arabica* coffee in the world, but little of it reaches the local market. The coffee drunk in Sulawesi is of the common *robusta* variety, frequently "cut" with maize, and prepared by simply pouring boiling water over fresh grounds and a teaspoonful of sugar in a glass. Or drink it with a dollop of sweetened condensed milk as an after-dinner treat. Unsweetened tea (*teh tawar*) is served everywhere with meals.

No account of food would be complete without mention of *tuak,* or palm wine. *Tuak* is tapped from a variety of palms—the best comes from the flower of the sugar palm (*Arenga saccharifera*). The liquid of the *lontar* palm of the drier regions of South Sulawesi is also quite good, while the sap of the coastal-dwelling *nipah* palm is considered inferior. Good *tuak* is a superb drink, slightly sweet but becoming more potent and acidic as the day progresses. The quality varies considerably—if you are not enchanted the first time, don't hesitate to try again.

Manioc (tapioca) roasted or deep-fried is also a popular snack. There are various kinds of meat-and-vegetable turnovers, called *jalan kote* in the South and *panada* in the North. Numerous *kue,* or cakes, come with an assortment of fillings. Not to be missed are roasted cashew nuts, a major product of the islands of Southeast Sulawesi but also grown in parts of South Sulawesi as well.

In the North, one should look for *halwa kenari*, a candy made of the *kenari* nut coated with local brown sugar, and various other confections such as *bagea*. Other treats are confections of brown palm sugar mixed with coconut or peanuts (*wajik*) wrapped in individual leaf containers. *Eskrim goreng* (fried ice cream) is another Manadonese specialty which should definitely not be overlooked on a gastronomic tour of the region.

The etiquette of eating

To eat in Sulawesi, as in most parts of Asia, means to eat rice. Indeed, in many of the languages of Sulawesi, the word for "rice" is identical to the word "eat."

Food is an important part of hospitality in Sulawesi. Even a very poor family will offer you at least a glass of boiled water, or send someone up a tree to cut a few coconuts. You should ignore what is offered to you until your host has invited you to eat and drink—apart from perhaps making a polite suggestion that your host or hostess should not go to any trouble on your account.

It would be impolite to refuse a host's offering, but then again don't polish off everything put in front of you—you could be eating your way through tomorrow's provisions. Food and drink on such social occasions are a way of initiating friendship and goodwill, and probably not an attempt to appease the appetites of ravenous travelers.

When in Sulawesi, you may be surprised to see someone seated in a restaurant look around the room and gesture for all present to join him in his meal. The invitation isn't meant to be taken literally—it indicates generosity as well as the social nature of eating in this culture.

—Tim Babcock

Opposite: *Dried fish for sale.*

PART II

South Sulawesi

Covering 82,768 square kilometers (51,730 sq mi), an area the size of England, the province of Sulawesi Selatan or South Sulawesi (often referred to as Sulsel), is geographically and culturally diverse. Sulsel possesses a fertile lowland rice bowl—the most densely populated region of Indonesia outside of Java and Bali—as well as towering mountains, an arid southern zone, and an unusually long coastline dotted with fishing villages, where thousands of boats and ingeniously designed traps of rattan and bamboo line the shore.

Southern Sulawesi is home to four major ethnic groups and several minor ones. In the northern reaches of the peninsula, fecund plains and rolling hills give way to 3,000-meter mountains, a region inhabited by some 550,000 people collectively designated as "Toraja," and known locally by a host of other names. The best known of these peoples, the Sa'dan Toraja, derive their name from the great brown river that courses through the mountains. (See Part III: "Tana Toraja.")

Nearly three million Bugis live along South Sulawesi's extensive coastal areas and throughout much of the fertile central lowlands. One and a half million Makassarese are concentrated in the southern part of the the province and around the port of Ujung Pandang, which is the largest city in eastern Indonesia. Along the peninsula's northwestern coastal strip live half a million Mandarese, said to be the finest sailors in all of Sulawesi. These three peoples are renowned throughout the archipelago for their skill and fearlessness as seafarers and (in the case of the Bugis) as colonizers of distant coasts.

The people of South Sulawesi draw their life from the land as well as the sea. Rice abounds in the well-irrigated paddies of the lowland plains, while the province's gently rolling hills yield important crops, including maize, cassava, sesame, pepper, cloves, nutmeg, coffee, cacao, coconuts and bananas. Silk weaving, lake fishing and trade provide additional cash income for many inland farming families.

Rulers in the lowland kingdoms first embraced Islam in the early 17th century, and the people of South Sulawesi are known today for their devotion. In villages one awakens to the hum of small boys and girls chanting the Koran. The chants are repeated daily for years until properly memorized.

Islam in Sulawesi, while important, is generally quite tolerant, and people have found ingenious ways of incorporating elements of older beliefs and practices into their daily lives. There is no contradiction in offering a prayer to Allah and a bunch of bananas to the spirits of the sea.

In the former kingdoms and petty states of Sulawesi, rank and status were paramount concerns, and were carefully demarcated. While the kingdoms no longer exist, the hierarchy of status is still important in the upper levels of society. Language, dress, how and where one sits, the utensils with which one is served, and numerous other cues serve to indicate one's social position.

Weddings, circumcisions, childbirth, and other life-cycle events are celebrated with style in South Sulawesi. Every family attempts to hold the largest, most splendid ceremony it can afford. A large gathering will include crowds of men smoking and drinking coffee under awnings erected outside the house. The women are inside, arranging platters of sticky rice cakes and bananas, or gossiping in the front room, clad in their best silk sarongs, fanning themselves to stay alert in the overpowering heat. The highest compliment that can be paid to a ritual is the word *ramai*, meaning crowded, noisy, and filled with energy and life.

—*Toby Alice Volkman*

Overleaf: *Bugis schooners unloading at Paotere Harbor, Ujung Pandang. Photo: Kal Muller.* **Left:** *A fisherman, the same harbor. Photo: J.-L. Dugast..*

PEOPLES OF THE SOUTH

Seafarers, Traders and Christians

South Sulawesi is home to four major ethnic groups: the Bugis, the Makassarese, the Toraja and the Mandarese. Each of these groups speaks a related but mutually unintelligible language. The Bugis and Toraja languages are quite similar, sharing many common terms, while Mandarese and Makassarese are more distantly related. Each language has numerous dialects, many of which are associated with the kingdoms into which Sulawesi was formerly divided.

Major groups

The Bugis, numbering about 3.5 million, are the most populous of the four peoples of Sulsel. Most Bugis occupy the central area of the peninsula, including the broad, fertile plain between Pinrang and Watampone. Although counted among the most staunchly Islamic populations in Indonesia, the great majority of Bugis, like their Makassarese and Mandarese Muslim neighbors, continue to observe some older, pre-Islamic customs.

The Makassarese, who number about 1,500,000, share close cultural ties with the Bugis. The lands they occupy are generally less fertile (with the exception of very productive land in the vicinity of Maros) and they depend to a greater extent than do the Bugis on the sea for their livelihood.

The Mandarese are also culturally close to the Bugis. About 400,000 Mandarese occupy the less hospitable northwestern part of the peninsula, as far north as Mamuju. Unlike the more prosperous Bugis and Makassarese people, who occupy better land, the Mandarese never developed extensive and centralized kingdoms, but lived in loosely-united and relatively autonomous villages.

The Toraja occupy the northern part of the peninsula, where they are distributed over a large and difficult terrain. They are divided into a number of sub-groups, including the Sa'dan, Rongkong, Seko, Mamasa and Mangki. About 330, 000 Toraja live in the central highlands known today as Tana Toraja, while another 200,000 live in the lowland towns and cities of South Sulawesi. Because they inhabit a mountainous area, the Toraja have insufficent wet-rice land to feed their population, and many make a living by growing coffee, rice and sago.

Social hierarchies

Bugis and Makassarese social life is characterized by a highly formalized class structure. Pre-colonial society was divided into nobles, commoners and slaves. While the nobility tried to maintain the divisions, capable young men could be "recruited" by marriage to a higher-status family.

The most desirable occupation today for a

Bugis is a high-level job as a government employee (*pegawai negeri*). But unlike the Javanese, the Bugis do not consider trade and business inherently low-status occupations. For centuries the Bugis have been known throughout the Indonesian archipelago as traders, pirates and settlers. Crawfurd, an early governor of Singapore, described the Bugis as being among "the most advanced people ... and the most enterprising of all the native tribes of the archipelago." Marsden, in his *History of Sumatra*, mentions their reputation for courage. Today, the Bugis are still regarded as one of the most enterprising and forthright peoples in Indonesia.

The Toraja share few cultural affinities with the Bugis, Makassarese and Mandarese.

Living in the remote mountainous interior, the Toraja were isolated from contacts with the European traders and Islamic teachers who influenced the lowlands and coasts. Not until the 19th century did Dutch missionaries make contact with the Toraja. Since then, some 60 percent have become Christians and 7.5 percent Muslims. The others, especially the older people, have remained adherents of *aluk to dolo*, the traditional religion.

Family

Most people in Sulsel live in small villages. Kinship and marriage is similar to Western patterns: individuals belong equally to their mother's and father's families, and a married couple lives in their own house.

The relationship between father and son is rather formal: it is considered improper for a son to contradict his father. Brothers—having equal status—are often great rivals. In the Chronicle of Tanete, a small west coast kingdom, constant quarrels between brothers cause their father to seek a successor to the throne from neighboring Segiri.

Mothers and daughters enjoy a closer relationship, but the most affectionate relationship is that between brother and sister. According to the Bugis and Makassarese, a brother is the protector and guardian of his sister. This is an important theme in the Bugis epic poem *I La Galigo*, which narrates the separation of Sawerigading and his twin sister Wé Tenriabéng, and their efforts to find one other.

A girl is the symbol of her family's honor. In earlier times, even an accidental meeting between an unmarried girl and a young man could have serious consequences, as custom required that the girl's brother seek vengeance by killing the offender with a dagger. In the tragic poem *I La Padoma*, the hero La Padoma is killed by his lover's brother, who catches them alone in her bedroom. Even today, a male visitor will sometimes cough before entering a house in order to give young women the opportunity to withdraw.

Between the ages of three and seven, most Makassarese and Bugis girls are submitted to clitoridectomy and ear-piercing. Boys are circumcised at ten to fifteen years of age. The feast accompanying the operation is often very elaborate, especially among the higher classes. Filing of the upper incisors and subsequent blackening with varnish, a practice dating back hundreds of years, once took place around the age of puberty for both sexes, but is no longer practiced.

Most marriages are arranged by the parents of the couple, usually with the help of a respected elder. There is a strong preference for marriage with one's relatives; the ideal marriage is between first cousins, but second- and third-cousin marriages are more common. In the competetive, status-conscious societies of South Sulawesi, an ambitious young man with an aggressive personality is a the ideal partner. A girl is supposed to have the complementary personality: obedient and timid. But today many more young people are choosing their own partners, often classmates from their school or university. If a couple cannot obtain their parents' blessing for marriage, they may elope.

Inter-ethnic rivalry is common. For

instance, the Bugis—still the dominant group in South Sulawesi—are quick to point out that Tana Toraja used to be a source of slaves and that today many Toraja work as domestic servants in Ujung Pandang. Their acceptance of such jobs, and their ignominious past as slaves, indicate that the Toraja are of a low rank. According also to Bugis wisdom, the Makassarese are hot headed, inferior farmers, and dubious Muslims. The inhabitants of Jeneponto, a dry and poor area in the extreme south, are the butt of numerous jokes.

—*Ian Caldwell*

Opposite and above: *Bugis children. Numbering over three million, the devoutly Muslim Bugis are the largest of Sulawesi's numerous ethnic groups.*

OLD MAKASSAR

Cosmopolitan Kingdom by the Sea

Generations of travelers have come to Ujung Pandang by sea, and this is still the best way to approach this charming city. The only Indonesian city which actually embraces the sea, Ujung Pandang curls along a narrow strip of beach ridges facing westward to the Makassar Straits. For Joseph Conrad it was "the prettiest, and perhaps the cleanest-looking, of all the towns in the islands."

One feels the sea most strongly on Jalan Penghibur, sipping a drink in one of the kiosks facing the sea, watching the odd fishing boat pass on its way to the islands; in the bustle of the *prahu* harbor at Paotere; or in one of the fish markets. The great mass of Fort Rotterdam dominates the central waterfront, and it is not difficult from its battlements to visualize a Makassarese galley, a Dutch East Indiaman, or Joseph Conrad himself on the bridge of his British trading ship, calling at these same shores.

The modern city stretches ever further inland, the road to the airport now taking the place of the waterfront as the gateway to Makassar. While the modern buildings of the central government and the regional House of Assembly lead the way in urban expansion away from the waterfront, most of the life of the city still remains in its historic heart—the commercial center stretching north of the fort where architectural relics dating back more than 300 years can be seen. Here one feels the pulse of a great Asian city—where Chinese, Indians, Europeans, Japanese, and every manner of Indonesian jostle each other in the streets and shops.

Traders and sea nomads

The city's original name, Makassar (or Mangkasara), is at least as old as the 14th century. In the 16th century it had become Sulawesi's major port and political power, due to the rising influence of the Gowa and Tallo kingdoms, as well as the maritime might of the Bajau "sea nomads."

Malay traders made their home in the city in the 1550s, and the first mosque was reportedly built for them two decades later. The city grew rapidly between 1600 and 1630, by which time it was one of the great trade entrepôts of Southeast Asia.

Tallo and Gowa had their own original centers, where kings were crowned and buried. The trading city and kingdom of Makassar developed between these two semi-sacred centers, and was defended by a series of forts and a long sea wall stretching along the coast. The most important fort was Sombaopu ("homage to the lord") at the mouth of the Jeneberang, which has now been partially restored. Sombaopu contained the elevated wooden palaces of the king and leading nobles, a round mosque, and various warehouses and living quarters. Just to the north of Sombaopu were the Portuguese and Gujerati quarters; to the south of the fort were the market, a large residential area including Ternatan and Makassarese *kampungs*, and the major port area.

After defeats by a combined Dutch/Bugis military force, Makassar was forced in 1667 to surrender the fort of Ujung Pandang, about seven kilometers north of Sombaopu. The Dutch renamed it Fort Rotterdam and made it the base of their operations against the Makassarese. In 1669 Sombaopu was razed, and the Sultan of Gowa was forced to live on the outskirts of the new Dutch town where he could be controlled.

The new Dutch city was a small one, dominated by the imposing figure of Fort Rotterdam. In 1730 the population was only 5,000, half of which were slaves. Company officials and soldiers were lodged in the fort, while the remaining Europeans, Chinese and Christians lived within the small walled city of Vlaardingen. This was bounded by present-day Jalan Nusantara and Jalan Jampea, and stretched north of the fort as far as Jalan Lembeh. At night it was kept locked and guarded. This area is the oldest part of the city, with many surviving 18th-century buildings. Its origins are remembered in the names *Kampung Belanda* ("Dutch village") and *Pintu Dua* ("two gates"), which locals still apply to the area.

Some of the Malay trading community of old Makassar eventually returned to live in Kampung Melayu, just to the north of the walls of Vlaardingen, at the end of the 17th century. A little farther north was Kampung Wajo, where the Bugis traders lived. The Vlaardingen area, gradually becoming more

Chinese in composition, was to remain the commercial center of Makassar until after Indonesian independence in 1945.

During the 19th century the economy of Makassar changed from one based largely on the fort and the slave trade, back to its previous role as a collecting point for all the produce of eastern Indonesia—pearls, sea-slugs, rattan, sandalwood, copra, and the famous "Makassar" oil from the nuts of the *bado* tree, which Western gentlemen of the time used to pomade their hair: whence "anti-makassar."

With its increasingly dynamic economy, Makassar grew rapidly. Estimated at around 15,000 in the early 19th century, Makassar's population reached 84,855 in 1930, and shot up to 708,465 by 1980. In 1938 Makassar had become the capital of a new Dutch super-province called "The Great East," embracing all of eastern Indonesia. The governor's mansion built on Jalan Sudirman was of a palatial opulence appropriate for the ruler of such an extensive territory. During the Second World War the mansion was occupied by the Japanese official responsible for an even larger chunk of Indonesian real estate, which also included Kalimantan. From 1947 to 1950 it was the residence of the president of the state of East Indonesia.

The rapid growth of Makassar in the 1950s, swelled by multitudes of refugees from fighting in the interior of the province, brought about many physical changes in the city. The former moat and parkland behind the fort was filled in to make room for a post office and other public buildings. The swamps and salt-pans which had bounded the city to the northeast were drained to provide a site for Hasanuddin University, officially founded in 1956. The eastward expansion of the urban *kampungs* continued. In the early 1970s many streets in the oldest part of the city were widened, sacrificing the traditional old storefronts to the freer movement of traffic. A vast Chinese and Christian cemetery was moved out of the city and replaced by the present Central Market and the commercial area around it.

Daeng Patompo, the city's mayor during this period of tremendous growth, also increased the area of Makassar by legislation in 1971. Makassar's growth, however, was the loss of neighboring regions like Maros and Gowa. As a concession, perhaps, the name of the city was changed to Ujung Pandang, the name customarily used by the Bugis and Makassarese of the interior. The name Makassar lives on, however, in local titles and organizations, and in the mythic presence of the city's exciting past.

—*Anthony Reid*

Overleaf and above: *Artists' impressions of the "Malay market" in Makassar. The Turkish flavor of the one above suggests that the artist never made it anywhere near the archipelago.*

UJUNG PANDANG

The Gateway to Eastern Indonesia

Ujung Pandang is the largest city and communications center east of Surabaya. It is the focal point not only for the populous province of South Sulawesi, but for the thousands of islands and hundreds of ethnic groups which make up the social fabric of eastern Indonesia. From these islands, people come to Ujung Pandang to trade, study, work, buy supplies, or simply to escape the constraints of village life and to step into a wider world.

At one level Ujung Pandang is a typical Indonesian city, with its government offices, Chinese and Indonesian shops and markets, Muslim and Christian places of worship, and a public life conducted in *Bahasa Indonesia*. You will soon discover, however, that Ujung Pandang is also a microcosm of the eastern seas, and that dozens of languages are spoken in its surrounding *kampungs*. The official government census reveals only the larger language groups in the city. At latest count, in addition to the large proportions of Indonesian, Makassarese, and Bugis speakers, there were 2000 speakers of Javanese, 300 of Sundanese, 380 of Batak, 130 of Minangkabau, and 100 of Banjarese, but tens of thousands in the "others" category which comprises most of eastern Indonesia's myriad languages.

The temples of the Chinese and Balinese are the most obvious signs of Ujung Pandang's cultural diversity; but there are also churches for the Ambonese, Minahasan, Torajan, Batak and Sangirese communities, and mosques favored by Gorontalese, Javanese, Madurese, or Ambonese. Clusters of people from the islands of Selayar, Buton, Tanimbar, Kei, Alor, Bonerate, and Banda live in *kampungs* near the city. In the tourist shops of Jalan Sombaopu you will find carvings from Irian Jaya and eastern Kalimantan, masks from Tanimbar and Bali, bronze drums from Alor, *ikat* weavings from Flores, wooden canes from central Sulawesi, clove ships from Ambon, betel-sets and metalware from the Bugis-Makassar area, Chinese ceramics, and old Dutch, British and·Spanish coins brought in from all over the archipelago. Ask the seamen at Paotere where they hail from, and you will understand how the life-blood of the eastern seas continues to pulse through this great city.

Fort Rotterdam

The massive walls of the waterfront Dutch fortress formerly known as Fort Rotterdam guard fine buildings of the 17th to 18th centuries. Now a museum and cultural center, the so-called "Benteng" now houses offices of the Indonesian Archaeological Service.

The name Ujung Pandang first appears as one of several forts protecting the heart of the Makassar kingdom. The first fort on this site, with earth walls, was built about 1550 under King Tunipallangga of Gowa. This fort was rebuilt in brick in 1634 by Sultan Alauddin to protect the northern suburbs of the city as it then was.

In 1667, it was specified in the Treaty of Bungaya that all the Makassar forts were to be destroyed except two. The king could remain at Sombaopu, though this was also destroyed two years later. The northern fort, Jumpandang, was to become the Dutch headquarters. It was described by the Dutch commander, Admiral Cornelis Speelman as "a strong fortress with a supply of good drinking water and situated in a healthy locality, possessing moreover a suitable harbor where our ships can shelter from almost any wind, so that it might well be termed a bastion of the valuable Easterly Districts."

Under Admiral Speelman the name was changed to Fort Rotterdam (his birthplace) and plans were made to transform it into a well-fortified castle, a center for administration as well as defence. A complete reconstruction in stone was begun in 1673, with a thousand workmen taking several years to complete the walls alone. Stone was brought from Maros, wood from Bantaeng and Tanete, lime from Selayar. The fortifications were completed well before their greatest test in 1739, when the forces of Karaeng Bontolangkasa launched several unsuccessful assaults against them.

Most of the buildings inside the fort were constructed in the late 17th or early 18th century to house the Dutch garrison and the offices of the Governor of Celebes. The Dutch traveler Stavorinus noted in 1775 that the lofty church in the center had been "neatly rebuilt a few years ago, and has room for

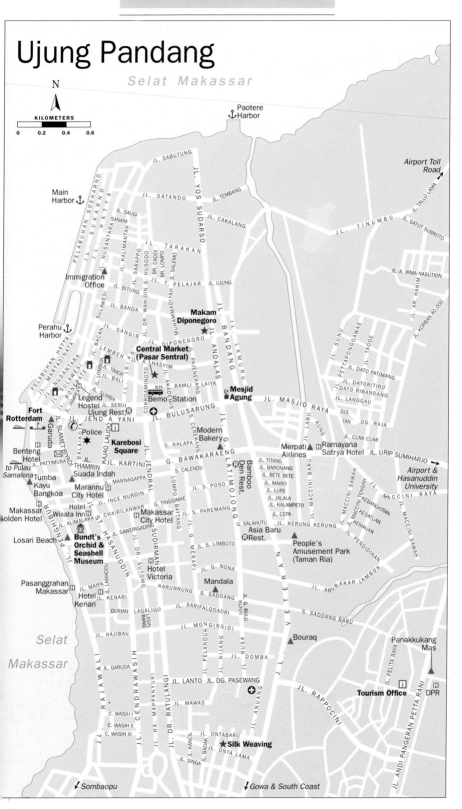

Ujung Pandang

Selat Makassar

N

KILOMETERS

0   0.2   0.4   0.6

Paotere Harbor

Main Harbor

Airport Toll Road

JL. SABUTUNG

JL. SATANDO

JL. TEMBANG

JL. CAKALANG

JL. TINUMBU

JL. GATOT SUBROTO

JL. SAUGI

SANANI

JL. PELABUHAN SOEKARNO

JL. SUKARNO

JL. HATTA

JL. NUSANTARA

JL. KALIMANTAN

TARAKAN

JL. A. IRMA NASUTION

Immigration Office

JL. SARAPPO

JL. BR. CADDI

BR. LOMPO

JL. HUSODO

JL. SALEMO

JL. T. PELAJAR

JL. UJUNG

JL. AR. HAKIM

JL. KORBAN 40.000

JL. BITUNG

JL. SULAWESI

JL. DR. WAHIDIN S.

JL. MUHAMMADIYAH

JL. BANDA

Makam Diponegoro

Perahu Harbor

JL. SANGIR

JL. BACAN

JL. LEMBEH

JL. DIPONEGORO

JL. ANDALAS

JL. BANDANG

JL. LAMURU

JL. SUNU

JL. PETTAPONGGAWAE

JL. TADDE

JL. DATO PATIMANG

Central Market (Pasar Sentral)

KH. HASYIM

JL. DATORITIRO

JL. DATO RIBANDANG

JL. MARTADINATA

JL. TIMOR

JL. BALI

JL. SUMBA

KH. AKADINIS

RAMLI

LAIYA

Mesjid Agung

JL. LANGGAU

Fort Rotterdam

JL. SERUI

JL. COKRAMINOTO

Bemo Station

JL. BULUSARUNG

JL. MASJID RAYA

SUL

TAN

DG. RAJA

Legend Hostel

Ujung Rest.

Police

Modern Bakery

JL. CUMI CUMI

Garuda

JL. SLAMET RIYADI

JL. JEND A YANI

JL. BALAIKOTA

S. CEREKANG

Karebosi Square

JL. KAJAO LALIDO

JL. KARTINI

G. BAWAKARAENG

S. KALAPA

Merpati Airlines

Ramayana Satrya Hotel

JL. URIP SUMIHARJO

Benteng Hotel

to Pulau Samalona

JL. PATTIMURA

JL. THAMRIN

Suada Indah

S. CALENDU

JL. MANNAGAPPA

Bamboo Den Rest.

JL. TITANG

JL. BARONANG

JL. BETE BETE

JL. MAIRO

Airport & Hasanuddin University

JL. MACCINI RAYA

Tumba Kayu Bangkoa

Marannu City Hotel

JL. INCE NURDIN

JL. S. POSO

JL. LURE

JL. JALALA

JL. KALAMPETO

JL. MACCINI BARU

JL. MACCINI SAWAH

JL. MACCINI TENGAH

JL. KEBANGKITAN

JL. KESATUAN

JL. KEMAUAN

Makassar Golden Hotel

Hotel Wisata Inn

JL. CHAIRILANWAR

JL. G. TINGGIMAE

JL. LOMPO BATTANG

JL. S. PAREMANG

JL. CEPA

G. SALAHUTU

Asia Baru Rest.

JL. KERUNG KERUNG

JL. PENDIDIKAN

Losari Beach

JL. ALIMALAKA

JL. SAWERIGADING

Makassar City Hotel

JL. G. MERAPI

JL. S. LIMBOTO

People's Amusement Park (Taman Ria)

JL. ABUBAKAR LAMBOK

Bundt's Orchid & Seashell Museum

JL. SUDIRMAN

JL. SUTOMO

Hotel Victoria

KARUNRUNG

JL. G. NONA

Mandala

S. SADDANG

JL. VETERAN

Pasanggrahan Makassar

JL. MAIPA

JL. LAMADDU

JL. KENARI

DURIAN

LAGALIGO

JL. SARIFALQOADRI

JL. G. BULU KUNYI

S. SADDANG BARU

Hotel Kenari

JL. HAJIBAU

JL. MONGINSIDI

Bouraq

Panakkukang Mas

Selat Makassar

JL. RAJAWALI

JL. GARUDA

JL. CENDRAWASIH

JL. HA. MAPPANYUKI

JL. PELANDUK

JL. KIJANG

JL. RUSA

JL. DOMBA

JL. PELITA RAYA

JL. DPR

JL. DR. RATULANGI

JL. LANTO

JL. DG. PASEWANG

JL. ANUANG

JL. RAPPANG

Tourism Office

DPR

C. WASIH I

C. WASIH II

C. WASIH III

JL. MAWAS

JL. RAPPOCINI

JL. KANCIL

JL. BADAK

JL. ONTABARU

JL. ONTA LAMA

Silk Weaving

JL. SINGA

JL. ANDI PANGERAN PETTA RANI

Sombaopu

Gowa & South Coast

two hundred persons. The seat of the governor is wholly gilt, and is under a canopy, opposite the pulpit."

During the Napoleonic period, when the English under Raffles took over Dutch claims in the Indies, a British detachment was sent to occupy the fort. A contemporary Malay diary recorded that on 26 February 1812 the Dutch commander solemnly surrendered the keys of the fort to commandant Roy Phillips. The (English) ships discharged their guns, all the ships' cannon firing, after which the guns around the fort fired. The (Dutch) Company's flag was lowered and the English flag hoisted on the flagstaff.

Within a few years the Dutch returned, and the range of their power was gradually extended. By the middle of the 19th century, the governor was able to move out of Fort Rotterdam into a more spacious abode (now the police office in Jl. A. Yani, just east of the Grand Hotel). Yet it was not until 1937 that Fort Rotterdam ceased to serve as a military installation, when it was handed over to the Fort Rotterdam Foundation for cultural uses. At the same time, it was listed as a historical monument in the register of the Archaeological Service.

During the Japanese occupation of World War II, the fort was used as a center of scientific research in agriculture and linguistics. After the war an attempt was again made to develop it as a cultural center, but the troubles of South Sulawesi were far from over. The fort was pressed into service as emergency housing for nearly twenty years, making proper maintenance impossible and causing extensive damage. The present restoration began in 1970 when the whole area was again available for cultural purposes.

The fort's original name, Ujung Pandang, can be variously translated as "the furthest visible point" (as seen from the south) or as "Screwpine Cape," from the screwpine or pandanus palm which grew at this point, and was used in making mats. It was also known as Benteng Panyu (turtle) because it looked like a huge turtle crawling to the sea. This creature was seen as a symbol of the Makassarese, who are based on the land but make their living at sea; moreover, the fort protected the people of Makassar, as the turtle's hard shell protects its body.

Construction of the fort

The walls of the fort are about two meters wide and seven meters high, forming a square with protruding bastions at each corner, and a fifth in the middle of the seaward wall, beside the main gate. Each of these bastions is traditionally named after a district or island in eastern Indonesia. The walls and bastions still stand intact except for the southern wall (behind the La Galigo Museum), which was demolished after World War II. At the same time the moat around the fort

was filled in and the two bridges, one to the main gate and the other to the postern gate on the east, were removed. A circuit of the present walls is best made by climbing the stone stairway in the barracks building (now a library) on the eastern side, then turning northwards and continuing around until reaching the seaward side. It is possible to descend in any of the three front bastions.

"Speelman's House," an imposing structure on the left as you enter, is the oldest of the present buildings in the fort, dating from 1686. Speelman himself had left Makassar by then—he became Governor-General of the Dutch East India Company in Batavia in 1681 and died in 1684—but the house did serve as governor's residence for nearly two centuries. The fine floors and doorways are particularly notable.

Unmistakably Dutch in style, the central chapel dates from well into the 18th century. Excavations on the eastern side of the building have revealed the foundations of an earlier building on the site. The present restoration of the chapel has been assisted by financial support from the Netherlands. The peculiar windows in the room on the south end of the building had to be completely rebuilt. It is now used for meetings.

To the east of "Speelman's House" and set at the same angle are the officers' quarters, while the troops lived in the building along the eastern wall—now a library. Before the war, this house contained the library and offices of the Matthes Foundation, now the Cultural Foundation of South and Southeast Celebes. At present it houses a collection of ceramics found in burial sites in South Sulawesi. The buildings between it and the troops' barracks date from the Japanese occupation of the fort.

Farther south along the eastern wall is the council house or main administrative building for the Dutch Company's local affairs. The arcaded porch is particularly elegant. The ground floor of the building served as a prison. Today the offices of the National Archaeological Service are located here.

The long south range of buildings, with its beautiful veranda, is an eloquent reminder that the primary purpose of the Dutch Company was trade. The great halls where the cargoes piled up ready for transshipment to Batavia and thence to Europe now make excellent exhibition areas for the new La Galigo Museum. Among the exhibits are a model of the fort, ethnographic displays, musical instruments, heraldry, reconstruc-

tions of archaeological sites, numismatics, and art objects. An excellent view of the fort is obtained from the dormer windows in the top loft at the eastern end of the building.

Behind the ground floor facade of the building in the southwest corner of the fort is a long, low dungeon sunk deep into the bastion behind and lighted only by a grill giving onto the small anteroom. This is reputed to have been the prison in which the famous Javanese rebel prince, Diponegoro, was held for several years until his death in 1855.

Visiting hours are 7:30-16:00 daily except for Mondays, when the fort is closed. Entry is free on Sundays.

The ports and esplanade

The Makassarese, the Bugis, and the Mandar are the great seafaring peoples of Indonesia. Their craft are remarkable for their sturdiness and grace, as well as for the exceptional skill of the ship-builders who still today fashion heavy ships purely from wood. The many different styles of fishing and sailing boats which ply the seafront in the harbor of Ujung Pandang give the town a unique charm and ambience. From the broad esplanade (Pantai Losari) a great variety of traditional sailing

Opposite: *Fort Rotterdam from the air.* **Above:** *The esplanade at Ujung Pandang, where townspeople regularly come to eat. Every evening foodstalls line the strand for over a kilometer.*

vessels can be seen making their way towards the port.

Among the many types of vessel to be found here are the *prahu pinisi*, the elegant ketch-rigged schooner which has become the symbol of South Sulawesi; the *pantorani*, which has two rectangular sails slung obliquely and is used to capture flying fish; the *lambo*, a stubby, single-masted cargo vessel; the *balolang* and many varieties of *lepa lepa*, sailing boats with outriggers.

There are three *prahu* ports in Ujung Pandang, all accessible only by *becak* or private transport. The busiest and most colorful of these is Paotere, to the north of the town along rough narrow streets. The maze of masts, rigging and brightly-painted *prahus* is picturesque, particularly at dawn or sunset. The scene is particularly lively with fishermen unloading their catch in the early mornings and mid-afternoon. Fish caught in bamboo fishtraps (*bagang*) far out at sea are collected each day in the early hours of the morning and brought into the city markets.

Some of the fishing boats sail with their catch to the fish market (Pasar Ikan, or Palelangan Ikan) on Jl. Rajawali. Here the fish is sold, usually about 6:00–7:00 a.m. and 3:00 p.m. It is worth a visit to appreciate the variety of fish which are spread out in heaps on the concrete floors of the market. They range in size from large swordfish, tuna, octopus, and rays to small prawns and tiny fish like whitebait.

The biggest *prahus* moor in the harbor which lies between the ports of Hatta and Sukarno, off Jl. Martadinata. They carry goods to ports such as Donggala (Central Sulawesi), Ambon, Banjarmasin, Samarinda, Surabaya, and Jakarta. Some will take passengers, but facilities are basic, and passengers and crew often remain on deck for the duration of the trip. The best time for sailing off Ujung Pandang is during the east monsoon, between May and October.

Chinese temples

There are four public temples in Ujung Pandang. The most important is Tian Hou Gong, or "Temple of the Heavenly Queen," on the corner of Jl. Sulawesi and Jl. Serui. It was probably built in the early 18th century, and was restored in 1738, 1803 and 1867.

The statue of the "Heavenly Queen," Tian Hou, to whom it is dedicated, stands at the back of the main altar, behind a wooden partition. Patroness of sailors, she is also associat-

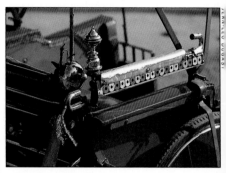

ed with fertility. There are a number of side altars. The first on the left is dedicated to the "Golden Mothers of the Golden Immortals;" the second to Xuan Tian Shang Di, venerated in Indonesia for his medical powers; the third to the Patroness of Fertility. The altars in the courtyard behind are dedicated to various Buddhist divinities.

The Long Xian Gong, or "Temple of the Apparition of the Dragon," at Jl. Sulawesi and Jl. Bali, was built in 1868. The central altar is dedicated to Xian Mu, "Mother of the Immortals;" that on the right to Mi Lo Fo, patron of jewelers; that on the left to Tu Di Gong, god of the soil and of wealth.

The Temple of the Association of Merchants of Guangdong, near the Long Xian Gong, was damaged when the road was recently aligned. It is dedicated to Guan Di, who is the patron of the Guangdong associations. The Chinese used to come here to swear oaths before testifying in court. On the left of Guan Di stand a horse and rider to whom mothers prayed that their children would be obedient. Since 1987 the Chinese community has been permitted to stage lion dances along Jl. Sulawesi during Lunar New Year celebrations (usually late January).

The fourth temple, located on Jl. Lombok,

Above, left: *Stall selling various dishes on the esplanade.* **Above, right:** *Detail of a* becak *pedicab.* **Opposite:** *Boat at Ujung Pandang.*

is relatively new. It was built after 1953 to replace an older one on Jl. Sulawesi which had been destroyed during the Japanese occupation of the island.

Orchids and sea shells

Mr. C.L. Bundt began to grow orchids as a hobby, but has gradually built up a business of world renown. His experiments in cross-fertilizing and breeding have produced some unique blooms which are registered in Sander's List in London. He has cultivated many rare specimens, as well as the common orchids of South Sulawesi which can be purchased at his home on Jl. Mochtar Lufti 15. There is also a large collection of seashells and coral on display.

To visit his three-hectare (7.5-acre) orchid garden outside the city, make a sharp right (not the adjacent oblique right) just before the electricity generating station 7.5 km (4.5 mi) out of Ujung Pandang on the main road north. At successive T-junctions turn left, then right, then right again, to find the garden tucked away at the end of the road, about 0.6 km from the main road. Remember that this is a private garden, and that you must seek permission before entering.

Diponegoro's tomb

Prince Diponegoro was born in 1785, son of Sultan Hamengkubuwono III of Yogyakarta. He led the last great Javanese resistance against the Dutch, in the "Java War" of 1825-30. He was captured through treachery and deported to Manado and then to Makassar, where he died in 1855. He has been declared a national hero.

His tomb, built in the Javanese style, is in a small but well-kept cemetery on Jl. Diponegoro. The family tree displayed on the wall of the tomb indicates that his descendants remained in Ujung Pandang. The custodian, his great-grandson, lives at Jl. Irian No. 83.

Silk weaving

Silk spun from cocoons grown near Soppeng is dyed and woven at Pertenunan Sutera Alam at 47 Jl. Ontah. The raw fiber is boiled for six and a half hours, when it becomes soft and glossy. It is then dyed in brilliant colors somewhat like the dyes for Thai silks, and then hung out to dry.

The skeins when dry are taken to a nearby room to be wound onto spools ready for weaving. In other rooms, on a number of large frames, silks in a variety of gorgeous colors are interwoven and blended—rich blues and purples; yellows, golds, greens, pinks, and reds. Some are woven in intricate designs; for others, the attraction lies in pure color and fine texture.

The factory management has opened a shop on the premises where silk is sold by the meter as well as in *sarung* lengths.

—*Anthony Reid*

JEAN-LÉO DUGAST

SIDETRIPS FROM U.P.

Coral Islands, Caves and Waterfalls

Just off the coast of Ujung Pandang lies one of the world's loveliest coral reefs. Magnificent coral formations and brilliantly-colored tropical fish combine to produce a superb underwater garden. Mushroom and fire corals vie for attention with rainbow-hued parrot fish, while blue-spotted stingray dart rapidly away if approached, leaving behind a fine cloud of sand. Grouper and silvery barracuda glide past, while curious blue- and white-tip sharks circle at a cautious distance.

The endangered reef

Sadly, in the last couple of decades the coral reefs around the scattered islands off Ujung Pandang have been seriously damaged, partly by explosives used to kill the fish, and partly because of depredation by thoughtless coral and sea-shell collectors. *Tridacna gigas*, the giant clam which serves as a baptismal font in many Dutch churches, is now extinct. The populations of corals and reef-dwelling creatures in this area, which was once one of the world's richest in numbers of different species, have declined sharply. It is still possible that the reef may be saved: dynamite has been banned (though the ban is not fully effective) and coral and shell collecting are discouraged.

Nevertheless, the area remains a delightful place to visit, offering much better swimming than the nearby mainland beaches. Some islands are uninhabited, or nearly so; others support large fishing or trading villages. Most offer shelter in the form of coconut, breadfruit and other trees. As you travel further out into the waters, the corals, seaweeds and coraline algae change with the physical features of the underwater realm: the first zone is all but dead, but from 6 to 60 km out (4 to 40 mi), where the underwater shelf plunges 2,000 meters (6,500 ft) down into the ocean's depths, the reef is still vibrant with life.

Islands and sand bars

One of the region's most pleasant spots for swimming and snorkeling is Samalona, an island of white sand beaches with plenty of shade and some coral. In the pre-independence days of Dutch colonial rule, the island was accessible only to members of the Makassar Yacht Club and the "De Harmonie"

society. Now, however, anyone who can afford to hire a boat is welcome.

Other nearby coral islands include Barang Lompo, Barang Caddi, and Kudingareng Lompo, all of which are populated. Barang Lompo, which has a population of some 3,000, supplies fresh drinking water for surrounding islands; a small *warung* there offers simple but good fish meals. Barang Lompo, Pandang Lae-Lae and Kayangan do not offer very good swimming. Further out you will reach Bone Tambung, a small island surrounded by a big reef.

Another very pleasant place to snorkle or dive is Kudingarang Keke, an uninhabited sand-bar which provides no shade other than a single wooden house. The sand here is white and dazzling, and the coral largely undamaged. Strikingly beautiful fish and the occasional barracuda glide by. The reef is large and falls off at its edge to a sandy bottom 35 meters (115 ft) down. Bring plenty of water and food. The journey out from the harbor takes about an hour.

Diving to remember

Experienced divers would do well to head for Kapoposang Island. Despite one to two knot currents, there are thrills to be had for even the most jaded scuba exponents. During two dives recently, we saw white-tip reef sharks in profusion and while this is no big deal for the hard core, that was not all. A school of some 150 batfish performed a complex choreographed dance, their bodies gleaming in the sun; a large crocodile fish, armed with its poisonous spines, kept a wary eye on us and refused to budge an inch; a school of at least two dozen lumbering bumphead parrotfish, bulldozed their way back and forth across the shallows; and the mother of fat Napoleon wrasses, a good meter-and-a-half long, played hide and seek in the fissure of a vertical wall of coral. A memorable dive. In this area there's also a good chance of close encounters with big groupers, tuna, hefty snappers, and the odd errant manta ray.

This rich fauna is present thanks to Kapoposang's location, at the edge of the wide shallows dotted with islands that extend west from Ujung Pandang. Beyond Kapoposang the sea gets deep: hundreds of meters to the sea floor before it rises again to form Kalimantan's "continental" shelf.

The island lies some 20 nautical miles from Ujung Pandang. The 1hr 45 minute speedboat ride out is no fun, even on relatively calm early-morning seas, but it's worth it. The reef wall drops to infinity, sometimes a sheer vertical, elsewhere it is broken with canyons or pierced by shallow coves and labyrinths filled with invertebrates. The visi-

Opposite: *One of many idyllic tropical islands near Ujung Pandang.* **Bottom:** *Corals and marine life, such as this lionfish, abound in the reefs.*

KAL MULLER

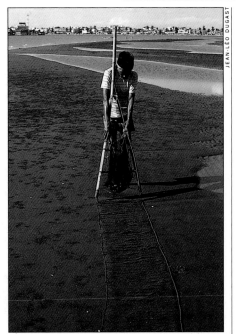

JEAN-LÉO DUGAST

bility is usually quite good, sometimes reaching 30m on the horizontal scale.

As the wind and waves usually pick up in the afternoon, it's either two dives before 1pm or stay overnight on the island, either in tents or among local Bugis people, a convivial bunch. Only the masochist would attempt a return trip in the late afternoon.

For those who consider Kapoposang rather beyond their sphere of competence, there are easier if less overwhelming dives nearer Ujung Pandang. Several wrecks have been located, including that of a Japanese gunboat—great exploration material if the water is clear (seldom). Or try Samalona Island, 15 minutes out from the city, which has cabins for overnight stays.

There are good coral formations here, especially staghorn, massive *Porites* and convoluted brain coral. We also saw lots of clownfish along with a fair variety of other reef fishes. As the drop off levels at a maximum of 15 meters onto sand, this is the best place to try night diving.

Rich scenery and prehistoric caves

Back on land, a short distance to the northeast of Ujung Pandang, lie the extraordinary limestone formations of the cordillera which stretches between Maros and Pangkajene. This is an area of great natural beauty, with rushing waterfalls and an abundance of butterflies. The limestone hills are also famous for their prehistoric caves, in which the remains of neolithic man have been found. Some of these are open to the public. A cave visit can be combined with a trip to the waterfalls at Bantimurung, 25 km southeast of Maros.

To get to the caves and the waterfalls at Bantimurung, you must first take a *bemo* to Maros, an hour north of Ujung Pandang, and then a second *bemo* east towards Bone. *Bemo*s for Maros leave from the central *bemo* terminal in Ujung Pandang; the journey takes an hour and costs Rp 500. As you leave the city, you may see men pushing two-wheeled carts laden with long bamboos, and cyclists carrying nipah palm leaves from the swampy areas to the northeast of the town.

For centuries these have been the basic roofing materials of the area. Note on the left the new building of the provincial assembly, which makes use of a five-layered structure in the roof eaves, a feature which was once the exclusive prerogative of Bugis and Makassar rulers.

About 5 km (3 mi) outside the city, the road passes the site of a vast Chinese cemetery covering about 12 hectares (30 acres). The oldest graves, at the rear of the site, have been there for over a century; most of the others were moved here in about 1970, after their removal from the old cemetery on the site of the present-day Central Market. All these graves were relocated yet again to make way for further government buildings. Another km down the road are the Hero's Cemetery on the right, predominantly for the military, and a Christian cemetery on the left.

Past the cemeteries, a sharp right turn just before the large power station leads to Mr. Bundt's orchid park. Continuing along the main road, cross the Tallo River, and a few km later you will see the new campus of Hasanuddin University on the left. The campus was built with assistance from the Asian Development Bank, and opened in September 1980.

Farther along the road, just before a military compound and half-hidden from the road (on the right), is a Balinese temple, Pura Giri Natha. Its syncretism is nicely displayed by the matching statues of Krishna and Buddha at the entrance. The first road on the left after entering *kabupaten* (region) Maros leads to the mosque headquarters of the Khalwatiah mystical order.

After crossing the Maros River you enter the town's new administrative center. Here you can take a *bemo* to Bantimurung for Rp 250. The road leads east towards Bone and

Bantimurung, through the older part of Maros town.

About 10 km (6 mi) later, a left turn leads to the Archaeological Park (Taman Purbakala Leang-Leang). The caves in this area are the most accessible to the public among all those in the region, and have prehistoric paintings dating back as much as 5,000 years. There are 55 such caves in South Sulawesi, where the limestone cliffs of the central ranges are tunnelled with fissures. The caves are a valuable source of information about the prehistory not only of Sulawesi but of Southeast Asia as a whole, and archaeologists are anxious to extend their knowledge of the area. Unfortunately their work is impeded by plunderers who destroy the sites in search of antique porcelain, as well as by farmers taking soil to replenish their exhausted terrain.

The caves at Ulu Leang appear to have been occupied between 8,000 and 3,000 BC The two caves which are sign-posted are Ulu Leang I, or Gua Pette, and Ulu Leang II, Gua Pettakere. A clear mountain stream which flows near the mouth of these caves is pleasant for swimming. To see the caves, follow signs to a ticket-office at the gate. A path leads to Gua Pettae, which measures about 15 by 20 meters (49 by 65 ft), and has stencils of human hands in a cavity on the wall.

Ulu Leang II (Gua Pettakere) opens from the south wall of the cliff, about 20 meters (65 ft) above the floor of Ulu Leang I, and has

other small passages leading to the cliff-face. It was probably used as a burial site, as it was found to contain a number of human bones. On the cliff above the opening is a painting of a *babirusa* "pig deer" which has unfortunately been badly defaced. If you carry a flashlight you can explore other parts of the cave, where there is another painting of a *babirusa*.

Farther along the road on the left are other caves, less clearly signposted but open to the public. These are the Leang Jarie, Leang Saripa and Leang Karrasa. They also have stencils of human hands.

Waterfalls and butterflies

From the caves you must return to the highway and hail a passing *bemo* to continue on to Bantimurung Reserve. You can't miss the entrance: the road leads beneath the legs of a 6 meter (20 ft) concrete monkey. This area, with its spectacular waterfalls, cliffs and chasms, and its butterflies and birds, has always attracted visitors. In 1856-57 the British naturalist Alfred Russel Wallace spent "some of the most pleasurable moments of [his] life" here, catching many rare specimens of insects, birds and butterflies, includ-

Opposite: *Clamming on the beach near Ujung Pandang.* **Above:** *Bamboo being floated down the Tallo River in bunches. Bamboo is a basic and versatile material, providing tools, building materials, containers, and even food.*

ing the *Papilio androcles*, one of the largest and rarest swallow-tailed butterflies. Wallace wrote, "Such gorges, chasms and precipices as here abound, I have nowhere seen in the Archipelago." His detailed descriptions have attracted numbers of archaeologists, prehistorians, and lepidopterists, including Vladimir Nabokov, who wrote a scientific article on the butterflies he discovered here.

Today Bantimurung has been proclaimed a protected area, as many species of its wildlife are threatened by overenthusiastic collectors. Nevertheless, visitors will find themselves beseiged by children with boxes of brilliantly-colored butterflies. The best time to see the butterflies in the living state is when the sun comes out after a rain, as they flutter over the water and nearby vegetation.

In the dry season the waterfall is a sheet of clear, surging water which falls about 12 meters (40 ft) from a rounded mass of rock into a deep pool below. Steep steps lead up beside the falls to the river above. From here, unless the torrent is too strong (as is common in the rainy season), you can wade along the edge of the stream to a bank 50 meters away on the left, where a shady patch leads through the bush to a second waterfall.

This fall is smaller but broad, and cascades into a pool of conflicting currents and eddies—the pool is stimulating but at times dangerous to swim in, as it forms whirlpools. Nearby, there is a cave which you will need a

flashlight to explore. This is a popular picnic spot, especially on Sundays, and a delightful place for walking, swimming, or just enjoying the scenery. The recent addition of large cement frogs has unfortunately robbed the waterfall of much of its charm. Walk up behind the falls to the river and the dark rocky gorge through which it flows.

Malino

Two hours and 70 km (42 mi) to the east of Ujung Pandang lies the refreshingly cool market town of Malino. It is a delightful place to visit if you have the time. Malino lies on the lower slopes of Mount Bawa Karaeng, and coaches and minibuses leave for here regularly from the main bus terminal in Ujung Pandang. The road leads south through Sungguminasa, and you can stop here and visit the ruins and the old palace before continuing on by mini-bus to Malino. (See "Historical Sights," page 80.)

After the Gowa palace, the road to Malino continues straight ahead at the main crossroads (the road to the right leads to Jeneponto and the south coast). Soon afterwards, you pass the Pabrik Kertas Gowa, the largest paper factory in Indonesia at the time of its establishment in 1962. It was seen as a sign of hope for a province long held back by polit-

Above: *Bantimurung waterfall.* **Opposite:** *Children playing in a stream near Ujung Pandung.*

ical turmoil. Built with Japanese help, it uses about 80 percent bamboo, with smaller amounts of acacia, mangrove and pine.

Opposite the factory lies Lake Mawang, once a favored location for boating among the prolific lotus blooms. The lotus have disappeared, along with the boats, but one can still picnic beneath the trees.

Continuing out of Ujung Pandang toward Malino, 29 km (18 mi) further down the road, on the left, is the entrance to the natural silk project. Since 1974, with Japanese technical assistance, Japanese and Chinese varieties of silk worms have been bred here to provide South Sulawesi farmers with eggs which they raise to the cocoon stage.

The road to Malino was completed in 1927, after which the town was developed as the hill resort of the Makassar area. In the colonial period, this was a hill station where Dutch officials and their families could escape from the heat of the plains. Marketday in Malino is Sunday morning, and this is when the quiet town comes alive. The area is famous for its fruits and vegetables, treetomatoes (tamarillos), passion fruit (*markisa*), and avocados, which are a bargain. Orchids, birds, and woven baskets are among the wares to be found here. Its greatest moment came in July 1946, when the "Malino Conference" laid the foundation for the ill-fated Dutch strategy of federalism for post-war Indonesia.

Twice a year, in May and November, Malino is ablaze with flowers from the tall red tulip trees which border the roads and parks. The cool mountain air is conducive to long walks among the pine forests and surrounding hills.

Hikes

There are lots of delightful walks through the area's pine forests and rice fields, surrounded by mountains, river valleys and cascading waterfalls. Two spectacular waterfalls can be reached from a winding road south of Malino, just past the Takapola bridge in Desa Buluttana. To the right of the road, the Balaniparang waterfall plunges 100 meters down a sheer cliff face. A little farther on, a smaller waterfall to the left of the road is better for swimming: take a footpath about 500 meters (0.3 mi) alongside the river to where the cascade sprays out into a deep basin.

Mount Bawa Karaeng can be climbed in about 3-4 hours from the village of Ngangre Apiang, at the highest point on the road beyond Malino. It is best to arrange for guides and to spend the night before your climb at Malino, so as to be able to set out early and avoid the likelihood of afternoon rain. Only from July to September can you be sure of wholly dry weather. It is a lovely walk among towering forest trees with lichen, orchids and numerous species of birds.

—*Anthony Reid and Kal Muller*

HISTORICAL SITES

Reminders of a Royal Past

The royal tombs, ruins, and sacred sites of Gowa and Tallo are today the only reminders of the vanished greatness of 17th-century Makassar. The two small kingdoms united in the 16th century to form the powerful Makassar kingdom which dominated much of the peninsula before its defeat by the Dutch and Bugis in 1669.

Gowa and Tallo each had their own centers of spiritual power, where kings were both crowned and buried, and where a large wooden palace on stilts housed members of the royal family. The royal ground of the kingdom of Gowa was the area now known as "Kale Gowa," situated on slightly elevated ground alongside the Jeneberang River, to the south of the city. The royal ground of Tallo was at the western side of the Tallo River, where the royal graves and coronation stone may still be seen.

Old Gowa

The royal tombs, graves, palace and treasures of Gowa can be visited by catching a *bemo* from the central terminal (fare: Rp350). Just before the portals of *kabupaten* Gowa, 8 km (5 mi) from Karebosi Square, a road leads off to the left to a complex of graves in the center of the old Gowa Kingdom (Kale Gowa).

The first tomb complex which you will see, on the left, is the most venerated grave in the Makassar area. Syech Yusuf (1626-94) was Makassar's foremost religious scholar. On his return in 1644 from a pilgrimage to Mecca, he taught the mystical Khalwatiah doctrine in Banten (West Java), married the daughter of Sultan Agung there, and became the soul of the resistance effort against the Dutch, who attacked Banten in 1682. He was captured in 1684 and exiled, first to Ceylon, and in 1693 to the Cape of Good Hope. Both in Ceylon and South Africa he is credited with a major role in inspiring their small Islamic communities.

Despite opposition from purist Muslims, the tomb is constantly visited by those seeking some favor—by pouring oil, scattering flowers, and lighting candles around the tomb. Although Yusuf is venerated as Tuanta Salamaka ("Our lord who grants us blessings"), it is not his tomb which receives the most attention, but that of his wife, who is said to be helpful to women wanting a child.

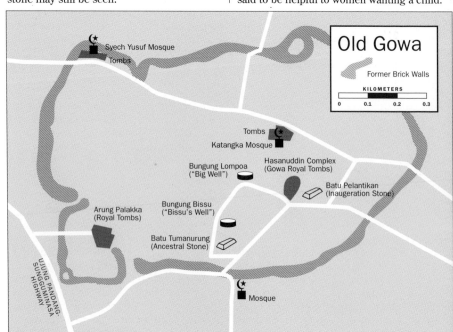

Ancient mosque and domed graves

A little farther along the road to the east, a sign at the entrance to Katangka Mosque announces that it is the oldest in South Sulawesi, built in 1605—the date when the kings of Gowa and Tallo accepted Islam. There is little evidence for this, although the solidity of the walls and the four central pillars suggest that parts of the present building date from the 18th century or earlier. The mosque is surrounded by the graves of the Gowa royal family of the 18th and 19th centuries, each dome containing the grave of a ruler and his close relatives.

From the mosque, continue eastward along the road for a few hundred meters, then take a sharp right turn onto a rough road leading up to the higher ground of Tamalate, the sacred center of Gowa and site of a 16th or 17th-century palace. On the highest point is the stone on which rulers of Gowa were inaugurated. The coronation established the new ruler's link with the sacred stone as well as to the heavenly nymph Tumanurunga, who on this spot married the mortal Karaeng Bayo and founded the Gowa dynasty.

Inside the modern enclosure are one of the domed graves like those of Katangka, and nine large stone graves shaped in the manner of many Islamic graves elsewhere, but on such an enlarged scale that one can move about inside an inner room containing the real tomb. No serious study has been made of the unique tomb structures of South Sulawesi, even though they provide important physical information on the early kingdoms. Since the dome-like structures require difficult arching, and most of them can be shown to date from the 18th century, it is assumed that this is a later form. This would mean that the one domed tomb in the Tamalate complex, that of King Tunibatta who ruled for only a month in 1565 before being killed in a war with Bone, was in fact built long after his death. It is nevertheless intriguing why this single pre-Islamic tomb should be here.

In general it appears that before Islam's arrival, rulers were buried only in earth mounds, perhaps with a wooden house-like structure above such as one still occasionally sees in Toraja. It is significant that Kale Gowa, more particularly the area around Syech Yusuf's tomb, is also referred to as "Lakiung," a variant of the Toraja term for the high house in which an aristocratic corpse is

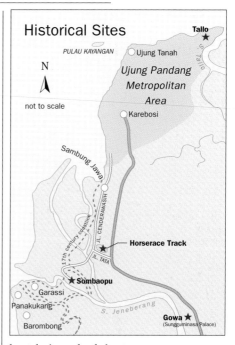

kept during a death-feast.

A little farther to the west, but also approachable from the main Ujung Pandang-Sungguminasa road, is another group of tombs dominated by that of Aru Palakka, the great war leader who rallied the Bugis and allied with the Dutch to defeat Makassar. When he died in 1696 he was the most powerful man in South Sulawesi, but he chose to be buried in this heartland of the Gowa he had conquered rather than in Bone, where he had been proclaimed king. Although regarded by many Bugis as a great liberator, he was understandably resented by Makassarese, and his tomb fell into great disrepair until the Dutch took it in hand in the 1930s. It may be significant that he also chose a burial spot close to the tomb of Karaeng Pattingalloang (d. 1654), the learned chancellor of Makassar who is said to have been a patron of the young Aru Palakka. Pattingalloang's tomb is a little to the east.

The Sungguminasa palace

Further up the main road at Sungguminasa is the royal palace of Gowa. The palace was built in 1936, in traditional style on stilts, with an imposing roofed flight of steps leading up to a large reception room. The rank of the occupant is shown by the maximum five wooden panels in the gable of the roof. Other than the architecture, the main points of interest are the treasure and royal regalia

KAL MULLER

(*pusaka*) kept locked in a room on the left. (Apply first at the *bupati's* office for permission to see the royal treasure.) The regalia was considered crucial for the validity and magical power of the rulers at coronations and other important ceremonies of state.

The treasure room is set up as if for a ceremony to honor the regalia, with incense, candles, offerings of betel, food, and various requisite herbs. The oldest parts of the regalia are closely connected with the mythological origins of the Gowa dynasty. The first female ruler, Tumanurunga, is held to have descended from heaven already equipped with the magnificent gold crown. The latter is displayed in a central showcase together with four gold bracelets made in the form of coiled serpents (*naga*) with realistic heads and gaping jaws. One of the snakes has two heads, and all have precious stones for eyes. Another important object claimed to have come from heaven with the first princess was a gold chain, I Tanisamanga, which was ritually weighed each year in the presence of the raja's council. If its weight had increased during the past year, this was taken as a good omen for the kingdom; if it had decreased, as a bad omen. Unfortunately, this chain has disappeared.

Of the three royal swords, the most sacred is the black one, Sudanga, said to have been brought by Lakipadada. According to the Gowa tradition he was the brother of the prince Karaeng Bayo, who married Tumanurunga to begin the Gowa royal line.

The spectacular *keris* studded with precious stones, its gold handle a *wayang* (shadow-puppet) figure, is Javanese and associated with the Islamic sultanate of Demak. It may have been a gift from the ruler of Demak or Mataram, in Java, in the late 16th or 17th century. In the same display case are spearheads; a delicate *keris* ornamented in gold; two sets of gold cymbals; and three gold medallions, two presented by the Dutch king in 1818 and 1829 respectively, the third by the British in 1814 to "Krain Lemban Parang, Rajah of Gowa, as a token of friendship and esteem and in testimony of his attachment and faithful services [in fighting Bone]."

In the opposite showcase the gold jewelery on display includes a chain necklace said to have come from Manila (*rante* Manila); eight heavy ornamental gold earrings; twelve rings, made mainly of gold with precious stones; and six braided gold epaulettes for ceremonial uniform.

Other exhibits include various musical instruments, ceremonial regalia such as a large parasol, brooms used for ritual sweeping after the harvest, and bamboo clappers to announce the birth of a royal child.

Old Tallo

The Tallo dynasty reportedly began with Karaeng Loe, a 15th-century prince of Gowa who sought to establish a new kingdom at the strategic point of land formed between the sea and the Tallo River. In the early 16th century this dynasty formed an alliance with the expanding power of Gowa, to make the Makassar state "one people with two kings." Although Gowa provided the senior monarch, Tallo frequently provided the court chancellor (*pabicara butta*) who exercised day-to-day control of the affairs of state.

This dualism was especially marked during the heyday of Makassar between 1590 and 1654. The greatest king of Tallo, Karaeng Matoaya or Sultan Awal-ul-Islam (r. 1593-1636), as Chancellor of Makassar was largely responsible for the Islamization of South Sulawesi. The first official Friday prayer for the newly-Islamized court of Makassar was

Above: *The grave of a Makassarese noble at Kale Gowa.* **Opposite:** *The palace at Sungguminasa in 1888, before it was rebuilt. The five gables denote royalty; non-ruling nobles were allowed three, commoners only one. The section between the steps and the house is an audience hall.*

held in Tallo in 1605. True to its seaside location, Tallo appears to have been consistently more open to external and commercial influences. With the Dutch conquest of Makassar in 1669, however, the Tallo dynasty gradually lost any real significance.

Tallo lies on the old road north, 3 km (1.8 mi) from the city center, on the near side of the Tallo River, where the low-lying fishponds (*empang*) make old Tallo almost an island. Since 1977 the royal graves have been gradually restored. The two tallest stone graves are from the 17th century. The one in the northwest corner is locally claimed to be that of the great Karaeng Matoaya, reverently known as "the white tiger of Tallo." His grave is more reliably located in Gowa: these two stone graves are probably those of the two subsequent rulers of Tallo.

Along the seashore you can see the stone foundations of the great sea wall of Tallo, built under Portuguese supervision in the early 17th century. The wall is 2.5 meters (8 ft) thick, and can be traced along the coast westwards for about 500 meters (0.3 mi), with some remaining mounds still 2 meters (6.5 ft) high. The total length of the wall was over 2 km (1.2 mi), enclosing almost all of the semi-island at the river's mouth. Like the other forts of Makassar, it was destroyed on Dutch orders in the 1660s.

A sacred coronation stone and well are also to be found within the old walled area.

The grave of Khatib Tunggal Datu ri Bandang can be seen in Kampung Kaluku Badoa, 300 meters to the left down a dirt road off Jl. Tinumbu, shortly before a prawn factory and Jl. Gatot Subroto. Datu ri Bandang was the Sumatran apostle who instructed Karaeng Matoaya in Islam, and is revered in many parts of South Sulawesi as the herald of the new religion. (Bantaeng and Selayar also claim his grave, though less plausibly.) The grave itself is unimpressive, though it is much visited as a *kramat* (miracle-working) site through which spiritual and material favors can be obtained.

Sombaopu

Sombaopu ("homage to the lord"), 7 km (4 mi) south of Ujung Pandang, was the mightiest of eleven great fortresses that once lined the coast of Makassar as far north as Tallo. It was the royal fortress, lying at the mouth of the Jeneberang River, serving as the personal residence of the ruler and the heart of the sprawling trading port which extended to the north and south. A Dutch map of the early 17th century shows houses on the east and northern sides of the fort, and two enormous palaces, storehouses and a mosque in the southwest. Outside the walls lay the southern and northern markets, the houses of the commoners and, stretching north along the coast, the Portuguese and Indian quarters.

The origin of Sombaopu appears to lie in a

Malay settlement just south of the Jene-berang. Here in the mid-16th century, a small group of Malay traders were encouraged to settle by Tunipalangga, the 10th ruler of Gowa. The Chronicle of Gowa relates how Tunipalangga promised not to enter the Malays' compounds, and to exempt them from seizure of property under Makassarese law. Tunipalangga is also remembered for standardizing weights and measures, and for building the brick walls of Sombaopu.

The Malay community grew steadily as Makassar began to make itself a major collecting point for spices from the eastern isles. The expansion in trade was accompanied by expansion in political control over the south coast, with military expeditions against Jeneponto, Bantaeng and Selayar. This coast was the first step on the route to the Moluccan spice islands, while Bira and Bulukumba were important ship-building areas. Together with Selayar, they also produced Makassar's major manufactured export, the checkered "Makassar cloth" which was in great demand throughout the archipelago.

By the 17th century, Makassar had emerged as the richest and most powerful kingdom in the eastern archipelago. The growing importance of the city as a source of spices also attracted Europeans. By 1625, as many as 22 Portuguese frigates visited the port every year. The English established a factory in Makassar in 1613, the Danes in 1618; Spanish and Chinese traders began to appear in 1615. The foreign "factories" were located north of Sombaopu, on the opposite bank of the Jenebereng River. Makassar was renowned for being a kingdom "kind to strangers." Despite the fact that it was an Islamic state, there were places of Christian worship and the city was home to a number of prominent refugees.

In June 1669, after months of bitter fighting between Makassarese and Bugis-Dutch forces, Dutch soldiers managed to mine and blow a 20-meter (65 ft) gap in the 3-meter-thick walls of Sombaopu, where the Makassarese had made their stand. The following day, fighting was so heavy, with Dutch musketeers firing 30,000 bullets, that "old soldiers have perhaps never heard its like in Europe itself." Dutch and Bugis troops, many sick with dysentry and tropical diseases, found themselves confronting reinforced dwellings which had to be taken in hand-to-hand street fighting. Not until nine days after the assault began and the sacred cannon *anak Makassar* had been captured, was Sombaopu firmly in Dutch hands. The mighty kingdom of Makassar lay in ruins. Surveying its burnt-out villages and settlements the following year, Speelman wrote: "And then comes Sombaopu, now razed and thrown into chaos."

After his victory in 1699, Speelman

ordered the complete destruction of Sombaopu. In subsequent years, the main channel of the Jeneberang shifted southwards, and a delta began to build up around Sombaopu, isolating it from the sea. The new colonial city grew up 7 km (4.5 mi) to the north, and the remains of Sombaopu were totally neglected. Over the following centuries the remaining bricks were used for Dutch buildings, or by locals for making wells and house foundations. By the 1980s, little was left. Here and there a rise in the soil

indicates the remains of a defense wall, but there is little to suggest Sombaopu's former importance.

Since July 1989 a team of Indonesian archaeologists has been working to preserve and protect this historic site. The restoration has been guided by two maps. One is a Dutch map of Makassar dated 1638, discovered recently in a European library. The other is an 18th century palm-leaf map written in the Makassarese script by an unknown author, showing the layout of the city and plans of the royal palace.

The excavations have produced many surprises, including strange hollow spaces built into the walls at 8-10 meter (26-33 ft) intervals. The reason for these spaces, which must have seriously reduced the defensive strength of the wall, is unclear. Many of them have produced evidence of cooking, suggesting occupation by troops. Other finds include stone cannon balls, bricks with pictures of boats and strange geometric designs etched on them. Others have the deep imprints of cats and dog's paws, indicating that animals were sacrificed as part of the building process. Perhaps the most intriguing find is a brick showing an unknown script, possibly an earlier version of the Old Makassarese script formerly used in the royal courts before the 18th century.

The palaces and houses of Sombaopu were protected by a single brick wall, except

on the north side, which in the 17th century bordered the main channel of the Jeneberang River. Here the wall was of triple thickness: a strong central wall made of large bricks and two lighter outer walls. In between, the walls were packed with earth, a sound defense against cannon fire. The bricks of this northern wall were also cemented. Iron slag and a bellows' mouthpiece show that iron forging, probably for weapons and cannon balls, took place within the fort.

In late 1992, Sumbaopu was a beehive of activity. Some of the ancient walls and foundations were being excavated and a new wall, presumably a replica of the original one, was being erected, facing the southern branch of the Jeneberang River.

Most of this large island, formed by the river's two branches, is being converted into a kind of South Sulawesi theme park. Large wood buildings copy the traditional house styles of the various groups in the province. Replicas of the various rulers' palaces were also nearing completion, along with an isolated cluster of Toraja houses. A sacred royal tomb (Mocinisombala's), where offerings are still made, is located on top of a low mound, it will soon have a large open building erected around it. Another area has been set aside for exhibitions and cultural shows.

The people who still live here occupy small, traditional-style homes. Sumbaopu aims to preserve a part of South Sulawesi's traditional way of life, hoping that the cultures will be able to preserve some of their identity in the face of today's rapidly changing world.

—*Anthony Reid and Ian Caldwell*

Opposite: *Crown of the former rulers of Gowa, now in Sungguminasa, probably dating from the 17th to 18th century. Note the spaces where the larger jewels have been pried out.* **Above, left:** *Brick with unknown inscription. Many bricks of this design have been found at Sombaopu.* **Above, right:** *An empty space in the wall at Sombaopu.*

WEST COAST

The Road North to Parepare

The journey north from Ujung Pandang takes you along a narrow, fertile coastline dominated by spectacular limestone ranges and shady, cool lagoons and inlets. Most visitors to Sulwesi will head along this road as far as Parepare, then inland towards the mountains. The west coast is home to some of the earliest-known kingdoms of South Sulawesi and some of its oldest traditions. Segeri, halfway between Ujung Pandang and Parepare, is famous for its sacred plough rituals and its "college" of transvestite priests.

Leaving Ujung Pandang, the road heads north through ricefields dominated by the spectacular limestone range, with its extraordinary honeycomb maze of steep outcrops festooned with tropical growth. These are said to be the remains of a coral reef dating from the Tertiary period. Their intricacy is best appreciated from the air.

Pangkajene, 53 km (33 mi) up the coast, lies on the border between the Bugis and the Makassarese regions. This area was part of the earlier kingdom of Siang, which before the 16th century and the development of Makassar was one of the liveliest commercial centers on the coast. Many ancient Chinese ceramics have been found in this district, as well as a few gold objects. Some of these are on display at the cultural office (*kantor kebudayaan*), together with musical instruments, arms, coats of mail, models of boats, etc. Ask to see the golden mask which is kept locked away. Probably a funerary mask, it is of a type not found elsewhere in Indonesia. Dating from the 14th to 16th century, it was found in 1967 in a tomb with other gold objects which have since been lost.

Several kilometers past Pangkajene are the Bungaro natural springs, on the right. A pool has been formed from a source in the limestone cliffs, but it is not very inviting. There are caves in the cliff face which the local people will guide you through with flashlights. Just past Bungaro (on the right) is the scenic road to the Tonasa II Cement Factory, which leads past limestone cliffs honey-combed with caves. Stalactites and stalagmites beneath the luxuriant vegetation give an air of unreality to the area, which is worth exploring on foot.

Segeri, 74 km (46 mi) down the road leading to the north, is a town of quaint but dilapidated painted houses, the former eminence of which is now reflected only in the remaining college of *bissu*, the transvestite priests in charge of the sacred *arajang* (regalia) of each Bugis kingdom. Segeri is the northernmost center of the region brought under the direct control of the sultans of Makassar (Gowa) in the early 17th century, and then conquered and annexed by the Dutch in 1667 as the Noorderdistricten (northern districts) of Makassar. Just as the Dutch conquered this rich rice-growing area between Segeri and Maros on their way to Makassar, so too did Bone at the end of the 18th century, and the region was not under firm colonial control until 1824.

The prominence of the *bissu* in Segeri dates from 1776, when a prince of Luwu settled there and was accepted as ruler. He brought with him a number of *bissu*, who were otherwise limited to the more powerful

Parepare

Polewali, Majene and Mamuju

Northern port (for bago fleet)

Market

Angin Mammiri Rest.

JL. LASINRANG

JL. HASSANUDDIN

JL. Pgr. Laut

Tana Toraja

JL. VETERAN

Municipal Offices

Western port

JL. DRS. A. MALLARANGENG

JL. OMBOPATAN

Bus Terminal

JL. MATIROTASI

JL. BAU MASEPI

JL. SILIWANGI

N

not to scale

JL. PENGABDIAN

Ujung Pandang

Opposite: *Stit fishing tower near Parepare. The fisherman seated on the tower hold the ropes leading to nets, which he pulls up occasionally.*

courts of Bone, Wajo and Luwu itself. They conducted the palace rituals, and looked after the *arajang*—in the case of Segeri a magical plough which had to be used during the *mapalili'* ceremony in mid to late November to begin the ploughing season. *Bissu* were shamans, able to communicate directly with the gods and speak in their special language, the *basa bissu*. In trance they are able to stab themselves without pain. Since the fall of the rajahs the *bissu* have lost most of their functions, and it is a sign of the times that their leader, the *puang matoa*, has become a Muslim haji. Only in the *mapilili'* ceremony is the *bissus* role still believed essential.

At Balusu, 119 km (74 mi) along the road, a detour just after the bridge leads one kilometer along an unpaved road to one of the few remaining examples of aristocratic architecture, dating from the late 19th century.

Shortly after Balusu, the road returns to the coast, as the foothills of the central range advance further into the plain. The remainder of the journey is a beautiful drive along the seashore, with good swimming at beaches about 12 km (7 mi) before Parepare. About 2 km (1.3 mi) before Parepare, the village of Bangange houses an "ethnology museum" run by Haji Hamzah, who is related by marriage to the former *arung* (ruler) of Bacukiki. He has a collection of traditional costumes and gold ornaments used for royal ceremonies, as well as ceramics, brassware, musical instruments and traditional tools of various sorts.

The town of Parepare

Parepare (population 86,000) has a relatively short history. It was formerly part of the kingdom of Suppa, which played an important role in the history of the area. The Portuguese claimed that the raja of Suppa and some of his nobles were converted to Christianity in 1543, more than 60 years before Makassar became Muslim.

Parepare, the second largest port in South Sulawesi after Ujung Padang, is now known chiefly as an important trade center, and a stopping-place for travelers between Ujung Pandang and Toraja.

The main animal export harbor in the province, Parepare has a regular boat service (not renowned for its safety) to Donggala, Kalimantan and Surabaya. Passengers travel above, and cattle below. There is also a freight service, mainly for cattle, to Java. Boats are built and repaired in the port.

There are views of the town and the bay from the hills to the north (turn right at the stadium and take the main road toward Pangkajene and Toraja). The bay can also be appreciated from the waterfront. There are magnificent sunsets and a lively night market here. At the harbor you can see the *bago*, a local type of *prahu*.

—*Anthony Reid*

MANDAR DISTRICT

Ship Builders of the Northwest

Mandar, a little-known ans seldom-visited region of fishermen, sailors and boat-builders, awaits the intrepid traveler who braves the bumps, grinds and dust of the coastal road leading north and west from Parepare. Stands of kapok and coconut trees, dusty villages, occasional sun-blinding glimpses of the Makassar Strait, and pastel-colored Buginese-style houses grace the journey north.

Mandarese culture is a complex amalgam of seaborne influences, particularly that of Islam, which arrived in the 17th century. The local ritual life reflects a rich diversity of cosmological conceptions, and a fervent belief in Islam is joined with ancient Indic practices (forehead, hands and navel are daubed with mixtures of herbs and rice flour at curing, birth and boat-launching ceremonies) and indigenous beliefs concerning local guardians, ghosts, and the spirits of flying fish.

Life in Mandar focuses on the Makassar Strait and its abundance of fish—silvery scads, long yellowfin and skipjack tuna, swordfish, shrimp and flying fish—as well as the produce of the land, such as bananas, papayas, pineapples and jackfruit. Hand-pressed, high-quality coconut oil and woven silk sarongs are also produced.

Until the 1930s, wind-powered Mandarese cargo vessels departed from Luaor village, near Majene (the district capital) and sailed to distant islands in the eastern archipelago—Morotai, Ternate, Tidore—doing a brisk trade in manufactured goods obtained in Makassar (from Indian and Chinese merchants), including plates, tobacco and hand-woven Mandarese rope. Six months later, moving west with the monsoon, they returned with fragrant cloves, cinnamon and nutmeg, as well as turtle meat and shells, copra and live plumage birds.

To many older fishermen, the ocean is a kingdom ruled by spirits who control the currents, whirlpools, waves, winds and weather. These spirit guardians also control man's fate at sea—determing whether fishermen will return from their journeys and whether fish will be captured. The flying fish is traditionally regarded as a divine creature endowed with the power to oversee everything that happens.

Foreign markets are driving the Mandarese to reevaluate their ideas of the marine world, its regulation and resources. Demands for seafood products have stimulated new industries in shrimp fry, shark meat and fins, red snapper, agar agar and tuna.

Visiting Majene

Majene, the capital of *kabupaten* Mandar, is a small and pleasant town on a wonderful half-moon-shaped bay. But, like the rest of Mandar, it is not well-equipped to handle tourists. Do not try to stay in the nearby villages overnight, as this creates problems with local police. In Majene itself, there are several rudimentary and rather depressing guesthouses (*penginapan*). Bring along plenty of mosquito coils.

A more attractive alternative is to stay at the pleasant and strategically located harbor home of Ibu Darmi Mas'ud at Jalan Amanna Wewang No. 12. The *warung* on Jl. Syukun Rahin is the best place in town to eat lunch; the fare is both savory and inexpensive (see "South Practicalities").

In the morning, walk along the Majene sea wall—the scene of bustling activity as tuna and scad boats return to land. By 8 am the sea wall is thronged with the wives, sisters, aunts and nieces of fishermen, who receive the fish, sort and price them—and amidst a cacophonous commercial roar—sell them to housewives and traders arriving on foot, by *becak*, and on motorcycles.

In the afternoon, walk north following the sea wall and turn left down the paved street leading past the green-and-white mosque of Pangali-Ali. This is a densely settled village of raft-fishing families and civil servants.

Walk through Pangali-Ali past the last house on your left, and follow a path that winds up the craggy, wind-blown promontory. Behind you and to the south stretches Majene harbor, while to the east east lies the deep-blue Makassar Strait. Continue north (the only way to go) through a rock wall until you reach Cilallang fishing village, its mosque's bulbous tin minaret shimmering in the sun. Tall *prahu sande* with twin outriggers and white sails squat like graceful water-spiders a few hundred yards offshore. Past Cilallang, turn right and continue on

CHARLES ZERNER

to the old graveyard at Ondongan—a site which is now being restored by the government office of historic remains and antiquities. On this high promontory you can walk among more than 600 graves, some antedating the arrival of Islam in the 17th century. Many are adorned with intricately carved, weather-worn markers in the shape of a female torso with hands on her hips, bird forms or cylindrical phallic shapes. At the southernmost edge of the graveyard you have a panoramic view of Majene town and harbor with the *bago* fleet lying at anchor; of the hills and mountains of Toraja-Mamasa; and of the expansive Makassar Strait. Find shade under a sacred tree (look for the signs of former offerings), relax and take shelter from the sun.

If you are inclined to hike to other, possibly older gravesites, ask for walking directions to Salabose. Here, in the hills above Majene, you may examine a ring of worn, black gravestones that suggest the memorial menhirs (*simbuang batu*) of Toraja. This worn ring of black stones, on a sacred headland overlooking the sea, stands as testimony of Mandar's pre-Islamic past and its links with the indigenous religions of the interior.

Salabose also has a smaller, more cluttered graveyard than the one at Ondongan. Here too are old, finely carved stone graves, as well as recent ones covered in pink and yellow tile. Unlike Ondongan, this site is still in use. It is a pretty place, filled with flowering frangipani trees. A building houses the tomb of Syekh Abdul Manan, said to have first brought Islam to Mandar from Mecca. Families visit his tomb to request blessings or favors, or to honor vows.

Back in Majene, shop around the market for some fresh fish, delicious fruits and a profusion of checkered silks. Although Mandarese silk-weaving is in decline, you may still wish to view and purchase some of the locally produced, finely woven silk sarungs, available in patterns of squares and checks, as well as in eccentric, eclectic, flamboyant Bugis-influenced patterns. Large flowers in shades of peach, electric green, and brilliant blues are shot through with sinuous lines of metallic silver and gold thread. Women weavers continue to work in Luaor and especially in Pambusuang (*kabupaten* Polmas). In Polmas, you may also visit the market at Tinambung, which is the center of the silk *sarung* production and trade.

The trip north to Mamuju is recommended if you enjoy torpid, slow-moving, unbearably hot Southeast Asian coastal towns. Muddy roads, less than indifferent food, and a decaying fishing pier await you under the glaring eye of an equatorial sun.

—*Charles Zerner*

Above: *Mandarese boat-builder. No nails are used; the ribs are attached with wooden pegs.*

SOUTH COAST

Maritime Makassarese Homeland

The southern coast of the peninsula is the Makassarese heartland. Boat-building and many other traditional crafts can best be seen here. There are excellent beaches, fine scenery, and a good main road. Modest hotels and restaurants are found at Bantaeng, Sinjai and Benteng (on Selayar Island).

By road, the trip from Ujung Pandang all around the south coast to Sinjai through Takalar, Jeneponto, Bulukumba and Kajang is 221 km (138 mi) long. The return journey can be made either by passing over the hills via Malino, or farther north via Watampone (Bone). Although a sidetrip to the boat-building center of Bira may involve a poor road, there are now places to eat and stay there before taking the ferry to Selayar.

Boats, pottery and flying fish

Coaches and minibuses leave regularly for Jeneponto and Takalar from the main bus terminal in Ujung Pandang. A direct coach to Bira leaves daily at 7.00 am and connects with the afternoon ferry to Selayar. Travel along the south coast is easy, and it is possible to stop off and explore the countryside along the way. From Jeneponto and Takalar, minibuses and *bemos* take you on to Sinjai and Bone. The distances given below are measured from Ujung Pandang.

Leaving Ujung Pandang, the road turns right to cross the Jeneberang River past Sungguminasa. At Limbung, 22 km (13 mi) from the city, a turn off to the right leads to Galesong (9 kms on a semi-paved road), through rice fields all the way to the coast. Galesong has always been one of the important Makassarese ports and political centers, but the progress of Ujung Pandang has scarcely touched it. The beach is a forest of small sailing craft, particularly in May and June, with hundreds of flying fish boats (*patorani*) drawn up on the sand. The people of Galesong are famous as experts with two-masted, tilted, rectangular rigs. They are also known for what is said to be the most spectacular boat ritual in Sulawesi—a feast and a race to a small island held on the day the fishermen leave in search of flying fish.

From Galesong a return can be made to Ujung Pandang by a poor but attractive coastal road north to Barombong, site of a new school for sailors and of the nearest

beach to the city, thence back by a short sealed road to the main southern highway. Or continue south from Limbung, past a region of brick kilns and monuments to heroes of the revolution. The Polambang-keng region of Takalar in particular played a big part in the fight for independence.

Takalar (34 km) is a new administrative center on the main road. To the right, 5 km (3 mi) away, lies Takalar Lama, the colonial capital of the district, with an old Dutch jail as the principal monument to those times. Takalar is famous for its pottery, and a little north of Takalar Lama women can be seen at work beneath their houses making clay pots for storing rice and water, burning incense, and cooking. Much of the pottery is sent out by sailing craft to distant ports in Kalimantan or Sulawesi. The gray clay of the rice fields is the basic material, with a reddish earth from the mountains adding the decoration.

Some 10 km (6 mi) past Takalar, you enter Jeneponto district, the driest, poorest, and in some respects most traditional region of South Sulawesi. The land gets progressively drier as you advance, with rice tending to give way to maize (a staple in Jeneponto), oranges, kapok, and the lontara palm. This palm thrives in dry conditions and provides the owners with leaves for fine baskets and mat-making; sugar; palm-wine (*tuak*), and the fruit itself (*buah lontara*), a refreshing jelly-like substance sold in beautiful little baskets

along the roadside. Don't eat the skins.

Horses are prominent everywhere in South Sulawesi (except Toraja), especially in hauling goods and people to market in little carts (*bendi* or *dokar*). Only in Jeneponto, however, do they rival the water buffalo as a symbol of wealth and strength. Horse meat is still often served at weddings and other feasts as a special honor to the guests.

One Jeneponto village researched in 1980 had a per capita annual income of only US $30. Many of Jeneponto's young men are forced to seek a living in Ujung Pandang as *becak* drivers, or in the Bone sugar factory or elsewhere. Unlike the Bugis however, they do not migrate permanently, but retain their roots in this stubbornly beautiful area. Jeneponto people have the reputation of being prouder than other Makassarese, more conscious of their *siri*, and ready to kill even close relatives when this appears to be required for the honor of the family.

At 57 km (38 mi) a very rough road to the right leads to the village of Cikuang, governed by a kind of theocracy of descendents of the original Arab *sayyid* who reputedly Islamized the village three and a half centuries ago. Its distinctive religious tradition is best seen in its colorful Maudu Lompoa festival in the Islamic month of *maulud*. There is a government resthouse on stilts here.

Opposite: *Fishing boats at Galesong harbor.*

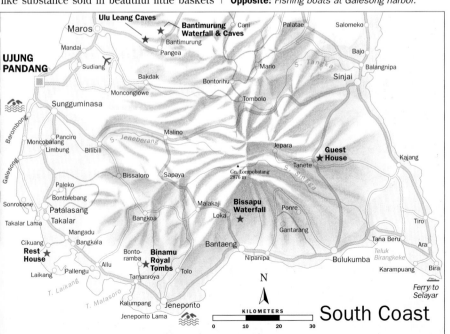

South Coast

At 63 km (39 mi) a fine view of the sea and the hills is offered as you approach Bangkala. To visit the former boat-building center of Pallengu, pass the mosque, cross a bridge, and follow the main road as it curves right. Immediately before a line of small shops there is a bumpy road to the right, leading 2 km (1.8 mi) down to the small village of Pallengu on a narrow estuary.

This was the former center of the fiefdom of Bangkala, the leading aristocratic families of which had a long history of shipping ventures. Most of the male population of Pallengu are seafarers, and their operations cover the whole archipelago. The largest shipowner is Karaeng Getah (Haji Akbar), whose shipping company is now centered in Jakarta. All the boats were built in his home village, however, using the master-craftsmen of Ara as well as some local labor. The dry season was the time for building.

In the early 1980s, the waterside still looked as though several Noahs had all decided to build their arks at once. Now, all boat construction has moved to Tana Beru. The broad motorized vessels (up to 1000 cu. meters) are less elegant than the *prahu pinisi* which predominated a few years back, but the miracle of construction entirely by hand is even more impressive as the size of the ships grows larger.

Hereafter the road is closer to the coast, offering a good view of salt pans in the dry season, which are converted to fish ponds (*empang*) during the rains. As the salt water dries the salt is raked up and sold by the roadside at pathetically low prices, in baskets made of *lontara* leaves. The fish ponds are more profitable, using the brackish water of the rainy season to grow the spawn of the *ikan bolu* as well as prawns.

Farther east there is an important subsidiary income to be had from scooping up the spawn of the *bolu* at the sea's edge (as this fish can only spawn in salt water) and selling it to the *empang* owners. Other than this, Jeneponto is not a fishing area, despite its long coast.

Continuing along the road, you will pass the Tirta Ria swimming resort (*pemandian*) on the right (74 km). The spot is generously endowed with bamboo groves and breadfruit trees which provide plenty of shade. There are sheds where you can change clothing before using a mediocre beach. More popular with local visitors on Sundays are two pools filled with spring water.

At 77 km, a road to the left leads upward 4 km to the royal graves of Bontoramba. Human and animal figures are carved on several of the graves of the Binamu dynasty, which was centered here before moving to Jeneponto Lama in the 19th century.

At 90 km, turn right for Jeneponto Lama, the pre-war capital and seat of the Karaeng Binamu. This has the predictable old colonial jail and *controleur's* house, and many fine aristocratic Makassar houses. If this road is followed past Jeneponto Lama, it skirts the coast closely enough to give access to a number of fine beaches. Just after Jeneponto, a poor road to the left leads up to the former Dutch hill station of Malakaji, which was fashionable before Malino opened in 1922.

As the road descends onto the coastal plain (108 km), there is a sweeping view of the valley, surrounding foothills and the sea. After this point the road runs along the coast for 20 km, past traditional villages and colorful *prahus* with their fishing nets hung out to dry. At various times of the year villagers can be seen working in groups netting eggs from the sea for their fish ponds, or taking fish from their traps.

Bantaeng

Bantaeng (123 km) was ceded to the Dutch under the terms of the Treaty of Bungaya (1667). It was originally occupied by Aru Palakka's Bugis, but later became a Dutch post. It became the capital of the southeast-

JEAN-LÉO DUGAST

ern region in the colonial period, but is now only slightly ahead of the other south coast capitals as an urban center. Bantaeng region is the best irrigated on the south coast, and provides rice and vegetables for Ujung Pandang.

For a spectacular waterfall (*air terjun Bisappu*) turn left towards Bissapu before Bantaeng. The waterfall, about 4 km north of Bissapu along a rough road, is about 100 meters (325 ft) high. In 1840 James Brooke, the raja of Sarawak, admired its "undisturbed solitude and complete seclusion," and on a weekday it still enjoys this claim. Brooke went on to climb Mount Lompobatang, or Bantaeng Peak, highest point in the southern cordillera; it took him three days to reach the summit from Bantaeng. Between Bantaeng and Bulukumba the road follows the coast, giving access to some good beaches.

Boat building

Kabupaten Bulukumba (146 km) occupies the rocky southeast corner of the province. As the road is rough and stony, the going is slow. After skirting the coast for a short time it turns inland, along a rocky terrain suitable only for forest and grazing. Cattle, buffalo, goats and horses are seen here. Further towards the coast there are *empang*, which attract flocks of white ibis.

Along the beach at Tana Beru (174 km, homestay available), you may observe tradi-

tional boat-building, noting the sign: "Lokasi Konstruksi Pinisi." At 178 km the road turning inland to Ara and Bira is well marked, the last signs you will see. At 181 km turn left at a fork in the road. At 188 km a T-junction: Ara to the left, Bira to the right. At 195 km begin a very steep, rocky descent to Bira (5 km): the center, as for centuries past, of the South Sulawesi boat-building industry.

There are three harbors in the little town of Bira, two for *prahus* and one for the vehicular ferry. The water is delightfully clear for swimming, and the white sand beaches shady and pleasant, especially near the ferry wharf. In the past, *prahus* gathered here to set sail for the Moluccas and Irian, when Bira was still a center for sailors and boat-owners. There are several hotels and eating places in Bira and nearby Tanateng. (See page 110.)

You may sail from Bira to Selayar by ferry; there is bus or private transport on the island. At least one night is necessary in Benteng on Selayar. It pays to arrive a little early, especially on the return trip. The crossing may be rough, as there are some treacherous currents in this area. However, it is generally calm, with crystal-clear water and lots of fish. The rocky coast and sandy beaches near both terminals are very inviting. (See "Selayar Island," page 98.)

Opposite: *A young Bugis girl at Tana Beru.*
Above: *A farmer on horseback at Jeneponto.*

JEAN-LEO DUGAST

Ara and Kajang

Returning from Selayar to Bira, continue back to the turnoff (a 5-km ascent) towards Ara, which lies about 13 km away. There are glimpses of the sea through the trees. Ara, a prosperous village, is famous for its shipbuilders, who travel all over Indonesia. The village has in fact no easy access to the sea (2 km away) nor to timber supplies. Still, 80 percent of the working males (about 1,000 in all) are employed in ship-building in various parts of Indonesia, always returning to their families in this village.

The signpost for the Ara caves (Gowa Purbakala Ara) on the main road gives the distance as 0.5 km. However, the way to the caves is through heavy brush and undergrowth and the caves themselves are disappointing; fairly open, with scattered remains of broken porcelain, coffins and bones.

Continue on the coastal road to Kajang to Tiro, a few km north of Ara. Here is the grave of Dato Tiro, Khatib Bungsu, one of the three Muslim holy men from Minangkabau who brought Islam to South Sulawesi in the 17th century. Tiro also has a pre-Muslim cliff grave similar to contemporary Toraja graves, in a cave overlooking the sea.

On the road east to Kajang there is a big government rubber plantation (formerly Dutch), the only one in South Sulawesi.

Kajang (266 km) is situated on a deep, pleasant bay. Travelers can stay overnight in Pondok Sisihorong, 10 km north.

Members of the Tanatoa religious sect centered west of Kajang wear black and have a formidable reputation for magic which has helped to protect their pre-Islamic culture.

Sinjai

The road to Sinjai is a pleasant, hilly drive around the slopes of Mount Lompobatang (2871 meters/9330 ft), an extinct volcano which according to local tradition was one of the first areas to emerge from the primordial sea. There is a mixture of crops on the terraced hills: cloves, some rice, corn, and fruits. The corn is hung out to dry in woven palm-leaf sheaths under the houses. As you reach Sinjai there is a fine view of the town and the coast.

Sinjai (221 km) is separated from *kabupaten* Bone by the river Tangka. The port lies in the adjoining town of Balangnipa, where there is a former Dutch fort, built in the 1860s. It is now used as a police office. From here, you can take a boat to Pulau Sembilan (Nine Islands), picturesque mountainous islands covered in jungle.

The road from here to Malino has recently been paved, and offers an alternate route back to Ujung Pandang. If you take this road for 1.5 km there are hot springs at Uwae. The sacred grave at this spot, which is looked after by a holy man (*sanro*), is frequently visited by the local people who come to pray and bring offerings. North of Sinjai, but difficult of access, are the caves, Gua Karampuang and Gua Bappajeng, and nearer Sinjai is a traditional aristocratic house.

The road to Bone travels along a flat plain cultivated in rice, with some grazing land. To the west of Marek, 30 km from Bone, are the hills where according to legend Prince La Darapung took refuge when exiled from Luwu because of leprosy. Having no other company but his dog, he had two children from this animal, humans with white skin and blue eyes. The horrified inhabitants of the area banished the family, who went off to populate Europe.

There is a sugar factory on the right as you continue, with 5,000 hectares (12,350 acres) of cane. The factory, the biggest outside Java, began production in 1975. Much of its labor force is seasonal, drawn especially from the poorer areas to the south.

—Anthony Reid

Above: *Women bathing in Sinjai.* **Opposite:** *A Kajang horseman carries his saddle on his head.*

TANA BERU

Craftsmen on the Brink of Change

Traditional wooden boats are built all along Sulawesi's south coast, but the epicenter of the industry is the village of Tana Beru (see map page 91). You can find hundreds of boats in the *bantilang* (boathouses) along the beach here. Tana Beru is the ideal location to witness this ancient skill, currently undergoing the pressures of modernization.

There are a number of traditional boat styles under construction in the village today. *Pajala* are small, sharp sterned 9 to 10 meter fishing boats. *Patorani* are decked boats from 10 to 18 meters long, used for fishing on open sea (mainly for *torani*, flying fish). *Paduwakang* are enlarged patorani, fitted with an aft deck (*ambeng*) and a low foredeck. These are used for extended sea voyages.

The most renowned and magnificent boats made in the region are the *pinisi*. These large, sleek Buginese schooners measuring 30 meters or more are sadly less common today because of high manufacturing costs.

Although many boats are now built to accommodate motors, nearly all of the smaller fishing craft and some larger vessels are still built according to the strict traditional rules of construction.

Plans, marriage and construction

Before building begins, the *panrita lopi*, or master boat builder, designs the vessel in a long night of contemplation. He must consider a number of factors: available timber, the size and shape of boat and the ways of combining this with the two classical construction patterns and his own family traditions.

One method of calculating the length of the main keel section uses the span of the future owner's hand as a unit of measurement. The piece is measured hand-over-hand while the five fates of the future boat are recited in the manner of "she loves me, she loves me not." These fates are: dying on land (returning to the place she was built); getting stolen; finding luck; sinking at sea; and being a reason for joy. When a favourable fate is cited near the right spot, the length is fixed. Construction proper can then begin.

The laying of the keel is an important event. The three pieces of a traditional keel are joined by mortice and tenon joints (called *telang*, vagina; and *lasso*, penis). The "marriage" of the keel is celebrated by a series of ceremonies in the *bantilang*.

A cake made from rice flour, coconut and red sugar is placed on the keel to mark the position of the first cuts. This tasty boiled cake has a special significance. Its name, *umba-umba*, means "that which always emerges": it floats to the water's surface when cooked. As the builders say: "first sinking, than coming up again, wouldn't that be a good boat?" Other offerings are also made, their ingredients dependent upon the future function of the vessel. The keel pieces are then left alone overnight, signifying the first night together for the "newlyweds."

The ceremonies held on the first day of building are the preamble to weeks of hard work. It takes two people some six to eight weeks to finish the shell of a 9 meter fishing boat. *Pinisi* take a ten-strong team many

HORST LIEBNER

Left: *Hull planks must be symmetrical. In the past, two sections of the same tree trunk were used as mirror images. Today, machine-cut timbers are employed.* **Opposite:** *The completed boat requires all available muscle to launch.*

months. Families often work together to build large boats, but you are just as likely to see men building by themselves. One man can complete a 14-meter *perahu* in under a year.

Convention dictates that the outside planks of the traditional hull must be assembled first, with supporting frames being installed afterwards. Getting the hull symmetrical is the trickiest part of construction.

Following the laying of the keel, the hull planks are then connected edge to edge with dowels made from a hard yet flexible mangrove. The internal frames are later fixed by dowels hammered through the planks from the outside. After being sealed with bark and rubber, the outside of the hull is then smoothed with a *bingkung*,—a square-bladed adze typical to Indonesian boat building.

Launching into the future

A big feast takes place on board the dry docked ship on the eve of a traditional launch. Water buffalo, goats and chickens are sacrificed then served to sometimes hundreds of guests. It is said that the greater the number of guests, the more fortunate the ship will be.

More ceremonies then take place within the hull. The most important is the cutting of the magic "navel" of the boat. The blood of two chicken combs is smeared on the spot where a hole is to be bored through the keel with a sacred drill. Once cut, gold is then dropped through the hole, to be collected by the builder's children. The hole is then temporarily sealed with a mixture of umba-umba and *haje*, sweetened black rice.

The following day the guests return to help with the launch. Men pull the boat, while women throw rice on the slipway, children run around and elders oversee the efforts. Singing and dancing used to accompany launches, but this is now rare.

The 1970s saw the advent of motorization in Tana Beru. This severely effected the longevity of traditional craft. Most of the first *pinisi* with engines didn't last longer than three years. Joints were weakened by the vibration of undamped engines: whole keel sections fell off, and seams split open when hit by heavy waves. Steel bolts and heavier timbers are now being used, but no satisfactory solution has been developed. Captains continue to bemoan the short lifespans of the motorized vessels: a drop from up to 60 years under sail, to a current maximum of eight.

Today half of boats built in Tana Beru are sold to other islands, and the owners seldom organize feasts. Electrical tools have recently come into use, and a government project encourages the use of modern glues and paints. The industry is being transformed from a traditional undertaking to a modern enterprise and there is a danger that the current generation of *panrita lopi* will be the last guard of Sulawesi's boat building heritage.

—Horst Liebner

HORST LIEBNER

SELAYAR ISLAND

Beaches and an Ancient Drum

Selayar's position as a long, narrow barrier on the trade routes to the Moluccas has thrust it into history despite the stubborn rockiness of its soil. Currents frequently wash wreckage up onto its 100-kilometer-long (60 mi) west coast, which perhaps accounts for the presence of a 2,000-year-old Vietnamese Dong Son drum. Yet Selayar must have been a trading center in its own right by at least the 14th century, when it is mentioned in the Javanese *Nagarakertagama* poem. An unusual abundance of Chinese and Sawankhalok (Thai) ceramics of about the same period has also been dug from grave sites on the island.

Islam appears to have come to Selayar in the 16th century from the eastern islands of Ternate and Buton. But it was Makassar which first imposed its political dominance over the island's many feuding principalities. Selayar was a valuable prize not only through its location, but because its coarse blue-and-white cotton "Selayar cloth" was in demand all over the archipelago. At least from the 16th to the 19th centuries, cotton was the major crop and export product of the island, and tribute had to be paid to its successive masters in this cloth.

Ternate (in the Moluccas) claimed Selayar in the Treaty of Bungaya, which carved up much of the Makassar empire (1667), but the Dutch wrested it back in the early 18th century. Thereafter the fourteen autonomous "regents" of Selayar had to bring their homage and their cloth to Fort Rotterdam. In the last 150 years Selayar cloth has declined to nothing in the face of factory production. The economy is now perilously dependent on coconut harvesting and whatever can be earned by other trade. The island's population has grown very little in the last century, as its earlier favorable location has given way to isolation.

This isolation (both internal and external) has sustained a surprising variety in Selayar, including the linguistic peculiarity of a Buton language surviving in the south. The southern village of Binanga Benteng was also the center of the Mahdi Akbar movement, a quasi-Islamic messianic movement centered around the mystical teachings of Abdul Sani ("Tuang Opu"), who died there in 1922. In the 1930s some of its adherents were led into the fold of Christianity and after 1966, when

the Mahdi Akbar moverment was banned by the local Moslem body, others took refuge under the umbrella of Hinduism.

The ferry to Selayar leaves daily from Bira at 14:00 and arrives at 16:15. A direct bus which connects up with the ferry leaves from Panaikan bus terminal in Ujung Pandang at 07:00. It pays to be a little early, especially on the return trip.

The inviting beaches to the north of the ferry are as good as most on the island. From Pamatata ferry, minibuses drive west across a barren, rocky terrain where the white coralitic rock is used for neat stone walls. Water is very scarce in this area, yet it has a prosperous and well-kept air despite the poverty of the soils. Along the west coast the road is asphalted but bumpy, fringed with rows of towering coconut palms. At sunset it is a picturesque drive down the coast past fishing villages to the main town of Benteng, where there is a clean new hotel.

In Benteng, the residence of the former *controleur,* which dates from the 1890s, overlooks the central green (*alun-alun*). On the north side of the *alun-alun* is a very solid-looking Dutch jail, which also dates from the 1890s. To the west, a sculptured figure with a *keris* lunges out to sea to repel invaders.

The *nekara*—the famous Dong Son drum of Selayar—is kept at Bontobangun, 3 km (1.8 mi) south of Benteng, in a wooden shed near the palace of the former raja of the area, Andi Arman, whose son now lives there. It was excavated around the 17th century at Papalohia (the center of a pre-Islamic kingdom). The drum is a magnificent specimen, measuring 95 cm high and 115 cm across (38 x 45 in), with four stylized frogs arranged on the sides of the top surface around a central raised star with 16 points. (One of the frogs was cut off but fortunately recovered.) Around this star there is an intricate pattern forming sixteen concentric circles.

On the sides, which are triple-tiered, are four handles, arranged in pairs. The pattern varies from tier to tier, with elephant motifs, birds and coconut trees around the base, abstract motifs in the middle section, and peacocks in the top section.

With the drum are kept three beautifully carved pieces of a wooden *prahu* wrecked at Metallallong and kept by the raja of Bontobangun as a magical craft in which he sailed to Gowa. These consist of the head of a *naga*, about 110 cm (43 in) high, with ornate wings, head and teeth; the tail, about 1.5 meters long, in a style reminiscent of Majapahit; and

an *anjungan*, the place where the captain sat to give orders to the boatmen. Inscribed in Arabic are the words "Sultan Abdul Malik, Tuban," suggesting that it dates from the 16th century, when Tuban was still a great East Javan port.

From a little below the microwave station overlooking Benteng you can walk east along a jungle track to the hilltop fort of Gantarang. One of the strongest pre-Islamic states in the region, Gantarang had links with Buton and Luwu. The village of about forty houses (it is said that formerly there were 700) lies on top of a hill reached only by three paths. The settlement is protected by nine-meter-high walls surmounting the natural stronghold.

The mosque in Gantarang is said to have been built in the 16th century at the behest of Datu ri Bandang, who spread Islamic teaching in the Makassar area. The old layered roof is supported on an ancient wooden frame on four pillars, with a short central pillar suspended from cross-beams. There is also a very old *mimbar* (pulpit), and two ancient *khotbah* (sermons) written in Arabic on sewn paper.

According to local legend a mark in the rock close to the mosque is the left footprint of the Bugus hero Sawerigading; the right is said to be in Mecca.

—Anthony Reid

Opposite: *The splendid Dongson drum of Selayar.*

BONE AND SOPPENG

Vanished Bugis Kingdoms

The capitals of three former Bugis kingdoms, located in the central and eastern parts of the peninsula, can be reached in just a few hours by bus from Ujung Pandang. Each has a distinctive character. Watansoppeng (Soppeng) is set among rolling foothills; Watampone (Bone) has old Dutch houses and spacious squares; while Singkang is a bustling market town overlooking Lake Tempe.

From Ujung Pandang, the road to Bone and Soppeng leads north, turning off to the right at Maros. After this turnoff, the road starts to climb over the limestone ranges. Soaring cliffs hung with tropical creepers are interspersed with the dense jungle of the National Forest. The crumbling rock lends itself to fantastic formations, caves and stalactites, with occasional waterfalls and glimpses of rivers far below. The area is rich in prehistoric remains. Camba, at 67 km (42 mi) from

Ujung Pandang, guards a pass in the southern range, dominated by Maros Peak, Bulu Saraung (1360 meters/4420 ft).

The road runs along a grassy plain with signs of severe erosion in the surrounding hills. At Lepangun (123 km), just after passing two *warungs* on the right, the road forks. The right fork leads to Bone, left to Soppeng. A little way up the road to Soppeng is Lamuru, a strategically important mountain kingdom on the pass between Bone and Soppeng. The tombs of the rajahs of Lamuru, Kompleks Makam Kuno, lie on the right just off the road about 10 km later. The guard on the left has a key and there is an information center on the left inside the gate.

Powerful kingdom of Bone

Capital of the most populous *kabupaten* in South Sulawesi, Bone was formerly the strongest of all Bugis states. The recorded list of Bone rulers goes back to the 14th century, when the original *tomunurung* came down from heaven, married a mortal, and began a dynasty. By the 16th century Bone dominated the region, linked with Wajo and Soppeng in the Tallumpocco alliance (1582) against the rising power of Makassar. In 1610-11 Bone accepted Islam and the loose hegemony of Makassar (Gowa) after being defeated on the battlefield. Renewed defiance brought a much more bitter defeat in 1640 and again in 1644, after which Bone was

they were naked to the waist, wearing only skull caps and sarongs, and preserving a profound silence."

After repeated difficulties, the Dutch sent another expedition against Bone in February 1859. The doughty female ruler retreated to the hills, but the Dutch expedition was a disaster and had to withdraw with its commander dead. A bigger force landed more cautiously in Sinjai in November 1859, taking Watampone in December and Pampanua in January. In 1931, after a long interregnum,

ruled as a conquered province. This led to the rebellion under Aru Palakka in the 1660s, and the alliance with the Dutch which ultimately destroyed Makassar in 1669.

Aru Palakka ruled in Bone from 1672 until his death in 1696. His victorious alliance with the Dutch added Bantaeng, Lamuru and parts of Bulukumba and Soppeng to his fiefdom, while in 1670 he conquered the vital Walanae (Cenrana) River outlet of Wajo to the sea. Bone continued through the 18th century to be the strongest Bugis power, supported by the Dutch until it began to threaten Makassar itself at the end of the century. The messianic Gowa rebel Sankilang held the most sacred Gowa regalia—the Sudanga sword—during his long resistance in the hills, but on his deathbed in the 1790s he passed it to the Bone ruler. This encouraged Bone's claims on Gowa itself, and from 1794 Bone attacked and dominated the Maros area to the north of Makassar. This forced the occupants of Fort Rotterdam to move against Bone—first the British (1816) and later the returning Dutch, who in 1824 briefly occupied and destroyed Watampone itself.

Nevertheless, Bone remained a substantial power. James Brooke found in 1840 he could achieve little among the Bugis without the Bone ruler, and when he finally gained audience in 1840 the scene was impressive:

"A body of 3000 or 4000 were ranged within and without the courtyard, dressed precisely alike, in skull-caps and blue sarongs over the kris. A dead silence was preserved as we passed through them, and afforded a striking contrast to the inexpressible tumult of our reception at Tesora [Wajo]. Eight or ten spearmen, clad in coats of bright chain armor, guarded the entrance, and presented the only display of arms we saw.

... Behind the monarch were half a dozen handsome boys, his own relations; and two rows of young rajahs were seated cross-legged on his right hand. Like those without,

Andi Mappanyuki was placed on the throne, which continued to be the most influential one in South Sulawesi until the monarchy was abolished in 1955.

Visiting Watampone

The devastations of numerous invasions of the capital, Watampone, have unfortunately not left a great deal of historic interest, except for one colorful wall of the *kabupaten* office, part of the 19th-century Bone palace which was taken to Makassar after the 1905 defeat and returned in 1931 to form part of the new palace. The royal grave complex, with 17th-century tombs similar in style to those of Gowa, is at Bukaka on the road leading north towards Singkang.

About 4 km (2.5 mi) east of the city is the port of Bajoe, which takes its name from the Bajau boat people who at one time inhabited the waterways throughout much of the archipelago. Many of them now live in houses over the water at the port. Legend links the origin of the Bajau with Luwu, where the

Opposite: *Palace of the ruler of Bone, built by the Dutch following his restoration to the throne in the 1930s.* **Above, left:** *Grave of Collipujie, an 18th-century ruler of Lamuru, said to have invented the letters of the Bugis alphabet.* **Above, right:** *the shield of the raja of Bone, kept in the Bone Museum. "Rose-style" brass studs represent the nine cardinal directions of Hindu mythology.*

Bugis hero Sawerigading felled a giant tree, forming an island, causing a flood, and washing the Bajau out to sea. The yolk from the broken birds' eggs which fell from the tree is supposed to have stained the Bajaus' hair a yellowish color (this was more likely due to a vitamin deficiency). On the strength of this legend, eggs are considered taboo among the Bajau. From Bajoe a ferry leaves nightly at 11 pm for Kolaka on the Southeast peninsula, arriving at about 6 am, whence there is a well-paved road to Kendari.

Limestone caves and a lost kingdom

The largest and most spectacular series of limestone caves in South Sulawesi, Gua Mampu, are 34 km (21 mi) north of Watampone. These comprise two upper caves lit by collapsed roofs, and two lower ones for which artificial light is needed. Take the road to Singkang, turning left at the village of Ulae. Guides and flashlights are available in abundance. This cave has been celebrated for centuries not only for its natural shapes, but for the legends associating it with the lost kingdom of Mampu. The members of the Mampu court are said to have been turned to stone, as the result of a curse delivered when a princess, Apung Mangenre, dropped her spool, and being too lazy to pick it up herself, asked her dog to do the job for her. There are varying versions of the legend, but all seek to explain particular strange shapes. James Brooke was so excited by the stories of a Mampu kingdom that he made enormous efforts to reach the cave in 1840 in the hope of discovering some vanished civilization. While his hopes were unfulfilled Brooke conceded the remarkable beauty of the cave.

Watansoppeng (Soppeng)

One of the prettiest towns in the province, Soppeng has won prizes for its gardens. Sprays of moon orchids frequently festoon the verandahs of Soppeng's buildings. One of the most remarkable features of the town is the vast numbers of bats which swarm in the tall trees of the town center, around the mosque and the office of the *bupati*. Local mythology has it that if the bats leave Soppeng, the town would collapse. Since they seem careful to only eat the fruit of non-Soppengers, they are never disturbed, but hang squeaking in their thousands, to take off in swarms at dusk and dawn.

The graves of the rajas, Taman Purbakala Kompleks Makam Kuno, Jena Lomoe, are located 800 meters from the town center, to

the left of the road to Ompo. Note the unique house-like structure of these stone graves. Continue on the road to Ompo and turn right upon reaching Ompo, heading for the springs and pool (*Pemandian Ompo*). Many villagers go directly to the springs behind the swimming pool to wash and bathe; but the pool is refilled every Friday with fresh spring water, and is very spacious, with pagodas along the sides to sit under. There is another natural pool at Lawo, nearby. Megaliths, some probably very old, are also to be seen in abundance in the village of Lawo, where the villagers use many of them for house supports.

Silk is now cultivated here as a home industry. Women take about a month to produce a piece two meters (6.5 ft) long. Visitors can stop to watch and to buy. Spinning can also be seen in small shops in the town. The main area for cultivating the silkworms is north of Soppeng, on the road to Pangkajene where mulberry trees are abundant.

Vanishing lakes

The road north to Singkang runs through a flat plain with *sawah* and tobacco production visible along the roadside. The tobacco leaves are dried, shredded and baked in bamboo tubes about two feet long in drying houses for two to three days. The cylinders are

Above: *Moslem children going to the mosque at Singkang.* **Opposite:** *Fish traps in Lake Tempe.*

simply sliced open for sale. Cabenge is the main marketing center of the tobacco-growing district, and is especially lively on market days (Monday and Friday), when villagers arrive in painted and decorated pony carts.

The road crosses the Walanae River, the only marine outlet for the Wajo people, who are nevertheless great seafarers. The river flows into Lake Tempe, which is gradually drying up because of heavy silting brought about by erosion. This has speeded a slow natural process of change, dating from the Pleistocene period, whereby large tracts of land have gradually emerged from the sea. Lake Tempe is the largest remnant of an inland sea which is thought to have originally divided the peninsula in two.

Nowadays the lake is hardly much more than two meters (6.5 ft) deep, and in the dry season vast areas dry up completely. In 1972 you could cross from Tempe to the other side in a horse and cart. Although Lake Tempe still provides fish for export, production is dropping. One specialty of the area is small shrimp (*lawa*), which are served seasoned and flavored with lemon juice.

At times the lake floods. People then move around by boat, and there are even floating shops. The birds in this area are particularly prolific. Boat races, which used to have a ritual significance, have been reintroduced for the celebration of Independence Day, the 17th of August.

Singkang: Bugis silks and dances

Capital of the *kabupaten* of Wajo, Singkang, along with its twin town of Tempe on the lakeside of Lake Tempe, retains a traditional character. From the government resthouse (*Baruga We Cudai*) situated on top of the hill across the square from the mosque, there is an excellent view over the two towns, each of which has a large mosque built in the Middle-Eastern architectural style. In the background glimmers Lake Tempe.

Singkang is renowned for its silk weaving. An energetic princess of Wajo named Andi Bau Muddaria, who takes particular interest in her people's traditions and culture, was the first to set up a local workshop modelled on Thai silk production, in a large house near the mosque. Other workshops have since followed suit. Sarongs and meter lengths of silk may be purchased at the silk factory on Jl. Sentosa Baru.

Andi Bau Muddaria is reviving a number of cultural traditions, such as a colorful Bugis wedding in the ancient style, reenacted in Singkang in 1981. Wajo dance groups are often asked to represent the aristocratic traditions of the Bugis people. There is an excellent dance group composed of local aristocratic ladies here, and a traditional orchestra including flutes, violins and *kecapi* (a kind of two-stringed lute).

—Anthony Reid

LUWU DISTRICT

Land Where the Gods Descended

The sign as you enter *kabupaten* Luwu from Siwa announces that this is "the land of Sawerigading." According to Bugis chronicles, it was in the vicinity of the Cerekang River, between the present towns of Wotu and Malili, that the gods first descended, and that their descendent, Sawerigading, performed his legendary deeds. The first Bugis kingdom may have been located here, perhaps in the 13th and 14th centuries, and may provide the historical basis for the tale.

In the centuries that followed, Luwu's main asset was always its cachet as the oldest kingdom with the most potent *bissu*. In reality the Bugis population of Luwu was always very small and its military and economic significance negligible, yet the sultanate managed to draw tribute from a host of diverse people from Tana Toraja to Poso and even Kolaka. The Dutch colonial regime after 1904 initially reinforced this shadowy authority, and it was not until the late 1940s that Toraja and Kolaka were separated from Luwu.

In 1937, however, Luwu began a new era as the open frontier of South Sulawesi, with new immigrants opening rice fields, where for centuries the main food crop had been the sago trees which grow wild in its vast forests. The Dutch sponsored the first Javanese "colonists" to the area of Bonebone and Wotu, though these had to undergo terrible hardships in the turbulent years that followed. When these years finally came to an end in the late 1960s with the crushing of the Darul Islam rebellion, both official "transmigration" of Javanese and Balinese and spontaneous migration of Toraja and others has been far more intensive, doubling the population of Luwu in the last ten years (1980 population 503,700). An ambitious irrigation and road-building project, "Project Luwu," has been under way since 1975 to provide the infrastructure for these migrants. In addition, one of the world's biggest nickel mines is now operating at the eastern fringe of Luwu.

Visiting Luwu

Buses from Ujung Pandang to Luwu leave in the early morning from the main bus terminal. The journey takes you north to Parepare (see "West Coast"), then inland to Pangkajene, capital of *kabupaten* Sidrap. The most prosperous rice-growing district in South

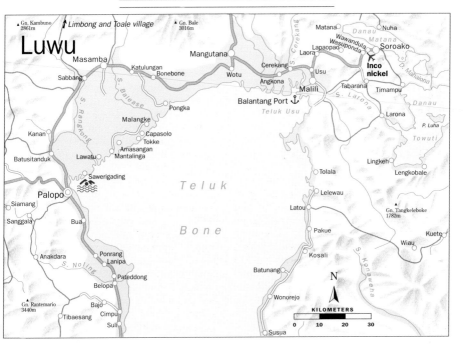

Sulawesi, Sidrap owes its fertility to the Sa'dan irrigation system set up by the Dutch in the 1930s, which has recently been upgraded. Double-cropping is thus normal here, and the commercialization and mechanization of agriculture has proceeded further than elsewhere.

Note the handsome old aristocratic house, brought intact from Wajo, which is now an annex to the government resthouse behind the *bupati*'s office.

From Anabanua, the road continues east through Siwa, a picturesque town on the river Tuguerange. The land is dry and barren at first, with coconut palms and some *sawah*.

Shortly after Pandangsappa the road draws near the coast, then moves a few kilometers inland again because of mangrove swamps. This is a scenic drive, with the mountains of Central Sulawesi looming mistily on the northern horizon. The approach to Palopo offers magnificent views of the bay, though even more so if you approach from Rantepao.

Palopo: gateway to the iron hills

To appreciate the setting of Palopo, the major town of Luwu, drive out onto the long pier which runs for 1.5 km (1 mi) alongside the river and out into the bay. It's a dirty and smelly area but there are several types of fishing boats to be seen. These include the twin-hulled *bagan*: a two-masted floating fishing platform with an orderly maze of wires stretching to their outriggers and used to haul up nets. Strings of lights attract the fish during moonless nights. There is good view of the bay from the end of the pier.

The Mosque opposite the post office, Mesjid Kuno Batupassi, is probably the oldest in South Sulawesi. Built around 1603 when the area was Islamized it is oriented to the west instead of the northwest as it should be. People now pray there facing the northwest corner. The stone walls are about a meter thick.

Said to have been built by the same artisan who built the mosque, the royal graves (*Makam raja-raja*) are in the single-domed pyramidal tomb (*lokkoh*) to the right. The caretaker next door has a key, but does not usually let tourists enter this holy tomb. It possibly replaces a wooden *lokkoh* such as the Toraja use if there is no cave available.

Other sites include the small Batara Guru museum in the house of the former rajas. There is a swimming pool at Latuppa, and beaches at Sawerigading (northeast of town), Songka, and Plywood Beach. It is pleasant to take a boat out to the small island of Lebukan.

From Palopo to Malili

This 188-km (118-mi) journey takes about six hours, thanks to a very good asphalt road developed as part of "Project Luwu." The

Opposite: *Palopo harbor.*

large dam 21 km (13 mi) from Palopo is part of an extensive irrigation project for the area. To the north lies the central mountain range, dominated by Mt. Kambuno (2,950 m/9600 ft) and to the southeast Mt. Bale (3016 m/9800 ft). Hardy travelers interested in walking could visit the traditional weaving centers of Rongkong, Seko, and Makki north of Sabbang. Each village has a different style of weaving. The aboriginal people of this area, the Toala, wear a distinctive form of dress. They are more hospitable here than around Poso, where they are suspicious of foreigners.

To get there, it is possible to take public transportation from Sabbang to Limbung. Then trek to Rongkong in a day or catch the *kijang* which runs once every six days (market day). From Rongkong to Seko it takes three days, then a further two to Makki. It is then a difficult six-day tramp from Kalumpang to Rantepao; or you could walk from Kalumpang to Tamlea, where you can take a river boat to Mamuju. This trip is only for the most adventurous, who must carry provisions and medical supplies.

From Masamba (61 km), the adventurous can hike northward to Lake Poso. The swampy coastal plain to the south of the road beyond Masamba, is a major transmigration area. 20 km (12 mi) past Masamba is Katulungan, one of the area's oldest settlements.

The center of the transmigration and irrigation projects of the region is at Bonebone (101 km). There is a fascinating mixture of peoples and cultures in this area. Toraja rice-barns and wooden churches exist side by side with mosques, Javanese bungalow cottages, and Balinese temples. Javanese *wayang kulit* or *gamelan* performances can be seen in some transmigration villages on special occasions.

At 139 km is Wotu, a small town with a *losmen*. The *prahu* port on the river to the east is worth a visit (not the harbor, which is 3 km away). This could be a scene from a Conrad novel, with houses on stilts built over the water, fishing boats and small industries such as sawmills on the water's edge.

From Wotu begins South Sulawesi's only road link to Central Sulawesi, the road north to Poso. The newly completed road to Lake Poso is occasionally blocked by landslides after a heavy rainfall, but traverses spectacular mountain country.

Cerekang, 175 km, is believed to have been the center of the old kingdom of Luwu. The Cerekang River is navigable for 15 km north towards Lake Matana, which can then be reached on foot. This area was in the past a source of iron for making knives (*badik*). The sacred graves upriver can only be visited with permission from the *kepala kampung* in Cerekang. According to tradition the god Batara Guru descended to earth here, and Sawerigading bathed in a small river in the hills nearby. Usu (184 km) reveals little trace of its prominent role in the *La Galigo* epic, though it long retained a magical significance for Luwu's kings.

Malili and Soroako

Formerly a picturesque riverside town near the bay of Usu, the town of Malili was destroyed by the rebellion during the 1950s, and was completely rebuilt as the port for the Soroako project. There are good swimming and boating from the sandy beaches of the island of Bulopeway, off the coast from Malili. According to legend, this island was formed when Sawerigading felled a huge *wailendring* tree, which shattered the land and sent the Bajau people out to sea.

In 1968 P.T. Inco began its operations in this area, when the Indonesian Government signed contracts with the Canadian-based company for the design and construction of nickel-processing facilities in the area of Soroako. All equipment and supplies for the plant passed through the port of Balantang at Malili. At first the headquarters were at Malili, but were later moved to Soroako, leaving only a small settlement at the port. Except for the port area the company seems to have hardly made a mark on the town, though a school and hospital were established there.

There is, however, a good road to Soroako which follows the spectacular Larona River gorge through the mountains for about 30 km, when the road leaves the river valley for the undulating valley which stretches to Lake Matana. The village of Wasuponda is the first satellite town of Soroako; a few kilometers farther on there is a turnoff to the second, Wawandula, where the river is dammed for a new electricity station. Schools have been constructed in all three towns, as well as a health center in Wasuponda and a hospital in Soroako for Inco employees.

The dense green jungle around Soroako has been razed for the massive mine complex, which transformed this area almost overnight from a village of shifting cultivators to a site of international importance, with the latest technological equipment. Airplanes and

helicopters fly daily into an area previously only accessible by long journeys on foot; motorboats and water-skis disturb the centuries-old silence on the lake; and the former ricefields are now a golf course and an air-conditioned village for workers. Besides the Inco guesthouse, which is expensive and intended for guests of the company, there is a *losmen* in the town; there are several restaurants, as well as the lavish Inco canteen.

One of the world's major nickel-producing plants, its massive machinery dominates the landscape. The westernized lifestyle of the predominantly Indonesian workers offers an extraordinary contrast with their environment. The plant has attracted workers from all over Indonesia, though Bugis and Toraja predominate. Naturally this has caused problems in the original village, which has grown beyond the limits of its facilities, and has also lost its original agricultural land. However there are compensations in the increased pay packets brought in by those employed by Inco, the side-benefits of improved communications, schooling, health, electricity and water supply. The company appears anxious to repair environmental damage caused by mining, and to avoid pollution of the lake, one of the great natural attractions of Sulawesi.

Lakes Matana and Towuti

One of the deepest lakes in the world, Matana has but few fish: an oddly shaped transparent fish called *botinu*; the *opudi*, and the *kolami*, a small crayfish. There are burial caves in the cliff edge around the lake, which is clear, cool and delightful for boating and swimming. At the head of the lake is Matana village, where there is a spring popularly believed to be the lake's source. "Matana" means literally "this eye."

The largest lake in Sulawesi, Lake Towuti is 48 km (30 mi) wide and stunningly beautiful. There is a bus from Malili to Wawondula and then to Timampu on the shores of the lake, but no tourist facilities.

This area at the northeastern tip of South Sulawesi encapsulates the attractions, the problems and the promise of future expansion for the province. Less than 15 years ago, Soroako was an isolated village. Today it has an up-to-date nickel plant, with two airstrips and a good highway to the sea.

Since the province opened to tourists several years ago, the number of visitors has rapidly escalated. Improved communications are rapidly breaking down the isolation which helped maintain its unique character. Whether the natural beauty admired in the 19th century by Wallace, Brooke and others will remain unimpaired by material progress is another question.

—*Anthony Reid*

Above: *600-meter (2000 ft) deep Lake Matana near Soroako in South Sulawesi.*

PART III

Introducing Tana Toraja

The long highway heading north from Ujung Pandang, after some 130 km (78 mi) of hugging the coastline of South Sulawesi, begins its fantastic, winding ascent to the mountains. Passing the "gateway" arch of Tana Toraja, the road leads through the small market village of Mebali. The traveler is now drawn into a majestic landscape of rugged grey granite outcrops and distant blue mountains. These form a sharp contrast with the vivid greens of fertile river- and rain-fed rice terraces and the rusty reds of the lateritic soil.

This is Tana Toraja—unquestionably one of the most beautiful regions of Indonesia. On hillocks in the midst of rice paddies, the curved roofs of houses pierce the thickets of bamboo and coconut palms. Children sit astride grazing water buffaloes. In the distance, a jagged ridge of mountains stretches north to distant, isolated valleys.

There are about 360,000 inhabitants of *kabupaten* (regency) Tana Toraja, also known as "Torajaland." Large numbers of Toraja have also emigrated in search of work outside the area. In spite of the splendid landscapes and the rice-field studded mountains, the region is actually land-poor.

Among the aristocrats there are some large landowners, but most people do not own enough land to provide them with rice year-round, and must supplement their diet with cassava, maize, and vegetables grown in small gardens. Rice, however, remains the preferred food in Toraja, and those who can afford it will buy the extra rice they need rather than eat cassava.

Rice is grown in rain-fed hill terraces, many of which must be dug by hand, as they are too narrow to allow the use of buffalo-drawn ploughs. Traditional strains are slow-growing and provide only one crop a year, but in many areas new high-yield varieties are cultivated with the aid of fertilizers and pesticides, permitting two crops a year or even five in two years.

Formerly, groups of villages forming one ritual community would coordinate their work and plant at the same time, each stage of the cycle accompanied by rituals. Death ceremonies would be delayed until the harvest was completed, so as not to mix the rites of death with those of life. Today, people tend to follow their own schedules, and the ritual aspects of cultivation are in decline.

Most Toraja are Christians. The 1990 census lists 87 percent of the population as Christians and 9 percent as Muslims. People in remote areas still tend to follow the traditional religion (now called *aluk to dolo*, or "ways of the ancestors").

For much of the population of Tana Toraja, life follows the familiar patterns of the past. After a simple breakfast of boiled rice or cassava, villagers head toward their rice fields or hillside vegetable gardens. Children go to the spring to fetch water in bamboo tubes.

In many areas there are no shops other than tiny path-side shacks selling necessities like salt, soap, matches, and paraffin for lamps. People must sell surplus rice, or a pig, to purchase what they cannot produce themselves, or in order to raise money for children's tuition at the local school.

In the evenings, a few men may gather under the tree of a local palm-wine tapper for a drink and gossip, or a game of dominoes may be played by lamp-light at home while dinner is cooking. In the absence of television, children provide the main form of entertainment at home, and most people go to bed early. When ritual activity breaks into the daily routine, people travel for miles and happily stay up all night eating, drinking, talking, and taking turns to join dancers who circle slowly, chanting songs in honor of the dead.

—*Roxana Waterson*

Overleaf: *A water buffalo about to be sacrificed at a Toraja death feast. Photo by Kal Muller.*
Opposite: *A Toraja noblewoman.*

HISTORY

Establishing a New Ethnic Identity

Islam came to to South Sulawesi's lowlands at the beginning of the 17th century. Before that, the culture and religious practices of the Toraja and Bugis peoples appear to have had much in common. The name "Toraja" probably derives from the Bugis *to ri aja*, or "people of the mountains." The Dutch adopted the term in the 19th century and applied it to many of the peoples of Central Sulawesi, as well as the South Sulawesi highlands. Central Sulawesi groups rejected the label, but the people of the Sa'dan region adopted it enthusiastically as a new sense of ethnic identity began to develop in relation to the outside world. The present boundaries of Tana Toraja more or less reflect the district boundaries set up by the Dutch; formerly the Toraja highlands had had no boundaries, or any political unity. No centralized state ever formed here, although in the south the three districts of Makale, Sangalla and Mengkendek had formed a federation and nobles there exercised more autocratic power than elsewhere.

Most people, however, owed their allegiance to petty chiefs or "big men" who held sway over individual villages or small groups of villages. The population was divided into ranks of nobles, commoners and slaves. Many of the Toraja nobility intermarried with the rulers of the small kingdoms of South Sulawesi, and some even sent their sons to stay at these courts. Traditionally some parts of Toraja stood in a tributary relationship to the kingdom of Luwu, though the gifts they sent were apparently more a sign of respect than of submission.

A degree of interdependence is reflected in myths which relate that the ruling families of the kingdoms of Gowa, Bone and Luwu are all descended from a common Toraja ancestor named Laki Padada. Up to the abolition of the kingdoms in the 1950s, a Toraja noble participated in the inauguration ceremonies of a new ruler in Luwu, and the ruling families of the old South Sulawesi kingdoms still send representatives to Toraja to take part in rituals celebrated by the house from which Laki Padada is supposed to have descended.

By the 19th century, however, Luwu was an economic backwater, and the more important contacts were with the southerly Bugis and Makassar kingdoms. Relations became troubled in the 1880s and 1890s when the kingdoms of Bone, Luwu, and Sidenreng sent their forces into Toraja to wrest control of the valuable coffee trade.

Guns and cloth were the main items offered in exchange for Toraja's high-quality *arabica* coffee. In slack periods, the coffee trade was augmented by slave-trading. The Bugis and Makassarese kingdoms desperately needed labor for rice cultivation, and slave-trading reached dramatic proportions in some areas of Toraja in the late 19th century. Toraja nobles with expansionist ambitions allied with Bugis mercenaries to raid remote districts for slaves. Some of these nobles had seized large amounts of land and were consolidating their new political power when the process was halted by Dutch intervention. Dutch troops entered the highlands in 1905, and in spite of the fierce resistance of several Toraja chiefs, who held out in natural rock fortresses in the mountains, Dutch control was imposed throughout the area by 1906. Pong Tiku, the Toraja warlord who defended the Pangala area with cannons and chili pepper squirters, was taken prisoner and later shot in Rantepao, purportedly while trying to escape. Today he is remembered as one of Indonesia's national heroes.

Functionaries and missionaries

The new colonial administration fixed boundaries, imposed taxes, established schools (initially reserved for the children of the nobility, who, distrustful of Dutch intentions, sometimes sent children of their slaves along as substitutes), and introduced Christianity. The Dutch Reformed Church sent its first missionary to the region in 1913. According to colonial policy, different churches were allotted specific regions of activity to prevent direct competition, so it was not until 1946 that the Roman Catholic church established a presence in Makale.

The Dutch also brought an end to the turbulence of the coffee and slave wars, and travel on the island became easier. For the

Opposite: *The traditional method of washing being applied to a new form of conveyence.*

first time, some Toraja began to leave the highlands to pursue education or to work. This widening of horizons in the 1920s and 1930s stimulated a new sense of ethnic identity among the Toraja (as they now called themselves).

The Reformed Church mission made uneven progress at first, and there were very few conversions, as the nobility suspected that Christianity would undermine their traditional authority. In the 1930s there was a small spate of conversions, brought about partly by the effects of education of the children of the aristocracy. When noble children converted, parents, relatives, and followers sometimes followed. But numbers fell away again with the depression years of the late 1930s, when local communities blamed the hard times on violation of traditional customs by the converted. The apostasy was aggravated by World War II and the Japanese occupation, when all the necessities of life were in very short supply.

After independence in 1950, primary and secondary education began to spread rapidly in Tana Toraja. But there were few opportunities within the region, with its subsistence-farming economy, to use one's education. Due to the area's poor infrastructure, travel beyond the highlands was difficult. Guerilla warfare, which raged throughout the region between Islamic rebels and the newly-established government during the 1950s, also made travel and expansion dangerous.

The population continued to grow, however, putting ever more pressure on already limited (and not especially fertile) village rice lands. Education had begun to open young peoples' eyes, and to awaken their curiosity about the world beyond the mountains. So it was no surprise that when peace returned to Sulawesi in the mid-1960s, thousands of young Toraja, motivated by scarcity of jobs and land at home, and intrigued by tales of urban wealth, began to leave.

The possibility of seeking work outside the highlands was furthered by Jakarta's new policy of opening up Indonesia's doors to foreign investors. In this period a large number of multinational companies established operations in neighboring Kalimantan, Irian Jaya, and elsewhere to tap the country's rich resources of oil, timber and minerals. Many young Toraja began to travel far from home to seek employment. Young men found jobs as laborers or mechanics, young women as household servants. The stream of migrants became a flood, as stories of success and the cash to prove it flowed home.

The flood continues unabated today. There may be over 300,000 Toraja migrants living outside of Tana Toraja. The impact of such movement is most dramatic in the villages, where grandparents and their grandchildren are often in the majority. In a society where family continuity and closeness is still

JEAN-LEO DUGAST

intensely valued, the absence of a whole generation may be quite devastating. The devastation is not just symbolic—old people are left without sources of support and everyday assistance, and everywhere people lament a labor shortage in the fields.

To leave the highlands in search of work or education is not, however, to abandon entirely one's social and cultural ties. Almost all Toraja migrants become Christians, since *aluk* or traditional religion is virtually unpracticeable away from a community of priests and practitioners. However, their experiences away from home in multi-ethnic settings often serve to heighten their sense of Toraja identity. And while they have left their kinship networks temporarily, paradoxically they have done so partly in order to provide for their ancestors (and more immediate family) at times of death. Virtually all migrants return to the highlands for a parent's funeral, to which they contribute great portions of their wealth earned abroad. It is this new wealth or "flying money" that has helped increase (some would say inflate) the amount of ritual activity seen in Tana Toraja during the last twenty years.

Shaking the social order

Traditionally, Toraja society was divided into three classes: nobles, commoners and slaves. What these categories actually meant varied regionally, but everywhere it was the case that one's rank determined the level of ritual performance to which one could aspire. A combination of heredity, marriage, political skill, and luck determined where one ended up in the social hierarchy. The Dutch began to undermine the foundations of this structure when they abolished slavery early in this century, and later when Christian missionaries began to preach the equality of man. The introduction of universal education for nobles and slaves alike further eroded the system, as did new sources of wealth and status. Perhaps the most radical shifts have been made possible by migration, as previously undreamed-of riches can now be earned by former slaves in distant lands where no one is aware of their status.

Even among low-status emigrant Toraja, however, ties to the highlands are incredibly strong, and most return for funerals and other important rituals. It is especially at these occasions that new wealth is poured into performances formerly discouraged by the colonial authorities, or restricted to a small, high-status elite. And it is in part

because of such rituals that Toraja ritual has become somewhat controversial even within the region. Is it wasteful and extravagant, or a successful form of distributing wealth? Is it fostering new forms of status competition, undermining the old social order? Or is it a vital link to Toraja tradition, an affirmation of a rich and distinctive culture once looked down upon as pagan and remote?

Whatever the answers, the rituals are a cultural institution of great interest—both in their practice and in debates about their meaning—for the Toraja as well as for the thousands of travelers drawn to the region.

A ritual renaissance

When Dutch missionaries began work in the highlands of South Sulawesi in the early part of this century, they outlawed most local rituals associated with life. "Smoke-rising" rites, for example, with their explicit supplication of the spirits, seemed irredeemably pagan to the Dutch. Ceremonies associated with death were viewed with more ambivalence. For one thing, it became clear that Christianity would make no headway if the rituals were banned entirely. Furthermore, the Dutch Protestants more or less had to admit that death should be accompanied by some sort of ritual.

The peculiar result of this colonial schizophrenia was that *aluk* (roughly, the elements of ritual life which Westerners would call "religious") became separated from *adat* (custom). The balance in the ritual cycle thus shifted, and funerals assumed increasing prominence as the Christian mission (and in later years the Toraja church) won converts. A Christian ritual could be edited, so that only the "customary" parts remained. Today, when the great majority of Toraja are Christians, funerals continue to flourish, while smoke-rising rituals are relatively rare.

Ironically, Christianity seems to have brought about a rise in ritual activity, for while the original tenets of Toraja *aluk* restrict participation in ritual according to a person's social position, Christianity does not recognize the traditional hierarchy. All Toraja Christians, therefore, may now perform even the highest, most elaborate rituals; thus the Toraja have continued to sustain a lively ritual tradition. With this has come a heightened sense of pride and prestige, as well as an increasing sense of Toraja identity in a multi-ethnic Indonesian state.

—*Roxana Waterson and Toby Alice Volkman*

Opposite: *Repainting a rice barn in Tana Toraja*

TONGKONAN

Elaborate 'Houses of Origin'

Toraja houses provide more than shelter, they are extremely important nodes in the kinship network—the points of reference through which one traces familial ties. People may be vague about genealogical links with distant relations, but they can invariably name the houses where their parents and grandparents were born, and are usually able to cite those of more distant ancestors. In a very real sense, they consider themselves linked to others *through* a particular house. The names of houses are often remembered in cases where the individuals have been forgotten, and in talking about kinship, a "house" idiom predominates. People say that their "houses join," or that they are "brothers and sisters within such-and-such a house," as a way of expressing their relationships.

Tracing relationships

There are two words for "house." Houses in general are called *banua*, while houses of origin are called *tongkonan*. The word *tongkonan* derives from *tongkon*, meaning "to sit." *Tongkonan* refers to the place where family members meet to discuss important affairs (marriage, inheritance), to arrange for the upkeep of the house, or to attend ceremonies. Any house where one's mother, father, grandparents, or other ancestors were born may be regarded as an origin-house.

Like many societies of western Indonesia, the Toraja trace descent bilaterally, through both mother and father. Instead of belonging to a single house, people, therefore, belong to several, though they may not necessarily live in any of them. It is almost impossible to trace the outlines of any group of house members, who only act together on rare occasions. This is also why it is possible to maintain membership in many houses. Only when a division of inheritance is imminent, or plans are afoot to rebuild a house or stage a ceremony, is membership activated.

If a house is being rebuilt, its descendants are expected to maintain claims to membership by contributing to the costs; if they are very poor, even a tiny token offering will do. Some say a single grain of rice suffices, embedded in a joint between posts and beams. Similarly, one may maintain membership claims by bringing a sacrificial pig to a ceremony. Sometimes a person may by this means attempt to assert a false claim to *tongkonan* membership. If the pig is refused, this amounts to a rejection of the claim, which, if recognized, might lead to later claims upon *tongkonan* property as well.

If one were to count back only eight generations, all the houses where parents, grandparents, great-grandparents, and so on were born would yield a total 256 houses. In theory, therefore, one could be related to hundreds of houses, and some aristocrats can name an apparently endless string of *tongkonan* to which they have ties. In practice, however, most people maintain relations only with their parents' and grandparents' houses, and after marriage, with the houses of their spouse. At first, these new ties are weak, but they become stronger after the birth of children—who themselves will have membership (and inheritance rights) in houses on both sides of the family.

Husband and wife are expected to pool their resources and help each other to meet the expense of participating in rituals held by either side. At the very least, this involves bringing a pig for sacrifice. Contributions to the family ceremonies on both sides should ideally be kept roughly in balance. This, then, is what effectively limits people's membership claims. It would simply be too expensive to keep up the ritual obligations of belonging to too many houses.

A *tongkonan* has its own stone grave (*liang*), and membership in the house gives one the right to burial there. The grave is spoken of in ritual poetry as "the house without smoke, (the) village where no fire is lit." Since people belong to so many houses, it follows that they also have considerable range of choice when it comes to selecting a final resting place.

House and rank

Not all houses are origin-houses, or qualify for the title of *tongkonan*. In some parts of Tana Toraja, relatively insignificant family origin-houses may be referred to as *tongkonan*,

Opposite: *Facing rows of houses in a traditional Toraja village, Nanggala.*

and it is said that "even the birds have their *tongkonan*," meaning that even those of low rank trace their ties through houses. But in areas such as Saluputti, the term *tongkonan* is reserved exclusively for origin-houses of the nobility. Only the nobility were allowed to have carved and painted houses; most people lived in plain bamboo shacks.

Tongkonan may simply be origin-houses, regarded as important only by a particular family, not by society in general. In the case of major aristocratic *tongkonan*, genealogies are long and carefully memorized, even going back so far as to include the names of famous mythical personages.

Traditionally, the houses of aristocratic chiefs were the visible embodiments of the nobles' wealth, power and ritual superiority. People of lesser rank were prohibited from imitating them and special ornaments could be added to the house façade only when certain expensive rituals had been held. The celebration of rituals was seen as an act of thanksgiving to the deities, and in itself drew supernatural benefits: fertility, prosperity, and general well-being. Since strict rules of social rank determined what rites one could hold, the ritual system served to enhance the prestige of ruling nobles and their houses.

Building and rebuilding

All over Tana Toraja one is likely to come across houses being built or rebuilt. The money for these new houses or restorations of existing houses often comes from successful migrant family members who have done well in distant cities.

The Toraja do not renew their houses just because they are in need of physical repair; often a perfectly good house will be pulled down and rebuilt, re-using some of the same timbers. Rebuilding in itself confers prestige on a house. A house built in one generation and renewed in the next already begins to be viewed as an origin-house; with susequent rebuildings, its claim over other houses grows stronger.

This process may coincide with the emergence of a person of particular energy and verbal skills, who becomes recognized as the spokesperson for the family. Such a person can persuade relatives to contribute to rebuilding a house in which they themselves will not be living, for the sake of enhancing the family's prestige.

All *tongkonan* have a pair of founders, a husband and wife. However, the original owners of the land may often be remembered and named as the founder. The famous *tongkonan* of Nonongan in the Kesu' district is regarded as having been founded by a woman, Manaek, because the house was built on her ancestral land. Since men most often go to live with their wives at marriage, a man often puts his energies into rebuilding a house that belongs to his wife. But should they divorce,

he is the one who must leave, though he may receive the rice barn as compensation.

Rice barns are easily dismantled and can be re-erected on another site, but houses should not be moved. When a child is born, the father buries the placenta in a woven reed bag on the east side of the house, the direction which the Toraja associate with life and the rising sun. Perhaps the strongest reason for which a house should never be moved is that numerous placentae are buried there. However far a Toraja may roam, it is said that

he or she will eventually return to the house, drawn by the placenta which is regarded as a sort of twin.

House ceremonies

Rituals traditionally accompany every stage of housebuilding, from the first felling of timber in the forest to the final placement of the bamboo roof tiles. With the scarcity brought about by present deforestation, however, most house timbers today are bought from lumber yards in Palopo. Throughout the building process, carpenters have to be supplied with food, coffee and cigarettes by the home-owners—an expensive proposition. Sometimes money runs out for a while, and the house remains half-built while the owners seek more funds.

The offerings made and the size of the final inaugural feast depend on social rank. At the inaugural ceremony, called *mangrara banua* (*banua* means "house," *rara* "blood") the poorest people might offer chickens, while those of middle rank sacrifice pigs. The largest aristocratic ceremony lasts three days and is called *ditallu rarai*, "three kinds of blood." This refers to the ritual sacrifice of chickens, pigs and dogs.

A huge house ceremony was held in 1983 for a *tongkonan* known as Nonongan in Kesu' district south of Rantepao. This *tongkonan* is one to which many noble families trace a link, and over 100 branches of the house descen-

dants attended, all bringing enormous pigs. The mythical ancestor Laki Padada, whose children are said to have founded the Bugis and Makassarese kingdoms of Goa, Bone and Luwu, features in Nonongan's genealogy. All these kingdoms sent representatives from their royal families to take part in the ceremony. Although themselves Muslim, the Luwu contingent brought a large pig. The house was magnificently decorated, resplendent with precious heirlooms hung from the façade: *ikat* textiles, ancestral swords, gold *keris* and ornaments, and beadwork ornaments or *kandaure*. The women of the house were also dressed in *kandaure* (whose patterns are identical to some house-carving motifs) as they greeted guests. On such occasions, even the most distant descendants of a house demonstrate their ties to the ancestral origin-site.

New wealth, new styles

While the traditional saddle-roofed *tongkonan* are enormously impressive from the outside, their interior space is actually quite small, dark and cramped. Many people today want to live in roomier, lighter houses with more room for furniture. A ground-built concrete bungalow has the cachet of modernity. Cheaper, but still offering some of these advantages, is a Bugis-style timber house, pile-built with large doors and windows. In the last decade, carpenters have also developed what might be termed a transitional style, cunningly combining the advantages of modern living with the prestige attaching to the *tongkonan* shape. This is a two-story house, the lower story square in plan, in the Bugis style, and above that a second floor built in true *tongkonan* style and decorated with traditional carvings.

When asked about the meanings of their house carvings, Toraja respond with a variety of explanations, sometimes the inspiration of the moment. Although very seldom does one hear an explanation relating to the carvings as an integral whole, a few general themes can be discerned.

On the weight-bearing wall studs, the buffalo-head (*pa'tedong*), is said by some to represent hope for wealth in the form of buffaloes, while others claim it represents the nobility who hold society together, just as wall studs hold the thinner in-fill planks which are grooved into them. On these planks many of the interwoven spirals are plant motifs. The plants represented are mostly humble ones: water weeds that grow in rice paddies, or perhaps pumpkin tendrils. Trailing plants indicate hope that house descendants, although forming numerous branches, will stay together just as spreading vines remain attached to the parent stem.

A number of other Toraja house motifs also have a water theme: tadpoles, crabs, or water-boatmen. The association with water suggests life, fertility, and flourishing ricefields, while tadpoles and water-weeds, which multiply rapidly, are also said to represent hope for many descendants. Some designs also represent ritually important species, including the banyan tree (*pa'barana'*), cordyline shoots (*pa'lolo tabang*), or betel leaves (*pa'daun bolu*).

The latter are always used in offerings, and they are typically found near the top of the house façade, beneath the design of cocks and sunbursts (*pa'barre allo*) at the top of the gable triangle. This part may be taken to represent the heavens, and some Toraja interpret the placement of the designs on the whole façade as representing, from bottom up, the gathering of the house descendants to make offerings to the deities.

The cock figures aptly as a mediator between earth and heaven, for when the cock crows, the sun rises. In several myths, the cock has the power to crow the dead hero back to life and to fulfil wishes. The cock also appears as a constellation in Toraja cosmology. Some people identify the cock on house facades as the cock of Tulang Didi' or Lapandek, two of the protagonists of Toraja mythology.

Still other designs represent objects, such as the hilt of a *keris* (*pa'pollo' gayang*), or the lid of a basket in which house heirlooms are stored (*pa'kapu' baka*). The latter, an eight-pointed design, as well as the cross-shaped *pa'doti* motif, both appear to have derived originally from Indian textiles which were long ago traded in the Toraja highlands and have since become valuable heirlooms.

The façades of the most important aristocratic *tongkonan* often have a realistically carved buffalo head with real horns attached, called a *kabongo'*. These are usually surmounted by a strange long-necked bird with a crest or protruberance on top of its head, called a *katik*.

Toraja offer various explanations for the appearance of this creature; some say that these carvings signify the greatness of the nobility, but a more convincing account is that each represents a particular type of ritual. The *kabongo'* buffalo head can only be added to the façade after the performance of one of the highest levels of funeral rites, while the *katik* means that the house has sponsored the celebration of the great fertility-enhancing *ma'bua'* rite, highest of the "rites of the east."

The *katik* is often described as a cock or a mythical bird of the forests, though some believe that it is really a hornbill, whose use as a motif is widespread and important in many of the islands of Southeast Asia. Together, the *katik* and *kabongo'* represent the totality of the Toraja ritual cycle.

—*Roxana Waterson*

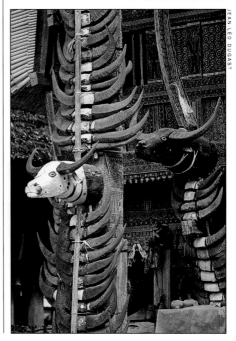

Opposite, left: *Painted decoration on a Toraja rice barn—the motifs are often quite playful.* **Opposite, right:** *An elaborate façade.* **Right:** *A buffalo head carving adorning the main pillar of a tongkonan, with buffalo horns from past sacrifices.*

RELIGION

Aluk—the Way of the Ancestors

Before the Dutch conquest of the highlands in the early 20th century, there was no word in the Toraja language for "religion" and no conception among the Toraja of a separate domain of thought and action directed toward the spirit world. Instead, there was *aluk*—a word which refers to the way in which both rituals and daily life are to be conducted—how houses are to be built, rice cooked (or avoided), children or village heads addressed. *Aluk* contains the rules for the number of buffalo to be sacrificed at funerals as well as the position of the stars when planting should begin. One of its basic tenets is that a constant exchange of gifts, blessings and even curses must occur between the living and the spirits of their ancestors.

Missionaries who followed on the heels of the first Dutch Colonial administrators on Sulawesi in 1906 could not help but notice that the Toraja inhabited a world populated by spirits and ancestors who required feeding and frequent sacrifice. In fact many Toraja today still refer to their religion as "feeding the ancestors," *pa'kandean nene'*.

The first representative of the Dutch Reformed Church was a certain A.A. van de Loosdrecht, who tried to win over converts but ultimately failed in his attempts to put a stop to the elaborate Toraja death feasts. He observed correctly that many people pawned and lost their land as a result of ritual obligations, but in 1917 his intrusion upon Toraja traditions culminated in an outburst of violence, during which van de Loosdrecht died of a stab wound to the chest.

The Dutch Reformed Church eventually refined its tactics and carved out a workable separation between "custom" (*adat*) and "religion" (*aluk,* or *agama* in Indonesian). To sacrifice a water buffalo was acceptable, provided that the meat was distributed to the living—a customary, social act—and not offered to the spirits. It was definitely unacceptable, however, to carve pagan images of the dead.

Thus, it might be said that ritual practices were allowed to continue, while the system of beliefs in which they were embedded gradually withered. Still, Christian conversions only reached 10 percent of the Toraja population during Dutch times. After independence, however, with Islamic rebellion creating tur-

moil and fear throughout the island, conversions increased dramatically, and by 1965 about 40 percent of the population were officially registered as Christians. Today, that figure is much higher and includes Protestants and Catholics together with a number of smaller denominations.

The national government declared in 1969 that the traditional religion of the Toraja, now labeled *aluk to dolo*, "the *aluk* of the ancestors," was officially recognised as a branch of Hinduism. This interesting development came at a time when Tana Toraja was being promoted as an alternative tourist attraction to Bali; and a Protestant Torajaland would appeal less to tourists than a "pagan" one.

But the governmental revival of *aluk* has not succeeded. Although some middle-aged intellectuals still count themselves as *aluk* adherents, most *aluk* people in Toraja are remote villagers, ritual priests (*to minaa*), the very old and the very young (not yet baptized or in school). Clearly, *aluk* will die out, particularly as the younger generation migrates in search of work beyond the highlands. But if *aluk* as an all-embracing way of life and thought is on the wane, as an *idea* it has been revived, and has given the Toraja a firm sense of identity.

Smoke rising, smoke descending

In 1972, a *National Geographic* team described its encounter with "a people so genial ... that even their funerals are more joyous than somber." While there is no question that Toraja funerals are remarkable, what is often overlooked is that funerals form only part of a ritual cycle that extends throughout the year. The article mentions a cycle of "smoke descending" rituals associated with death (*rambu solo*), and "smoke rising" rituals associated with life (*rambu tuka'*). In fact, this opposition does not do justice to the richness of the ritual cycle, which is profoundly linked to agricultural cycles of death and rebirth—to planting, nurturing and harvesting rice. Although such a cycle has no real beginning and end, we can take as a starting point the first soaking of the new year's seed.

Me'datu: rice of the new year

In many parts of Tana Toraja, the season of death and mortuary ritual is brought to a close in September by a rite known as *me'datu*. In the past, *me'datu* also referred to the time when some Toraja brought tributes of gold and chickens to the ruler, or *datu*, of Luwu, in exchange for blessings on the rice seed. Today *aluk* families prepare seed and offer tiny chicks, along with prayers, to the spirits responsible for the fertility of the fields and grain. A visitor is not likely to see

Opposite: *Chanting the* ma'badong—*a lament in memory of the deceased.* **Below:** *A buffalo-fight held as part of an elaborate funeral ceremony.*

KAL MULLER

this furtive ritual, which is performed quietly in house-yards, fields, and springs—wherever the spirits, or *deata*, reside.

Following the mini-sacrifices, tidbits of chicken are given to children and others who may be present, while the ritual priest or *to minaa* receives the head. The rice seed is taken from the granary, pounded (not, as is usual, by hand, but in this ritual instance by foot, as women loosen their hair and tread upon the grain). It is then sifted in winnowing trays and transferred to baskets (*baka*) which are brought to flooded fields where they will be immersed for several days.

Rice seed is scattered in nursery beds to sprout. The timing varies from village to village, but if you are lucky enough to be visiting in November or December, you will see a patchwork landscape of lush green seed-beds, interspersed with newly cleared rice fields whose flooded surfaces reflect the sky.

When the seedlings are four or five inches tall, it is time to perform the *maro*, a ritual associated with the fertility of the fields and with the fulfillment of desires for wealth, for progeny, and for the greatness of the ancestral house. If the seed has grown well, and if a family has sufficient resources (and, formerly, high status), the *maro* may be held before transplanting.

The *maro* blessing

The *maro* involves the construction of a tall cloth-and-bamboo tower (*bate*), which visually represents the transformation from death to life. At a funeral, a similar tower is erected, the bamboo's tip thrust into the earth. At the *maro*, the bamboo points toward the sky, the direction of growth.

Like many Toraja rituals, the *maro* includes many days of barely visible activity, much of which consists of speech. Toraja priests use a special form of "high language," rich in metaphor, allusion, and repetition. Such speech is considered potent. Its audience consists of spirits, and many people say they do not understand the words. Still, it is essential for the efficacy of the ritual, and men who have mastered its intricacies and memorized hours and hours of such talk are highly respected. At the *maro*, six nights of ritual speech precede the more dramatic and public activities.

Inside a small house, its central room lit only by a hissing pressure lamp, a dozen men sit on woven mats on the wooden floor. Small boys sprawl over older men's legs, others lie in dark corners of the room, asleep. Women, gossiping, are busy at the hearth, preparing rice, boiling water for coffee to keep chanters awake throughout the night. The men, all of whom are *to minaa*, chant in unison, following the cues of their leader, the "mother of the chant," a man with a mellifluous voice and an authoritative air. The men chant, sometimes robustly, sometimes soporifically,

KAL MULLER

between outbursts of laughter and even argument. The theme of the chant is the *bate*'s quest for riches. The *bate*, they say, bends like a tree to places as near as the next village, as distant as America or "the edge of heaven." The riches it finds will bring blessings to the assembled family.

At dawn on the seventh day, one or more *bate* are assembled in a public arena and given offerings. Each *bate* is carried in boisterous procession to a field where, under the noon sun, to the accompaniment of the chanting *to minaa*, all kinds of spirits are enticed to descend, to draw near, and to enter the bodies of those now dancing and entranced. Men and women whirl about, loosen their hair, jump on drums, stamp on sharp upturned blades, and cut themselves with swords (but draw no blood). Possession by the spirits may last several hours. The spirits' power prevents maiming. By late afternoon, the spirits depart and exhausted trancers go home. The *to minaa* bless the *bate* and take it apart.

Funerary rites

The funeral rite is so important in Toraja that it is held even when a person dies at sea or in a distant land. In an *aluk* rite known as "capturing the wind," family members and a *to minaa* climb to a mountaintop, where they call the wind to fill a sarong. When it billows out, the sarong is closed for a moment, then released. A length of bamboo representing the corpse is then brought home and given a proper funeral.

All funerals in Toraja, however grand or simple, are intended to transport the soul safely to the next world, whether to the *aluk* Puya or to a Christian heaven. All funerals are also intended to free survivors from their attachments to the deceased, and to reintegrate them into the world of the living through some form of sacrifice. For poor people, a symbolic sacrifice will do: a chicken egg, or even just the striking of a chicken basket or a pig pen. But although a symbolic sacrifice may satisfy the spirits, genuine animal sacrifice is at the heart of a socially acceptable ceremony in Toraja.

Aluk requires a strict separation of life and death. When the last rice is harvested from the fields, the mortuary season begins. (In many areas, this happens to coincide with school holidays and the tourist season, from July through September.) The seasonality of such ritual is made possible by the fact that the Toraja do not immediately bury their dead. When a person dies, the body is wrapped in layers of cloth and kept in the house for months, sometimes even for years,

Opposite: *Teams of young men engage in the sport of kick-fighting at a funeral.* **Above:** *Cuts of ritually slaughtered meat are distributed according to the rank and status of the funeral participants.*

while preparations are made for the complicated mortuary rites. Dispersed family members must be brought home and tremendous resources—money, livestock, followers and friends—are mobilized for the event.

Funerals vary according to the region and the status of the deceased: from simple rituals accorded to former slaves or children, to extravaganzas that receive national or even international media attention. The latter may entail the slaughter of hundreds of pigs and water buffalo, and the reception of thousands of guests in specially constructed temporary bamboo shelters. A visitor to Tana Toraja is likely to see something in between.

Behind the scenes

An *aluk* death ceremony begins in earnest after its timing has been agreed upon among family members and village leaders. It must be coordinated with other rituals and with the phases of the moon. The onset of socially acknowledged death is marked by sound and sacrifice: the striking of a gong and a distinctive, death-announcing drum beat echo throughout surrounding villages.

Relatives who have probably been sipping coffee or chewing betel nut out in the yard now enter the house to witness the transition of the corpse from "hot" to "dead," a change which is effected by the sacrifice of a chicken and, later in the day, a pig and one or two young water buffalo. The surviving spouse is

wrapped in a large cloth, and for several days will be allowed to partake of no food which has been cooked.

On the next day, the *to mebalun* ("the one who wraps") encloses the corpse in many layers of cloth. During the next few days, there are small sacrifices as relatives and friends appear, helping with the preparations and spending the night chanting *ma'badong*, a lament in memory of the deceased. Men, clad in sarongs stand in a circle in the yard, hands joined, swaying rhythmically and stamping their bare feet in unison. A fire burns in the center, where a pig is later cut, singed, and divided among all present. *Ma'badong* tells the story of the deceased's life in high ritual speech, while women, sitting on the sidelines, sing another form of mourning chant, *ma'londe*, simultaneously. It is said that the voices should sound as though they are "one breath."

Ritual activity continues to build in the house-yard for several more days, as more animals are sacrificed and chants intoned. An effigy of cloth and bamboo is constructed, and mourners, effigy, and corpse all eventually make their way to a special field (*rante*) ringed with a circle of stone boulders which are monuments to important ancestors. This is the site of the climax of the ceremony, the long-awaited moment which either spells glory or shame for the sponsors of the ritual and their guests. This is also the part of the ceremony which is most likely to be viewed by outsiders.

Guests and debts

On the day before the burial, guests arrive in formal processions, or *rombongan*, leading water buffalo and carrying pigs, rice baskets (at a Christian funeral), and huge vats of palm wine (or perhaps cases of beer and whiskey). Next follow men in single file. They are ranked in approximate order by age, status, and even size. Women, ranked in the same way, follow. Before the *rombongan* enters there is a great flurry of activity as the line is reorganized, sarongs straightened, scarves folded.

A gong is sounded to announce the group's arrival, and the procession slowly walks around the ritual field, which is lined with temporary shelters housing guests who cluck approval at the girth of a buffalo, the number of pigs, or the composure and fine attire of the visitors. They may also (and often do) mutter disapproval if the animals are scrawny or the guests in disarray.

Following a ceremonial greeting and betel offering to the leaders of the *rombongan*, its members retire to shelters where they are offered coffee and cookies by the hosts. Later they will be served rice. Much of the success of a ritual depends upon the smooth operation of the kitchen, which is managed by the women of the sponsoring family. For a

funeral involving hundreds or even thousands of guests, meticulous coordination and timing are required.

As the day wears on, the ground is strewn with squealing pigs, and buffalo accumulate on the sidelines. The great attention paid to these animals is not simply in anticipation of meat. In fact, each animal represents a debt, and therefore a social tie. The history of a pig is a complex story that stretches back many generations of pig-exchange between the hosts (normally the children of the deceased) and relatives. If a pig represents the payment of a debt, everyone will know that "the pig has eaten the vegetables," the debt is clean.

Water buffalo also represent debts. One may bring an entirely new buffalo to a funeral in a particular person's name, thereby initiating a new debt relationship. Any Toraja has intricate networks of such debts, acquired by inheritance, adoption, loyalty, or other peculiarities of personal history.

All debts are carefully noted in writing (in the past they were simply remembered). The government also sends a representative to collect a slaughter tax.

The slaughter

The slaughter of the buffalo, when done correctly, is very quick: a single blow to the jugular vein with the long-bladed *la'bo* knife. As the animal collapses, small boys with bamboo tubes rush forward to collect the steaming blood (used in cooking). The meat is hacked up and either distributed from the center of the yard, or thrown down from a tall bamboo platform. With each throw "the divider" (*to mentaa*) shouts the name of someone in the crowd below. As the meat thuds to the ground everyone seems to know exactly who is called, and (in spite of what appears to an outsider as chaos) to see exactly what size and cut of meat is thrown.

It is not at all unusual for tourists to be given a share of meat on such occasions, sometimes a prime cut, dangling from a thin rattan string. This is a sign of honored guest status, and should be graciously accepted. The presence of foreign guests is welcomed, as they help transform the ritual field, if only for a moment, into what it ideally is: the center of the social universe, drawing prestigious visitors from afar.

—Toby Alice Volkman

Left: *Clothing a* tau tau *or wooden effigy for the spirit of the deceased.* **Opposite:** *Installing the coffin in its final resting place—a cliffside grave.*

TAU TAU

Effigies for the Spirits of the Dead

The death of an *aluk* noble occasions the creation of an effigy, or *tau tau* (meaning "small person" or "person-like"). Such effigies are of two kinds: *tau tau nangka*, carved of the durable gold-toned wood of the jackfruit (*nangka*) tree, and *tau tau lampa*, ephemeral effigies of bamboo and cloth.

The *tau tau* are thought to be the receptacle of the ghost (*bombo*) of the deceased. Males are clad in a fine batik sarong with a European-style shirt and and oversized sport jacket. Around his neck are hung tubes of incised gold and invulnerabity charms fashioned of boars' teeth. For the headdress, rows of old silver coins are threaded between buffalo horns and crowned with clusters of red-and-yellow parakeet feathers or a bird-of-paradise plume.

Females are more modestly attired in a sarong with lacy blouse or *kebaya*, a betel pouch, a wide cummerbund of silver coins, gold and shell beads and bracelets, and a black cloth tied behind the head to form a bun. On the head is placed a tiny white porcelain plate, reminder of her connection to the kitchen. The faces of both male and female effigies are wrapped in vivid red cloth to which are added white paper or wooden eyes.

When the effigy is complete, the *to mebalun* (who is also responsible for wrapping the corpse) kneels before it and spins the figure around to "awaken" it. He presents it with an offering of pork and rice, and a tiny tube of palm wine. Relatives offer betel and tobacco, requesting blessings and a ripe old age. Later, women mourners embrace the *tau tau*, press their faces to its blood-red face, and utter long, stylized wails. Together with the corpse, the effigy is then carried to the ritual field. At the end of the funeral, when the corpse is brought to the grave, the *tau tau* is stripped of its ornaments and clothing. All that remains on the ritual field is a green bamboo skeleton: the body has gone to its "house without smoke," the ghost has gone south to Puya, and the living have gone home.

In wealthier, more stratified areas, a permanent wooden effigy is carved in addition to the ephemeral *tau tau lampa*. These are the statues that stand in ledges cut high into the limestone cliffs or in volcanic boulders all around the landscape. Like the temporary *tau tau* they too are considered receptacles

for the spirit; their role, however, is both to guard the tombs which are chiseled into the rock behind them, and to provide blessings to descendants.

These effigies are expensive and time-consuming to produce, and their carving is fraught with many taboos. Although infrequently made these days, both because of the expense and the decline in *aluk*, such figures are still treated by the Toraja—*aluk* and Christian alike—with reverence. But only *aluk* Toraja may participate in a ceremony held every few years to honor the ancestors. At this ceremony ancestral graves are reopened and the *tau tau* reclothed and repaired. Offerings of betel, tobacco, cigarettes, rice, pork, and wine are presented in exhange for continued blessings imparted to the living.

The presence of carved wooden effigies installed in sheer limestone cliffs overlooking the rice fields captured the imagination of the first Europeans to visit Tana Toraja early in this century. Today they still fascinate—their austere, geometric, yet startlingly lifelike faces and wide, staring eyes gaze hauntingly over the lush landscapes; while their soft, faded cotton shirts, caps, sarongs, and betel bags belie their place in the ritual system of their society. *Tau tau* "galleries" are natural outdoor cliffs, not stuffy museums—combining death, art and ritual into one.

Although Dutch missionaries banned their creation early in this century, in recent years *tau tau* have been fashioned for some prominent Christians. This has led to great debate, as some Christians argue that Toraja culture must be maintained and even revitalized at all cost, and that besides the effigies are merely representations. Like photographs, it is said, they have no power.

Defined as "art" by the international market, hundreds of *tau tau* were stolen from their graves during the 1980s. Today the figures have found (and continue to find) their way into museums, galleries and living rooms in Jakarta, Europe and America. The Toraja, Christian and *aluk* alike, have reacted with shock, anger, bitterness and dismay. In desperation, many families have reclaimed their ancestors' effigies and hid them in caves and other secret places.

In 1989 the government commissioned local artists to create "replacements." The crudely carved statues that fill the niches at Lemo are modern substitutes. Elsewhere, locks and barbed wire now shield the once powerful ancestral protectors from the depredations of the living.

—*Toby Alice Volkman*

Opposite: *Cliffside graves guarded by* tau tau *effigies. Note the empty spaces—the result of thefts instigated by international "art" dealers.*
Below: *A close-up of striking* tau tau *figures.*
Overleaf: *Early morning mist rising from the hills around Paken, Tana Toraja. Photo by Deborah Hill.*

KAL MULLER

ROAD TO RANTEPAO

Ascent to the Tana Toraja Highlands

Out of Parepare, the road to Rantepao turns inland and begins to wind steeply upwards into the rolling hills above the town. From time to time one glimpses entrancing views of the town below, with its glittering, tin-roofed mosques. In the distance beyond sparkles the sea with its rocky outcrops. Houses are replaced by grassland as the road pushes upwards over a low range of hills, past picturesque villages and scattered rice and corn fields and tapioca. Bananas, papaya and jackfruit grow in luxuriant profusion. Wooden and bamboo stalls piled with fruit and vegetables line the road, where travelers stop to buy treats for the families they are going to visit. Then, almost without warning, a magnificent view to the east signals the brief descent to the plain below.

Shortly after it reaches the plain at the village of Lawada, the road forks: the road to the left leads across an open expanse of rice fields—the major source of South Sulawesi's rice surplus—and into the market town of Rappang. A right-hand fork leads to Sidrap and Palopo (see "Luwu," page 104). Rugged peaks beckon on the horizon. Along the side of the road, women sit in the shade beneath wooden houses, weaving colorful silks on backstrap looms.

Rappang is an attractive little town with winding, tree-lined streets. Wooden shops with overhanging jettys sell rattan furniture. On market day the town comes to life, as cart-loads of produce and wide-horned cattle negotiate the narrow streets. As you leave Rappang, you might even spot a Bugis wedding, identifiable by the awnings set up in front of the household and crowds of people in their best silk sarongs, with loudspeaker systems amplifying music and speeches.

More rice fields. On warm evenings, thunderheads gather as you head for the forested mountains. The road narrows as it enters the foothills, where bamboo groves alternate with little cultivated valleys, and the occasional house nestles between the trees. Near Kabere you catch your first glimpse of the Sa'dan River, now wide and brown after its long journey through the mountains.

The next town is picturesque Enrekang, where the Sa'dan and Mata Allo Rivers meet. It is a predominantly Muslim town—impressive mosques and *pesantren* (Islamic reli-

gious schools) line the roads. Enrekang is also famous for *danke*, a cheese-like delicacy made from fried buffalo milk, which is often available in the town's largest *losmen*, overlooking the river and bridge.

Leaving Enrekang, the road narrows and begins its steep, winding climb into the mountains. Roadside engineers and wet-season landslides fight for possession of the sandy soil; in recent years fast-growing casuarina pine trees have been planted along the road to combat the erosion caused by deforestation. This section of the journey offers breathtaking, panoramic views of rugged mountains and valleys, with villages clinging to the steep slopes. Perhaps you will stop at Kotu, where you can buy *baje'*, a favourite local sweet made from glutinous rice and palm sugar wrapped in rice husks.

This region is known as Bamba Puang, after the spectacular mountain which dominates it. The area is rich with mythic and historical significance. Toraja and Duri legends hold that the first human beings descended here from the heavens by means of a celestial ladder. The gods subseqently hurled the ladder to earth in a fit of anger, shattering it into pieces. Older Duri and Toraja folk will point out the fragmented remains of the ladder, now metamorphosed into rocky terrain. In the early years of the 20th century, the mountains were the backdrop for battles with Dutch forces attempting to annex the region.

Some 20 km (13 mi) past Enrekang, Butu Kabobong ("erotic mountain") can be spotted across the western ravine. The terrain on the slopes of the mountain is said to resemble male and female genitalia. Local legends recall how an incestuous couple was punished by being turned into stone and made to lie side by side, eternally separated by the river that runs between them.

A few kilometers beyond Butu Kabobong you reach Puncak Lakawan, where a cluster of unpretentious restaurants offers expansive views of now badly-denuded canyons and mountain ranges. Strong Sulawesi coffee and surprisingly tasty local cooking revive you for the remaining three-hour drive to Rantepao. In the limestone hills across the river below are old burial cliffs with hollowed-out niches containing ancient wooden coffins. For a closer inspection, drive 4 km to Cakke, then turn right onto the road to Barakka. Keep going another 3 km until you encounter the burial cliffs on your left.

Leaving the restaurant, the road continues upwards, past mulberry fields where silk-

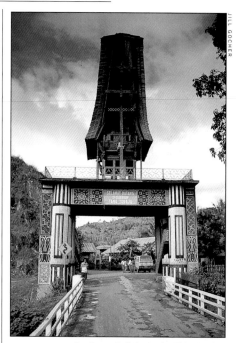

worms are raised, to Salubarani. This is the gateway to Tana Toraja. Here the road passes under a large cement arch topped with a miniature *tongkonan*. From the top of the arch you can look down over the river and town. Here you are 800 meters (2,650 ft) up in the south-central mountains. The inhabitants of this area hold more closely to their traditions than the Toraja of other regions, as ideas, like other commodities, travel less quickly through the area. The Toraja are predominantly Christian, but this southern region has a higher percentage of Muslims and *aluk to dolo* adherents.

Eventually the road opens out onto a hilly plateau, passing clove plantations, pine forests, and pockets of lush rice fields. Then the road begins its gradual, 200-meter (660-ft) descent into the Makale and Rantepao valleys. From Makale the road climbs up into the narrow, winding valley which the deceptively tranquil Sa'dan river has carved out of the limestone mountains. The early morning mists hang over tranquil villages nestled between verdant rice fields and swift-flowing streams. As the road nears Rantepao, ornately carved *tongkonan* complete the magical picture. Here at last is Tana Toraja.

—*Kathleen Adams and Ian Caldwell*

Opposite: *Two boys and a friend play in the Sa'dan River.* **Above:** *A raised* tongkonan *welcomes visitors to Tana Toraja.*

MAKALE AND RANTEPAO

The Growing 'Downtowns' of Tana Toraja

The steep hills of Makale, the administrative capital of Tana Toraja, 17 km (16.5 mi) south of Rantepao, are crowned with church spires, while the valley floor is dominated by large new government buildings, many of which have borrowed themes from traditional Toraja architecture. For many years Makale has been expanding northward along the road to Rantepao. In the last two years alone, several new government offices, a new hospital and new hotels have sprung up along this road. Fearing that tourists would be frightened off by all of this development, the *bupati* (head of the regency) issued a decree that all new buildings along the main road should be embellished with Toraja motifs. The result is a hodge-podge of styles that has stimulated comment by anthropologists and architects alike.

Few tourists stay in Makale, though there is now a large new Marannu hotel just out of town. The town is a good base for visiting west Toraja and nearby Tondon, Suaya and Sangalla. There are several good walks in the region, and the town is clean and pleasant.

On market day, every six days, the town becomes a hub of activity, as people from distant villages arrive with produce, livestock, hand-crafted mats, baskets and knives. If you follow the road running up the hill directly behind the market, look to your left for a trail leading to some very old limestone burial cliffs. Although many of these graves have been desecrated by thieves in recent years, there are still a few old bones and skulls and the odd coffin to be seen.

Rantepao

Rantepao is a dusty, bustling town that initially conjures up images of the American Wild West, with its long, wide streets and drifting tumbleweed plastic bags. Mountain villagers carrying bamboo tubes of foaming *tuak* lope into town, while *bemo*s packed with plastic buckets, sacks of rice and kerosene bounce in the opposite direction along the pot-holed road.

The main intersection of the town is distinguished by a miniature *tongkonan* set on what appears to be a pink champagne glass, but which is in fact a ceremonial serving dish. (Real antique wood ones can be purchased in the antique shops close to the mini-*tongkonan*.) From here, coaches and mini-buses set out for the long, gruelling ride to Palopo, Soroako, Poso and Palu. On market day this intersection is particularly lively, as passenger-filled trucks, *becaks*, jeeps, tourist vans and motorcycles cruise through town and out towards the market. A money changer, bank, the Post Office and Rantepao's largest general store cluster round this intersection.

Market day. *Bemos* laden with pigs, sacks of coffee beans, corn, rice and sago bounce unsteadily along Rantepao's pot-holed roads. Women carry fruits and vegetables on their backs in baskets, men balance long bamboo tubes filled with frothy palm wine, or carry bundles of carvings and hand-forged knives. Stacks of finely-plaited hats (most of them made at the leper colony just out of town) sit precariously on the heads of small, wiry village women, while men swing bamboo carriers containing squealing piglets or cradle roosters in their arms. Fishmongers transport their goods on bicycles equipped with deep basket saddlebags, while men from distant villages lead large buffalo to the market on foot, stopping for a bath in the river before putting the animals up for sale.

The entrance to the market is a large muddy field crowded with men and buffalo. On market day, hundreds of buffalos can be seen tethered in the field. *Bemos* bounce and sway across the dirt track cutting through the field and through the market, dropping off and picking up passengers and goods. The market is a loose arrangement of different sections. The pig department is a place of great interest: specimens ranging from day-old piglets to large sows and boars lie trussed up, flanks heaving, in neatly arranged rows. Prospective buyers step gingerly between them, discussing their respective merits. When a purchase is made, porters hoist the hogtied merchandise onto a stout bamboo pole and heave it into a passing *bemo*; smaller swine are carried off like handbags. Packed meals to take home—rice, vegetables, eels from the ricefields and pork—are sold for those too tired to cook after their big day at the market.

—*Kathleen Adams and Nancy Caldwell*

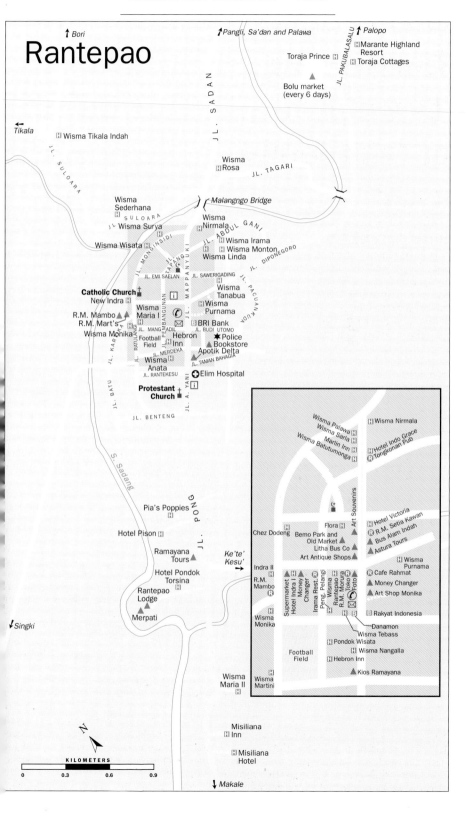

Rantepao

↑ *Bori*

↑ *Pangli, Sa'dan and Palawa*

↑ *Palopo*

JL. PAKUBALASALU

H Marante Highland Resort
H Toraja Cottages

Toraja Prince H

Bolu market
(every 6 days)

←
Tikala

H Wisma Tikala Indah

JL. SULOARA

Wisma
H Rosa

JL. TAGARI

Wisma
Sederhana
H
SULOARA
Wisma Surya
JL. MONGINSIDI
Wisma Wisata

Malangngo Bridge

JL. SADAN

JL. ABDUL GANI

Wisma
Nirmala
H Wisma Irama
H Wisma Monton
Wisma Linda

JL. DIPONEGORO

JL. EMI SAELAN

JL. SAWERIGADING

JL. PACUANA

Wisma
Tanabua
H Wisma
Purnama

Catholic Church
New Indra H
R.M. Mambo
R.M. Mart's
Wisma Monika
Wisma
Maria I
Football
Field
Hebron
Inn

BRI Bank
JL. BUDI UTOMO
★ Police
▲ Bookstore
Apotik Delta
JL. TAMAN BAHAGIA

JL. KARUAJA
JL. RATULANG
JL. PEMBANGUNAN
JL. MANG PADIL
JL. MERDEKA

Wisma
Anata
JL. RANTEKESU
**Protestant
Church**
JL. BENTENG
JL. A. YANI

✚ Elim Hospital

JL. BATU

S. Sadang

Pia's Poppies H

JL. PONG

Hotel Pison H

Ramayana
Tours

*Ke'te'
Kesu'*
→

Hotel Pondok
Torsina

Rantepao
Lodge

▲ Merpati

↓*Singki*

Wisma
Maria II

Misiliana
H Inn

Misiliana
Hotel

↓ *Makale*

Wisma Palawa H
Wisma Sarla H
Marlin Inn H
Wisma Batutumonga H

H Wisma Nirmala

H Hotel Indo Grace
▲ Tongkonan Pub

Art Souvenirs

Chez Dodeng
Flora H
Bemo Park and
Old Market
Litha Bus Co
Art Antique Shops

H Hotel Victoria
▲ R.M. Setia Kawan
▲ Bus Alam Indah
▲ Astura Tours

Indra II

R.M.
Mambo

Supermarket
Hotel Indra I
Money
Changer

Irama Rest.

Wisma
Peng. Pelangi
Rantepao
R.M. Mcnura
Toko
Foto

H Wisma
Purnama
● Cafe Rahmat
▲ Money Changer
▲ Art Shop Monika

Wisma
Monika

H Rakyat Indonesia
Danamon
Wisma Tebass
H Pondok Wisata
H Wisma Nangalla

Football
Field

H Hebron Inn

Wisma
Martini

▲ Kios Ramayana

N

KILOMETERS
0   0.3   0.6   0.9

VISITING TORAJA

Lush Valleys, Tongkonan and Gravesites

Most of Rantepao's attractions lie within half an hour's drive by car or public *bemo*, providing delightful walks through the surrounding countryside. Many places of interest are close to one another, which means you can visit several in a day. It is best to set off for the more distant villages in the early morning, while it is still cool and the light is good for photography, returning to Rantepao for lunch. If you are not too tired, nearby villages can then be visited in the afternoon.

Most *obyek wisata* (official "tourist sites") charge an admission fee, usually around $1, with additional charges for such things as "offerings" of flower petals ($0.50—a custom imported recently from Bali), a guide ($1), the rental of a storm lantern for caves ($1), and so on. At several of the sites there is an admission fee for cameras (another $1). At the more popular sites, such as Londa and Lemo, you will be lucky to get change back from your Rp 10.000 note.

During the tourist season, you will be pestered continuously by children (and occasionally adults) asking for money and sweets. Children will pose for photographs (at $1 per head), and try to sell you handicrafts from Flores and Bali. Several villages are building walls to keep out visitors who find it all too expensive and insist on looking without paying. There is no point in getting offended by all of this—after all, you've paid a lot of money to airlines and travel agents to get you here, and there is no reason that the local residents should not receive something too.

Visiting sites during the off season is a completely different experience. Often the villages are deserted and you are on your way to the next place by the time the admission book has been located. People have time to chat in between sales, and even the children are reasonably behaved.

Food is not generally available at these sites, though small *warungs* and restaurants are starting to appear. You will usually have to return to Rantepao for lunch, or take food with you. Most of the sites in the area around Rantepao can be visited in about four days, provided you have the stamina.

Karasik and Londa

Karasik is the first village south of Rantepao on the road to Makale. As you reach the edge

of town, watch for the Karasik marker indicating a trail up the hillside to the left of the road. Karasik consists of a number of colorfully painted bamboo houses fringing a large ritual field (*rante*) with several stone menhirs. The houses were originally constructed as temporary pavilions for a large funeral ritual held about a decade ago. Normally, such constructions would be dismantled after the funeral, but these houses were reinforced and used for subsequent funerals. Several of these houses have been made into permanent homes, but in 1986 a violent storm destroyed a number of structures, and today Karasik has the feel of an abandoned ghost town.

Another 5 km (3 mi) down the main road is **Londa**, one of the most frequently visited cave burial sites in Tana Toraja. Catch a *bemo* headed for Makale and ask to be let off at the entrance to Londa, then walk one kilometer east; the road is clearly signposted.

Adjacent to the caves is a balcony filled with *tau tau* gazing out over a lush rice field. Traditionally, only certain nobles were allowed to have *tau tau*. Today, Christian religious officials are ambivalent about this practice and some ministers from the Toraja Church have been known to refuse to officiate at funeral ceremonies where *tau tau* are present. The Catholic Church, however, has proven itself much more tolerant as regards the use of *tau tau*.

After a number of the Londa effigies were stolen for resale on the international art market in the 1980s, villagers installed a sliding metal grate, and the few remaining *tau tau* are locked into their balcony each night. (Much to the local people's disgust, some of the stolen *tau tau* are due to appear in an exhibition at the Smithsonian Institute in 1991.) It is sadly ironic that effigies that were once supposed to protect the living must now be protected from the living.

The sheer limestone cliff-face above these effigies is the burial site for numerous aristocrats. Those Toraja who could afford to have the most elaborate funeral rituals are buried farthest up the cliff.

The two burial caves are said to stretch on for a couple of kilometers. Although only the mouths of the caves can be easily viewed, they stretch deep into the hill in a network of caverns. The caves are filled with coffins and bones of both Christian and *aluk to dolo* adherents, with skulls and bones artistically arranged for visitors.

Kerosene lanterns for cave exploring can be rented from the ticket booth at the entrance to Londa for $1 with a guide. If you want to see it by yourself, make sure you bring a powerful flashlight. Drinks and sou-

Opposite: *Rantepao seen from the hills above the town.* **Below:** *The tuak (palm wine) commerce at a market in Rantepao.*

JEAN-LEO DUGAST

venirs are also available here.

A trail to the east of Londa brings you to **Pabaisenan** (Liang Pia). Here you will find a hearty old tree where infants who died before teething are laid to rest. The corpses are placed in cavities cut into the trunk, and these are then sealed so that the tree eventually grows around the infants' remains.

Returning to the main road, a further 3 km (1.8 mi) will bring you to the turnoff for the pool at **Tilanga'**. Turn left at the signpost and follow a somewhat bumpy road for another 5 km (3 mi) to this clear natural swimming hole lodged in a bamboo forest. The water is cool and refreshing, although the pool is to be avoided on Sundays when the local crowds come out in full force. From here you can head on south 2.5 km (1.4 mi) to Lemo, a nice walk through rice fields.

Lemo and Ke'te' Kesu'

Lemo, 12 km (7 mi) south of Rantepao, is one of the most impressive cliffside grave sites in the entire region. To get here, turn left at the marked signpost and head east a few hundred meters.

Dozens of effigies stand solemnly in niches overlooking the valley below. Adjacent to them are carved wooden doors which seal the remains of the deceased in tombs hewn out of the cliff. Sadly, most of the original *tau tau* here were also stolen in the 1980s—only the few effigies in the upper rows are origi-

nal. The rest are replacements provided by the government in 1988. This site is heavily visited by tourists, and the viewing platforms, souvenir stands and parking lot are reminiscent of sites in Bali. Still, the limestone burial cliffs are dramatic and there are lovely views of the surrounding countryside. For the best photographs, go early in the morning.

Two kilometers (1.25 mi) south of Rantepao on the road to Makale is a left turn which leads into a parallel valley with many interesting villages and ritual sites. The turn-off is clearly marked "To Ke'te' Kesu'."

Buntupune, one kilometer (0.6 mi) from the junction , has two turn-of-the-century traditional houses and six rice barns. The *tongkonan* on the western side was erected by Pong Maramba, a nobleman who was the first district head during Dutch colonial times. When his plan to revolt against the Dutch was discovered, he was exiled to Ambon. After his death his body was carried back to Tana Toraja and buried in the mountain just north of Buntupune.

Another 2 km brings you to **Ke'te' Kesu'**, one of the region's oldest and most-visited "traditional villages," idyllically situated in a virtual sea of rice fields.

On the little hill at the turn-off to the village, you can watch carvers at work. The village itself has four well-kept *tongkonan* and a long row of rice barns. The residents of the village sell handicrafts on the porches of these traditional houses, and the bottom floor of Tongkonan Kesu' (in the middle) has been converted into a small museum.

The path at the far end of the village leads to several mossy menhirs, reminders of the funerals of important aristocrats. To see the village's ancestral burial cliffs, take the trail behind the museum. The large cement tomb adorned with a strikingly realistic *tau tau* belongs to F.K. Sarungallo, a charismatic *tongkonan* leader, church figure and politician who died in 1986.

Just beyond Sarungallo's tomb are hanging graves and burial cliffs with elaborately-carved coffins and bones. There were once 27 *tau tau* here, but 13 of them were stolen one night in 1984 while the entire village was away attending a funeral ritual. The villagers removed the remaining effigies for safe-keeping, and today remain doubtful that they will ever be able to return them to their rightful place in the burial cliffs.

No one lives here anymore. During the summer months it is not unusual for 50-100 tourists to visit this village in a single day.

Tickets must be purchased at the entrance and when tour groups arrive local children will race to hold tourists' hands and sing French songs which end with requests for "bon bons." Despite its commercialism, Ke'te' Kesu' merits a visit.

Just a little further on from Ke'te' Kesu', off the side of the main road, is the village of **Sullukang**. Here there are several large menhirs installed on the *rante*. A group of *tau tau* were once housed under the overgrown shack on the rocky platform, but they have now also been removed for safekeeping.

Palatokke (also known as Mengke'pe') is a seldom-visited village and grave site which can be reached via an idyllic path from Sullukang. As the path wanders through terraced rice fields and quiet villages, you will need to ask directions (you can also hire a guide for $1).

In addition to magnificent scenery, at Palatokke you will find an imposing cliff with stone and hanging graves. Some Toraja maintain that "Palatokke" is a reference to people who are as adept as geckos at clinging to sheer cliffs, and who mounted the *erongs*, or hanging graves, on the cliff-face without the benefit of ladders.

Metalworkers and hot springs

The metalworking village of **La'bo** can be reached by continuing southeast from Palatokke, or by returning to the main road

from Sullukang and continuing on for 3 km (2 mi). Listen for the sound of metal-pounding coming from a small cluster of houses on the right side of the road. Here you will find blacksmiths forging scrap iron into fine knives (*parang*). Their impressive bellows are made from hollowed logs with feather-lined air pumps. The name of the area, La'bo, is a Torajan term meaning "large knife."

Leaving La'bo, the road splits, with the right fork leading to another blacksmith's village called **Randanbatu**. Another 12 km (7.2 mi) down the road lies **Sanggalla**, the site of a bamboo palace constructed on top of a levelled-off hill and a few graves.

You might want to catch a *bemo* from Rantepao to Sanggalla (22 km/13 mi for 30 to 60 cents), and then walk northeast through some delightful countryside for about two hours to Buntao, where you can get a minibus back to town.

A shorter alternative would be to walk southwest from Sanggalla to Suaya, then go 4 or 5 km (2.5 to 3 mi) along a good trail to the Makale-Rantepao highway. (Suaya can also be visited in a morning from Makale.) The trail to Suaya is on the right, leading up the hillside, starting 1.5 km (around a mile) south of Sangalla.

Opposite: *Cave graves at Londa.* **Above:** *A "tree grave" for deceased infants.* **Left:** *A decayed wooden coffin with skulls in Ke'te' Kesu'.*

Follow the trail for approximately 2 km (1.2 mi), where you will reach **Buntukalando**. The town has a small museum run by local aristocracy. Although modest in size, the museum houses some interesting royal paraphenalia and household objects. Another kilometer brings you to **Suaya**, one of the best places to see *tau tau*: more than 40 are crammed into three galleries. There is a lovely church here too.

Go 3 km (1.8 mi) south from the turnoff to Suaya to get to the hot springs at **Makula**. There is an old government rest house here; the rooms have large tubs for running spring water. In front is a small concrete swimming pool fed by the hot springs behind the house. Although the water is not always clear, it's a wonderful place to soak after a long hike. Both the private rooms and swimming pool can be used for a nominal fee. It is sometimes possible to spend the night here.

A left-hand fork at La'bo leads to **Buntao'**, an interesting village to visit on market day. Ask at Rantepao which day of the week the market falls on. Buntao' has a *patane* (house grave) and there are some old graves on the hill above the village, which is 15 km (9 mi) from Rantepao. **Tembamba**, 2 km further down the road, is a mountain pass village with old graves and a magnificent panorama.

Sites east of Rantepao

Marante and Nanggala are the two important ritual sites on the main road east of Rantepao. **Marante**, approximately 6 km (3.5 mi) east of Rantepao, has several large *tongkonans* and rice barns. If you walk along the dirt road just beyond Marante, there is a large cliff with stone and hanging graves. As with other Toraja burial sites, many of these graves have been ravaged by antique hunters. Some coffins, skulls and a cave remain as reminders of what once was.

Nanggala is a traditional Toraja village 15 km (9 mi) east of Rantepao. Turn right off of the main road onto a small dirt road leading to the village. Here you will find a sweeping row of 14 magnificent rice barns with interesting carvings blending old and new themes.

North and northeast of Rantepao

Some of the most attractive and least visited places of interest in this area are north of Rantepao. The easiest way to visit these sites is to take a *bemo* 6 km (3.6 mi) north to the turnoff for Deri. The road quicky deteriorates into a pot-holed, single-lane track which winds alongside the east bank of the Sa'dan River. On the far side lie rice fields and the occasional outcrop dominated by a glittering tin-roofed *tongkonan*.

The first village of interest is **Pangli**, 8 km

Above: *A man feeds a water buffalo which is about to be sacrificed at a funeral.* **Opposite:** *Fertile fields line the valleys around Rantepao.*

(4.8 mi) from Rantepao, where you can see the house grave of a noted Toraja, Pong Massangka, who fought against the first Dutch missionaries but who was later converted to Christianity. The house-grave is 200 meters uphill, just above the new church on the right. In front is a strikingly realistic stone likeness of Pong Massangka.

You can reach Pangli on foot from Rantepao along a parallel trail. Take the road running north out of town, and after crossing the bridge veer left, then turn right at the next fork in the road. A pleasant, leisurely 7 km (4 mi) walk brings you to **Parinding**, a traditional village with impressive *tongkonan* houses and rice barns. **Bori**, another kilometer down the road, has a large *rante*. A short walk will bring you to a T-junction, where you turn right for Pangli (1 km).

From Pangli, the trail continues north along the Sa'dan River to **Palawa**, on the left. A rice barn and a few bogus *tau tau* welcome visitors to the village, where rather splendid *tongkonans* double as kiosks selling souvenir items from all over Indonesia. Children ask for the inevitable money and sweets.

Another 4 km (2.5 mi) down the track, a left-hand fork 500 meters before a bridge leads uphill to **Sa'dan Sangkombang**, a relaxed, friendly village. Here women can be seen weaving traditional textiles beneath their houses. Continuing along the main road 400 meters, a left turn just before the bridge brings you into **Sa'dan To'barana**. At the back of the village are four rice barns set on a manicured lawn; alongside them are some kiosks selling textiles. The village is worth visiting for the spendid views of terraced rice fields and distant mountains to the west.

To the southwest

A pleasant walk southwest of Rantepao along the western bank of the Sa'dan river leads to **Singki'**, set on a hill overlooking the town. The summit of the hill offers an excellent view of the surrounding countryside. From the center of Rantepao go south on the road that parallels the river, then go right over the bridge (there is a Singki' signpost here). Some 50 meters up the road take the trail leading off to the right. Although it's a short walk from here to the peak, the trail is overgrown and slippery in the wet season. You can often ask directions from the neighborhood children—in fact, they will probably follow you up the peak with the hope of being rewarded with a treat.

The road to Singki' continues on to **Siguntu'**, a traditional village 5 km (3 mi) southwest of Rantepao. To get to Siguntu', go beyond Singki' village and follow the road until you spot a road branching off to the right up the hill. Siguntu' offers three elaborately carved *tongkonans*, rice barns and pleasant sunset views of the valley.

—*Kathleen Adams*

TREKS

Finding the Hidden Hamlets of Tana Toraja

The treks in Torajaland reward walkers with some of Sulawesi's most breathtaking mountain landscapes as well as the chance to experience the hospitality of Toraja village life.

Before launching into multi-day adventures it's worth making one or more shakedown treks, lasting from a few hours to a full day, to see how you handle it. Some of these you can walk without a guide and without a knowledge of Indonesian, but a basic grasp of the language can save an awful lot of hassles.

For the more ambitious treks—west to Mamasa and north to the weaving villages of the Toala group in the mountains—you will definitely need a guide. If you're contemplating really serious treks, such as the route to Rongkong, take only the most experienced guides. Be warned, some will claim to know the way, then get lost. Consequently for this kind of expedition we suggest contacting Ramayana Tours for a reputable guide.

Short Treks

Nanggala to Buntao' (4 to 5 hours). Take a *bemo* northeast out of Rantepao to Nanggala then climb upwards to Pedamaran through a coffee plantation. Walk down to Paniki and cross the ridge to Buntao'. Here you can catch a *bemo* back to Rantepao.

Deri to Tikala (one day trek, 6 to 7 hours, or shorter if you're based in Batu Tumonga or Pangala; no guide needed). Take a *bemo* from Rantepao to Deri, you'll see rock graves set into the hill to your left. A leisurely hour and a half walk will bring you to Lempo, where there's a Catholic church and a *warung*. Continue for another hour and a half to Batu Tumonga, which has a couple of homestays and small restaurants.

From Batu Tumonga, a clearly defined track continues on to Lo'ko'mata. Just before you arrive you'll see an enormous boulder with rock graves hewn into its side. To return to Rantepao, walk back 3 km (1.8 mi) to a turn-off to the right, which leads to Pana

where there are also rock graves. After Pana, another hour's walk down the small trail beginning 300 m before the school, up a bank to your left, will bring you to Tikala where you can catch the *bemo* back to Rantepao.

Gentengan to Sangalla (one day trek with a guide). From Makale, take a *bemo* to Gentengan then walk uphill along the well-defined path through rice fields to Palipu. Continue to Suaya, where you will find some *tau tau* and graves, then walk one km to Tampangallo, where there's a tree in which bodies of infants were formerly placed. From Sangalla catch a *bemo* back to Makale.

Longer expeditions

Pali to Rembon (3 days with guide). Catch a *bemo* from Makale to Bittuang, then one of the jeeps going to Ponding. Get out at the turnoff to Pali. If you get there early enough, continue through the forest to Sasak, you can bathe in the river while lunch is prepared. After lunch walk to Bau, an easy three-hour stroll. Spend the night in a *tongkonan*.

Next day continue to Battayan, then up to Balepe and stay overnight in a Bugis-style house. The following morning head towards Pasapa, then through the forest to Snik and To'lamba. From To'lamba go to Tobone, Malimbong and Rembon, from where you can catch a *bemo* back to Makale.

Getengan to Buntao (3 days with guide). Take a *bemo* 8 km south of Makale to Getengan and walk to Marinding, then on to Dulang and overnight in one of the 100 or so *tongkonan*. Next morning, continue down to Malimongan and To'duri, then on to Kambelangi. Leave your packs in a *tongkonan* and go for a bath in the hot spring at Makula one km below the village. There's also a *losmen* here. From here either take a *bemo* back to Makale or continue to Buntao the next day and return to Rantepao by *bemo*.

Pangala to Rongkong (about a week, with guide). This is probably the most interesting, difficult and unusual trek in the region: it is very rarely attempted. Start from the Losmen Sando in Pangala and trek two days to Pula Pula via Baruppu.

From here it's about four days of mountain trekking to Rongkong, one of the traditional Toale villages. From Rongkong, it's easy to reach the Transul Highway at Sabbang (especially on Rongkong's market day, every six days) and there's public transportation to Limbong, which is connected by a good road to Sabbang.

—*Nancy Caldwell and Kal Muller*

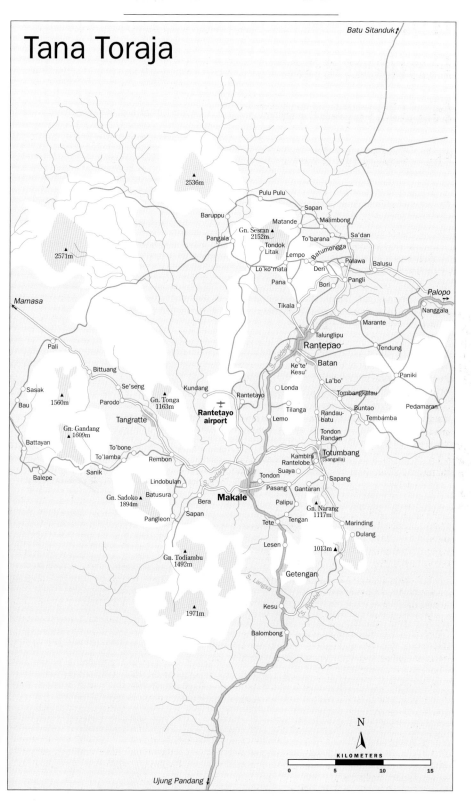

Tana Toraja

Batu Sitanduk↑

2536m

Pulu Pulu

Baruppu
Sapan

Matande
Malimbong

Pangala
Gn. Sesran
2152m
To'barana'
Sa'dan

2571m
Tondok
Litak
Lempo
Batumongga

Lo'ko'mata
Deri
Palawa
Balusu

Pana
Bori
Pangli

Mamasa→
Tikala

Palopo→
Nanggala

Marante

Pali
Talunglipu

Rantepao
Tendung

Bittuang
Ke'te'
Kesu'
Batan

Paniki

Se'seng
Kundang
La'bo'

Sasak
1560m
Parodo
Gn. Tonga
1163m
Rantetayo
Londa
Tombangkalua

Pedamaran

Bau

Rantetayo
airport
Tilanga
Buntao
Tembamba

Tangratte
Lemo
Randau-
batu

Gn. Gandang
1609m
Tondon
Randan

Battayan
To'bone

To'lamba
Rembon
Kambira
Ranteobe
Totumbang
(Sangalla)

Balepe
Sanik
Suaya
Sapang

Lindobulan
Tondon
Gn. Sadoko
1894m
Batusura
Pasang
Gantaran

Bera
Palipu
Gn. Narang
1117m

Makale
Pangleon
Sapan
Tete
Tengan
Marinding

Dulang

Lesen
1013m

Gn. Todiambu
1492m
Getengan

1971m

Kesu

Balombong

N

KILOMETERS
0   5   10   15

Ujung Pandang↓

TO MAMASA

Trekking into the Remote Highlands

The westward trek from Bittuang to Mamasa takes three days, walking 6 to 7 hours a day. The rewards make it well worth while. Most trekkers stick to the eastern Toraja region, but those with time and a spirit of adventure will not be disappointed with the spectacular mountainscapes and turbulent rivers of the Mamasa region. This trek also provides an alternative return route to Ujung Pandang.

While the journey requires a degree of fitness, one heavy-smoking, fifty-something man did it with no problems, aside from sore leg muscles by the end.

The trail itself is a wide track which will eventually be the road between Makale and Mamasa so climbs and descents are not too steep. The first section and the final few kms, can be navigated by four-wheel-drive vehicles, but the remaining 66 kms or so are too rough. The track is cleared of vegetation and

stunning panoramic views open up at every turn. The only disadvantage comes from the hot sun as most of the track is without shade.

Bittuang to Ponding

From Makale take either a *bemo* or a rented jeep for the two-hour (22 km), 500 m climb north to Bittuang (elevation 1,300 m). A market is held here every six days, according to the traditional Toraja calendar, but even on non market days, there are at least a couple of public minibuses a day plying this route. This number will increase as the government is clearing several hundred hectares near Bittuang for coffee trees, a Toraja cash crop for over a century.

The first leg of the three-day trek covers the 24 kms from Bittuang to the village of Ponding, where a weekly market is held every Saturday. On market days several open jeeps run between Bittuang and Ponding, while during the rest of the week they are usually only two trips a day. The fare is cheap, but they are inevitably crowded: 20 passengers plus bags of coffee is not unusual. Hanging on for dear life while having your ribcage crushed can spoil the appreciation of the spectacular roadside scenery, and we suggest either hiring a jeep to drop you off at Ponding, or walking it.

From Bittuang, the road skirts a mountain but there's a short cut for trekkers. About 3 km out of Bittuang, the road drops into a val-

ley at the bottom of which lies Bulupala village. There's a big school full of boys who will greet you with loud choruses of "hello meester." From here it's a gradual 9 km climb to Pasangtau, a little roadside settlement just beyond the mountain pass at 1,500 m.

There are a few small stores here (some have beer!) simple meals can be ordered, but they will take a while. You can spend the night here, but that would be dropping out of the game a bit early. Ask if a young man named Yupri is around: he speaks some English and can help you order a meal or arrange accommodation.

Beyond Pasangtau, the road drops steeply into a deep valley. The scenery is magnificent as the road descends into the Paku area, then flattens out to Belau about 7 km from Pasangtau. Here a roadside *losmen* Pa'Aru, has double beds with mattresses and also serves meals to weary trekkers. Stay here or continue another 5 or 6 km to Ponding which bustles on Saturdays, but is otherwise tranquil. There's an unmarked homestay off the market with one double bed and a mosquito net.

Ponding to Timbaan

If you don't have a guide, ask for the way out of Ponding to Mamasa—this is the only place where the route is not obvious. The track cuts through this sprawling village then drops down to the Masupu River, crossed by a bamboo suspension bridge. At just under 600 m, this the lowest point of the route.

The Masupu marks the division between the two main Toraja groups which speak different dialects, but are mutually understandable. The traditions and architecture of the two areas are also divergent. The magnificent *tongkonan* and decorated rice barns are absent in the Mamasa-Toraja area, but there are some impressive nobles' homes featuring elaborate decorations and huge coffins in the shape of water buffalo. There is also traditional weaving, and a lack of package tourists.

On the other side of the bamboo bridge, the wide track begins again, climbing gently along the western slopes of the sparsely covered mountains which enclose the rapids of the Masupu River. The river stays in sight for the first five kms or so, dropping away very gradually as the trail rises.

As you turn a corner and head northwest into the adjacent valley, the slopes become sheer and thickly wooded, except where impossible gardens have been hacked into the valley walls. Far below, you can hear the muffled roar of the Mawai River, a tributary of the Masupu. A couple of kms after the turn lies the village of Mawai (Friday market), nestled in the valley at about 850 m elevation.

The first house along the trail offers

Opposite: A fully laden coffee caravan on the trail near Bittuang. Below: The bamboo bridge over the river Masupo marks the trail's lowest point.

KAL MULLER

homestay facilities under the direction of Pak Theofilus, a very pleasant elderly man who speaks some English. Even if you don't spend the night, drop in for a cup of delicious, invigoration coffee. If you stay a while, try one of his hand-rolled cigarettes: local tobacco mixed with bits of home-grown cloves and wrapped in corn husk. Expect a very long prayer before meals.

Past Mawai a wooden bridge crosses the Mawai River. There are pools beneath for bathing. From the bridge the road climbs some 200 m to Timbaan, the usual overnight stopping place marking the end of the second day's trek. Off to the left of the road, before reaching Timbaan, is the small village of Pokko where the inhabitants still follow the traditional Toraja religion of their ancestors.

There are two homestays in Timbaan, one with mattresses on the floor, the other with real beds. Both provide meals and a nearby store sells beer. There's also a place to bathe here: water pouring from a bamboo tube, with a wall of sorts providing partial privacy.

Timbaan to Mamasa

The last day starts with the trek's toughest ascent: from Timbaan, at about 1,075 m, a 5-km-long stretch rises to a mountain pass at just over 1,700 m. There's no real difficult climbing—it's just a long grind upwards.

Strategically located bamboo tubes channel water from mountain streams along here, as elsewhere along the three day trek. We drank often, with no ill-effects. Here again, the road winds along steep, thickly wooded valley sides, punctuated by coffee bushes, cacao trees, occasional rice paddies and clearings where cassava-like tubers are planted.

A wide open space marks the mountain pass, the perfect spot for a much-needed rest. It's downhill all the way from here. The trail is wide and steep at first, then leads through grass where growth has reclaimed the road.

You have to wade across a stream without a bridge near here. Beyond the stream vegetation becomes thicker, with few open spaces and a good chance of afternoon rains. A roadside house at Lombonan, 3 km down from the pass, offers shelter should it pour. After Lombonan the road improves considerably as the first rice fields appear alongside.

There may already be some traffic along this stretch, with the chance of a ride to nearby Pakassasan or Mamasa beyond, but don't count on it. From Pakassasan it's a level 10 km to Mamasa (1,150 m) with the occasional passing minibus, most likely on Mondays, Mamasa's market day. Three kms before Mamasa, stop at Rantebuda village for a look at a great tradition house with lots of carvings—it's only 50 m from the main road.

—*Kal Muller*

Below: *A rice barn amid a hillside paddy field in the Mamasa heartland.*

MAMASA TORAJA

New Frontiers in Western Tana Toraja

The Toraja homeland is divided into two distinct halves, bisected by the Masupu River which runs north-south from the Quarles mountains to meet the Sa'dan River some 20 miles south of Makale. The Tator Toraja people live in the eastern region around Makale and Rantepao and number some 300,000. This is the area most frequently visited because of its numerous grave sites, elaborate funeral rituals and fairly good access roads.

The Mamasa Toraja, who inhabit the region west of the Masupu, have twice as much land as the Tators, yet only number 100,000. There is a road planned to link Mamasa with Bittuang (scheduled for late 1993 or 1994) which will undoubtedly bring change to the western region, but in many ways the Mamasa area today resembles the Tator of 20 years ago, before the advent of mass tourism.

A lack of sufficient arable land in Tator has forced many people to move away, and it is said that between 200,000 and 400,000 live outside their homeland. In contrast, only about 20 percent of the Mamasa Toraja have departed. There is sufficient rice land here, and a much smaller proportion of Mamasa's land is controlled by wealthy landowners than is still retained by the descendants of chiefs and noblemen in Tator.

Taken as a whole, the Mamasa Toraja culture is not as visually spectacular as that of their Tator cousins: there are no cliffside graves with the carved figures of the deceased (*tau-tau*), for example. However, the region has many fine traditional houses, as well as spectacular highland landscapes.

The houses, called *banua sura*, stand on low logs and are more elongated than the *tongkonan* of Tator. Although lacking the water buffalo horn adornments of the latter, each *banua sura* is covered with carved panels and features a wooden water buffalo head, a horse head or, occasionally, human figures. These impressive sculptures jut out from the main pillar which supports a long roof extending way beyond the front entrance.

Traditional cloth, known as *sambu*, is woven in some areas. In a few villages, thread

Below: *A magnificent Mamasa banau sura. The extraordinary roof extension and a lack of buffalo horn decoration show it is not a Tator tongkonan.*

JILL GOCHER

is spun from cotton and natural dyes are used in the *ikat* technique before the women get to work on the backstrap loom. But in most places, store-bought thread and dyes have replaced the fine traditional materials.

Exploring Mamasa

There are only four small *losmen* in Mamasa and the only way to reach many of the surrounding villages is by motorcycle or on foot. Almost all foreigners traveling through Mamasa are trekking from Tator, and they generally overnight in this small town, then leave the following day for Ujung Pandang or Bittuang. This is a mistake: the Mamasa area is well worth exploring for at least a day and preferably a week or more. Travelers with initiative, a sense of adventure and the ability to survive with few creature comforts won't regret it.

Short trips from Mamasa allow you to explore the villages and hamlets close to the area's few roads. Longer trips, all involving trekking and overnighting, open a world of traditional villages rarely visited by outsiders.

One kilometer south of town, in the front of the *camat*'s (sub-district head) office, there's a 200-m dirt road which leads to Buntu Kesisi village. There are a number of traditional houses here, and the highlight is a very baroque *banua sura* which has about a dozen human figures scattered about its facade. A warrior straddles a beam, wielding a double-headed spear; a crudely carved, ferocious fanged figure holds a *parang* machete and another has joints to allow movement. While it is said that these sculptures are relatively new, most of them are well excecuted and artistic.

It is not traditional to decorate houses with so many figures, but the overall effect is nevertheless highly impressive. This house also sports a wooden water buffalo head, the traditional sign of wealth, along with a horse head, a more recent status symbol.

Locals consider the *banua sura* of Orobua village to be one of the best around. It's eight km east of Mamasa, at the end of a roughly paved road which is good for the first five km but turns to dirt (and mud after rain) for the remaining three. As this road climbs out of Mamasa, there are panoramic views to the west, with Gandang Dewata mountain towering behind an expanse of rice fields.

From Orobua, it's about 150 meters to a small compound of thatched buildings, dominated by the *banua sura*. It is almost as big as the one in Rantebuda and is said to be 400 years old. An imposing carved buffalo head, partially covered with a skull, juts from the front pillar, and a giant set of water buffalo horns decorate the entrance.

Coffins in Mamasa-land were formerly each cut out of a single, huge tree trunk and carved into the shape of a water buffalo (*tedong*) or a canoe (*bangka*). Unfortunately,

many of the heads from these coffins have been cut off for sale to art dealers.

The most impressive collection of coffins in the region is at Tedung-Tedung (meaning "graves") 1.5 km from the main road to Polewali. Start at the bridge at Pena village, 9 km south of Mamasa. After a short climb, it's level strolling to a large, open-sided building, erected by the government in 1990 to house and protect the area's ancient tombs. There are 18 of them here, some of the boat type, others in the shape of water buffalo. All the occupants' bones have been unceremoniously dumped into a coffin at the front.

The only other place with an intact set of tombs (two of them) is Paladan, southeast of Mamasa. One retains its original water buffalo head while the other sports a newly carved horse's head. All the rest of the region's tomb carvings have been cut off and sold.

If you have time and energy, continue on the path from Tedung-Tedung (also known as Minanga) to the village of Buntuballa, about one km south, where there is a traditional house and a cave along the way.

The traditional village of Bulo is nearby, and beyond is Batarira (6 km from Tedung-Tedung). Here you can see traditional weaving, a fine *banua sura* and occasionally the *simbong*, or war dance. The dances last some two hours, involve about 20 performers, and are accompanied by bamboo flute playing. With enough advance warning, performances can be arranged for about $75. *Simbong* can also be set up at nearby Rante Balla, the village at heart of the most traditional area in the Mamasa sub district.

The villagers in Taibassi make top quality traditional *sambu* cloth using hand-spun thread and natural dyes. In contrast, the roadside weavers at Rante Sepang, on the Mamasa to Polewali road, use store bought thread and colors and are only really worth visiting if you've never before seen a backstrap loom being used.

An alternative route from near Buntuballa leads to Pidara village (1 to 2 km), then on to Ballapeu, five km from Tedung-Tedung. Some 15 to 20 percent of Ballapeu villagers follow the traditional animist religion. The large *banua sura* here is considered the finest and most original in the entire Mamasa region. There's also a great view over the waterfall at Allodio from nearby Mussa village.

It's around an hour from Ballapeu to Dama Dama which lies on a good road between the town of Mambi and Malabo village. This road continues to Polewali along the scenic coastal highway, 18 km south of Mamasa.

An extended trek

For a good long trek, start off by crossing the bridge just outside Mamasa, in the northwest. Head for Buntubuda and Taupe. Taupe village is the center of the regional handicraft industry, with half of the population earning a living making souvenirs, mostly for sale in Tator.

Continue to Ulu Mambi, a day or so away (6 to 8 hours). On the way, there's a towering 100 m waterfall. Ulu Mambi is one of a group of five traditional villages which straddle the Mambi River. There's great scenery on the way and throughout the five-village area.

The *To Kapé*, or ancestors' religion, is still practiced by a high percentage of the population here. If you are there around April, ask if the harvest ritual (*menari pare*) is happening soon. The animists hold funerary rituals, but like their Christian brothers in the area, do not sacrifice nearly as many water buffalo as in Tator, mainly due to the relative poverty of the Mamasa Toraja.

From here it's about a one day trek west to Mambi, a small town and sub district capital. There's a *losmen* here and public transport south to Polewali or back to Mamasa.

—Kal Muller

Opposite: *One of Mamasa's few remaining buffalo coffins, minus legs.* **Below:** *A detail from the many carvings adorning a banau sura house.*

PART IV

Introducing Central Sulawesi

The province of Central Sulawesi (Sulteng) is a jumble of towering, forest-clad mountains where rain falls almost every afternoon of the year. Yet its most fertile area, the Palu Valley, is also the driest region in all of Indonesia, averaging only 40-80 cm (15-30 in) of rainfall a year. Minutes away from coconut groves and irrigated rice fields are barren, cactus-studded plains riven by empty watercourses, where emaciated oxen and cows wander in search of shrubs.

Religious contrasts abound as well. Scattered in the highlands west of Palu, east of Ampana, and along the ridge of the northern neck, are dozens of relatively isolated ethnic groups practicing shamanic religions. While the Dutch Reformed Church and the Salvation Army have made minor inroads in the area, over 75 percent of the population is Muslim. The proportion is even higher in the densely populated coastal and valley regions, where traders, farmers, and fishermen of Bugis, Mandarese, and Gorontalo origin have settled, bringing Islam with them.

Geologically, too, the province is a stunning mosaic. The volcanic and tectonic activity which created the island left in its wake a network of streams and ravines, along with massive rifts and craters that later became rivers, lakes, and upland plains. Covering 68,033 sq km (26,270 sq mi, roughly the size of Ireland), Sulteng is the largest of Sulawesi's four provinces.

Though classified as a single province for administrative purposes, Central Sulawesi is still at best a tenuous geographic entity. Communication remains difficult in a terrain dominated by mountains. Forests cover 64 percent of the land (over 95 percent of the province's income derives from timber exports, mainly ebony). Between many points along the coasts, travel is still faster by motorized boat than by road, despite the presence of the Trans-Sulawesi Highway.

Even with a population of over 1.5 million and a growth rate approaching 3.5 percent (in part due to the influx of transmigrants), the province still averages only 22 persons per sq km. Furthermore, the vast majority (almost 90 percent) are distributed along the coasts, meaning that the hinterlands are very sparsely inhabited. Many inland settlements are linked only by horse trails or walking tracks. As a result, the social and cultural life of the province is amazingly varied—groups living quite close to one another (as the crow flies) may speak very different languages and follow different customs.

While much of Central Sulawesi remains isolated, a degree of unity has been brought to the area by the Indonesian government and by Islam and Christianity. Even villagers in the most remote settlements have heard and seen something of government development programs. Gradually, the diversity of this hitherto inaccessible area is being eroded by the influx of traders and officials. Crafts such as bark cloth manufacture are on the wane, and baskets and mats are being supplanted by plastic buckets and vinyl floor coverings.

Still, Central Sulawesi remains one of most culturally diverse provinces on an island known for its diversity. Government publications list 12 different ethnic groups and 24 distinct languages for the province, and a trip through Sulteng will give the visitor a chance to witness a sort of microcosm of the multicultural "Indonesian experience" within a small geographical area. This is a rugged province whose natural attractions are best appreciated by the trekker with a sense of adventure and a knowledge of at least a few words of Indonesian. For those with the time and the patience, a trip through Sulteng may be a vastly rewarding experience.

—*Greg Acciaioli*

Overleaf: *The huge megalith known as Palindo, in the Bada Valley. Photo by Kal Muller.* **Opposite:** *A woman from Tentena. Photo by Alain Compost.*

BARKCLOTH

Rare 'Paper Cloth' of the Highlands

"It is in this Kingdom where Men and Women are clad in nothing but Paper, and that not being lasting, the Women are always working at it very curiously. It is made of the Rind of a small Tree we saw there, which they beat with a Stone curiously wrought, and make it as they please, either coarse, fine or very fine. They dye it all colours, and twenty paces off it looks like fine Tabby. A great deal of it is carry'd to Manila and Macao, where I have seen excellent bed-hangings made from it; they are the best you could desire in cold Weather. When it rains, Water being the Destruction of Paper those People strip, and carry their Clothes under their arm."

Thus wrote the Spanish friar Domingo Navarette, after a month-long visit to the Palu Valley in 1657. At the turn of this century, when Dutch colonial officials, European explorers, and Western missionaries began to penetrate the mountainous jungles of Central Sulawesi, they found the local inhabitants still wearing clothing made from processed tree bark.

Never having been introduced to the technology of weaving, and having little contact with outside peoples, the interior peoples of the area, largely migratory farming and hunting groups, made use of locally produced barkcloth for all of their clothing needs. Although some groups possessed woven cloths which had been traded from India, Europe, or South Sulawesi, these were not worn, but kept as heirlooms.

A variety of barkcloth fabrics were manufactured by stripping the inner bark of certain trees (mostly wild fig and breadfruit species), then cooking and fermenting or soaking the strips for several days. The softened bark strips were then washed and later pounded together on a wooden board with a set of wooden and grooved stone beaters.

The felted cloth thus produced in one to two weeks' time was treated with a preservative and dye fluid derived from one of several plant species called *ula'* (meaning "red" in many Austronesian languages). The finished barkcloth was fashioned into tube-shaped blankets or cut and sewn into regionally distinctive clothing styles.

Men's traditional daily wear consisted of simple brown loincloths. Adult women wore full multi-layered, finely pleated skirts and tunic blouses. Black cloth was obtained by soaking the natural reddish-brown material in mud. In some areas, chips of mica stone were added as sequins, or appliqués of differently colored barkcloth were sewn onto the garment with hemp fibers to create geometrical designs. Rough-textured monochromatic daily wear was replaced with finer clothing

for important occasions such as feasts and celebrations.

For feasts a thinner, softer, white barkcloth was produced from paper mulberry trees specially cultivated for this purpose. The resulting fabric was intricately painted with plant dyes to create colorful designs for men's headscarfs, sarongs, and women's blouses.

Although today the interior peoples of Central Sulawesi are not generally recognized for their artistry or technical skills, their 19th-century barkcloth manufacture stands out as among the most refined barkcloth production systems ever developed. Prior to the 20th century, Central Sulawesi barkcloth was exported to other islands as clothing material, paper, and even as "canvas" for Balinese calendar paintings.

The period between 1910 and 1940, however, marked the beginning of the end for the barkcloth industry. At this time, the Dutch government and Protestant missions began to assert their presence more aggressively in highland Central Sulawesi. Contact increased with outsiders, including Indonesians from other areas of the country; as a result, woven cotton cloth was quickly adapted in the interior for clothing.

The use of barkcloth for everyday wear had almost vanished by World War II, when manufactured cloth became suddenly unavailable due to the Japanese occupation. From 1941 to 1945 almost no cloth could be obtained in interior Sulawesi, and local women returned to their ancestral technology in order to clothe their families. Today, Western-style cotton or polyester clothing is in general use, but barkcloth for blankets and ceremonial dress is still sometimes produced in the highland regions of Pandere, Kulawi, Pipikoro, Tobaku, Bada, and Besoa.

The production of barkcloth in Sulteng is principally the responsibility of the women, although in some regions male relatives may be enlisted to cut down large trees, strip bark, or make the wood, stone and rattan tools that are used for beating the fermented bark. Only in areas such as Napu, Besoa and Bada were male transvestite priests allowed to practice the art of barkcloth painting for ritual clothing to be used in major ceremonies. Elsewhere, all young girls were taught to beat and decorate barkcloth by their mothers, and girls were expected to produce a full set of ceremonial clothing before their marriage day.

When a Kulawi bride was six months pregnant, she was presented with a white barkcloth blouse, which she donned in another ceremony at the seventh month, and was not allowed to remove the blouse until the baby was born. The fact that barkcloth making had important connections with fertility and womanhood is also shown by a Kulawi ceremony formerly carried out after the birth of a child.

When the child was born, its sex was announced to the village by a set of symbolic objects placed in front of the house. For boys these consisted of a sword, a shield and a brass bell; for girls, a basket of agricultural tools and a set of barkcloth beaters.

The production itself was always regulated by a number of ritual taboos. Women were forbidden to make barkcloth within the agricultural field and settlement areas, or inside the village houses, for fear of disturbing spirits with pounding noises, or even accidentally hitting one.

Nor could cloth be produced after sunset, during the harvest season, during or soon after epidemic illnesses, or during mourning periods following the death of a relative or a noble. Before production began, offerings of betel nut were always put out for the spirits, and in the Poso region elder women would formally appeal to the souls of the ancestral residents of the land. The ancestors were asked not to be angry with the noise, but to wait patiently for the barkcloth that eventually would be shared with them.

LORRAINE V. ARAGON

Prior to the arrival of Christian missionaries, barkcloth was used as a vessel for spiritual power. In some regions, the noble descendants of community founders would bless their community's fields by giving each household a strip of barkcloth. This was to be hung on poles in the fields as a talisman warding off evil spirits and pests. Many of these practices are still followed today, although barkcloth is now produced mostly in Christian areas where the women now also refrain from beating barkcloth on Sundays.

—Lorraine V. Aragon

Opposite: *A Bada woman beating barkcloth under the shade of the family granary.* **Above:** *A woman models a barkcloth blouse made by her mother.*

PALU

The Bustling Capital of Sulteng

In his early 18th-century writings on the Indonesian archipelago, the missionary François Valentyn likened the appearance of the area around Palu to the gentle beauty of Holland. With a bit of imagination (block out the coconut palms and mountains which surround the region), it is possible to travel homeward with the writer as he describes "a flat land and its black clay soil ... a gloriously beautiful view upon the fields, pleasant enough by themselves, which are full of all sorts of livestock: fatting cows, buffalo, horses, sheep, goats and all sorts of wild animals. Above all they yield a great abundance of paddy and rice, as the paddy fields are usually worked by these buffalo. It is indeed a blessed land ..." But, adds the priest, "in manner of life, it is an accursed Sodom."

During Valentyn's time, Palu was only one among a number of chiefdoms located in the Palu Valley and the surrounding coasts, inhabited by a people known as the Kaili. The original settlement from which these people spread seems to have been a village on the east shore of Palu Bay.

A century after Valentyn, the Spanish monk Navarette records his shock at the local practice of male transvestite priests or *bajasa* being taken as wives by respected community members. (Was this the source of Valentyn's moral outrage?) Navarette was also impressed, however, by the natural riches of the area—where people subsisted on bananas and produced vast quantities of coconut oil, much of it sent as tribute to Makassar. He also noted the absence of wet-rice cultivation, which is of recent introduction to the area.

Although Palu was not a major town during the colonial period, it is now a rapidly-growing provincial capital (population 150,000), and the starting point for an investigation of the Kaili area. Situated at the foot of Palu Bay, the city is bisected by the Palu River, with downtown and major shopping areas on the west bank and the main government offices and airport to the east.

A general outline of the attractions of the whole province can be obtained by visiting the provincial museum on Jalan Sapiri. Designed on the general plan of a *lobo* or ritual meeting house, the museum includes replicas of the Lore region's megaliths and great stone vats, exhibits of traditional arts and

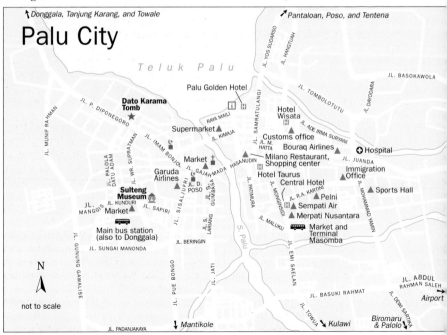

Palu City

Donggala, Tanjung Karang, and Towale

Pantaloan, Poso, and Tentena

Teluk Palu

JL. YOS SUDARSO
JL. HANGTUAH
JL. BASOKAWOLA
JL. TOMBOLOTUTU
JL. DAYODARA
Palu Golden Hotel
Dato Karama Tomb
Hotel Wisata
RAYA MAILI
JL. ADE IRMA SURYANI
Supermarket
JL. KIMAJA
JL. SAMRATULANGI
Customs office
JL. P. DIPONEGORO
JL. MUNIF RA. HMAN
JL. IMAM BONJOL
JL. SUPRATMAN
JL. PALOLA DATU ADAM
JL. WR. SUPRATMAN
JL. GAJAH MADA
HASANUDIN
JL. M. HATTA
Bouraq Airlines
Hospital
Market
Milano Restaurant, Shopping center
Garuda Airlines
JL. D. POSO
Hotel Taurus
Immigration Office
JL. JUANDA
Sulteng Museum
JL. KUNDURI
JL. S. GUMBASA
JL. PATIMURA
Central Hotel
JL. R.A. KARTINI
Sports Hall
JL. MANGGIS
JL. SISALU FRI
JL. SAPIRI
JL. MONGINSIDI
Pelni
JL. MOHAMMAD YAMIN
Market
JL. S. LARIANG
JL. MALUKU
Sempati Air
Merpati Nusantara
Main bus station (also to Donggala)
JL. BERINGIN
S. Palu
Market and Terminal Masomba
JL. SUNGAI MANONDA
JL. GUNUNG GAWALISE
JL. PUE BONGO
JL. JATI
JL. EMI SAELAN
JL. ABDUL RAHMAN SALEH
Airport
N
not to scale
JL. PADANJAKAYA
Mantikole
JL. TOWUA
Kulawi
JL. BASUKI RAHMAT
JL. DEWI SARTIKA
Biromaru & Palolo

crafts, as well as household utensils and weapons. Its collection of heirloom cloths (*mbesa*) is particularly fine.

There are *ikat* cloths from Kalumpang and Rongkong in South Sulawesi, and *patola* cloths from India, still used in marriage exchanges among families of noble descent (and modern wealth). Also to be seen are the locally produced *kain Donggala*—darkly colored silks with supplementary embroidery or *ikat*, sometimes including a tic-tac-toe double *ikat* design, thus making the Kaili region the only one in the archipelago aside from the village of Tengganan in Bali to make use of this difficult technique. Different types of bark-cloth—long the primary material for secular and ritual clothing in the highlands of the province—are also on display.

Live performances of local dances are given in the *Gedung Olah Seni* (GONI) on Jalan Professor Muhammed Yamin SH in the eastern half of the city near the immigration office. Inquiries can be made at the helpful Central Sulawesi Tourist Office on Jalan Cut Mutia. These performances are often held in conjunction with arts festivals where youth groups representing various subdistricts and villages compete in the presentation of newly choreographed adaptations of traditional dances such as the *dero*.

Essentially a city created by the Japanese during World War II, Palu has the feel of a bustling town assiduously asserting its mo-

dernity, rather than the elegiac torpor exuded by many former Dutch colonial towns. There is little to remind the traveler that the Dutch once brought their gunships to the banks of the Palu River (now an impossibility due to silting at the river's mouth) to issue demands for taxes and obedience.

What can still be witnessed is the role of Palu in disseminating Islam throughout the region. In Kampung Lere, to the west of the city, can be found the tomb of Dato Karama, the missionary who is said to have come from West Sumatra to propagate Islam in the Palu Valley and northern coasts. The mosque he built in the 17th century, reputed to be the oldest in the province, can be visited on Jalan Kyai Haji Agus Salim.

In the *pasar* on the west bank of Palu, hundreds of hawkers (most of them Bugis) squat in their stalls selling fish, cloth, utensils and a host of other items. This was once the center of the city, just north of the intersection of Jalan Gajah Mada and Jalan Teuku Umar. Although major banks and shops (*toko*) are still located here, the central *pasar* has relocated to Jalan Sapiri just past the provincial museum. Another market has recently been erected for the eastern half of the city on Jalan Walter Monginsidi, the main road leading south out of town.

—*Greg Acciaioli*

Above: *Spinning silk for local* kain Donggala.

DONGGALA & THE NORTH

Old Port and the 'Northern Neck'

Forty kilometers (25 mi) north of Palu along a well-surfaced road lies the ancient and picturesque seaport of Donggala. For more than a thousand years, ships from the east coast of Borneo have been calling here to trade, bringing with them Indian textiles and weaving techniques that have inspired the famous silk cloths of the Kaili region. On the opposite side of the huge Bay of Palu stretches Sulawesi's long northern neck. Often considered just an obligatory stretch of territory connecting Central and North Sulawesi, this region is actually quite interesting as a midpoint between Sulawesi's contrasting highland and lowland cultures.

The old port of Donggala

Donggala has been a port of importance for most of its long history, particularly among the traders of South Sulawesi and the east

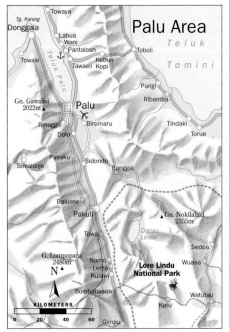

coast of Borneo. The Indian-inspired silk weavings of this area, called *kain Donggala*, are still made at Towale village. Over the centuries, Bugis sailors and traders have settled in Donggala, first integrating with then largely replacing the indigenous Kaili inhabitants. When the Dutch decided it was time to bring Central Sulawesi under their control at the very end of the 19th century, Donggala was chosen as the colonial administrative center.

The seaport lost much of its importance during and after the Second World War, when the capital was shifted to Palu. More recently, new port facilities at Pantoloan across the bay have further eroded the town's importance. Pelni and other larger ships no longer call at Donggala, though Bugis schooners continue to do so, shuttling back and forth to Surabaya. There are at least a half dozen of these vessels in port at any one time, bringing cargoes of foodstuffs, cement and consumer goods which are then transported by small boat or truck to Palu. On the outward journey, these schooners are crammed full of copra, Donggala's main export and primary source of wealth. It is thanks to copra money that the Donggala area has so many *haji*, Muslims who have made the (expensive) pilgrimage to the holy Islamic city of Mecca.

A trip to Donggala provides a pleasant change from the bustle of Palu. It is a sleepy provincial town. The harbor still teems with sea craft of all sorts and, invigorated by sea breezes, the town itself is a delight simply to walk through, enjoying views of the harbor and the vegetable gardens in the hills above, with a brief stop to watch fresh fish being brought into its small *pasar* or market.

The town lies on the protected inner shore of Palu Bay, near the very tip of the mountainous peninsula which defines the bay's western shore. The best view onto Donggala's picturesque harbor is from a narrow paved road leading north to Tanjung Karang and Boneage, especially during the late afternoon. From the edge of town, it's a pleasant two-kilometer (1.25 mi) stroll on this road to where it forks; the paved left-hand fork leads to Boneage and the unpaved right branch heads to the water's edge at Tanjung Karang. At Tanjung Karang, the best beach is fenced off and a small entrance fee is charged to swim. The beach is deserted during weekdays.

Off the beach, the bay's transparent

Opposite: *View of Donggala harbor from Tanjung Karang, with the "northern neck" behind.*

waters gradually shift to richer shades of turquoise, abruptly changing to deep blue some distance from the shore and across to verdant hills on the other side. There is usually a variety of sailing craft here, including graceful sailing catamarans, posed for countless photo opportunities.

Further down the coast at Boneage, 7 km (4 mi) from Palu, an incredibly fine sand beach lines a two-kilometer-long, two-house-wide village.

Another paved 12-km (7-mi) road from Donggala cuts across the tip of the peninsula, passing by a golf course to Towale village on the western coast. Nearby, a sunken salt-water pool called Pusenasi provides the setting for an unforgettable swim. Access to the pool is via a notched tree which reaches some 7 meters (22 ft) down to the surface.

From Towale, an unpaved road of sorts runs southward to Suranama village, at the border with Sulsel, 24 km (14 mi) away and continues south as far as Pasangkayu. From there, bits and pieces of unconnected road head south to Mamuju. However, it's a lot easier to get there by boat.

While the snorkeling off Tanjung Karang is nothing spectacular, there is good diving closer to Donggala as well as off Towale village. During the 1959 Permesta Rebellion, five ships commandeered as troop transports by the Indonesian military were sunk by an American-piloted rebel airplane just off Donggala. One of these ships, the Mutiara, lies on its side, just off the old pier next to the Dutch-built Quonset-hut warehouses used to store copra and rattan. While the water tends to be a bit murky here, just a bit further south, close to shore, there are lots of coral species, a fair variety of anemones, purple-veined white and yellow tunicates and some reef fish. An outrigger canoe for snorkeling and exploring the harbor can be rented quite cheaply, complete with paddler.

About 8 km (5 mi) to the south of Donggala on the road to Palu is the Loli Indah recreation park, with swimming pool and children's playground. There is also the smaller port of Wani, whence small boats depart for local destinations along the northern arm up to Tolitoli and down the west coast on the Strait of Makassar and to destinations in South Sulawesi.

Dive resort

Just before the end of the road to Tanjung Karang, a right hand turn leads through coconut trees to the Prinz John's Diving Resort. Here you find a little tropical paradise. This resort has simple but very well built wood-and-thatch cottages and rooms, excellent meals, no electricity, a white sand beach, and year-round water sports, including scuba diving. The calm, shallow waters off the beach are perfect for children.

While there is good snorkeling a few

KAL MULLER

meters from Prinz John's, the real attraction is afternoon windsurfing and sailing as well as year-round scuba diving. Beach-entry diving and a shallow slope make this location perfect for beginners. Intermediate divers will want to go out a bit further where depths reach just over 30 m. Big bumphead parrotfish and harmless white tip reef sharks regularly cruise these waters, dominating a good variety of reef fish: we saw 50-odd species after a couple of dives and an angelfish expert spotted 11 species of his prey. Offshore we saw a great cloud of fish: a mixed school of two species of fusiliers and surgeonfish, an unusual sight. Intermediate and advanced divers will want to check out the drop-off at Enu, a 50 minute boat ride to the opposite side of Palu Bay. The vertical drop-off plunges over 60 meters and in one stretch rivals Bunaken.

Expert divers can explore the wrecks just off Donggala Harbor. While snorkeling is possible on the wrecks close to shore, the best one for diving lies on her side, between 32 and 50 meters. The boatman at the Prinz John's knows where to find it. But it's not easy, especially in a current. However, it is well worth it: this is a magnificent wreck, in good condition, with a fair amount of coral encrustations, at least one monster grouper, big jacks and other large fish hanging around. Make certain that the boatman hangs a full tank with regulator over the side of the dive boat at five meters, to use in case decompression time is needed.

The 'Northern Neck'

The Kaili-speaking regions around Palu and Donggala and along the coasts of the "northern neck"—the long and narrow strip of land connecting Central and North Sulawesi—offer a number of attractions, accessible either by rented car or by any number of minibuses that ply the main roads.

The coasts of the northern neck have long been settled by migrants of Gorontalo, Mandarese, and Bugis origin, who have dominated the fishing villages and established extensive groves of coconuts to produce both oil and copra. The cordillera of mountains is inhabited by scattered tribal groups (*suku terasing*)—including the Tajio, Pendau, Lauje, and others—collectively called "Da'a" by coastal dwellers (seemingly a reference to the indigenous Dayak peoples of interior Kalimantan). These highland groups have traditionally subsisted on dry crops, including sweet potatoes, taro, maize and swidden rice, making the descent to the coast occasionally to market forest products and such cash crops as onions, garlic and coffee.

This traditional pattern of highland-lowland relations has changed significantly in recent times. Members of mountain tribes now work alongside Filipino loggers cutting down ebony and other precious woods in the montane forest. The government has resettled whole villages on the coast, providing these local transmigrants with basic housing, implements and seeds to open up wet-rice fields or establish hybrid coconut plantations. As a result, distinctions between the various ethnic groups are no longer easily made according to geography.

The west coast up to Tolitoli

The west coast of the neck still has no surfaced road connecting Palu directly to the town of Tolitoli. Despite its inaccessibility, however, the Tolitoli regency is well worth a trip by local boat from the harbors of Pantoloan or Wani, or by plane from Palu. Approaching by air, the traveler cannot help but be amazed by the endless stands of clove trees below. This region is an ideal one for clove cultivation, as the hills around Tolitoli continuously receive the sea breezes which enable these trees to thrive. Indeed, in the last two decades Tolitoli has been transformed into a veritable boomtown by the income from lucrative cloves.

But there are quiet spots to be found nearby Batu Bangga beach, 12 km (7.5 mi) north of Tolitoli, provides opportunities for swimming or just taking in the scenery, as do the beaches of Lutungan Island, a quick kilometer to the west of Tolitoli and easily reachable by chartered boat.

On the island, the tomb of a former raja of Tolitoli still is a site for pilgrimages. To determine whether their wishes will be fulfilled, the supplicants to the tomb thrust a palm leaf rib into the ground, checking to see whether upon extracting it the stick is longer (a good sign) or shorter.

At Salumpaga, a village about 70 km (44 mi) north of Tolitoli, you will come across the remnants of another monument to earlier rulers. The towering walls of the crumbling Dutch fort there still evoke the tenuous hold the colonial regime maintained over distant outposts such as Sulawesi.

—*Greg Acciaioli and Kal Muller*

Opposite: *Bringing vegetables to market by the shores of Lake Lindu, in Kulawi district.*

LORE LINDU

Exploring the Western Highlands

Fifty kilometers south of Palu lies the huge Lore Lindu National Park. Covering more than 231,000 hectares (570,570 acres), the park straddles the border between Donggala and Poso districts. This vast and rugged area includes Mt. Nokilalaki and Mt. Tokosa, the entire Lindu Plain with its large lake, the Besoa Valley, and the western sections of the Bada and Napu Valleys. In these three valleys are found the mysterious stone statues and cisterns of a long-vanished culture whose traces continue to intrigue archaeologists.

Most of the park is covered in dense montane forest, inhabited by many of Sulawesi's endemic species—including *babirusa, anoa*, Sulawesi macaques and tarsiers. Though it is often hard to catch a glimpse of these creatures, the avian life of the park is abundant, accessible and very watchable. Whether stalking green imperial pigeons, hornbills, or egrets and herons, the avid bird watcher is not likely to be disappointed. Starting at 300 meters (990 ft) above sea level and rising to 2,610 meters (8500 ft), the park's landscapes are richly varied—dense forests alternate with grassy plains and swampy upland valleys.

While no permits are required to enter Lore Lindu, such projects as climbing Mt. Nokilalaki do require permission from the Nature Preservation office KSDA (formerly PPA) on Jalan M. Yamin No. 17, Palu. There are many points of access to the park. From Palu, minibuses may be taken on a small road through the Palolo Valley to Wuasa (the capital of North Lore, in the Napu Valley), or south through Kulawi as far as Gimpu.

South from Palu

Two roads travel south from the city along either side of the Palu River. Zipping along the main artery on the eastern bank you encounter a succession of Kaili villages, recognizable by the characteristic stilt houses which bear a strong resemblance to Bugis homes, only without the multi-layered gables that denote rank in the South.

At a major intersection near Kalukubula, just south of Palu, you can make a detour to the east to visit Biromaru and Bora, center of the former Sigi rajadom. Here once lived the most powerful *magau*, as Kaili rajas were called—the overlord of the western highlands. Sigi preserved longest the rites per-

GREG ACCIAIOLI

formed by transvestite *bajasa* priests, but unlike the *bissu* of the South, the *bajasa* have now disappeared in this staunchly Islamic area. The mineral waters of the hot springs at Bora are still reputed for their healing properties, and occasional circle dances are performed. (Aficionados of hot springs might also wish to try those at Pesaku in the Dolo subdistrict, some 25 km [16 mi] south of Palu on the main road.)

You can also take the smaller road leading out of Palu along the western banks of the river. This brings you through the Marawola district, with its starkly-eroded mountains towering above sparsely-inhabited savannahs. Farther south towards Binagga, wet-rice fields appear in the midst of ever denser groves of arched coconut trees, now being replaced by dwarf hybrid varieties whose quicker maturation and higher yields, it is hoped, will reinvigorate the local economy. This road then crosses the river to meet up with the main road about 10 km (6 mi) south of Palu, at Dolo.

Continuing south past Sidondo, the main road passes massive irrigation works fed by the Gumbasa River, which drains Lake Lindu. It then begins a gentle ascent into the hills at the village of Pakuli. A steep, winding climb begins in earnest at Tuwa, at the lower end of the Palu Valley. Now the traveler is no longer in the lowland Kaili regions, but has entered the western highlands.

The western highlands

In pre-colonial days the western highlands consisted of a congeries of small chiefdoms paying tribute and performing corvée as warriors for Sigi and other coastal and valley Kaili rajadoms. These upland groups worked swidden fields of rice and tubers cut from the slopes of the mountains and collected sago, supplementing their diet with the plentiful game of the surrounding forests.

Although the Dutch established outposts on the coast as early as the 18th century, it was not until 1903 that colonial forces began to conquer the interior. The fiercest resistance was offered by the people of Kulawi in their fortress on Mt. Momi. Battles raged for 3 months in 1904, until finally an aristocrat of Tuwa was captured and tortured (baked over an open fire at the command of a Dutch officer) to reveal an alternate pathway to Kulawi along the Miu River. After the capture of the Kulawi leader, Toi Torengke, his forces surrendered. The defenders of the neighboring Napu Valley continued to offer resistance,

however, until being defeated in a decisive battle at Peore in 1907.

The Dutch set about restructuring local settlements, forcing people down from the hills to open up wet-rice fields in the plain surrounding Lake Lindu. The western highlands were then divided between the rajas of Kulawi and of Lore, who ruled under Dutch supervision and became powerful as a result.

Social changes accelerated once missionaries moved into the area. Soon after establishing a Javanese transmigrant colony in the Palu Valley in 1913, the Salvation Army began to convert highland groups from a center in the southern highlands village of Kentewu.

Today, the peoples of the western highlands are overwhelmingly Christian, though in towns such as Kulawi, Gimpu, Wuasa and Gintu, numerous Muslim traders of Bugis, Arab and Pakistani descent are to be found. Towering wooden church spires—Salvation Army, Dutch Reformed, and the more recent Pentecostal and 7th Day Adventist—greet the traveler on arrival.

There is little of the syncretism that characterizes the Christianity of Tana Toraja here. Still, local groups are proud of their *hada* customs, clothing styles (including ceremonial barkcloth vestments), dances, ways of greeting and serving guests, as well as forms of recognition and punishment that continue to spice marriages, funerals, harvest thanksgiving and other ceremonies that are now performed under the auspices of the Church.

Visiting Lore Lindu

The village of Wuasa lies on the eastern edge of Lore Lindu Park, about 100 km (60 mi) southeast of Palu (a bit over 3 hours by minibus when road conditions are good). Walking trails lead from here west into the Lindu Plain or across to Toro, east of Kulawi. These are infrequently used, however, and hiring a guide willing to spend two or three nights traversing the park may be difficult.

The park is more accessible from the western side from Toro, just southeast of Kulawi on the main road, about 80 km (50 mi) south of Palu. Local agents at the PPA office in the village will be able to help arrange a guide for day-trips or for the trek across to Wuasa or to the Besoa Valley. The central part of the reserve accessible from Toro is its most thickly forested section, with a watershed of steep ascents and descents.

Another approach to Lore Lindu begins even before Kulawi at Sidaunta, some 70 km (42 mi) south of Palu, and there is now a road

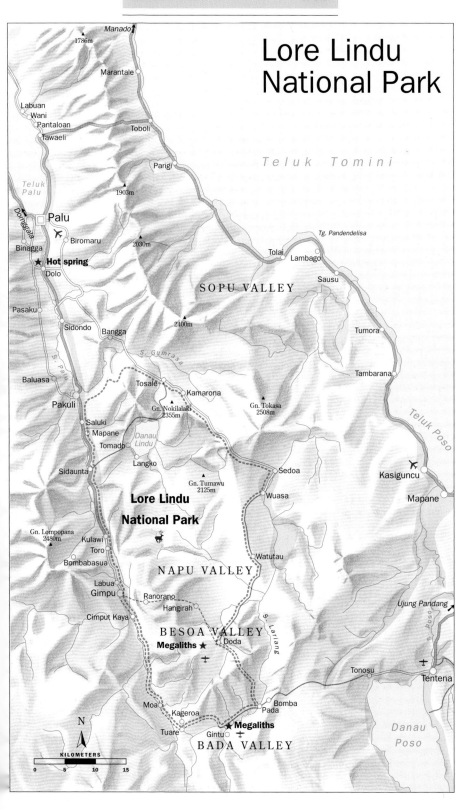

Lore Lindu National Park

adequate for a 4-wheel-drive vehicle from Sidaunta to Lake Lindu. A bit after noon each day, horse caravans start out to carry goods for the four villages around the lake. One can walk with them, paying a nominal fee to let a horse carry the bags, or even rent a horse to ride. Riding can be hazardous, however, as horses frequently tumble into the ravine below the trail. The horses and their drivers usually make the trip in a little over 4 hours, but the weary walker may require up to 7 hours to traverse the 20 km (12 mi) to the village of Tomado on the lakeshore.

Accommodation in villagers' homes can be arranged with the headmen of Tomado, Langko or Anca. Sometimes there is space available in the Le Petit Soleil research laboratory at the edge of Tomado. (Note: The laboratory was set up to study the schistosome blood flukes which proliferate in bodies of standing water in the area—do *not* walk barefoot in this region, as schistosomiasis is very common. Rubber boots are strongly recommended for tramping around the highland plains of Lindu and Napu.)

Trekking in south Lindu

Three highland valleys around Lore—from north to south: Napu, Besoa and Bada—are not only ideal for trekking or horse travel, but also feature a scattering of megalithic remains of unknown origin. While Wuasa in the Napu Valley can be reached by minibus, Besoa can only be reached on foot or by jeep from Wuasa—or by MAF flights.

From the end of the road at Gimpu, a well-used trail leads eastward across the southern stretches of Lore Lindu Park, over the watershed at Ranorano to Hangira in the Besoa Valley—a hard day's walk. A shelter with roof and raised floor at Ranorano can be used if permission has been obtained from the KSDA in Toro.

If instead one proceeds south from Gimpu on horse or on foot in one of the numerous horse caravans that periodically leaves with supplies, one can reach Moa in the southern Pipikoro region in a good day's journey. After having spent the night in a villager's house, another long day of trekking brings you through a stretch of magnificent forest at the very southern tip of Lore Lindu Park to the grassy plains that announce the Bada Valley. Upon arrival, accommodation can be arranged in Tuare or Kageroa, or with the *camat* of Gintu, capital of Lore Selatan.

You may frequently run into groups of local people walking up to the highlands, and it is possible to join up with them. There are no facilities along the road, so you will have to depend upon bargaining with local people for food and accommodation.

—*Greg Acciaioli*

Above: *Net fishing in huge Lake Lindu in the highlands.* **Opposite:** *A cistern in the Bada valley.*

BADA VALLEY

Remote and Rugged Land of Megaliths

An imposing phallic figure, minimalistically carved to represent a human form, projects out of the earth at an angle. The face—a few curved lines defining large, round eyes and slightly parted lips—stares westward with a timeless expression as impassive and impenetrable as that of the Sphinx.

This magnificent work of megalithic art—massive, simple and eloquent—retains its awesome, mute power in spite of increasing efforts to develop the area, and even despite the soap scrubs which guardians have recently applied in an attempt to wash away the effects of natural weathering.

Ancient art and modern man

Palindo, as the statue is known locally—along with 13 other statues and many large stone vats—inhabits the Bada Valley which extends 15 kilometers (9mi) south of the Lore Lindu

National Park. The Lariang River runs the length of the valley, spanned by three suspension bridges. Along with its tributaries, the Lariang serves to irrigate the valley's rich soils, which are parcelled into neatly terraced rice paddies. Gintu, the capital, is the principal village of the Bada sub-district, with about 1,500 inhabitants. It dominates the area with its handful of government offices, shops and the valley's three TV sets. All in all, some 7,000 Bada people are scattered among 14 villages which dot the valley.

Nothing definite is known either of the origin or the purpose of the megaliths. When the Dutch missionary Dr. Albert C. Kruyt (whose efforts, incidentally, are largely responsible for the high proportion of Protestants in the region) reached Bada in 1908, the megalithic culture had long since disappeared. The inhabitants could provide no clues other than that the statues were already there when their ancestors first arrived in the valley.

The megaliths at Bada draw small numbers of tourists and archaelogists to this remote area. The rugged terrain makes an impressive backdrop for the works of stone: eroded embankments and low-lying mountains two kilometers away complement the rugged grace of the carvings. But for some, this natural setting was not enough.

In 1984 the government persuaded people living in the Bada Valley to construct a huge

KAL MULLER

wooden house next to the Palindo statue at Sepe, along with a vaguely traditional building which sits behind it. Neither serve any apparent purpose and both are beginning to show signs of shabbiness. For the *coup de grâce*, cement walkways and a number of stone slabs were set up around the statue. There is also a rice barn, with a shaded platform under a raised, rat-proof, but empty storage area. As with the statues themselves, the purpose of the barn remains a mystery, though it provides a good shady spot to sit and look at the back of the statue.

The first Europeans to arrive in the valley, Paul and Fritz Sarasin, trekked through in 1902 but did not notice the megaliths. Dr. Kruyt does mention that propitiatory offerings for abundant harvests were taken to one of the statues; and when rain was lacking, offerings of betel nut were laid in front of the statue known as Tarai Roi. Other early visitors also mention offerings being made to some of the megaliths.

The Besoa Valley, a hard, leech-filled day's walk north from Bada, also has a number of human statues, along with *kalambu*—the large stone jars which are covered with carvings lacking on the ones found in Bada. One of these stone vats has a cover with five carved animals at the edge, very much like the bronze Dong Son drums which made their way to Indonesia from Vietnam in prehistoric times.

Mysteries in stone

No definitive research has yet been done, and estimates of the dates of the statues vary from 3000 BC (most unlikely) to AD 1,300. It is likely that the Bada statues, along with those of the Besoa Valley to the north, are remnants of a megalithic tradition which once spread throughout Indonesia (and continues today in places such as Sumba). In Central Sulawesi, aside from the stone statues and large jars, there is a variety of stone objects which are probably products of the same culture. Walter Kaudern, who lived in the area from 1917 to 1920, gives the best account to date of the megaliths in his *Megalithic Finds in Central Celebes*.

Although the statues of the Bada Valley vary considerably in size—from less than one meter to over four—they are stylistically quite similar. All are roughly oval in shape, with disproportionately large, round faces. The eyes, also round (or slightly oval), are framed by a single curved line which outlines the chin, cheeks and eyebrows. While the faces are carved in high relief, the arms, hands and genetalia (erect penis or parted vagina) are barely raised from the surface of the stone.

It has been suggested that westward-gazing Palindo, the largest of the statues, may be associated with death. For the Toraja, who live some four to five days' walk to the south,

west is the direction of death. Linguistic and other cultural similarities between the Toraja and the Bada peoples lend at least partial credence to the theory. The Bada, even after conversion to Christianity, insist on burying their dead facing west, and the Toraja until recently erected megaliths (the stones were roughly shaped but never sculpted) as part of their funerary rituals. The Toraja, like the Bada, sacrifice water buffalo for the souls of the deceased.

Visiting the megaliths

Getting around the Bada Valley to see the megaliths is a wet, muddy affair for nine months of the year. A jeep track links some of the villages; wide footpaths connect the remaining ones. There are frequent stretches of mud, except during the drier part of the year, in June, July and August. Logs span most creeks, but crossing the Malei River's waist-high waters requires some skill or a steadying hand—the bed rocks are slippery. While some of the megaliths can be easily reached from the main tracks or paths, others require navigating through irrigated rice fields and occasional knee-deep mud.

Slogging through the rice fields is in itself a lesson in rice irrigation techniques. You will

get a view of water buffalo or teams of oxen churning up the earth to prepare the land. After plowing, the rice shoots which have been raised for 40 days in bamboo-fenced plots are transplanted. A period of alternate three-day floodings and three-day dryings of the fields then takes place, followed by the harvest. The four species of rice planted here require different maturation times: three, four, five or six months. The longest time is for the preferred local variety; the others have been introduced recently into the valley.

Bada economy

Although not overly rich in monetary terms, the Bada Valley's more than 7000 inhabitants enjoy a very comfortable standard of living. The terraced and irrigated rice fields regularly yield a surplus, and coffee is grown as a cash crop. Under government initiatives, cacao and clove trees are being tested. A recently completed government irrigation scheme added 1,000 hectares (2,500 acres) of paddies to the region. Agricultural experts are trying to convince the people of Bada to sow more than one rice crop per year.

Local gold panners work several of the valley's creeks and rivers, and concentrate on the Malei. According to one local Chinese shopkeeper, the revenue from gold panning accounts for close to 50 percent of the valley's cash income. It can, however, be a risky occupation: in 1986, 25 men drowned in a

Opposite: Water buffalo "plow" a rice paddy.
Above: The giant Sepe statue known as Palindo.
Right: Oba ("the monkey") squatting in a field.

flash flood as they lay sleeping on a small island in the middle of the Malei River.

Even before gold added considerable cash to local incomes, many people were well enough off to prefer taking the MAF plane (service started in 1978) to Tentena, rather than making the two-day hike.

Domestic animals such as water buffalo, cattle, horses, pigs and chickens are plentiful in the valley. Cattle are worth as much as water buffalo (traditionally the most highly valued possessions in many parts of Indonesia) on the barter scale, and prized for their flesh as well as their usefulness as draft animals. Both are used to draw crude plows in the local rice paddies, but water buffaloes are actually more serviceable, as they can plow in areas of deep mud which would be unmanageable for the weaker cattle.

The water buffalo is perfectly adapted to the agricultural conditions of Central Sulawesi. Its reputation as the "tractor of Asia" is well merited. The irrigated rice paddies require extensive aeration before the rice shoots can be planted. Herds of water buffalo, up to two dozen, are driven back and forth in the small, partially flooded paddies, churning the soil with each lumbering step.

The Bada use the water buffalo as a bride price for the traditional marriage ceremonies which usually precede the church ritual. While the aristocracy has lost much of its former privileged status, a noble daughter is still worth a dozen water buffalo, which is quite a sum in real terms. The less blue her blood, the fewer water buffaloes she draws. In deference to "modernization," however the Bada have begun to accept hard cash as part of the bride price if the groom's family and relatives can not come up with enough water buffalo.

If the Bada Valley regularly produces surplus rice and coffee (during the past two decades, the rice crop has failed only once, due to bad weather), getting these items to the market at Tentena is not easy. The twice-weekly MAF flight charges about 14 cents a kilo for freight, and the Cessna's carrying capacity is limited. Men with pack horses levy a fee of about 9 cents per kilo for goods brought to Tentena. So until the road surface improves, the Bada people will receive less for their exports while paying more for essentials such as fuel, matches, tools, soap and clothing. This is typical for the more remote parts of Indonesia.

Funds for construction have been approved but the road work has not yet started. As soon as the roads improve, public transportation will be able to reach the Bada Valley, making it much easier to visit the "Land of the Megaliths."

—*Kal Muller*

Above: *The statue known as Ari Impohi, in Bewa.*
Opposite: *A formerly tortuous part of the now complete Trans-Sulawesi Highway.*

POSO AND TENTENA

A Huge and Enchanting Highland Lake

Poised precisely in the center of Sulawesi, Lake Poso appears as the jeweled head of a cosmic pivot about which the pinwheel arms of the island flail as if blown by massive forces. According to local legends, this area is indeed the pivot around which heaven and earth revolve—and long ago a rope connecting the two was located in the vicinity of the huge highland lake.

The inhabitants of the hills and mountains of the Poso area—formerly known as the Bare'e-speaking or East Toraja—were once famous for their inter-tribal raiding and head-hunting expeditions. Though they were at one time united under a powerful raja, when the ruler was captured by Bugis warriors sent by the ruler of mighty Luwu, the people decided to secede. They symbolized their claim for separation by ramming a tremendous stone pillar into the ground on the hill named Pamona above the shores of Lake Poso. This pillar remains here to this day.

The Pamona people of this region, as they are now called, are considered the great success story of Christian missionization in Indonesia. The Dutch Reformed Church missionary Albertus C. Kruyt landed on the southern shores of Tomini Gulf in 1892 from his post in Gorontalo, and began his efforts in the town of Poso. Displaying incredible patience and tolerance—all the while documenting local customs that his missionary work would eventually cause to disappear—Kruyt waited 17 long years before celebrating his first baptism. Within 5 years after that, however, a school for missionaries had been founded at Pendolo at the southern tip of Lake Poso, and in 1947 an independent Church of Central Sulawesi was established. Today most of the highland Pamona are Christians.

The upland region around Lake Poso and the town of Tentena makes a perfect resting spot on the long Trans-Sulawesi Highway, and is a good jumping-off point for visits to the surrounding area, including the Bada Valley and its mysterious megaliths. The road connecting Tentena to the north with Poso and Palu is quite good.

The tidy town of Poso

The modern district capital of Poso is a clean, shady town breathing an air of efficiency,

with its Dutch-inspired churches and administrative buildings.

Most of the town's main hotels and eating establishments are within a two-block radius of the Poso River, which empties into the Gulf of Tomini. You will find them clustered together on the east side of town, in the vicinity of the harbor (from which you can catch boats across the gulf to Gorontalo). On the west side is the central *pasar*, which can be reached by small outriggers that periodically ply the river.

Sadly, the beaches of Poso have pretty well succumbed to urban pollution. Swimming and snorkeling are still possible, however, at the fishing village of Kayamanya to the northwest of the *pasar,* and at Polande, a two-hour drive to the west.

About 7 km (4 mi) south of Poso along the lilting road to Tentena is the village of Tagolu. This is the place to pick up ebony wood carvings, as works from around the province are on display in stores and shops. Although shops throughout the province (and even the Mutiara Airport in Palu) sell the sets of sprouting coconuts, miniature hornbills, and other mass-produced items worked here, the workshops themselves offer these at far lower prices (bargaining required), and feature a far greater and more imaginative variety of carvings—from lamp tables to humorous miniatures.

Tentena

The small church town of Tentena lies 57 km (35 mi) to the south of Poso on the northeastern corner of beautiful Lake Poso, with enchanting views across this huge inland lake, whence cooling breezes waft across the town. There are several very comfortable, if not luxurious, hotels right at the water's edge. Where the Poso River empties the lake, a quaint covered-bridge connects the two sides of Tentena. Most facilities, including the lakeside docks, are on the town's eastern side, although the western side contains the Missionary Aviation Fellowship (MAF) airstrip.

The recently discovered Saluopa waterfall, quite close to Tentena, consists of jungle-clad cascades punctuated by falls, the largest of which offers a natural pool for a refreshing dip. The path to the falls starts just past Kampung Bali, located a couple of kilometers past Tonusu on the road to the Bada Valley. It's about 3.5 km of flat walking and five river crossings to reach the base of the falls. A wood house about a half kilometer from the falls, on the path, offers floor space for sleeping and simple meals.

In Tentena itself are several caves full of human remains and roughly carved mini-coffins called *peti mayat*. The most accessible of these lies but five minutes' walk from behind the Protestant Church's regional headquarters. This is an overhang rather than a true cave—bones and coffins lie scattered about, while the skulls have been neatly stacked in parallel rows on top of each other.

It takes somewhat longer to reach the Latea caves, and the going is a bit more muddy and slippery, involving two crossings of Latea creek (Kuala Latea). There are two caves at this spot. The lower one holds a few clay pots with bones and coffins; the higher one is full of coffins, mostly dilapidated. Don't bother crawling into the caves; there's nothing to see other than the bats that you will find swishing about you.

There are also the well-known Pamona Caves, located at the far side of the Poso River near the Theological School. Nine chambers but no human remains. Nearby there are pleasant places to sit and watch small canoes paddled or poled around the entrance of the Poso River.

Lake Poso

About 37 kilometers (23 mi) long and 13 kilometers (8 mi) at its widest point, Lake Poso covers approximately 32,000 hectares (80,000 acres). It lies at an elevation of 515 meters (1675 ft), bounded by steeply sloping mountains to the west and gentle hills to the east.

A kaleidoscope of greens blanket the surrounding shores—dense, primary rain forest and lush plantations of cloves and coffee, as neatly arranged as 18th-century European armies—are broken only by a dozen villages with neighboring expanses of terraced rice fields whose sensuous, velvety greens turn gradually to a golden yellow when the grain is ready for harvest.

Locals, quoting a foreign expert, proudly proclaim that Lake Poso is the "second clearest" in the world. Be that as it may, the waters are transparent indeed—ranging from a light turquoise color near the shore to a dark blue out in the lake's depths.

Of Lake Poso's five indigenous fish species, two have almost become extinct due to the introduction of carp and catfish (*lele*) from Java. Most impressive of the native species are the huge eels, which reach over two meters (6.5 ft) in length and can weigh up to 20 kg (44 lb). The eels are caught in

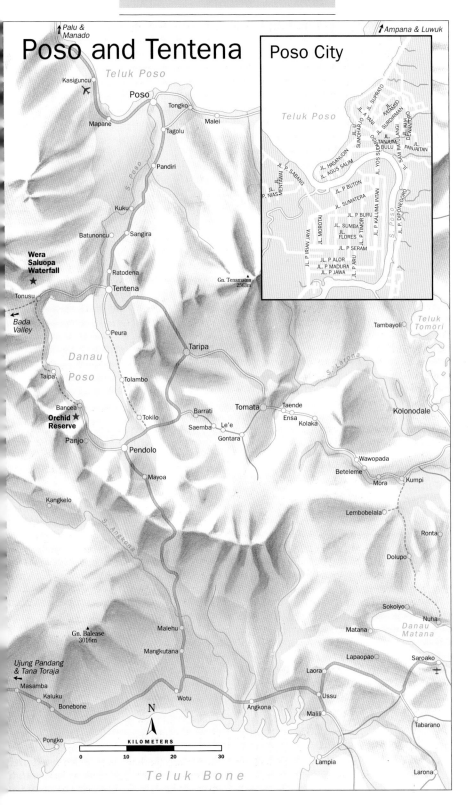

Poso and Tentena

Poso City

wide, V-shaped traps just downstream from the covered bridge at Tentena in the waters of the swift-flowing Poso River. It is perhaps these large eels which are at the root of rumors about the sighting of a huge dragon-snake with a body well over 30 meters (98 ft) long. But then again, perhaps the Loch Ness monster has a cousin in Lake Poso.

You can charter various types of craft for a trip around the lake: outriggers, canoes or motorized boats. The views are spectacular. Get an early start and bring some food. Plan on returning by mid-afternoon, for the waters start to get choppy then and the waves can capsize small boats. If things get too rough, you might have to pull into the nearest village and spend the night. There are worse fates.

A boat trip straight around the lake non-stop takes four to five hours. You might want to stop, however, to watch the fishermen or to take a swim. If you have goggles, take a look at the lake's crabs and exotic shellfish. Lake Poso is quite deep—440 meters (1430 ft).

Landing at Taipa village on the western shore, you can hike 3 kms (1.8 mi) up to a steep promontory which juts a short way over the lake—the perfect spot for photographs. You could also go up the steep hillside directly from the shore to the vantage point, but it's rough and slippery going.

Further down the western shore, the lakeside Bancea Orchid Reserve offers seven hectares (17 acres) and some 45 species of flowers, which bloom in January, May and August. Along the shore, you might see water buffalo bathing.

The main road to the east and south takes you through mountains inhabited by the Mori people. In precolonial times the Mori were constantly warring with Pamona groups and with the sultanate of Bungku on the east coast. The road does not offer any views of the lake, however—you only see it again when approaching Pendolo at the lake's southern tip, as mountains cut off the view. There is, however, a short 12-km (7 mi) road south along the eastern lakeshore leading from Tentena down to Peura village, which climbs up to reveal spectacular panoramas then cuts through a stretch of rice fields.

Along the western side of the lake, a track to Pendolo hugs the shore, climbing a hill just beyond Taipa village. It is rumored that someday this trail may even be covered with asphalt, which would make it one of the most lovely roads in the world.

—*Greg Acciaioli and Kal Muller*

Above: *Experts consider Lake Poso's crystal clear water to be the second-purest in the world, after famous Lake Baikal in Siberia.*

EASTERN PENINSULA

'Fire Cape' and Other Rarities

The eastern arm of Central Sulawesi, including the Banggai archipelago nestling below the head of this peninsula, is the province's least-known region. Many ethnic groups inhabit this isolated area—several of the small groups living in the rugged interior were once coastal dwellers who fled to escape the exactions of the Sultan of Ternate and the Raja of Banggai, who acted as his local representative. These peoples subsist on sago and shifting tuber agriculture in infertile mountain terrain, living in scattered groups of two to ten families. The other major ethnic group in this region are the Bajau, the so-called boat dwellers (though all of them are now found in houses on land near the sea).

The majority of peoples along the coasts and in the foothills were Christianized in the early 20th century, and like the Mori and Pamona to the west now have their own independent church. The coasts are full as well of Muslim fishermen and traders. As a vassal of the Sultan of Ternate, the Islamic raja of the Banggai Islands is of reputed Javanese descent and maintained Islam as the dominant religion of these small islands until recent Christian intrusions.

Ampana

The small port of Ampana, 150 km (90 mi) and 6 hours by jeep or motorcycle from Poso (the condition of unbridged rivers permitting), is a town of some 15,000 souls that serves as a focal point of land communications between Poso and Luwuk, as well as providing a sea link between Poso, the Togian Islands in the Gulf of Tomini, and Gorontalo in the north. The area's chief exports are rattan and copra, followed by damar resin, candlenuts and cloves.

Ampana has seen just enough foreigners that you will be deluged with cries of "hello-meester" along with "where you from" and "wasurnem" (What's your name?). Comic relief comes in the form of unusual phrases such as "bad man"—somehow learned by cute little girls—along with the occasional "I love you" from their older sister. Don't get excited, they don't mean it.

While the town lines a wide bay for a kilometer or so, all the action focuses on a small market by a dock and bus terminal. Just in

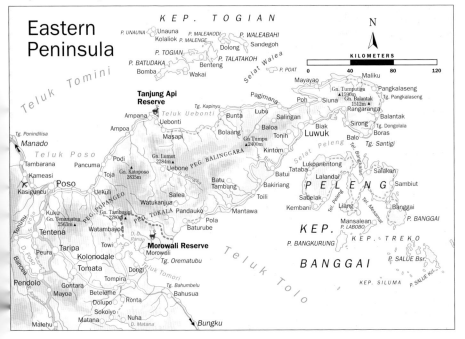

front of the market are local horse-drawn carriages or *bendi*, some quite colorful. Drivers tend to zoom out of the lot with Ben-Hur racing spirit. They charge Rp 200-500 for a ride, depending on distance.

A visit to 'Fire Cape'

The Tanjung Api Reserve lies on the coast a few kilometers east of Ampana, less than an hour's ride by motorized outrigger. The ride there and back can be beautiful, except during December and January, when the seas become rough. As you pull away from shore, Ampana falls rapidly into relief: a cluster of nondescript buildings lined by a sea of coconut trees along the bay with steep hills behind. Fishing boats with colorful sails ply the waters, which are incredibly clear. Steep, vegetation-clad slopes plunge directly into the sea, and around each promontory a new cove is revealed. Schools of dolphins are often sighted along the way.

The name Tanjung Api literally means "Fire Cape" and natural gas seeps up at several points offshore, gurgling to the surface through sand and coral formations. Gas also escapes through cracks in a small cliff next to the shore, and is said to ignite spontaneously upon contact with the air, though a match helps. Strangely, the gas does ignite if water is thrown on the rocks or the earth nearby. Best to see this unique phenomenon during a shower or at night. There is a small shelter here but all supplies must be brought along.

In the immediate vicinity, a small crocodile or two may scurry away but that is all the game you will see. A well-trodden path through the sparse underbrush of the forest gives the opportunity for pleasant walks across the cape. It may be possible here to catch a glimpse of the larger endemic species that inhabit the reserve—including Sulawesi macaques, cuscus, tarsiers, babirusa, pythons, wild boars and deer.

While the swimming in this area is fine, the snorkeling tends to be disappointing as much of the coral has been destroyed by dynamite fishing. Near the gas seepages there is less dynamite damage, but the sea floor sprouts only reed-like seaweed.

A bit over an hour northeast of Tanjung Api, the tiny island of Bukabuka harbors a small fishing village known for its delicious coconut crabs, which fetch $3 or more apiece at Ampana's market.

The Togian Islands

To get really off the beaten track, hop on one of the small boats running between Ampana and Gorontalo (in North Sulawesi), with stops along the way at the Togian Islands in the middle of the gulf. Several mixed cargo/passenger boats crisscross Tomini Gulf on relatively fixed schedules. The boats usually stop at Wakai, Ketupat and Dolong—villages which look better from a distance than up close. The waters under the picturesque stilt-houses serve as sewers and garbage dumps, and are only partially cleaned by the tides. Foreigners in these parts are few and far between, but the locals have all learned the dreaded "hello meester."

The islands' forests are one of the main habitats of the babirusa, while the beaches along the coast function as hatcheries for sea turtles and frigate birds. The Togian Islands are also unusual in being surrounded by all major types of coral reef environments.

While the islands may be a naturalist's delight, they also possess latent powers of destruction. The eruption of Mt. Colo, which blew apart Unauna Island in 1983, was one of the most devastating in recent history. A cloud of ash 15,000 meters (9 miles) high covered 90 percent of the island, destroying all houses, crops, animals, coral and shore fish except in a sheltered narrow eastern strip. Miraculously, all the island's inhabitants were safely evacuated.

The Togian islanders are a diverse bunch. Indigenous ethnic groups include the Kaili (on Unauna), the Pamona (on Togian and Batudaka, the two large, westernmost islands) and the Saluan (on the other islands; they also occupy parts of the eastern peninsula). Also present are Bugis and Bajau immigrants. The Bajau language has become a kind of *lingua franca* in these parts, and Islam has been well established here since the 17th century, having arrived from Gorontalo.

Fishing is the primary way of life, so you see scores of tiny boats with striped, triangular sails, sometimes supported by spidery outriggers, cruising to and from fishing grounds that are often quite far out to sea. On the open sea, flying fish scurry along, their beating tails forming overlapping circles on the surface until they gain enough altitude to swoop amazingly long distances.

Most of the commerce is controlled by the local Chinese who own the larger stores, importing foodstuffs and household items while purchasing and exporting sea products that include dried and salted fish, trochus shells, *trepang*, sharks' fins and mother-of-pearl. Pearls, including the occasional rare black one, are taken to Gorontalo for sale.

Edi Jusuf, a local Chinese-Indonesian at the village of Wakai, has equipped a boat with a hookah rig for pearl oyster gathering. He is also planning to purchase scuba gear, both for pearling and to rent to tourists. Edi knows the good dive spots where coral formations are intact and reef fish abound.

Several boats also connect the islands with the town of Pagimana, about 160 km (100 mi) east of Ampana on the peninsula. A church on a rise just in back of the port area

here gives a panoramic view of the bay and Tongkabu village just across the bay, dominated by a mosque and settled by Bajau people. At Pagimana you are within 62 km (38 mi) of Luwuk, often hard to reach by road from Ampana as rains and rushing rivers tend to make the minibus passage a long, masochistic endeavor.

Luwuk

Luwuk, the capital of Central Sulawesi's easternmost district, rose in importance when occupying Japanese forces made it a government center during World War II. Prior to that, Banggai, the seat of a powerful sultanate, was the region's de facto capital.

A successful transmigration program, started in 1964, brought in 70,000 of the district's 350,000 inhabitants. Some of the formerly dirt-poor Javanese farmers now own cars and satellite receptors for their color TVs. Whereas previously the district had to import almost all of its rice requirements, it now produces a surplus, exported to Gorontalo and the Moluccas. However, copra remains Luwuk district's prime cash crop, with a factory processing the bulk of the production into oil. Rattan from the jungles, cultivated pearls and dry fish are also exported.

Because of the transmigration program, the roads have improved considerably in the past few years. While the main link road to Poso still needs some bridges and surfacing

(especially between Ampana and Bunta), it is in far better shape than a couple of years back. And a brand-new road from Luwuk heads southwest along the coast, soon to reach Baturube, with another road heading that way from Kolonodale. This coastal road, when completed, will make access much easier to the Morowali Nature Reserve.

The existing road from Luwuk already reaches the maleo egg hatcheries at Batui and Bakiriang. You must obtain a permit from the KSDA/PPA office before visiting the hatching grounds, which are active between November and early March. Following an age-old tradition called "sesaji tumpeh," the inhabitants of the Batui region offer the 100 first maleo eggs gathered to the family of the last sultan. The ritual, complete with traditional clothing, takes place at Banggai on November 20 every year. Visitors are welcome and photography allowed—but no one has shown up so far.

Small scale rituals for planting (May and December) and harvest (September and April/May) are still held in the area. Not long ago, in the Balantak-speaking tip of the peninsula, these were great, month-long ceremonies, with dancing every night, but "progress" has ended this. But in marriages, the bride price still includes an old metal gong, from a stock formerly forged locally.

Pulau Tikus

The water was crystal-clear over the sheer wall, plunging straight down beyond the limits of visibility. There were fish everywhere - fusiliers, parrotfish, surgeonfish and wrasses, trumpetfish, butterflyfish, angelfish and Moorish Idols. I swam straight down into this fairyland, down to 10 meters and to the limits

Above, left: *Fisherman spread their haul of trepang—dried sea cucmbers—near Pagimana.*
Above, right: *Coasting in a small craft off Batudaka Island in the Togian Archipelago.*

of my lung capacity and still saw no end to the wall: sea floor nowhere in sight. My kingdom for scuba gear.

But swimming off Pulau Makailu Island (called Pulau Tikus by the mainlanders) was fine, as was snorkeling at the southwest edge of the reef, some 300 meters away from the white sand beach and coconut tree island. Less than a kilometer in circumference, Makailu has fresh water but no permanent inhabitants. Some locals from the nearby sub district capital, Tataba, spend time on the island to make copra and use it as well as a base for fishing. The government has erected some picnic stands on the beach and these can serve as beds until a few simple bamboo guest houses are built.

Banggai Archipelago

The large island of Peleng, a dozen medium-sized islands, and a sea full of tiny ones make up the Banggai archipelago. Enough for a lifetime of exploration. Or a day.

The town of Banggai, on the island of the same name, offers a dawn and dusk spectacle of a variety of small boats, along with a morning market. Stroll down to the main dock just before 7 am to see the canoes paddled in from nearby villages, laden with passengers and fish for sale. The large passenger boats from Luwuk arrive between 7 and 8 am.

A back alley from the rusting pier leads to the far end of the market area, to where the fish are sold. Smoked fish arrives skewered and neatly arranged in racks—but most of the night's catch is fresh and glistening in the morning sun. Around the edges of the market, shark fins and *trepang* dry in the sun.

After the market concludes, it's best to get away for at least a day's swimming, snorkeling, lazing on nearby white sand beaches.

Several locals had warned us about the number of sharks in the nearby seas and some of the drying shark fins we saw at the market attested to the size of the critters. But, we were assured, the big ones were far away, off Pulau Sago, the southernmost of the archipelago.

Be that as it may, the two pairs of blacktip sharks we saw on the seaward side of Kokungan Island were big enough to leave a lasting impression. But when we plunged down for a closer look, the first pair turned chicken, swimming off at impressive speed. The second pair, slightly larger, did not panic, but circled instead, keeping however at a respectful distance and well away from decent camera range. Typical, in our experi-

ence. While most people panic at the mere mention of a shark, they are damn hard to approach in real life. So take the sighting of a shark as the magnificent spectacle it is. No need to jump into the boat if you spot one.

There were no sharks, and because of fish-bombing, very few reef fish off the twin Bandang Islands, about a half hour's motoring from Banggai. But the water was clear and warm, and there was a good white sand beach in back of a Bajau fishing village. The condition of the coral—and the number of fish—was far better off Kokungan Island, opposite the Badangs.

But our favorite snorkeling was at a pearl farm on the landward side of Kokungan. There are five pearl farms in the archipelago, four of them managed by Japanese who do not allow visitors. The pearl farm at Kokungan is owned by a local businessman, and permission to visit it was easily obtained.

The shallows around the pearl farm were very rich in fish life and the scene—with seeded pearl oysters dangling in mesh cages, was very interesting indeed.

On to Kolonodale

Kolonodale lies on the southern shore of Tomori Bay, a westward protrusion of the Gulf of Tolo, 160 km (100 mi) east of Tentena. Formerly a minor trading town within the Bungku rajadom, Kolonodale has a history of contact with incoming Bugis traders, as well as with the Bajau sea people who have long plied the shores of east Sulawesi, fishing and gathering *trepang*.

The side road from Taripa on the Transul Highway to Kolonodale remains a bone-jarring 5–6 hours until the surfacing is completed. But it's worth it to see Tomori Bay, huge and convoluted, with some near-vertical mountainsides plunging into the waters. Motorized boats can be hired to circle a part of Tomori Bay, revealing outlines of prehistoric hands "stenciled" with red hematite, thatch-roofed villages, and grand views.

Pulau Pingia Island (also called Kepiting) offers a spectacular 80-meter plus limestone cliff which dives into the sea to continue under the surface, sprouting tunicates, sea fans, bushy coral and the odd barrel sponge. Snorkeling here and off other islands reveal some decent coral formations, although some is damaged from bombing.

Kolonodale is best known as the gateway for the Morowali Nature Reserve, a 160,000-

Opposite: *A dramatic sunset at Ampana.*

hectare (395,200 acre) wilderness area of unspoiled rain forest, containing three substantial mountains—Tokala, Tambusisi and Morowali—and five major rivers. The name 'Morowali' means "rumbling" or "growling" in the Wana language, referring to the sound of the rivers streaming across their stony beds. The Ranu Lakes here are eerily quiet, as the exhalation of marsh gases keeps birds and other animals away.

Morowali Reserve

In 1980, the British expedition Operation Drake conducted a four-month survey of endangered species to celebrate the quadricentennial of Sir Francis Drake's running aground on a reef off Morowali. (He was only able to free the *Golden Hind* by jettisoning eight tons of spices and eight heavy pieces of ordnance).

As a result of this survey, the area was declared a reserve rather than being developed as a transmigration site. Morowali hosts hundreds of unique butterflies and beetles in addition to *anoa,* babirusa and maleo birds.

Care should be taken during the rainy season (from March to September, especially in May), as heavy rainfall can transform the low-lying areas into swamps and suddenly change the courses of the major rivers.

Make sure to take a guide: foreigners have been lost there for several days. The local Wana are said to make excellent guides.

Unless you have lots of time, patience and luck, you probably won't see many animals except perhaps a wild pig, so don't go strictly to see the rare fauna: the *anoa,* babirusa, huge butterflies and what is claimed to be the world's smallest bat. But this area is a botanist's paradise.

The Wana people are friendly, and quite traditional in their religious beliefs, but dress in ordinary western clothing. They practice slash-and-burn agriculture and hunt with blowguns.

Treks into the Morowali Nature Reserve start with a 1.5 hr. boat ride across Tomori Bay from Kolondole. You land your boat near the Morowali River and trek 4–6 hours to the Wana settlement at Kayupoli. From there it is 2–3 hours walk west to the Ranu Lakes, or a day's walk northeast to Taronggo. This last segment is very difficult during the rainy season. You can also enter from Baturube. This takes about a half a day by boat and hiking to Taronggo, and from there, again, a long day's trek to Kayupoli.

A group in Kolonodale, the Sahabat Morowali (Friends of Morowali) have set up a tourist information center in town to advise travelers about the Wana people. They feel that excessive visiting by outsiders will almost certainly change an already fragile culture. This outfit can recommend local guides who know and respect Wana lifestyle.

—*Greg Acciaioli and Kal Muller*

PART V

Introducing North Sulawesi

"The little town of Manado," wrote the great English naturalist Alfred Russel Wallace after visiting the area in 1859, "is one of the prettiest in the East. It has the appearance of a large garden containing rows of rustic villas, with broad paths between, forming streets generally at right angles with each other. Good roads branch off in several directions towards the interior, with a succession of pretty cottages, neat gardens, and thriving plantations, interspersed with wildernesses of fruit trees. To the west and south the country is mountainous, with groups of fine volcanic peaks 6,000 or 7,000 feet high, forming grand and picturesque backgrounds to the landscape ... I had heard much of the beauty of this country, but the reality far surpassed my expectations."

A land of plenty

Wallace's description still holds true today, and this is indeed one of the most prosperous and spectacularly scenic areas in Indonesia. Made up of three large districts (Minahasa, Bolaang Mongondow and Gorontalo) and one smaller one (the Sangihe-Talaud Islands), the province of North Sulawesi (Sulawesi Utara or Sulut) occupies the long (600 km/ 360 mi) and narrow (average width is only 50 km/30 mi) northern arm of the island.

Much of the beauty and fertility of the region derives from its towering volcanoes. Many are extinct or dormant, but Mt. Lokon near Tomohon erupted in 1986 and 1991, and Mt. Soputan in central Minahasa in 1989. Earth tremors are not at all uncommon. Wallace experienced an earthquake in the hills overlooking Tondano, at Rurukan, that shook the earth at frequent intervals for an entire week.

"We feel ourselves," he wrote, "in the grasp of a power to which the wildest fury of the winds and waves are as nothing; yet the effect is more a thrill of awe than the terror which the more boisterous war of the elements produces."

Volcanoes are only one aspect of a geologically active complex that includes fumaroles and hot springs in the Minahasa district. Studies have been carried out to ascertain the feasibility of generating electricity from geothermal energy here. More importantly, the volcanoes are responsible for the exceptionally fertile soils that are the province's major economic asset. North Sulawesi indeed possesses some of the most fertile land in Indonesia outside Java and Bali. Agriculture, in the form of coconut, clove and nutmeg tree cultivation, forms the basis for great wealth in many parts of the province.

The northermost district comprises the thinly populated volcanic islands of the Sangihe and Talaud groups, which depend on fishing, spices and coconut production. These islanders frequently travel to the mainland to work as coconut harvesters, among other occupations.

Minahasa, the hinterland of Manado, is the most heavily populated and highly developed district. Only 20 percent of its land remains under forest cover, and the population density has soared to over 300 persons per square km (750 per square mile)—less than half that of Java but still very high.

The Minahasa area is extremely mountainous (Mt. Klabat, the highest peak, stands at 1995 m/6,000 ft), but has a narrow coastal fringe where coconuts thrive, and an interior plateau around Lake Tondano (altitude 600 m/1820 ft; surface area 46 sq km/18 sq mi) where irrigated rice fields provide abundant harvests. The upland hills are covered in clove trees, while in the cool highland areas to the south, near the border with Bolaang Mongondow, vegetables such as potatoes,

Overleaf: *The clear waters around Manado are rich with marine life.* **Opposite:** *Coral reefs and volcanoes provide the North with major scenic attractions. Both photos by Jill Gocher.*

carrots and cabbages are grown.

To the west of Minahasa lie the districts of Bolaang Mongondow and Gorontalo. Both are very mountainous also, with an even narrower coastal plain and only a few small, inland valleys, where agriculture is less intensively practiced than in Minahasa. Both districts contain small village settlements created through government-sponsored transmigration from Java and Bali.

The Dumoga Valley to the west of Kotamobagu, for example, supports two prosperous Balinese farming villages (and several Javanese settlements) that have benefitted from the area's fertile soils, extensive irrigation system and good road network. Transmigration settlements have been remarkably successful in North Sulawesi, but local population pressures and a shortage of arable land have led to a virtual cessation of sponsored transmigration into the province.

North Sulawesi is also blessed by abundant rainfall, more or less evenly spread throughout the year, and by a richness of marine life in the surrounding seas. But erosion and the consequent silting of waterways, from deforestation, can be seen in both Minahasa and Gorontalo.

Rice and coconuts

Products of the soil (and a quest for souls) first drew Europeans to North Sulawesi in the 16th century, and agriculture still underpins the wealth of the province today. North Sulawesi is indeed relatively wealthy, ranking in the top ten of Indonesia's 27 provinces in terms of per capita GNP, with a growth rate well above the national average. In the areas of education and health care, North Sulawesi also outstrips most Indonesian provinces.

Rice was the first crop to interest outsiders. The Dutch, based in the food-poor Moluccan "Spice Islands," looked to nearby Minahasa for their provisions. Ironically, the province now imports rice. Coffee was important during the 19th century, but copra, coconut oil and their by-products are the major revenue earners today. Many of the province's more than 25 million coconut trees are old and less than optimally managed, however, and now need replacement.

Coconuts, like all other agricultural crops in North Sulawesi, are with few exceptions grown not on large estates but by individual smallholders, providing many villagers with a good income. Visiting rural areas, travelers will notice coconut meat being dried in the sun or smoked in cribs to produce copra—a big money-earner.

'Clove fever'

More recently, fortunes large and small have also been made from cloves (*cengkeh*). Native to the neighboring Moluccan Islands, cloves have long been grown in North Sulawesi, but in recent decades this crop has caught on in

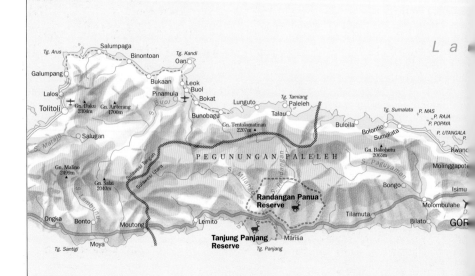

North Sulawesi

a big way. The phrase "clove fever" well describes the atmosphere of the 1970s, when everyone seemed to be planting, growing, harvesting or trading cloves. Prior to the "great harvests" (which occur periodically between more normal annual harvests), consumer goods flood into the villages, supplied by traders as advance payment for specified quantities of dried cloves.

At peak harvest times work in offices and schools grinds to a halt, since the labor-intensive picking of cloves has to be carried out in a very short time. The unmistakable fragrance of the spice then perfumes the air. Picked when still greenish-yellow in color, clove buds are spread on mats to dry in the sun, and quickly turn a dark brown. They are then stored against future price rises, or more often delivered immediately to middlemen as repayment for advances.

Cloves are mainly grown on the slopes of the Minahasa region. Even the possession of a few trees can mean important cash income for a family. The cloves are exported to Java, largely to be used in scented *kretek* cigarettes, which provide the visitor with a distinctive sensory memory of the country. (*Kreteks* contain as much as 50 percent clove powder by weight, but beware—the World Health Organization has recently rated these the world's most harmful cigarettes.) Clove oil is also pressed from the leaves of the tall clove trees; the oil is used for relief from tooth-

aches, among other things. The relative prosperity one notices in parts of Minahasa is largely due to this wonderful tree.

Another important tree crop in North Sulawesi is nutmeg. A sourish fruit that grows on tall trees, the hard kernel produces nutmeg spice while the beautiful lacey vermilion covering surrounding it is dried and ground to become mace. Candien, the nutmeg fruit, is a pleasant treat. Besides nutmeg, vanilla is enjoying some popularity now, too, though production is still limited.

Aside from corn, cassava and rice agriculture, the sea is also of substantial importance to the province, whose waters are rich in various species of tuna. A fishing port with modern processing facilities has been developed at Aer Tembaga on the northeastern coast near Bitung, but much fishing is still carried out by small craft instead of by the large seagoing vessels once envisaged. Significant quantities of freshwater fish are also taken from Lake Tondano or raised in fishponds.

A bit of manufacturing, largely the processing of agricultural products such as coconut, is found throughout the province, mainly in the Manado-Bitung region. There is also some mining, including widespread panning for gold in Bolaang Mongondow. Gorontalo has sizeable reserves of copper. Like the rest of Sulawesi, however, the North is still primarily an agrarian region.

—*Tim Babcock*

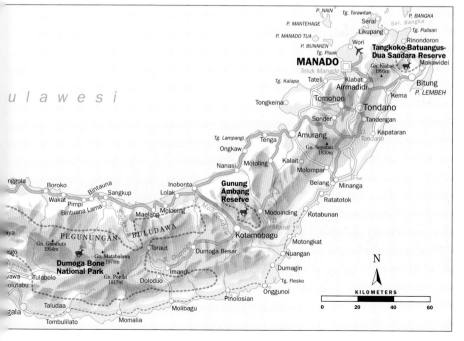

HISTORY

Colonial Stronghold in the North

Legends, archaeological remains and linguistic analyses are the only evidence we have of northern Sulawesi's history prior to the 16th century. No "high" civilization such as was known on Java and Bali ever developed here, and the pre-colonial peoples of the region left behind no written records.

The languages of North Sulawesi are closely related to languages spoken in the Philippines. On the basis of this and other evidence, scholars have suggested that the area was settled from the north, though this no doubt involved a complex and millennia-long process of migrations and adaptation.

Minahasans and other peoples of the province have a different sort of origin story: the myth of Toar and Lumimuut. The primal ancestress Lumimuut was born out of foam from a coral rock thrown up from the sea and impregnated by the wind. She and her son Toar set out in different directions to search for mates. Years later they met but did not recognize one another and so married, giving birth to many children. It is said that Lumimuut gathered her offspring at a sacred stone called Watu Pinabetengan and allocated different parts of the realm to them. This stone, with its undeciphered pictographic carvings, is still *in situ* near the town of Langowan.

At the time of Europeans' first contact with the area, North Sulawesi was inhabited largely by inland and upland peoples who practiced shifting cultivation. The Minahasans were not organized into states, though unions of villages did exist. Petty coastal kingdoms had been established in Gorontalo, as a result of Islamic influence emanating from Bugis kingdoms to the south and from the sultanate of Ternate to the east.

Ternate, a mighty maritime power which then controlled the world's supply of valuable cloves, wielded considerable influence over northern Sulawesi. The language of Manado contains numerous words originating from the non-Austronesian languages of the Moluccas, and some traditional titles in Bolaang Mongondow and Gorontalo derive from the Ternatean language.

The first Westerners to visit the area were the Portuguese; in the mid-1500s they sent a priest to spread the faith. During the next century, the Spanish arrived via the Philippines; though they never settled in large

numbers, their influence is still visible. They introduced corn, tomatoes, chili peppers and horses. Indigenous words for horse are variations on the Spanish *caballo*, and other Spanish and Portuguese words not found in Indonesian are preserved in the regional *lingua franca,* Manado Malay (*Bahasa Manado*). Two other cultural peculiarities of rural Minahasa which appear to be inherited from the Iberians are Christmas mumming—a tradition once widespread throughout western Europe—and, oddly enough, square-dancing (locally called *katrili,* presumably from the French *quadrille*).

In the 1650s the Dutch, under the aegis of the United East Indies Company (VOC), supplanted the Spanish and established a post at the site of present-day Manado. In 1673 the Dutch constructed Fort Amsterdam here (which was bombed during the Second World War and, unfortunately, later razed to the ground). Not until the early 1800s, however, did they penetrate the interior. The Minahasa highlands were subjugated in 1808-1809, and rapid and massive conversions to Protestantism, along with the forced cultivation of coffee, began to take place soon after.

Christianity became an emblem of Minahasan culture and identity and helped reinforce a local attachment to European culture, as well as in some cases an identification with Dutch interests. The Church and the Dutch administration were instrumental in spreading education and basic health services throughout the district. By the turn of the century, there was a school for every 1,000 people in Minahasa, whereas in Java the ratio was one to 50,000. Thus by 1930, Minahasa registered the highest literacy rate (in Malay as well as Dutch) in the country. Minahasans made up a significant portion of the colonial bureaucracy as well as the army; needless to say, their status as colonial "Tories" did not greatly endear them to other Indonesians.

The Japanese occupation was followed by Dutch reoccupation, and by revolutionary activity that eventually brought independence in 1949. Not everyone in North Sulawesi initially supported the revolution; for a long time, in fact, pro-Dutch sentiments among Minahasans earned the region the nickname of the "twelfth province" of Holland. On the eve of independence many Minahasans emigrated to Holland. Today, however, such things have long been forgotten and most of the talk is of economic development. Government policies in the New Order era have focused mainly on this, and have been remarkably successful in bringing progress to even remote areas of the province.

—Tim Babcock

Opposite: *Fort Amsterdam in Manado as it appeared in the 19th century.* **Above:** *The regalia of the kingdom of Sekoyo in North Sulawesi, guarded by a nobleman and female exorcists.*

PEOPLES OF THE NORTH

Lively, Fun-Loving and Extroverted

Over the centuries four main ethnic groups have coalesced out of the dozens of interrelated peoples that formerly inhabited North Sulawesi. Their names parallel the names of the province's four districts: Minahasa, Gorontalo, Sangihe and Mongondow. In practice, people still recognize and identify many local subgroups, distinguished mainly by language or dialect.

Outside the province they are often all referred to as *orang Manado,* though in other contexts this term refers more specifically to (Christian) Minahasans, the outgoing group who make up half of the province's 2.5 million inhabitants. Although Minahasans were once the educated and professional elite, in recent decades other groups have been catching up. Gorontalo people in particular are known as successful petty traders.

The North also contains significant immi-grant populations, of whom the most notice-able are the Chinese, concentrated in the towns and engaging in wholesale and retail trading. Over the years there has been much intermarriage between Chinese and Mina-hasans, and inter-ethnic tensions here are less pronounced than in other areas.

Small Arab communities (primarily in Manado and Gorontalo City) engage in com-mercial and professional occupations. Bugis and Makassarese from the South are found in small numbers; about one percent of the pop-ulation is made up of Javanese or Balinese transmigrants. Coastal settlements of Bajau also exist, though not in the numbers found in Central or Southeast Sulawesi.

In Minahasa, 95 percent of the population is Christian—mostly Protestant with a small Catholic minority. While there is an estab-lished, dominant Protestant Church (descen-ded from the Dutch Reformed Church), per-haps 50 other sects exist. Gorontalo and Mongondow people are almost entirely Muslim, the latter group having undergone conversion in the 19th century. In Manado and Bitung, the Christian and Muslim popula-tions are more evenly balanced.

In spite of the impact of Christianity, Islam and the West, traces of indigenous culture remain. Today among Minahasans (and pre-sumably other groups as well) there is still a lively (though often covert) belief in a super-natural world populated with *opo-opo*—gods,

culture heroes, or similar helpful or harmful beings. These can be contacted either directly or with the assistance of ritual specialists (who may be devout Christians or Muslims). Offerings and spirit-possession are common; the sacred ancestor stone, Watu Pinawetengan, is especially favored for such activities. Also popular are the pre-Christian stone burial chambers (*waruga*) found at many locations. Coconut shells left as offerings here are said to be a modern substitute for the human skulls left in earlier times.

Today, what is generally propounded as "traditional culture" by the Department of Education and Culture and the national television network, TVRI, is limited to the visual and performing arts and devoid of much of its original ritual significance. Alas, North Sulawesi is no Bali, nor even a Tana Toraja, though a number of interesting forms of dance, for example, do exist and with some effort may be seen by the visitor.

Perhaps the most accessible of the local performing arts is Minahasan singing. The fun-loving Minahasans are famed throughout the country for their vocal skills, displayed to best advantage during their huge ritual celebrations, when wine and song flow in equally copious quantities. Songs are often accompanied by a *kolintang* orchestra consisting of several wooden xylophones. *Kolintangs* are found in almost every village and occasionally at popular seafood restaurants in the Manado area. Cassettes are also sold locally.

A variety of modernized and secularized dance forms are often performed to greet important visitors, or in competitions, rather than in their original community-rooted context. *Maengket* and *marambak* are forms of Minahasan group dancing, often with verses sung as accompaniment, that once had connections with harvest ceremonies and inaugurations of new houses. The *cakalele* war dance, known throughout the province and in the Moluccas (from where it may have originated), is danced by men dressed in red, waving swords and shields and uttering ferocious cries to frighten the "enemy."

Of sculpture, painting, and other plastic arts there is little today, though there is a tradition of ebony carving in North Sulawesi, most notably in the Sangihe-Talaud Islands. Weaving died out in Minahasa some time during the last century, but an attractive form of pulled-thread embroidery called *krawang* is made in the Gorontalo City area, and is widely available in the form of ready-made clothing (shirts, dresses), tablecloths, sheets and pillowcases. One can also buy the material as dress- and shirt-length pieces of cloth ready for custom tailoring.

—*Tim Babcock*

Opposite: A cakalele *war dance.* **Above:** *A group of kids outside Manado screaming the inevitable "Hello Meester" at our female photographer.*

MANADO AND BUNAKEN

Thriving City and World Class Diving

Manado, bustling capital of North Sulawesi province, sprawls inland across low, palm-clad hills around a wide bay fringed with luxuriant tropical vegetation. In the distance, a backdrop of three volcanoes completes the city's spectacular setting. With a limited number of intrinsic attractions, Manado's main interests for the traveler are its convenient location as a base for exploring the Tondano region, and the splendid underwater scenery of Bunaken.

Manado first acquired its importance during the early colonial period and only very gradually became the focus of Minihasan culture, traditionally centered around Lake Tondano. The city (population 300,000) is predominantly Christian—a legacy of centuries of Portuguese and Dutch domination. There are 349 places of worship, including 266 churches, and more are still being built. The church plays a key role in society here and on Sundays the streets become filled with smartly-dressed churchgoers.

Manado was a major seaport until the early 1960s, but the harbour has silted up and now large ships call at Bitung, on the other side of the northern peninsula, which also has better weather protection thanks to Lembeh Island. However, passenger boats from Manado's harbor sail to the major islands in the Sangihe–Talaud archipelago to the north: Siau, Sangihe (Tahuna), Salibabu (Lirung) and Karakelong (Beo), as well as to Ternate, Toli-Toli, and Ambon.

City sights

Manado has a wide variety of shops, hotels and restaurants. As a service and administrative center for the entire province, it is also the site of numerous educational institutions, banks and government offices. There is little architecture of note to reward curious strollers, although shoppers will be amply rewarded in the city center, which is full of busy stores selling goods of every description at bargain prices.

Early morning risers should head to the **wholesale fish market**, just off the north side of the harbor. Large snappers, mackerel, tuna, barracuda and smaller fry are auctioned here. The action is already well underway by 6 am.

Pasar Bersehati, next to the fish market, is the largest food market in town and has an overwhelming quantity and variety of fresh produce, meat, fish and chicken. One section of the market is devoted to freshly butchered dog, a delicacy much appreciated by local gastronomes. Watch out for the signs proclaiming "RW," a euphemism for dog meat, to either avoid or sample man's best friend, served flaming spicy hot. Foreigners seldom venture into this market, so be prepared for stares and lots of attention.

The **Ban Hian Kiong Buddhist Confucian Temple** (on Jl. Panjaitan in the center of the city) was built in the early 19th century and rebuilt in 1974, after being partially destroyed by vandals. Two weeks after the Chinese Lunar New Year, the large Cap Go Mei (15th of the first lunar month) celebration held in Chinese communities throughout Southeast Asia is held at this temple.

You may see local residents practicing various forms of divination and geomancy, and if you ascend to the top floor of the temple you will be rewarded by an excellent view of downtown Manado. Oddly, the temple also has a display of Portuguese artifacts, and the top floor features a couple of ancient V.O.C. muzzle-loading cannon pointing to the rusting tin roofs of the downtown area.

The **North Sulawesi Provincial Museum** on Jl. W.R. Supratman (open every day 8 am to 2 pm except Sundays and holidays; Friday closing at 11 am) has interesting displays of historical and cultural relics from all around the province. Although labeled only in Indonesian, the displays are interesting and include miniatures, curious wind instruments and a very mean set of brass knuckles sprouting spikes. Guides are well-informed, though their English may be far from fluent.

The broad **Piere Tandean Boulevard** which hugs the shoreline for 4 km from the southern outskirts of town to the harbor is a good place to catch magnificent sunsets with small fishing craft in the foreground and Manado Tua looming out of the sea in the distance. This area comes alive after dark, with numerous food stands and plenty of evening strollers.

The downtown area, crowded with shops and traffic, covers a relatively small area to the south of the harbor, near the Jumbo Supermarket and the central *bemo* station where the main arteries converge. You can catch a minibus from here to a dozen areas around the city's periphery where you then transfer to destinations beyond.

Bunaken Marine Reserve

For the past decade, the fame of the reefs of the Bunaken group has spread among lovers of the underwater world. And rightly so: the 75,000 hectare Bunaken–Manado Tua Marine Park, one hour by boat from Manado, offers excellent snorkeling and scuba diving.

While several years ago the service and equipment of the dive resorts left much to be desired, this has improved considerably over the past couple of years. The rental gear is now well maintained, boats have been upgraded and dive guides are (slowly) learning to speak English.

The clear waters, with an average temperature of 27°C, harbor a tremendous amount of marine life: reef fishes in great variety; healthy, diverse coral growth and just about every invertebrate on the evolutionary scale, from sponges to squids.

There are some eighteen dive spots off the five islands in the marine reserve. The safest and most popular are in a large, sheltered bay off the south coast of Bunaken

Island, and offer excellent wall diving, as well as a dozen homestays which serve meals. Commercial activities are banned in the reserve, along with dynamite fishing, coral, live shell or fish collecting and spear fishing. Most foreign visitors to Bunaken stay with one of the dive companies located outside Manado.

While the area offers several different kinds of dives (drift, deep, and wreck), the prime attraction is the vertical walls. Pierced by shallow caves and crevasses which provide shelter and protection for reef fish species, they are also covered with a layer of invertebrate marine life. Hard and soft corals, whip corals, sponges and filter feeders all cling to these walls in a dazzling kaleidoscope of colors.

Schools of pyramid butterfly fish, black triggerfish and the clouds of bright orange and purple anthias swarm around the reef edge and the upper part of the wall at around five meters, making this a great spot to spend your decompression time or just safety stop. This is also the best place to see, and follow, the black-and-gray–banded colubrine seasnake as it slithers around, checking out nooks and crannies for snacks. Although very poisonous, these mild-mannered snakes are very difficult to rile—guides show off by

Above: *A view of the green hills surrounding Manado Bay.*

grabbing their tails and pulling them out from under rocks. Don't try it yourself.

While the walls offer an ever-changing tableau of marine ecology, don't forget to glance out at the open water occasionally: that's where the big fellas lurk. The guides are excellent at spotting and pointing at what's out there: rays, sea turtles, schools of barracuda, Napoleon and bumphead wrasses and the occasional shark, usually of the harmless, reef white-tip variety.

Don't worry about sharks, but keep a wary eye out for the Titan triggerfish, especially if you see one with no other fish around. They defend their newly laid eggs against one and all, attacking even sharks and humans who inadvertently wander into their territory. While their mouths are too small to cause fatal damage, their strong back-teeth could nip off a chunk of your ear, or bite through enough flesh to require stitches.

Be extremely careful when approaching sting rays, especially big ones. They are *not* manta rays. An Italian diver made that fatal mistake and tried to ride one. The spine on the ray's tail pierced his chest cavity. He barely made it to the surface, then hemorrhaged to death on his way to the hospital. Remember the basic underwater law—look but don't touch!

Beginner and intermediate divers will be fully satisfied with any number of plunges off south Bunaken. Expert divers—those with experience in strong currents and depths of over 30 m (bring your computer!)—might want to try some of the sites on the backside of Bunaken: Sachiko's Point, for a good chance to see large tuna and turtles, or Mike's Point, for a nice concentration of reef fish and invertebrates.

Deep divers might want to try Batu Kapal, on Pulau Nain, so-named for an outcrop in the shape of a stone boat, at 42 m. A narrow canyon begins here and plunges way down – to at least 90 m where an overhang may shelter big jacks.

If you go this deep, leave your cameras behind. The last couple who tried this (on a single tank) were a startled to see both their underwater lights and one of their depth gauges implode! Better try the shipwreck close to Molas, lying between 25 and 40 meters. Night dives at Bunaken are an exciting option for experts and beginners alike.

Aside from the usual lunch along with fellow divers on Bunaken Island, there are several other day-time options. One is to visit the friendly Bajau community on Montehage Island. The whole village lives in houses perched on stilts in the shallow estuary just north of the island.

Volcanoes and dolphins

You could also climb part of the way up the dormant Manado Tua island-volcano. It's not

worth going as far as the summit crater at at 822 m; thick vegetation fills the crater and obscures any views of the sea. However, from part of the way up the steep slopes, there are stupendous views of Bunaken Island surrounded by shallow turquoise seas, blending into the deep blue, with Mt. Klabat on the mainland rearing up in the distance.

On the various boat rides, keep a lookout for the occasional pilot whale or school of dolphins. Sometimes the sea swarms with several groups of leaping dolphins.

Nonswimmers can enjoy many of the sites of the coral reefs from glass bottom boats which make the run to the marine reserve when there are enough clients. Stay away in the December–February period, when strong winds and turbulent seas could make boat rides very rough indeed.

Bangka Island

Divers, snorkelers and camp followers interested in a long boat ride offering lots of scenery can visit Bangka Island most of the year round. The scuba diving off Bangka was pioneered by Dr. Hanny Batuna of the Murex Dive Centre and this outfit offers a delightful trip to Bangka, with the option of returning overland.

The boat ride to Bangka is unforgettable. As you depart mainland Sulawesi, leaving the Lokon and Mahawu volcanoes behind, cloud-wreathed Manado Tua looms large in the north behind low-lying Bunaken Island. In the early morning and late afternoon small sailboats ply the passage between Bunaken and the mainland.

As you head towards the tip of the Minihasa Peninsula, the magnificent cone of Mt. Klabat, (1,995 m) which lies east of Manado, dominates the mainland and becomes a reference point throughout most of the journey. Passing Tanjung Tarawitan, mainland Sulawesi's northernmost point, the mountains amid the Tangkoko-Batuangus–Dua Saudara Reserve appear in the south, Talisei Island lies north and Bangka sits dead ahead. The large white buildings you can see on Talisei are part of a Japanese-run pearl culture operation, which attests to the purity of the surrounding waters.

Bangka Island, with its contorted bays

and many hills, has few white sand beaches as tropical vegetation grows to the waters' edge in most places. There are rich fishing grounds off the coast, and you may see teams of boats either setting up their huge circle nets, or hauling them in, writhing with tuna as they near the surface.

Jagged pinnacles rise out of the waters off southern and southeastern Bangka and it is here that Dr. Hanny Batuna, the owner of Murex, pioneered some outstanding dive locations. The pinnacle scenery continues underwater, and the spread and variety of soft corals here is truly outstanding. This is also a very good area for snorkeling.

At some drop off points, shoals of fish swirl around in such profusion it's like entering a wind-driven snowstorm. There are also a few big fellas around Bangka: we spotted a decent sized shark in the distance which fled when we tried to get closer; several hefty Napoleon wrasse and a dozen large barracuda with unusual yellow tails. Some small shark hide under the table coral. There is often current here, and it is best to have some experience before attempting to scuba dive in the area.

Lunch is usually eaten under a shelter on a picturesque sandy beach in a deep bay. But sadly the scene is not entirely idyllic: all fish-lovers will be disgusted by the sight of the floating house with large nets attached to it in the bay. This operation was set up in 1991 with the sole purpose of capturing groupers and Napoleon wrasse alive. They are then shipped to Hong Kong. It takes many years for these fish to reach their large size, and to see yet another example of man's exploitation of nature for a quick profit, in such a beautiful spot, leaves a bad taste in the mouth.

For the return journey to Manado, you have the choice of a scenic one-hour drive back from the mainland village of Likupang, or to take the boat back the way you came with the possibility of seeing a great sunset off Manado Tua.

Lembeh Strait

Several operations will take divers to the Lembeh Strait, around the point from Bangka, or there is a diving resort—Kungkungan Bay—right in the strait. This area has just recently opened up to diving, and it is a very special place, particularly for richness of marine life. National Geographic Explorer TV has already filmed an underwater documentary in the area.

—Kal Muller

Opposite: *Diving off the coast of Bunaken, just an hour north of Manado by boat. The reefs here feature a dramatic, 1,000-meter vertical drop and lots of exciting tropical marine life, all of which adds up to some of the best diving in the world.*

EXPLORING MINAHASA

Extraordinary Day Trips from Manado

Roads radiate outward from Manado in several directions, all of them, it seems, leading somewhere interesting. Since the best hotels and travel facilities are in the city, and since most of the surrounding sights can easily be reached in a series of day-long excursions, your best bet is to base yourself in Manado and make a number of trips into the hinterland by rented car, minibus or public transport. This can actually be done in any number of ways, and the itineraries given below are merely intended as suggestions that neatly encompass many of the major sights.

Tomohon via Tasik Ria

This round-trip excursion follows the coast south out of Manado to Tasik Ria beach and on to Tanawangko, then cuts inland via Taratara to the highland town of Tomohon, offering a delightful combination of a visit to the beach, a taste of delicious Minahasan cuisine, and spectacular views of coastal coconut groves and highland clove plantations, all the while passing through picturesque rural villages. Start out early to fully enjoy the sights.

Tasik Ria is about 30 minutes from Manado, and is worth a stop to collect seashells, have a swim in the warm Sulawesi Sea and watch the local fishermen. There are tennis courts here, a children's playground and several cottages for rent by the beach. On Sundays it gets very crowded. Manado Seaside Cottages, on the road from Manado before Tasik Ria, offers excellent fresh seafood.

The village of Tanawangko, further south along the coast, has a deserted beach which fits perfectly most peoples' image of a tropical island paradise. At the southern end of the village, just after the Pentacostal Church and a bridge, turn right along a small, rough road that leads 2 kilometers (1.25 mi) to a long, sandy beach bordering on a wide bay. The swimming here is excellent; gentle waves lap the shore and there are plenty of seashells. Look out for falling coconuts, however, and be aware of unconfirmed rumors of small crocodiles said to inhabit the rivers flowing into the ocean at this spot.

Back at the north end of Tanawangko, turn inland to the mountains and follow a road that winds up through coconut plantations to the highland town of Tomohon

JILL GOCHER

some 45 minutes away) via Taratara. Along ne way the magnificent active volcano, Mt. Lokon (1595 m/5181 feet), looms into view.

The village of Tara-Tara at the southern)ot of the volcano is a regional center for tra-itional music and dance. Performances of ne *kolintang* (wooden xylophone) orchestra, ne *cakalele* war dance, the *maengket* song nd dance group, and the *lancier* dance roup are held here at the Kemer open-air uditorium by prior arrangement.

The hilltop town of Tomohon, known cally as the "City of Flowers," sits in a sad-le between two volcanoes, Lokon and Mahawu. The climate is delightfully temper-te; fruits and a wide range of flowers—hibis-us, angel trumpets, bougainvillea, lilies, ladiolas, carnations and irises—are grown ommercially to supply markets in Manado. he town's main road is lined with flower alls, every yard seems to overflow with lush oliage, and the roadsides are planted with eep red croton plants. Well-proportioned onies pull beautifully-decorated horsecarts, nown as *bendi*, often leaving little room for notorized traffic. On Tuesday, Thursday and aturday mornings a local market sells rats, ats and dogs (ingredients in the notorious cal cuisine). Tomohon is famed as an edu-ational center, and there is a large auditori-n atop Bukit Inspirasi, a hill that gives a riking view of the town with Mt. Lokon in e background.

If you wish to climb Lokon, head back on the main road north toward Manado and obtain permission first from the village head (*lurah*) of Kakaskasan, a small village just to the north of Tomohon. The ascent begins just behind the village; any of the small lanes leading up the volcano will eventually bring you to a large stone quarry. From here, fol-low the lava flow up to a large side vent in the crater. At this point the landscape takes on the appearance of a charred moonscape. To reach the top takes a total of about 2 hours; be sure to bring sturdy footwear.

The half-hour journey back to Manado along a winding mountain road affords spec-tacular views. Excellent Minahasan food is available at restaurants in the town of Tinoor, from where you also have a panoramic view of Manado Bay. *Durian, langsat* and other locally-grown tropical fruits are also sold from stands along the wayside, as is *dodol*—a sticky-sweet concoction of dried palm sugar, coconut milk and nuts wrapped in bamboo leaves.

Further along, a turn-off to the right at the distinctly Sumatran-style gate at Pineling leads after about a kilometer to the Mauso-leum of Imam Bonjol, the Islamic cleric who led Minangkabau resistance against the Dutch in West Sumatra. Bonjol was captured

Opposite: *View inside Mt. Lokon before the 1991 eruption.* **Above:** *Sunset at Tasik Ria beach.*

in 1837 and exiled to Ambon, then later to North Sulawesi. He died in 1864 near the site of the grave.

Lake Tondano

The main road out of Manado to the east to Airmadidi and Bitung leads through coconut groves past a large factory, P.T. United Coconut Tina Indonesia, which is a good place to see the ubiquitous nuts being processed. Every part of the coconut is used—to produce oil, charcoal, animal fodder, coconut milk and mountains of copra or dessicated coconut meat. If phoned ahead of time, Bapak Dengah (Tel: 52108) can arrange a tour if the factory is currently in production.

Also on this road is Taman Anggrek, an orchid garden containing more than 80 varieties of orchids from the different parts of North Sulawesi. Over 10,000 specimens, including 2,000 hybrids, are on display in gardens and greenhouses. All varieties bloom only part of the year, at different times. If you are lucky you may see the rare Anggrek Hitam, a black orchid which usually blooms in November and is found only here and in Kalimantan. Hours are 08:00 to 17:00. There is a children's amusement park next door.

Just beyond Airmadidi (30 minutes from Manado) a road to the right leads south to Tondano. The village of Sawangan, five minutes further on, is the site of the largest collection of ancient sarcophagi or *waruga* in the province. A small sign (on the right) indicates a narrow road to the left. The cemetery contains 144 *waruga* and a small museum.

Dating from as early as the 9th century, the *waruga* are rectangular stone burial chambers with holes in the middle and prism-shaped lids. According to legend, people knew of their death shortly before it occurred in pre-Christian days. Endowed with supernatural powers, they singlehandedly carried a mammoth stone tomb to a chosen site, with the top balanced on their head. The sarcophagus was placed above the ground and the deceased was later arranged inside, sitting upright on a porcelain bowl. Tradition decreed that valuable jewelry adorn the body, but no clothing was permitted. The lid was placed over a layer of sealing material. However, the temptation offered by the jewelry was often too great, and many *waruga* have been opened and plundered.

In 1828 an epidemic in Sawangan forced the colonial government to ban the practice of above-ground burials. In 1977, most *waruga* in the area were moved to Sawangan, and

the cemetery and museum were officially opened in 1978. The location downwind from the village is thought to provide protection from evil smells or anything untoward (of a spiritual nature) emanating from the graves.

Each *waruga* is decorated with carvings denoting the occupation, cause of death or characteristics of the owner. One shows a woman giving birth and women with fertility problems come here to pray for a child. The oldest resident of Sawangan conducts a ceremony beside this *waruga* on the night of the full moon. All *waruga* face the rising sun.

The museum displays salvaged contents of some of the *waruga*. There is a traditional belief that ancient Minahasans were of large physical stature, and the rings and bracelets on display do nothing to disprove this.

Beyond Sawangan, the narrow, winding road continues on up into the hills, arriving at the town of Tondano after half an hour. It follows the course of the Tondano River, with spectacular views of the gorge, skirting a recently expanded hydro-electric power station at Tanggari which supplies electricity to the region. Shortly before Tondano, caves used by the Japanese during World War II to store ammunition can be seen on the left.

Just before Tondano town, a sharp turn to the left (at a point where the main road turns sharply to the right) takes one through the historically and culturally unique village of Kampung Jawa. Its name ("Java Village") indicates that some of the population descend from fighters captured in the Java War of 1825-1830, and exiled here by the Dutch.

Visit the unique Javanese-style Alfalah Mosque, which has been reconstructed several times on this site. It features old pillars inside as well as an intricately carved pulpit dating from 1868. The culture of the inhabitants of the village is a fascinating blend of elements. The language they speak is Tondanese (with a sprinkling of Javanese words), but many of the rituals and art forms derive from Java and Sumatra.

The road through Kampung Jawa and on past nearby Wulauan leads to a Muslim cemetery containing the recently renovated mausoleum of Kyai Modjo, the leader of the exiles. The hillock on which the mausoleum stands offers a dramatic view of Lake Tondano and the surrounding area (as do points further along the road should you wish to continue on up the mountain).

Tondano town, the administrative center of the Minahasa region, lies on the northern shores of Lake Tondano. It is a small town

Minahasa

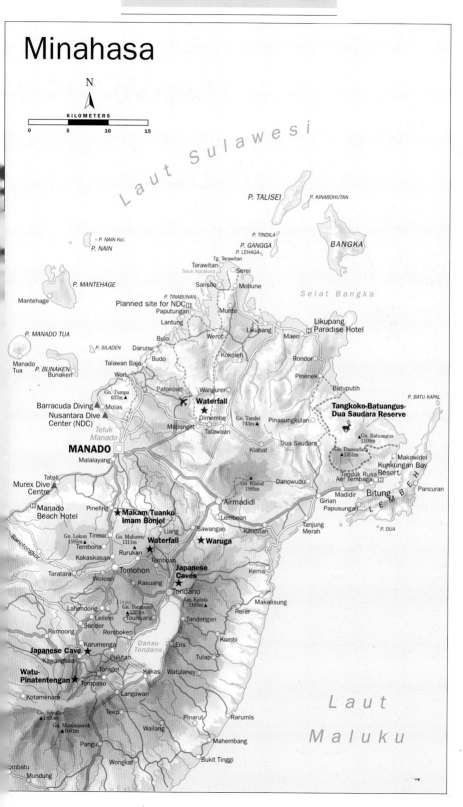

N

KILOMETERS

0   5   10   15

Laut Sulawesi

P. TALISEI   P. KINABOHUTAN

P. TINDILA

P. GANGGA   BANGKA
P. LEHAGA

Tg. Tarawitan

Tarawitan
Teluk Korakora   Serei

P. NAIN Kcl.   *Selat Bangka*

P. NAIN

Sansilo   Mobune

P. MANTEHAGE

P. TINABUNAN

Mantehage   Planned site for NDC

Paputungan   Likupang
Munte   Paradise Hotel

Lantung   Likupang

Bulo   Werot   Maen

P. MANADO TUA   Darunu

P. SILADEN   Kokoleh   Rondor

Manado   Budo

Tua   P. BUNAKEN   Talawan Bajo   Pinenek

Bunaken

Wori   Batuputih   P. BATU KAPAL

Gn. Tumpa   Patokoan   Wangurer
637m

Barracuda Diving ▲ Molas   **Waterfall**   **Tangkoko-Batuangus-**
Nusantara Dive ▲   **Dua Saudara Reserve**

Center (NDC)   Dimembe   Gn. Batuangus
Mapanget   Gn. Tandei   1109m
Teluk   743m   Pinasungkulan

Manado   Talawaan   Gn. Duasudara
1351m

MANADO □   Klabat   Dua Saudara   Makawidei

Malalayang   Kunkungan Bay
Resort

Tateli   Gn. Klabat   Danowudu   Tanduk Rusa

Murex Dive ▲   1995m   Aer Tembaga   Pancuran

Centre   **Bitung**

Manado   Pineling   **Airmadidi**   Madidir

Beach Hotel   Lembean   Girian

Makam Tuanku   Papusungan

Imam Bonjol   Sawangan

Gn. Lokon Tinoor   Liang   Kauditan   Tanjung

1595m   Tembona   Merah   P. DUA

Waterfall   Rurukan   Kema

Kakaskasan

Waruga

Taratara   Temboan

Woloan   Tomohon   **Japanese**

Kasuang   **Caves**

Tondano

Gn. Kaluta Makalisung

D. Linau   1163m

Lahendong   Gn. Tountusu   Tandengan   Rerer

1203m

Leilem Tountsaru

Rumoong   Sonder Remboken

Karumenga   *Danau*   Eris   Kombi

Tondano

Japanese Cave Kawangkoan Pulutan   Tulap

Watu-   Toraget   Kakas   Watulaney

Pinatentengan Tompaso

Kotamenara   Langowan

Gn. Soputan   Teep

1830m   Pinarut   Rarumis

Gn. Marimporok

1661m   Wailang   *Laut*

Pangu   Mahembang   *Maluku*

Wongkat

ombatu   Bukit Tinggi

Mundung

laid out with straight streets crisscrossing at right angles. Dr. Sam Ratulangi, an early Swiss-educated nationalist leader and the first post-war governor of Sulawesi, was born here, and there is an impressive monument to his memory in the north of the town.

Smaller roads from Tondano skirt both shores of the lake, and a trip all the way around it provides ever-changing vistas of the nearby mountains, rice fields and the lake itself. At the town of Remboken on the lake's western shore there is a government-operat-

ed tourist development which includes a small park, a hot spring-fed pool (open Thursdays, Saturday afternoons and Sundays) and a restaurant with a view of the lake. Boats may be hired for a spin around the lake, and there are cottages for rent. It is quiet and peaceful, except on Sundays.

Not far from Remboken, past the village of Kaima, is the small village of Pulutan where pottery is made. Just inside the village gates is a small factory where you can watch pots, vases and the like being made on a kick-wheel. You can buy the finished products for a few thousand rupiah.

Backtracking to Remboken and continuing on south around the lake, the road eventually brings you to Kasuang. Here a number of restaurants serve traditional Minahasan cuisine, which you can watch being baked in bamboo tubes over a large, open barbecue. The Tondano Indah Restaurant, on the eastern shore of the lake between Eris and Tondano, is also a good place to stop for food.

Once back at Tondano town, instead of returning directly to Manado along the main road via Tomohon, you might want to take a scenic detour. Follow the narrow little road from Tondano up to the mountain village of Rurukan, half an hour away. This is a lovely excursion through small coffee stands and vegetable gardens. Once in Rurukan, turn left up a hill to a small area known as Temboan ("lookout"). It is only about 100 m

away, but the road is so bad that you might as well walk. At the top of this hill you will find one of the most spectacular vistas in Minahasa—high-altitude, terraced vegetable gardens spread out before you in every direction, with Bitung, the Molucca Sea and Lake Tondano visible in the distance. From here a road leads down to Tomohon and thence to Manado.

Sonder to Watu Pinabetengan

The beautiful and varied scenery on this day-long trip beyond Tomohon to the south makes it well worth the effort. Added bonuses are visits to a natural hot spring and to the most sacred spot in all of Minahasa.

The road south of Tomohon to Sonder passes first through Lahendong, where seething energy just below the earth's surface is dramatically apparent. A hut and a green sign on the right mark the head of the well-marked trail to the springs. These are interspersed with ominously hissing fissures and gurgling pools of mud. There is a primeval feel about the site, and the sulphuric odors are powerful. The largest hot spring provides a place for bathing, and there is a small changing hut.

Past Leilem, a village known for its handsome handmade furniture, you come to the village of Sonder, which in the 1970s had the highest per capita income of any village in Indonesia. Many of the people here got rich when clove prices were high. Unlike many other Minahasans, however, they diversified their investments and survived the subsequent drop in prices relatively unscathed. The people of Sonder are known throughout the region as energetic businessmen; indeed, they are involved in everything from selling cookies in small villages to running large

Above, left and right: *The scenic highland town of Tomohon.* **Opposite:** *Ancient stone sarcophagi (waruga) at Sawangan, south of Manado.*

businesses in the city.

The nearby Toar-Lumimuut tourist resort has a lovely swimming pool and park, and is a good place to relax and cool off after the drive from Manado.

About 15 minutes south of Sonder, and shortly before Kawangkoan, are the Japanese Caves—large tunnels built with forced labor where the Japanese hid ammunition and supplies during World War II. Enter this extensive cave system if you don't mind the pitch blackness and the bats flying around you. A guide from the restaurant across from the biggest cave will escort you with a flashlight.

Continue south from Kawangkoan toward Langowan, turning right just after the Minaesa Institute of Technology. A pretty drive through terraced rice paddies then brings you to Watu Pinabetengan—a stone believed to be the most spiritually powerful site in Minahasa. Through the ages, this has also proved to be a politically potent gathering spot for Minahasan leaders.

According to legend, Lumimuut, the primal ancestress from whom all Minahasans are descended, divided up her people at this stone and drew maps on it denoting the territory of each group. Later, seven Minahasan chieftains negotiated a unification of the area here. In 1642 a meeting was held to devise a defense against the invading Spaniards. Later in the 17th century, the Minahasan chiefs met at the stone to plan strategy during a war with neighboring Bolaang Mongondow. Dr. Sam Ratulangi, subsequently the first governor of the province, gathered here with other notables in 1939 to pray for success in the struggle for independence from the Dutch, and when this was achieved in 1949 another large meeting was held here to bless the newly-formed republic.

Pictographic carvings on the stone have never been deciphered, and most had unfortunately already been encased in concrete along with much of the stone before the government declared it a public monument. Ceremonies involving chicken and pig sacrifices are still held during the full moon, and people come here to consult with the spirits of their deceased ancestors. A local elder acts as medium.

Back on the main road, shortly before Langowan, a left-hand turn at the village of Toraget leads to another small village by the name of Karumenga, where you will find baths fed from a clear, sulphurous hot spring. Villagers boil eggs in the main pool, cooking them from the inside out to produce a firm yolk and soft, wobbly white. A five-minute walk through the jungle from here leads to bubbling mud pools.

Climbing Mount Klabat

Those with the agility of a mountain goat will welcome the opportunity to climb Mt. Klabat. Located directly to the east of Manado, this

dormant volcano is the highest peak in Minahasa at 1,995 meters (6,500 ft)—offering fine views from the summit across the entire northern end of the peninsula.

A well developed trail begins just behind the police station in Airmadidi (see above under "Lake Tondano" for sights along the road leading here from Manado). You will need to stop here first to register. They will be somewhat concerned if you plan to make the climb without a guide, and local children will be appointed to lead you to the trailhead. Here, you'll have to pay a small "tax" on all cameras. Receipts are issued, and the children can be dispatched with a small tip.

Follow the trail to the first sign, marked "Pos 1," and take the left-hand trail up the hill. There are shelters midway up where you can spend the night if you get caught in a sudden storm. It takes most people 7 to 8 hours to reach the summit—but you had best plan an overnight excursion, climbing up the first day and spending the night on top to wake up early to catch the sunrise. Be sure to bring along warm clothing, a good sleeping bag and plenty of food and water.

Climbing or descending after dark can be risky along stretches of the trail because of the severe erosion, and should only be attempted with headlamps, as both hands are sometimes needed. The vegetation is quite dense, and moonlight would not be adequate. Water is only available at a few spots. On a Saturday night, expect to have company at the summit as this is a popular weekend outing for university students.

Into the tropical rainforest

The entire tip of the peninsula to the north and east of Mt. Klabat is covered in lush, tropical rainforests which have been declared a nature reserve. The Tangkoko-Batuangus-Dua Saudara Reserve, as it is known (the name refers to three peaks in the reserve) encompasses 9,000 hectares (22,230 acres) ranging from sea level up to 1,100 meters (3,400 ft). This is a spectacular area which offers you the possibility to see not only some of Sulawesi's unique animals and plants, but also a wealth of corals and fishes.

The most notable species in the reserve is the endemic maleo bird (see "Maleo Bird" page 203). Alfred Russel Wallace visited the area in 1859 to collect specimens along the black sand beach. Sadly, the maleos have disappeared from this site, largely because of over-exploitation of their eggs after the village of Batuputih was established here in 1913. The few remaining maleos now lay their eggs inside the reserve.

The reserve also offers excellent opportunities to see the bear cuscus. This arboreal marsupial is fully dependent on a few species of trees; usually the guards know where to look. Tarsiers, macaques and wild pigs are also common. The anoa is rare and usually found at higher altitudes, but the babirusa is thought to be extinct here.

A wide variety of birds can be seen, notably the lilac kingfisher and a relative of the maleo—the much smaller Phillipine scrubfowl. The latter deposits its eggs between the decaying roots of trees, where heat generated by the decomposition of the wood incubates them. Flying lizards, gliding from tree to tree, are more numerous than in Dumoga-Bone. Mudskippers are common on the stones and rocks along the shore. Frigate-birds, white-bellied sea-eagles and other marine birds are often seen soaring overhead or fishing offshore.

Though it is only 60 km (38 mi) from Manado, access to the reserve is difficult and several days are required to see it properly. If you don't have the time, you can also simply hike into the rainforest from Danowudu along short, well-maintained trails. Danowudu is reached by taking a turn-off to the left (north) at Girian, just before Bitung.

After Danowudu, a narrow and dangerous track composed of loose volcanic scree runs north through the village of Dua Saudara to Batuputih, at the northern end of the reserve near the coast. Jeeps can make the trip in the dry season, but during the rainy season (November to March) you will have to hike three hours from Dua Saudara. You can also get to Batuputih by hiring a boat from Bitung—only an hour's journey. (See "National Parks of the North" page 199.)

Bitung

The port of Bitung is the other main point of interest in this area. Neatly laid out with wide boulevards, it boast two bizarre replicas of the Eiffel Tower and a striking church. Bitung is the main port of North Sulawesi and has a fine natural harbor protected by the island of Lembeh. This is also the center for commercial fishing in the region. There are several excellent restaurants in Bitung serving Chinese-style seafood.

—*Kal Muller*

Opposite: *Fishing boats at Gorontalo, a quiet, rarely visited town that retains a colonial feel.*

GORONTALO

Scenic Drive, Old Forts and Lake Limboto

Halfway along the south coast of Sulawesi's northernmost peninsula, on the eastern shore of Lake Limboto, where the lake and three rivers drain into the sea, lies Gorontalo, North Sulawesi's second-largest city. Unlike most towns in eastern Indonesia, Gorontalo escaped Allied bombing during World War II and in its architecture, and feel, has retained a certain air of pre-war Indonesia.

The city (pop. 120,000) is staunchly Muslim and mosques here begin their calls to prayer unusually early. A cacophony of shrill and unsynchronized loudspeakers will wake all but the heaviest sleeper. Take advantage of this reveille to venture out for an early morning stroll along tree-lined avenues past gracious colonial architecture in the harbor area. The best way to get there is either on foot, or by horse-drawn *bendi*, which should cost about $1 an hour after some bargaining.

There are still some 50 colonial style houses in Gorontalo. Some of these former Dutch homes have suffered greatly from time's vicissitudes, but a few are still in excellent condition, with two of the best located on Jl. A. Yani, near the post office. Few foreigners visit Gorontalo, and while touring the streets one still occasionally hears exclamations of "Belanda-Belanda" (Dutch man) along with the usual "Hello meester!," be you man or woman.

While you're in the downtown area, take a look at the shops on Jl. Jendral Suprapto which specialize in the local *krawang* embroidery for which Gorontalo is famous. Try **Toko Matahari** or **Toko Palapa**—and bargain hard before buying.

In the evening, visit the **Pasar Jajan** which specializes in selling fruit, as well as Indonesian and local food. Here you can sample a local delicacy known as *milu siram,* a tasty mixture of fish stock, corn (*milu*), lemon, and freshly grated coconut.

Lake Limboto

Over the past 30 years erosion has caused the level of Lake Limboto to drop by some five meters, and it has also silted up considerably—its maximum depth is now just two meters rather than the 15 meters of three decades ago. While there is still some fishing in the lake, large areas of its dried periphery have been turned into pasture or planted.

KAL MULLER

The chief crops grown in the area are rice, corn and vegetables.

The best spot from which to view the lake is from **Fort Otanaha**, about 8 km out of town. The fort, built in 1525, was restored in the early 1980s. Take a *bemo* toward either Batudaa or Dembe (15¢) and ask to be let off at the side road to Benteng (Fort) Otanaha. The way up is indicated by a large sign.

It's a short walk from the main road to the base of the steps leading to the fort: all 353 of them. There's a number on every fifth tread for your reading pleasure as you puff upward, and using the several rest stops along the way will help prevent heart attacks. Climb up in the early morning or late afternoon to avoid heat stroke.

Once you arrive, the view from the top is magnificent, with a sweeping vista of the Lake Limboto area and of another smaller fort nearby.

Back on the main road, which leads away from Fort Otanaha and skirts the southern edge of the lake, there are still more impressive views, and a couple of kilometers beyond the fort you come across an old terminal building with a broken down pier. This is a decrepit reminder of the once booming Catalina passenger seaplane service which operated here in the 1950s.

Dumoga-Bone by the back door

About 15 km east of Gorontalo along a paved road, the large hot water public swimming pool at Lombongo marks an entry point into the Dumoga-Bone National Park. While there is frequent *bemo* service directly to the pool on weekends, when local crowds invade, on weekdays the place is deserted and the *bemo* route slightly more complicated.

To get there during the week, take a *bemo* to Pasar Minggu (20¢) about 2.5 km from the pool. From there, it's about 1.5 km to the park rangers' office. Ask the *bemo* driver to drop you off there, which with a bit of bargaining should cost you around 50¢.

While the usual entry to the park is via the headquarters 50 km west of Kotamobagu, this "back door" entry is perfectly legal, if you check in with the rangers and go with one of them as guide ($1.50 per hour, $7 all day, very little English).

There is a series of waterfalls not too far into the park and while it's no Niagara, the possibilities of seeing animals during the three hour climb are quite good, especially during the early morning and late afternoon. If you're lucky, you might spot hornbills and kingfishers, as well as black macaques, babirusa and wild pigs. This is an easy one-day trip. For longer jaunts you need to bring a tent, food and a pair of legs in good shape.

To the sea

Gorontalo's heavy shipping activities are concentrated on the eastern shore of Gorontalo Bay, a couple of kilometers from downtown. On the opposite side of the bay, small fishing boats tie up and sell their catches, which are then taken to town in bicycle-borne baskets.

Just past this fish market, the road bends around a cliff and leads to nearby Lahilote, a village with the only sand beach close to town. Unfortunately the beach is nothing special, and you will be stared at continuously if you go there. A better bet is to take the "high road," which climbs just before Lahilote and soon gives a commanding view across the sea. Far below, fishermen in small outrigger canoes cast nets in large circles, then draw them tight. In the shallower waters near the coast, they stand or swim to perform the same chore.

A paved road heads eastwards out of the harbor area and follows the southern coast. It hugs the shore for some 20 km, through little fishing villages and past seascapes dotted with the tiny rectangular and V-shaped sails of outriggers. Just before the village of Oluhuta, there's a beautiful little cove, accessible from the road, which is perfect for secluded swimming and snorkeling.

From Oluhuta, which lies on a bay backed by hills, the road winds inland for 8 km, rising 200m and affording views of impossibly steep slopes which have been cleared and planted with peanuts: the perfect crop for the dry climate.

The road reaches the coast again at a little village and continues towards Bilungala (Sunday market), the capital of the sub district. From there you can continue for about another 35 km to the village of Taludaa (Wednesday market) which sits in an affluent clove-producing area. While there is a morning and late afternoon *bemo* service to Bilungala (50¢), public transportation only occasionally reaches Taludaa. From there during the dry season, it is said that 4-wheel drive vehicles can follow the coast all the way to the gold mining area of Ratatotok, which is connected to Manado by a paved road.

—*Kal Muller*

Opposite: *Dense tropical rainforest inside the Tangkoko–Batuangus–Dua Saudara Reserve.*

Visiting the Nature Reserves

Sulawesi is home to an incomparable range of wildlife which can be seen by those who take the time and make the effort to visit the national parks. Ten-meter reticulated pythons, flying lizards, the tusked baribirusa or "pig-deer," the *anoa,* a dog-sized buffalo, woolly-necked storks and whistling ducks, are just some of the wealth of strange animals found here. The fact that 62 percent of Sulawesi's native mammal species and 88 species of birds are found only on Sulawesi, means these sanctuaries can provide a window onto the exclusive natural world east of Wallace's Line.

North Sulawesi's extensive national parks cover 13 percent of its land area. They give a measure of protection to the area's unique flora and fauna (see pp. 20–22), but park rangers are sadly burdened by a lack of funds and ridiculously low salaries. They do what they can to stop the poachers who kill *anoa* and black macaques, but the problem is so extensive that the meat of these protected animals is sold openly in the markets.

The most shocking example of the depredation caused in recent years comes from the Tangkoko-Batuangus–Dua Saudara Reserve. In 1979 the population of crested black macaques was estimated at 20,000 and bands could easily be seen during a short stroll from the Reserve headquarters. By 1992, the number of these animals was reduced to between 2–3,000 and current research indicates that the decline continues.

This Reserve's headquarters are much easier to reach now than in the late 1970's. The formerly awful road from Girian to Tangkoko is now paved as far as Batuputih, providing access even during the rainy season.

Another paved road, via Likupang, Maen and Rondor, comes close to the Reserve headquarters, but there is not much public transportation here and the last few kilometers are passable only with 4-wheel drive vehicles. There are good trails in Tangkoko, which is not the case in the much bigger Dumoga-Bone Park. But access to the Dumoga-Bone park headquarters, near Dololduo village, is quite easy from Kotamobagu.

While maleo birds (see page 203) are very difficult to find in the Tangkoko Reserve, this Reserve holds excellent possibilities for spotting tarsiers, black macaques,

large colorful butterflies, hornbills and other birds, including many of Sulawesi's endemics. Forget about seeing babirusa here or at Dumoga-Bone. In Dumoga-Bone, there is a slight chance of an encounter with an *anoa*, but you are more likely to see cuscus and maleo birds. Tarsiers, black macaques (a different species from those in Tangkoko), birds and butterflies are relatively easy targets here for binoculars and telephoto lenses.

The 45,000 ha. Panua Reserve is said to be the best for *anoa* and babirusa with lots of maleos also. But there are no facilities, and access is difficult. First get to Marisa, far away on the south coast of North Sulawesi. From Marisa, it's a jeep ride, then a couple of hours by boat up the Randangan River.

Two small islands off the province's north coast, Pulau Mas (also called Diyonumo) and Pulau Popaya, are egg-laying grounds for green turtles and the occasional huge leatherback. These two islands and Panua, east of the border with Central Sulawesi, require a strong dose of initiative and a willingness to rough it for the duration. Hardcore enthusiasts should inquire at the PHPA Sub-Balai office in Manado, or at the port of Kwandang.

Access to the Gunung Ambang National Park is much easier. Consolation for not finding the *anoa* could be the sighting of a Malay civet. Failing that, there are tree ferns, *Pigafetta* palms and sulfur fumeroles at the summit.

Tangkoko Reserve

The entire tip of the peninsula to the east of Mt. Klabat is covered in lush, tropical rainforests which have been declared a nature reserve. The Tangkoko-Batuangus-Dua Saudara Reserve, as it is known (the name refers to three peaks in the reserve) encompasses 9,000 hectares (22,230 acres) ranging from sea level up to 1,100 meters (3,400 ft). This is a spectacular area which offers you the possibility to see not only some of Sulawesi's unique animals and plants, but also a wealth of corals and fishes.

The most notable species in the reserve is the endemic maleo bird. Alfred Russel Wallace visited the area in 1859 to collect specimens along the black sand beach. Sadly, the maleos have disappeared from this site, largely because of over-exploitation of their eggs after the village of Batuputih was established in 1913. The few remaining maleos, estimated at only 7-10 pairs in 1994, lay their eggs at two open spots inside the reserve.

The reserve also offers rare opportunities to see the bear cuscus. This arboreal marsupial is fully dependent on the leaves of a few species of trees; usually the guards know where to look. Tarsiers, macaques and wild pigs are also common. The *anoa* is rare and usually found at higher altitudes, but the babirusa is thought to be extinct here. Three groups of macaques have been the focus of scientific research over the past three years and are habituated to humans. This provides wonderful photo opportunities beacause you may approach calm animals. It is important to remember that these are wild monkeys; do not feed or pursue them. You must approach on their terms, not yours.

Tangkoko is famous for its high densities of endemic red-knobbed hornbills. During months when their favorite fruits, figs, are readily available, densities may soar as high as 80 birds per square kilometer—these are the highest reported densities in the world for forest hornbills. Hornbill breeding season is between July and January; reserve guides can lead you to any one of the 60 known nest trees for observation.

A wide variety of birds can be seen, notably the lilac kingfisher and a relative of the maleo—the much smaller Phillipine scrubfowl. The latter deposits its eggs between the decaying roots of trees, where heat generated by the decomposition of the wood incubates them. Flying lizards, gliding from tree to tree, are more numerous here than in Dumoga-Bone. Mudskippers are common on the stones and rocks along the shore. Frigate-birds, white-bellied sea-eagles and other marine birds are often seen soaring overhead or fishing offshore.

Several good trails give access to the forest, to the maleo nesting grounds, and to the summit of Mt. Tangkoko, which is covered in moss forest.

Mt. Batuangus, a relatively recent addition to the landscape, was thrown up by a volcanic eruption in 1836 and is worth a visit. The slopes facing the sea are still black and bare of vegetation. While in the vicinity, take mask and snorkel to check out the cove. An inlet of the sea wanders half a kilometer inland and has particularly fine, dense coral formations. You can hike out of the Reserve in six hours, from the headquarters to Dua Saudara. It's a good trail, enjoyable but tiring.

The management of Tangkoko Reserve is impressive and it is clearly run by farsighted people. They have initiated a program to introduce locals to the importance of nature and, in order to raise critically needed funds, the Reserve sells T-shirts ($5) and glossy prints of animal photos ($1-$2.50): buy some. To enter the Reserve, guides are required, most charging fees of around $5 per walk. Some of the guides speak good English and a few know the scientific names of many of the plants. For the best wildlife watching, get up at 5 am for a walk with your guide.

Tangkoko also offers the sea as a bonus.

Aside from the snorkeling at Batuangus cove, there's a 3km-long black sand beach near Batuputih, offering decent underwater scenery or a vantage spot for watching tiny boats sailing by. Avoid snorkeling between January and March, when big waves come crashing in. Turtles come to nest on this beach around May and August, when it's a life-and-death competition for the eggs between the rangers and the locals. *Losmen* in Batuputih charges $5–$10 for room and meals.

Dumoga-Bone National Park

The Dumoga-Bone National Park is a large and fascinating reserve unlike any other, which merits at least several days' exploration. Naturalists from Indonesia and elsewhere often conduct research at the park, and you may make some interesting acquaintances in addition to enjoying the region's natural wonders.

Dumoga-Bone Park consists of 300,000 hectares (741,000 acres) of virgin rainforest lying between Gorontalo and Kotamobagu. Its primary function is to protect the water-catchment area for the new irrigation project. It was set aside as a national park in 1984, following severe deforestation of the surrounding hills that resulted in erosion and flooding, upsetting the irrigation plans. As a bonus, the unique flora and fauna of this large primary rainforest has been preserved as well.

Parts of the park ascend to 2,000 meters (6,600 ft). Most of it is impenetrable because of dense vegetation and steep hills. Several forest types, each with its own characteristic vegetation, can be recognized. Visibility in the lowland rainforest, with its undergrowth of rattan and giant *Livistona* palm leaves, is often less than 10 meters. At 800-1,000 meters the more open montane rainforest with pandanus trees begins, and at 1,500 meters, this gives way to cloud-covered upper montane forest. Here bright-green moss covers the ground, and trees covered with beard-moss give the forest a fairy tale air of enchantment.

The interior of the park is extremely rich in animal and plant life. Most of the island's 80 endemic bird species are found here. The best place for bird-watching is the forest edge, where magnificent hornbills, beautifully colored kingfishers, parrots, pigeons and birds of prey are common.

Wild pigs, Dumoga-Bone macaques and

Opposite: *A red-knobbed Hornbill* (Rhyticeros cassidix), *one of the island's many unique birds.*

the tiny, night-hunting spectral tarsier, which produces high-pitched, insect-like sounds, are all around. *Anoa* and babirusa can be seen, but they are shy and normally inhabit higher altitudes. Insect life is abundant and fascinating. Butterflies (especially common on sandy riverbanks), moths and dragonflies are present in an unbelievable rainbow of colors. The humming of cicadas fills the air and beetles of all sizes seem to be everywhere.

Although there is little to fear from ferocious fauna inside the park, some animals and plants can be a nuisance. Leeches are common at higher altitudes, and are always eager to tag along. Shrub-mites, practically invisible, will dig under your skin and cause incredible itching. A mixture of dibutylphtalate (5%) and benzylbenzoate (5%) in soapy water, splashed on your socks and clothes, is sufficient protection from these pests, even after wading through rivers. Fortunately, mosquitoes are not much of a problem.

Snakes are common, but seldom seen. Pythons grow up to ten meters (30 ft). Poisonous pit vipers and kraits will not cause you any harm unless you disturb them. Rattan is covered with sharp spines which can rip your clothes. Good boots and proper clothing are therefore de rigueur. If you want to spend the night in the forest, you are advised to bring a hammock and a mosquito net instead of a tent. At higher altitudes you will definitely need a sleeping bag, for the nights can get cold.

Park headquarters are at the eastern entrance near the village of Dolodo, 50 km (30 mi) west of Kotamobagu (an hour by car or minibus). Over 200 scientists participated in Project Wallace in 1985—the largest international entomological expedition ever mounted—and their basecamp and a newly constructed laboratory at Toraut close to the headquarters may now be used by tourists and students. Accommodation and hospitality are assured, and the park guards will act as your guides. Near the entrance are several small restaurants offering excellent food.

Several day-long excursions can be made. Ask at the office for the best routes to follow. Tambun and Tumokang, two major maleo nesting grounds heated by hot springs are in the vicinity and offer you the opportunity to watch the birds and their chicks closely. The Kosinggolan floodland—an artificial wetland resulting from the irrigation project—harbors darters, woolly-necked storks, herons, whistling-ducks, rails and eagles.

Mt. Mogogonipa, an isolated peak rising 1008 meters (3,325 ft), has a beautiful forest with pandanus trees and tree ferns; the top of the peak itself is covered with moss. If you'd prefer to just relax, you can sit on the veranda of the guesthouse and read, or go for shorter strolls in the forest just behind the headquarters. June, July and August are generally dry and the best time to visit.

—Kal Muller

MALEO BIRD

Sulawesi's Endangered Megapode

The unique flora and fauna of Sulawesi are characterized by both Asian and Australian features. One of the island's most spectacular birds, the maleo or *Macrocephalon maleo,* is of Australian origin. This endemic megapode does not lay its eggs in a nest or incubate them with body heat, but buries them on beaches or in volcanic regions where they are hatched by the sun or geothermal heat.

The unmistakeable long and rolling call of the male, one of the characteristic sounds of Sulawesi's tropical rainforest, betrays the presence of the maleo. Male and female are always seen together, looking for snails, insects and fruit on the forest floor or resting in trees. They are the most colorful of all megapodes (mound-building, large-footed birds native to Australia and eastern Indonesia), with their black-and-salmon plumage and strange, featherless helmet.

During egg-laying season, the maleo (which is abut the size of a chicken) digs a deep hole in which they bury their enormous egg (200-250 grams or 7-9 ounces). After the egg has been hidden away, the birds disappear into the forest and do not take any further care of it. The large size of the egg is an adaptation to the maleo's strange reptilian-like incubation process. It contains a large yolk, guaranteeing adequate nourishment during incubation.

The maleo chick can fly immediately after hatching and is completely independent, surviving without any form of parental nurturing. However, before it can fly away, it has to free itself from the burrow in which the egg was laid. This often requires struggling through more than 50 cm (20 in) of sand; it can take several days and is fraught with danger. Monitor-lizards, feral dogs and ants are never far away, ready to prey upon the chickling.

Maleos are found nowhere but on Sulawesi; there are approximately 50 communal nesting sites known on the island, most of which are situated on the northern peninsu-

la. The national parks offer excellent opportunities to watch the birds closely. You can even see the chicks raised, as part of a conservation project, under semi-captive conditions in hatcheries at the Tambun and Tumokang nesting grounds in Dumoga-Bone.

An endangered species, the maleo has a tenuous claim on its future survival. A considerable number of nesting grounds have been abandoned by the birds because of deforestation and the island's ever-expanding urban population. At other nesting sites, maleo eggs are heavily over-exploited for human consumption. Until recently, egg-collecting was traditionally supervised by local authorities, and enough eggs were left behind to guarantee viable populations. Despite regulations in force since 1970 which prohibit collection, nearly all eggs are harvested by human predators. Some of the eggs even find their way to markets as far away as Jakarta.

Hopefully, increased attention on the international scene will stimulate greater awareness among the local population as to the precarious existence of the maleo. Its preservation is important from a conservational point of view, and also simply because it is a unique part of the life of Sulawesi.

—*René Dekker*

Opposite: A newly-born maleo chick burrows its way to the surface. **Above:** The author examines a maleo egg for signs of activity.

SANGIHE-TALAUD

Seascapes and Isolated Islands

The Sangihe-Talaud archipelago, 77 islands scattered north of Manado, rewards travelers who have the urge to explore. The real adventures begin once you get away from the major towns and head into more remote locations. Little English is spoken here and a basic knowledge of Indonesian can come in extremely handy. (See map pg. 276.)

The area is known for its fertile soil, its high quality nutmeg and its palm trees. There are several active volcanoes here, including Mt Awu on Sangir Island, which has claimed over 7,000 lives in recent years.

Forty seven of the islands are inhabited (by a total population of 260,000)—the rest are deserted becasue of an absence of drinking water. Three principal islands constitute the population and communications centers of the group: Sangihe Besar, location of the political capital Tahuna; Karakelang, the largest island; and Siau.

Air and sea communications from Manado are good: there are daily flights and numerous boats to Tahuna, and twice weekly flights and frequent boats to Melanguane and Beo on Karakelang. There are plans to build an airstrip on Siau Island, but meanwhile the port of Siau Ulu has daily, or more frequent, passenger ships from and to North Sulawesi.

Lirung port, on the island of Salibabu next door to Karakelang, is served by frequent passenger ships, but the rest of the islands in the archipelago are linked only by sporadic, unscheduled boats.

Sangihe Besar and Karakelang

Tahuna is the largest town and capital of the archipelago with a population of some 24,000. There are a half dozen *losmen* here, including a couple which could qualify as hotels. Thanks to still-active Gunung Awu volcano, the island is fertile and yields high quality nutmeg and cloves, and copra from coconuts.

While you're in town, shop for ebony carvings, especially the models of traditional canoes. There's also embroidery from the nearby island of Batunderang. Early risers should check out the morning catches of the small fishing boats, these often include hefty-sized tuna caught by hand line.

There are some gold mining operations on the island for geologists to peruse, while trekkers should climb Awu. First go to the volcano monitoring station at Tulusau near Tahuna and, if no major explosions are expected, climb to the summit in a couple of long but easy days for magnificent views.

A 22,000 ha. nature reserve covers much of the interior of Karakelang island. Although the most predominant species found here are wild pigs and cattle of limited interest, the reserve is said to be a birder's paradise.

A four hour walk from Essang village leads to Leang Buidane cave; a must for those interested in archeology. This site yielded considerable pre-historical information thanks to its material remains (see pg. 26). Rumors tell of another cave, containing ancestor skulls, near Arangkaa village.

Saltwater crocodiles thrive in the Rai River, two hours' motoring north of Beo. This is one of the few areas remaining where they have not been hunted to extinction for their skins. Stay well away from these monsters which can reach well over 7 meters in length. A safer option is to enjoy the island's white sand beaches and snorkel over pristine coral formations.

Siau Island

Aim to arrive on Siau at daybreak: the night's logistical problems are quickly forgotten during the dawn approach to the island, crowned by 1,827 meter Karangetang (The Highest) volcano (a.k.a Gunung Api Siau). As you stand on the roof of the boat taking in the magnificent scenery, the other passengers, who see nothing extraordinary in the view, stare at your extraordinary behavior on the roof.

As the craft enters the passage between Siau and Buhias islands, the pitch ceases as the boat advances into what is almost an enclosed lake; the drowned crater of a long-extinct mega-volcano. The verdant slopes of Buhias glide by on the right, while Siau's six stepped peaks flank the left. Karangetang stands sentry furthest north, spewing out a stream of sulfurous gas from its crater.

Disembarkation is a bedlam of porters and friends boarding the ship as passengers struggle to be first off. Wait for things to calm down before heading off to the only decent accommodation in town, a homestay with the

Mohede family.

The town of Siau Ulu hugs the coastline, with the main street separated from the sea by narrow shops and houses. There's a lively market in the early morning, especially at dawn when local fishing boats bring in the night's catch. You'll see cloves, nutmeg and mace drying in the sun all over town, and the wealth from these lucrative crops has financed several ostentatious two- and three-story houses, topped by satellite dishes.

The Volcano

In 1974 an earthquake, accompanied by volcanic activity from Gunung Api Siau, shook the island every 10 minutes for two whole weeks. Houses crumbled, roads disintegrated and most of the 40,000 inhabitants fled to Manado. Gunung Api Siau's last major eruption, in 1976, killed one overly curious local.

The trek up Api Siau is a tough 1,748m climb which takes two days. Bring a sleeping bag, food and water. Dense jungle on the way up requires a guide with a *parang*. Don't be discouraged by locals who will try to talk you out of the idea of climbing this volcano, which they say is haunted.

At times during the ascent a combination of volcanic activity and wind can causes smoke clouds to engulf you as you struggle upwards. Once on top, with luck, you will see a minor Strombolian explosion which usually happens every few hours. Even if there are no explosions, the difficult climb is rewarded with incredible vistas of Siau and the nearby tapestry of islands. On clear days, you can see as far as Mt. Klabat on the mainland.

The road system on Siau has been rebuilt and extended since the destruction of 1974. Most of the island's 50 km circumference is now paved, plus an 8 km. cross-island stretch to Ondong on the west coast. Minibuses runs regularly on this fairly good road.

From Ondong, it's a two hour outboard-powered ride to Makaleli Island. This paradise, with a lake in the middle, is inhabited by very tradition-minded folks who practice leaf-plaiting and basket weaving. There are a wealth of bird species here and there's reputedly a cave, full of ancestral skulls. On Makeleli and elsewhere, a yearly traditional festival called Talude, with song and dance, takes place on January 31.

Mahoro Island is a pristine, uninhabited island with a broad white sand beach, with good snorkeling, a view of Gunung Api Siau and a source of brackish water which is good enough for rinsing off. The harbormaster at Siau can help to arrange for you to take a small boat there, complete with a two-man crew to spear fish for meals. But you need to bring drinking water and food.

—*Kal Muller*

Above: *The live-aboard dive boat the* Cehili *stops at one of Sangihe-Talaud's many small islands.*

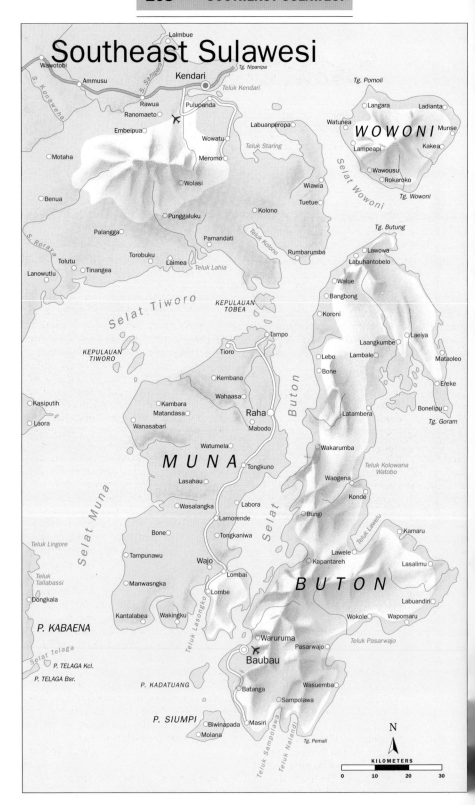

Southeast Sulawesi

Lalmbue
Wawotobi
Ammusu
Kendari
Tg. Nipanipa
Tg. Pomoli
S. Konaweha
S. Sampara
Teluk Kendari
Rawua
Pulupanda
Langara
Ladianta
Ranomaeto
Watunea
WOWONI
Munse
Embeipua
Labuanperopa
Lampeapi
Kakea
Wowatu
Teluk Staring
Motaha
Meromo
Wawousu
Rokaroko
Wolasi
Wiawia
Tg. Wowoni
Benua
Tuetue
Selat Wowoni
S. Roraya
Punggaluku
Kolono
Tg. Butung
Palangga
Pamandati
Rumbarumba
Lawowa
Tolutu
Torobuku
Teluk Kolono
Labuhantobelo
Lanowutlu
Tinangea
Laimea
Teluk Lahia
Walue
Bangbong
Selat Tiworo
KEPULAUAN TOBEA
Koroni
Laeiya
Tampo
Laangkumbe
Mataoleo
KEPULAUAN TIWORO
Tioro
Lebo
Lambale
Kembano
Bone
Ereke
Kasiputih
Wahaasa
Bonelipu
Kambara
Raha
Latambera
Tg. Goram
Laora
Matandasa
Mabodo
Wanasabari
Watumela
Wakarumba
MUNA
Tongkuno
Teluk Kolowana Watobo
Lasahau
Waogena
Buton
Konde
Wasalangka
Labora
Bungi
Bone
Lamorende
Teluk Lawelu
Kamaru
Tampunawu
Tongkaniwa
Selat
Lawele
Lasalimu
Manwasngka
Wajo
Kapantareh
Teluk Lingore
Lombai
Teluk Tallabassi
Lombe
BUTON
Labuandiri
Dongkala
Kantalabea
Wakingku
Wokole
Wapomaru
P. KABAENA
Waruruma
Teluk Pasarwajo
Selat Telaga
Pasarwajo
P. TELAGA Kcl.
Baubau
P. TELAGA Bsr.
P. KADATUANG
Batanga
Wasuemba
P. SIUMPI
Sampolawa
Biwinapada
Masiri
Molana
Tg. Pemali

N

KILOMETERS
0   10   20   30

Southeast Sulawesi

The province of Southeast Sulawesi (Sulawesi Tenggara, or Sultra) covers a total area of 38,000 sq km (23,750 sq mi, or slightly smaller than Ireland). Much of the peninsula is mountainous. Menkongga, the highest peak, is 2790 meters (9070 ft) high. The southern plains are covered in the west with forest, and in the drier east with swaying fields of *lalang* elephant grass, while the low-lying area around Aopa, probably once an inland sea, is mostly swampland. Southeast Sulawesi has the feel of a largely undiscovered wilderness.

During the 17th century, the island of Buton off Sultra's east coast was an important stop for VOC ships en route from their headquarters at Batavia (Jakarta) and Makassar (Ujung Pandang) to the Moluccan "Spice Islands" in the east. The peninsula itself, however, was virtually unknown to the West until the early 19th century.

While Southeast Sulawesi is still the remotest, least developed and least-traveled area of the entire island, links with the outside are fairly good. There are daily flights from Ujung Pandang and Palu to Kendari. A well-paved road with a regular bus service connects Kendari with Kolaka on the west coast (140 km/85 mi away) in under four hours. Ferries link the peninsula with Bone in South Sulawesi, with Buton and Muna to the south, and irregular small boats sail to the remote Tukang Besi Islands to the southeast. Smaller interior settlements are joined by unpaved roads and footpaths, which are often impassable in the wet season.

The province is sparsely populated by Indonesian standards. Its 1,220,000 inhabitants comprise several ethnic and linguistic groups. The Tolaki and the Tomekongga number 250,000; some 40,000 Tomoronene, who speak languages akin to those of Central Sulawesi, inhabit the Rumbia Poleang district and the island of Kabaena. On the islands of Buton, Muna and Kabaena there are 25,000 speakers of Wolio—the language of the former sultanate of Buton. Munanese is spoken on the northwest coast of Buton.

Bugis and Makassarese immigrants have settled along the coasts, as have groups of Bajau. More recent arrivals include transmigrants from Java, Bali and Lombok. In some parts of Southeast Sulawesi, new settlers actually outnumber natives. While there are occasional flare-ups between native inhabitants and the transmigrants, inter-ethnic relations in the province are generally smooth.

Rice and maize are the main crops on the islands, supplemented by cashews, cacao and teak. The sea yields trepang, tuna, shellfish and mother-of-pearl. The agricultural staple on the mainland is dry rice, though sago and various tubers are also planted. Fruits, soya, coconuts, cacao (especially in the area north of Kolaka), cashews, coffee, kapok and pepper provide additional income as cash crops. Forests yield valuable ebony and rattan.

In former times, the peoples of the interior bred water buffalo, which they traded as far away as the Toraja highlands. During the civil conflicts of the 1950s and 1960s, however, the buffalo population of Southeast Sulawesi was virtually decimated—plundered for food by rebel and government armies alike. Today goats, poultry and a bovine species imported from Bali are the most common domestic animals in the region.

On the west coast of the peninsula, where annual rainfall is as high as 3,000 mm (120 in), several thousand Bugis from Bone on South Sulawesi have planted more than 10,000 hectares (24,700 acres) of cacao gardens. Every weekend, a small flotilla of Bugis vessels makes the six-hour sea crossing over the Bone Bay into the Southeast, where the commuter-farmers tend their crop.

—*Dinah Bergink*

Overleaf: *Canoers in Napabale lagoon on Muna Island. Photo by Kal Muller.*

KENDARI AND KOLAKA

Major Towns of the Southeast

When a Dutch seaman named Vosmaer sailed into Kendari Bay in 1830, he "discovered" a tiny trading village made up of some 30 houses. Situated on a natural harbor in a narrow passage between steep cliffs, its entrance hidden from storms and invaders by a small island, Kendari was little known even to most local seafarers. The town was populated by various Bajau, Bugis and Makassarese merchants, who traded with the native Tolaki for forest and agricultural products.

The Tolaki trace their origins to the highlands north of Kolaka, near Andolaki at the source of the Konaweha River. As the "Brave People" (*to laki*) moved gradually southward, they pushed the peninsula's original inhabitants, the Tomoronene, down to Rumbia Poleang and onto Kabaena Island.

Kendari today is a growing town of 115,000. The provincial capital of Southeast Sulawesi and its largest city, Kendari is the key point of entry for travelers to Sultra, most of whom fly in from Ujung Pandang or Palu. The city consists of a long main road running along the north bank of the bay. On this road you will pass every building of importance in the city—government offices, hotels, restaurants and shops—as you head toward the rather shabby business district around the ferry terminal. As the administrative center for the province, Kendari is home to all major government agencies, along with entities such as oil-exploration companies.

The morning flight from Ujung Pandang gets in at about 10:00. The time between your arrival and the next afternoon's ferry to Buton and Muna should be just right to see what the area has to offer. While most visitors hit Kendari as a stopover on their quest for the thrills of Southeast Sulawesi's rugged, unspoilt natural charms, the town does offer a few incentives of its own.

Silversmithing, introduced by the Chinese about 150 years ago, is still practiced here, and there are high-quality works of gold and silver filigree for sale. There is also an 18-hole golf course, Kendari's main attraction, with well-kept greens and friendly caddies.

The area around Kendari offers some of Sulawesi's most scenic wilderness. The spectacular seven-level terraced waterfalls at Moramo, 75 km (45 mi) south of Kendari, are not to be missed. The trip by minibus takes

edge of thinly-forested hills, then crossing a rickety cantilevered bridge before moving into the grasslands which precede Raterate.

Here the vegetation is richer. Low hills covered with bright green *lalang* grass stand out sharply against the darker trees and bushes. Fruit trees line the road, and women gather firewood from the hills. After passing through Raterate, the road makes a gentle ascent before reaching a wide plateau. Roadside stalls along the way offer local produce: wild honey, pomelos, jackfruit, guava and *ubi-*

about two hours. The area near the waterfalls is home to a goodly number of West Javanese transmigrant families.

The fresh, cool water at the falls makes for excellent swimming, and enterprising locals there sell all kinds of drinks, including beer. The falls are best visited after heavy rains which swell the Kali Osena River, on which the falls occur. The river's source is two large mountain lakes 7 km (4.2 mi) distant. You can hike up to the lakes, a leechy business as there are no trails.

You can water-ski in nearby Moramo Bay (get there by speedboat from Kendari), which offers white sandy beaches and unpolluted waters. For more white sand beaches along with secluded rocky coves, head for Pulau Hari, half an hour by boat from Kendari harbor. The translucent green water and virgin coral gardens are ideal for snorkeling.

From the town itself, you can take a short 2-km stroll to an area with waterfalls and mature rainforest. Start out from the huts and Javanese-run shops (which cater to the hordes of local weekenders) at one end of the town's road. Some of the roadside trees have labels, though none in English except for those of the handsome ebony.

The road to Kolaka

Starting out from the Wawotobi bus terminal 8 km (4.8 mi) outside of Kendari, the minibus to Kolaka follows a reasonably good road through scenic countryside, albeit relatively unspectacular by South Sulawesi standards. About 40 km (24 mi) out of Kendari, after passing through a stretch of broad, marshy plains, the bus may stop at the town of Ammusu. Here you can enjoy a delicious meal of grilled river fish, spicy soup, rice and freshly squeezed lime juice.

Continuing on across the wide, muddy Kumbuti River (where you will see canoers poling their craft slowly by), the bus twists up through a hairpin-bend pass, skirting the

ubi, a tuber which many people in this region prefer to rice.

The view across the plateau, just before reaching Mowewe, is splendid—fields and houses quilt the broad expanses of the plain. The road cuts a long curve through more hills before winding down to Kolaka. Here the road follows a sparkling, rust-brown band of river through lush greenery. Flocks of goats slow the bus, and a large lizard occasionally scampers across the road.

Kolaka is a small, dusty town lying on a vast, sweeping bay set against a background of jungle-clad hills rising from the shore. Horse-drawn carts and stray goats saunter down the narrow back lanes of the town. In front of the decaying bus terminal, *bemos* and minibuses vie for passengers for the four-hour westward journey back to Kendari.

There is little to see or do in Kolaka, which is primarily a transit point between Kendari and Bone. Kolaka is, in addition to Kendari, the only practical port of access to Southeast Sulawesi. Travelers in South Sulawesi may wish to take the ferry from Watampone to Kolaka, then make the above overland voyage to Kendari in reverse (see "Southeast Practicalities" for details).

—*Dinah Bergink, Ian Caldwell, Kal Muller*

Opposite: Southeast Sulawesi boat-builder.
Above, left: View of Kendari from the water.
Above, right: The steps of the Moramo waterfall.

BUTON

Palace of a Powerful Sultanate

The little town of Baubau is set on the water's edge at the southern entrance of the Buton Strait. Including the nearby district of Wolio, Baubau has a population of some 52,000 inhabitants. From the hill above you can see the narrow strait stretching far to the northwest. On this hill sits the former fortress and palace of the rulers of Buton, an Islamic sultanate which traces its roots back over 30 generations to a goddess.

The kingdom of Buton

Legend tells of four immigrants from Johore who settled on the island of Buton. Moving inland, they founded a village on the site of the present-day palace of Wolio. The village became four separate districts, ruled over by the sons of the original settlers.

One day, one of the rulers chanced upon a bamboo stalk, inside of which he found the goddess Wakaakaa. She became the first queen of the territory, and even married a prince of the famous Javanese Majapahit kingdom. Their descendants became the royal line of the Wolio kingdom, whose influence extended throughout the region.

In 1540, the sixth ruler of Buton converted to Islam, becoming the first sultan. The sultan of Wolio was seen by his people as God's representative on earth, and was held responsible for the welfare of his country. If disaster struck the realm, the sultan could be forced to abdicate.

In its heyday, the sultanate of Buton included four vassal states: Muna, Tiworo (northern Muna and some small islands); Kalingsusu (northern Buton) and Kaledupa, one of the Tukang Besi Islands. The sultanate is mentioned in records of the Dutch East India Company as early as 1613. Buton sought support for its struggle for independence against the expanding kingdom of Makassar and the Ternate sultanate, of which it had been a vassal state in former days. After the Makassar kingdom was defeated by the Dutch in 1669, Buton became part of the territory administered under the Pax Neerlandica. This provided some protection for Butonese traders, but the Dutch monopoly excluded them from the spice trade.

In 1906, the sultanate was incorporated by the Dutch colonial government as a self-governing state. After independence, Buton was

integrated into the Republic of Indonesia. The last sultan, the 38th of the royal line, died in 1960, though his descendants still live in the *kraton*, or palace, of the ruler.

The palace of Wolio

The Wolio *kraton* is a large and relatively modern building built of teak in the traditional style. For a small fee (plus an official contribution) local children will show you inside; the palace is still inhabited, and is full of memorabilia. Of particular interest is the

cloth money once used in Buton—a handwoven forerunner of the modern banknote.

Inside the *kraton* grounds is the *mesjid agung*, "great mosque," a rusting, tin-roofed affair claiming to be the oldest (16th century) mosque in eastern Indonesia. Inside the mosque is a sacred stone with two footprints, on which the newly elected sultan had to place his feet upon his enthronement.

The walls of the fort, built of white coral, stretch for nearly three kilometers (1.8 mi) round the summit of the hill. The walls were built in 1613 following clashes with the Dutch East India Company. In 1637, the Dutch general Anthony van Diemen (who gave his name to what is now Tasmania) tried to take the *kraton* with 700 soldiers, but was forced to relent because of the "terrible steepness" of the mountain, on top of which lay the city. Today the walls are in ruin, though restoration is beginning. Rusty cannon, many bearing the blazon of the VOC, lie at the walls pointing out to sea, or half-buried and forgotten in groves of banana plants.

The hilltop area encircled by the walls of the fort contains a number of wooden houses as well as several smaller *kratons,* the residences of former sultans (each new sultan built his own palace). Next to the mosque is an interesting creation—an ancient, weathered, teak flagpole-looking structure.

There is also an enclosed area in front of the mosque which appears to have had some

sort of ritual function. The "*yoni*" (female genitalia) half of a *yoni-linggam* stone altar is kept in here. Unfortunately, the male part is broken off and reportedly lost.

Next to the mosque lies the combined grave of Buton's first sultan and its last raja. Also in the vicinity of the mosque-grave complex are a few craftsmen turning out fine brass items. With the dissolution of the sultanate, most of the court arts have disappeared. However, the brass works (known as *kerajinan kuningan*) are still around, along with some pottery and silver. Traditional Butonese weaving, a dark blue or black cloth with silver stripes, is also still worn here as sarongs, shirts and jackets.

If you are planning to spend more than half a day in Baubau, you could hire an English-speaking guide. Expect to pay about $10-12 a day; you can ask your hotel to contact the office of the *camat*, or district head (tel. 318), to make arrangements.

A good white-sand beach called Nirwana is located about 10 km (6 mi) outside of Baubau. On Thursday and Sunday mornings from around 5:30 to 8:00, fishermen from the area sell their fresh catch here. You can buy a large fish for less than $1, and grill it for a picnic at the beach. The place gets pretty crowded with locals on Sunday.

For more beach activity, the Tukang Besi Islands can be reached in about 11 hours by freighter (usually daily) from Baubau, or in 6-7 hours from the port of Pasar Wajo down the road from Baubau. At the town of Ambuea on Kaledupa Island, you will find some magnificent coral gardens. There is no scuba equpment available in the area, so it's swimming and snorkeling only.

—Dinah Bergink and Kal Muller

Opposite: Morning mists hang over Baubau.
Above, left: A "Mongol" helmet at the Wolio fort; said to be a momento of Genghis Khan's army.
Above, right: Dutch cannon at Wolio.

MUNA

Stallion Fights and Cave Paintings

Red horses of all sizes and shapes, some mounted by stick-figure riders, cover the off-white walls of a large chambered cave near the town of Raha on Southeast Sulawesi's Muna Island. Other tableaux vie for space and the visitor's attention, but the horses run away with the show.

Barely a couple of dozen kilometers away from the caves and their stylized equines, the ancient practice of horse-fighting remains an integral part of local rituals, even though most of the inhabitants of Muna converted to Islam long ago.

Heady stuff, cave paintings and horse-fighting, complemented by one of the most beautiful turquoise-colored lagoons anywhere in the world. Raha, the capital of Muna district, is the undisputed highlight for travelers with the initiative to make it to these rather remote parts.

This would not necessarily be evident to the traveler who has just disembarked at Muna. While the docks, located at the end of a long jetty, have a touch of the picturesque at night when the ferries from Baubau or Kendari call into port, the town itself is one of those many places in Indonesia which seem to exist quite happily with no redeeming features. Rusting tin roofs, "hallo, meesters" and stares at foreigners.

Like many nondescript towns in Indonesia, however, Raha is the gateway to a fascinating hinterland. Accommodations here are inexpensive and quite passable, if far from international-class. In addition, Muna has a surprisingly decent network of paved roads, part of Indonesia's unheralded but rapidly improving infrastructure.

As in most parts of Indonesia, seeing the hidden virtues of Muna requires some initiative and a few words of *Bahasa Indonesia*. The owner of your hotel can arrange for you to find an English-speaking guide, or you can try to find Pak Suarnadi, who speaks English, at the office of the local *bupati*. You can also pick up an English-speaking guide in Kendari. If you really want to play it safe, you could also join a tour out of Jakarta, Ujung Pandang or Kendari.

A minimum of two days is suggested for the vicinity of Raha, and at least double that if you want to explore other parts of Muna Island. First thing after arrival is to send

word to Latugo village if you want to see horsefighting. It will take a day for the villagers to get the horses and their act together. Also send word to Bolo village that you will need a guide early the following morning to visit the caves with the prehistoric paintings. It's 9 kilometers (5.5 mi) by paved road from Raha to Bolo.

Visiting the caves

You want to get an early start to see the paintings, starting no later than 7:00, as there's a good hour's brisk walk to get to the main cave, and the sun can make life a bit too warm for comfort. You will be hot enough on the way back. Also, you might want lots of time to see other caves. Eighteen of the caves here have paintings, but only dedicated archaeologists will want to visit them all. Nine are readily accessible, and visiting these will be enough for a full day.

Leaving Bolo village, you pass through groves of cashew trees whose nuts are by far the most important cash crop for the locals. While you may be able to arrange for a motorcycle to take you most of the distance (around 6 km/3.6 mi) to the main cave, we suggest walking to simplify things. Taking short cuts, it's about a 4-km walk (2.5 mi), a bit over an hour at a brisk pace.

As you head out of Bolo village, the road takes you through fields of corn and cassava, staples in the local diet. Walls of coral block surround the fields to keep out wild pigs as well as the native *babirusa,* who would otherwise gorge themselves on the fruits, so to speak, of man's labors. (To further "enhance the region," as they say, police teams from Java have been coming on a yearly basis to have fun and practice their marksmanship on the animals. In 1989, a group of 150 military police bagged over 5,000 of them. The bodies were buried, as Islam forbids the consumption of pork. Though *babirusa* do look like pigs, technically they are ruminants, and *halal* or "kosher" under Islamic law.) Huts set on tall stilts serve as watchtowers to keep monkeys out of the fields—another pest against which crops must be guarded.

Taking shortcuts means clambering over the stone walls, but there are crude notched-log ladders to facilitate passage. Otherwise, the walk is an easy one, encompassing a series of low, rolling hills. The landscape around the caves is actually created from raised coral bumps and ridges, some with bare sides but most covered with vegetation.

Less than a half hour out of Bolo, just off the trail, you pass a large block of coral vaguely resembling a dugout cave. A few minutes further, you come to the first "cave," Liang Lasabo, which is only an overhang protecting the paintings—all red here as in the

Opposite: *Horsefighting at Latugo.*
Below: *Coin-divers in the Buton Strait*

KAL MULLER

other caves—of horses, people and (perhaps) deer. There used to be an impressive store of human bones and carved coffins here, as well as at other caves, but all the goodies were removed in a series of raids by Jakartan archaeologists between 1984 and 1986. The locals were not very happy with this plundering, but appear resigned to the wisdom of the central government.

Don't linger too long at this first cave—a better one, Liang Toko, is just over half an hour away. This is the most important of all the caves, with the most and the best paintings. A huge chamber cave, some 15 to 20 meters (50-65 ft) deep, it is filled with rounded stalagtites and stalagmites, covered with a layer of (clothes-staining) green. The ceiling drips and there is a trickling stream in the back. One of the rounded walls is covered with paintings, mostly large horse-like creatures, the biggest one of which has two riders. The other paintings, whose themes include suns and insect-like figures, vie for the white space. A magical place.

Evidently, the locals also think that there is some magic going on here. There are three permanent cave-keepers living close by, and offerings of food (topped by a white flag to attract spirits' attention) are made here at regular intervals. Every year in mid- to late January, during the lull in the rainy season when the planting of the corn takes place, a week-long ritual is held here, with dances, carousing and discreet drinking by the nominally Muslim villagers. The ceremony is called *tolak bala,* literally meaning "warding off disaster."

The village head, after consultation with the people, decides on the exact date every year. Aside from averting disasters such as epidemics and boats overturning at sea, the ritual also proposes to ensure abundant harvests. During one part of the festivities, groups of young people, boys on one side and girls on the other, recite formulaic quatrains

made up on the spur of the moment (*pantun*) to each other as a way of showing off their wit. Kick-fights between the young men are also held.

At harvest time, in late August and early September, many places on Muna hold festivals. There are dances where guests must participate, pulled out of the ranks of spectators by a pair of comely maidens. Food is cooked overnight on hot stones in a covered pit. Bamboo tubes filled with cassava paste and red sugar are a local speciality which is always served here. The harvest festival is held at or close to the time of the full moon, and lasts anywhere from one to three days.

Near Liang Toko, there is another similar—if somewhat smaller—cave, Liang Kobori, with but a few small paintings. These are primarily interesting because of their motif—they represent men in tiny ships. If you still have the stamina, there are other caves nearby to explore. Or you can head back for something completely different.

The emerald lagoon

About 16 kilometers (10 mi) south of Raha is the Napabale lagoon, a local recreation spot. Crowded on weekends. Low but steep coral walls surround this breath-taking natural gem. You can rent canoes here; one of the outriggered or double-hulled jobs with a connecting plank platform helps prevent heart attack for those carrying cameras.

KAL MULLER

You can paddle your own canoe or rent one with one or two paddlers. At one end of the lagoon, a low cave allows passage to the next lagoon at low tide. This second lagoon is connected to the sea through the Strait of Buton. A small island, easy to circumnavigate, protects the entrance into the lagoon. There's a white-sand beach there and clean waters with seaweed.

The swimming is great everywhere, but the snorkeling is mediocre, as there are few fish around. In the inner lagoon you might see some long, thick, worm-like beasts feeding on the bottom. This is a wonderful place to spend a couple of hours but, especially on weekends, you are the main attraction for the crowd of locals.

Mustang machismo

Horsefighting goes on everywhere on Muna, but it's easiest to arrange and see at Latugo village, 24 kilometers (15 mi) outside of Raha. While it was—and still is—primarily a ritual practice, locals are willing to stage the event for visitors, provided they are given at least a day's notice.

A wide field is used for the event. Two troops of mares are "shown" to each stallion to "put them in the mood," as the villagers say. Then, with ropes around their necks, the two contestant stallions are introduced to each other, with obvious results. Rearing up and looking for a likely hold for their power-ful teeth, the stallions fight savagely for supremacy of the passive mares, with the crowd cheering for their favorite.

Eventually, one of the stallions decides that flight is the better part of valor, and gallops off the field to the jeers of the audience, which bother him not at all. Another challenger is brought in to dispute the hard-won victory. Although they do bite and kick each other quite enthusiastically, the damage is seldom serious. If it looks like the fight is getting too rough, the horses are pulled apart. It's a magnificent spectacle, much appreciated by the villagers, but somewhat unsettling to faint-hearted foreigners.

Horsefighting appears to be a remnant of the island's heathen days before the advent of Islam. Apparently, it was once performed to celebrate the return of victorious war parties and their booty of human head trophies. Stallions also fought at various festivals held among the aristocracy—weddings, first haircuts, 40 days after birth, etc. Then, as now, the spectacle was enlivened by lady jockeys riding astride piles of pillows and men with *parangs* (local machetes) demonstrating the art of horseback deer-hunting.

—*Kal Muller*

Opposite, above: *Ancient art at Liang Toko cave.*
Opposite, below: *An Islamic Muna boy during the celebration of his circumcision.*
Above: *A quiet corner of the Napabale lagoon.*

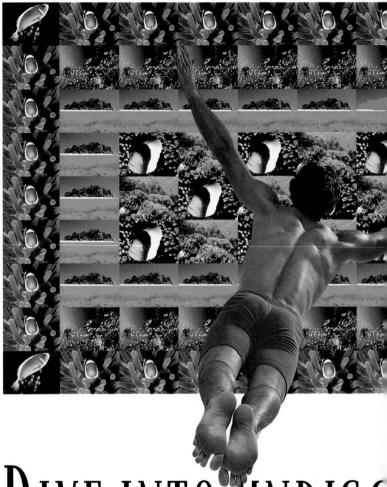

DIVE INTO UNDISC

There are some cities in Indonesia that no tourist bus can ever take you to. T are the lost cities of corals, sponges and sea fans.

Where the walls are ever changing - alive with the most diverse marine imaginable. Where the caves, crevices and overhangs have so far yielded t secrets only to schools of Moorish idols, Bamboola steamfish, devil rays, unicorn f some of the 3,000 kinds of fish that have yet to glimpse a mask or a flipper.

Where there are wrecks still to be discovered. Where the only shadows are ones that are cast by manta rays.

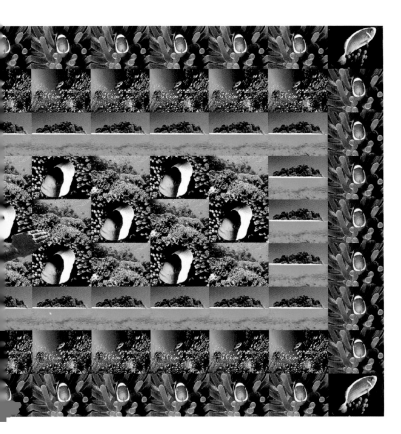

ERED TREASURES.

To the experienced diver, the hidden depths of Indonesia represent the richest

ng experience in the world.

And to the snorkeller or the beginner, there are more than enough secrets of

reef in the shallow coral gardens.

And who is better equipped to take you there than Garuda Indonesia? We have 18

its a week from Europe that will take you to some of the 17,508 islands that are

nesia. Contact your travel agent or Garuda Indonesia. We'll also give you an idea of

paradise that awaits you above water.   **Garuda Indonesia**
THE AIRLINE OF INDONESIA

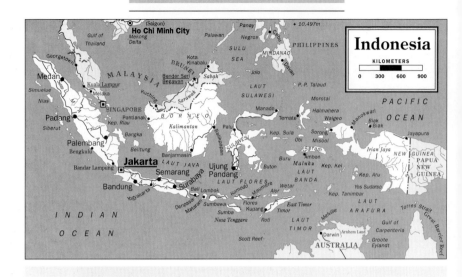

Indonesia at a Glance

The Republic of Indonesia is the world's fourth largest country, with 197 million people. The vast majority (88%) is Muslim, making this the world's largest Islamic country. More than 400 languages are spoken, but Bahasa Indonesia, a variant of Malay, is the national language.

The nation is a republic, headed by a strong President, with a 500-member legislature and a 1,500-member People's Consultative Assembly. There are 27 provinces and special territories. The capital is Jakarta, with 9.3 million people. The archipelago comprises just over 2 million square km of land. Of 18,508 islands, about 6,000 are named, and 1,000 permanently inhabited.

Indonesia's $133 billion gross national product comes from petroleum, textiles, lumber, mining, agriculture and manufacturing, and the country's largest trading partner is Japan. Per capita income is $680. Much of the population still makes a living through agriculture, chiefly rice. The unit of currency is the rupiah, which trades at approximately Rp2,200 to $1 (Feb 1995).

Historical overview The Buddhist Sriwijaya empire, based in southeastern Sumatra, controlled parts of Western Indonesia from the 7th to the 13th centuries. The Hindu Majapahit kingdom, based in eastern Java, controlled even more area from the 13th to the 16th centuries. Beginning in the mid-13th century, local rulers began converting to Islam.

In the early 17th century the Dutch East India Company (VOC) founded trading settlements and quickly wrested control of the Indies spice trade. The VOC was declared bankrupt in 1799, and a Dutch colonial government was established.

Anti-colonial uprisings began in the the early 20th century, when nationalism movements were founded by various Muslim, communist and student groups. Sukarno, a Dutch-educated nationalist, was jailed by the Dutch in 1930.

Early in 1942, the Dutch Indies were overrun by the Japanese army. Treatment by the occupiers was harsh. When Japan saw her fortunes waning toward the end of the war, Indonesian nationalists were encouraged to organize. On August 17, 1945, Sukarno proclaimed Indonesia's independence.

After the war, the Dutch sought a return to colonial rule. Several years of fighting ensued between nationalists and the Dutch, and full independence was achieved in 1949.

During the 1950s and early 1960s, President Sukarno's government moved steadily to the left, alienating western governments and capital. In 1963, Indonesia took control of Irian Jaya, and began a period of confrontation with Malaysia.

On September 30, 1965 the army put down an attempted coup attributed to the communist PKI. Several hundred thousand people were killed as suspected communists.

In the following year, Sukarno drifted from power, and General Suharto became president in 1968. His administration has been friendly to Japanese and western investment, and the nation has enjoyed several decades of solid economic growth.

In 1994 we held back the ocean

At Makassar Gate Beach Hotel, just walking distance from the bustling heart of Ujung Pandang, a peaceful haven awaits you. Spacious guest rooms, all business facilities you may require, attentive service and fine cuisine, right on the water's edge.

In 1995 we will walk on it

Traditionally styled Bugis cottages, adjoined by timber decked pathways, and set amid lush tropical gardens appear to float upon the calm waters of Makassar Bay. A refurbished Pinisi schooner offers a seafood restaurant and cosy lounge bar. Exciting new developments such as these are tailored to tantalise the most discerning adventure traveller.

Plans for 1996?
We will keep you in suspense.
Ujung Pandang is famous for surprises.

MAKASSAR GATE
Beach Hotel

Jl. Pasar Ikan No. 10, Ujung Pandang 90111, Indonesia.
Tel : 62 411 325791 (Hunting), Fax : 62 411 316303

Head office : Wisma Barito Pacific Atrium 3, Jl. Letjend. S. Parman
Kav. 62 - 63 Jakarta 11410, Tel : 62 21 5487158, 5487161, Fax : 62 21 5306337

LIMBUNAN
TOURS & TRAVEL SERVICE

Explore the Mysterious and Unique Cultures in Sulawesi, East Kalimantan, Maluku, Irian Jaya, East Nusa Tenggara, Sumatra and Java

Unspoilt Indonesia outside Bali, with its natural beauty, promises a real exciting experience to adventure. See the unique traditions and mystical life of the TORAJA in South Sulawesi, the impressive, traditional dances and houses of the MINAHASA in North Sulawesi, the national orchid park in BANCEA, the beautiful Poso Lake, nature waterfall and megalith culture in Central Sulawesi. Experience an exciting river cruise and jungle adventure on the Mahakam River in East Kalimantan, and the exotic MALUKU Islands. See also the Stone Age Villages of the natives with their unique way of life in Irian Jaya.

Come to East Nusa Tenggara (Flores, Timor, Sumba, etc.) to see the Giant Lizard wild life KOMODO, the contrasting three-colours of lake KELIMUTU, megalith cultures in BAJAWA and also other unique cultures/traditions in NIAS North Sumatra and Java ■

Special services:
◆ Car rental
◆ Off the beaten track
◆ Ticketing
◆ Hotel reservation
◆ Convention
◆ Specialist in
   East Indonesia

Head Office: 40-42, Jalan Gunung Bawakaraeng, Ujung Pandang 90115.
Tel: (062-411) 321710, 315010, 318810, 323333, 316350 Fax: (062-411) 314344, 314567
Telex: 71185, 71328 LIMTURIA Cable: LIMCO P.O. Box 1097
Branches:
Jayapura: Jalan Argapura Raya No. 68 Tel: (0967) 35430, 35498 Fax: (0967) 35377 Jayapura 99222
Labuan Bajo: Bajo Beach Inn, Kecamatan Komodo Manggarai, Labuan Bajo-Flores Tel: (0385) 41008, 41009
Manado: Jalan Sam Ratulangi No. 159 Tel: (0431) 52009, 52100, 52110 Fax: (0431) 52117 Manado 95113
Wamena: The Honai Resort, Jalan Pikhe Tel: (0969) 31515, 31516 Fax: (0969) 31513 Wamena 99511

Practicalities

TRAVEL ADVISORY, TRANSPORTATION, AREA PRACTICALITIES

The following Practicalities sections contain all the practical information you need for your journey. **Travel Advisory** provides background about traveling in Indonesia, from the economy and health precautions to bathroom etiquette. It is followed by a handy language primer. **Transportation** is concerned exclusively with transportation: getting to Indonesia and traveling around Sulawesi.

The **Area Practicalities** sections focus on each destination and contain details on transport, accommodations, dining, the arts, trekking, shopping and services. Most include local street maps. These sections are organized by area and correspond to Parts II to VI in the first half of the guide.

Indonesia At A Glance 218

▶MAP OF INDONESIA 218

Travel Advisory 221

What to Bring Along, When to
    Travel, Climate 221
Time Zones, Money and Banking,
    Tax and Tipping, Office Hours,
    Mail, Telephone..................222
Telephone Codes, Electricity,
    Tourist Information,
    Etiquette..............................223
Security, Health 224
Accommodations, Finding
    Your Way 227
Food and Drink 228
Political Organization, Spelling,
    Calendar 229
Shopping, Photography,
    Tours and Guides 230

Indonesian Language Primer 231

Transportation 233

Getting To Indonesia 233
▶MAP OF MERPATI ROUTES   234–235
Traveling In Indonesia 235
▶MAP OF PELNI ROUTES   236–237
Air Travel 236
Sea Travel..............................237
Travel Overland......................238

1 Ujung Pandang Practicalities 242

Getting There..........................242
Transportation in Town,
    Accommodations 243
Dining 244
Nightlife 245
Shopping, Medical, Travelers'
    Services, Travel Agencies......246
Nearby Islands, Historical Sites,
    Scuba Diving 247

2 South Practicalities 248

Parepare 248
    Facilities...............................248
Majene 248
Southeastern Peninsula............248
    Facilities 248
Selayar Island 249
Watampone (Bone) 249
    Transportation,
    Accommodations.................249
    Dining, Shopping 250
Watansoppeng (Soppeng).........250
    Accommodations, Dining.........250
Singkang 250
    Transportation,
    Accommodations.................250
    Dining, Shopping 251
Pinrang................................251
Palopo 251
    Transportation,
    Accommodations.................251
East of Palopo.........................251

3 Tana Toraja Practicalities   252

Rantepao 252
Getting There, Local
Transportation.....................252
Accommodations 253
Dining 254
Nightlife, Shopping.................255
Travelers' Services, Rafting 256
Trekking in Toraja 256
Guides 256
Trailside Accommodations.......257
Mamasa..................................257
Transportation, Accommodations,
Guides, Souvenirs 257

4 Central Practicalities   258

Palu...258
Transportation 258
Accommodations, Dining,
Handicrafts 259
Travelers' Services.................260
Donggala 260
Local Transportation,
Accommodations,
Scuba Diving 260
Poso 260
Transportation,
Accommodations 260
Dining, Money Changing 261
Tentena 261
Transportation,
Accommodations 261
Guides 262
Pendolo 262
Accommodations, Bancea
Orchid Reserve.....................262
Bada Valley 262
Getting There, Food and
Accommodations, Megaliths..263
▶MAP OF BADA VALLEY MEGALITHS   264
Megalith Hikes 265
Ampana 265
Transportation 265
Accommodations 266
Togian Islands.........................266
Kolonodale 266
Transportation,
Accommodations, Guides......266
Trekking in Morowali 267

Luwuk and Banggai 267
Transportation, Accommodations,
Pulau Tikus / Makailu Island ..267

5 North Practicalites   268

Manado 268
Transportation 268
Accommodations 269
Dining.....................................270
▶MAP OF MANADO   271
Health, Tours...........................272
Travelers' Services, Local
Activities, Scuba Diving 273
Shopping 275
Bitung 275
Transportation 275
Diving/Accommodations..........276
▶MAP OF SANGIHE–TALAUD   276
Sangihe–Talaud 277
Transportation,
Accommodations.................277
Minahassa 277
Accommodations 277
Gorontalo 278
Transportation,
Accommodations, Dining.......278
National Parks 278
Gunung Ambang, Dumoga
Bone, Tangkoko-Batuangus ...278

6 Southeast Practicalities   279

Kendari....................................279
Transportation, Accommodations,
Dining, Tours and Sights 279
Handicrafts 280
Kolaka 280
Buton Island............................280
Transportation 280
Accommodations and Food...281
Muna Island 281
Transportation, Food and
Accommodations, Guides......281

Further Readings   282

About the Authors   283

Index   284

Side tabs: 1 Ujung Pandang · 2 South · 3 Tana Toraja · 4 Central · 5 North · 6 Southeast

Travel Advisory

WHAT YOU SHOULD KNOW BEFORE YOU GO

WHAT TO BRING ALONG

When packing, keep in mind that you will be in the tropics, but that it gets chilly in the higher elevations, and sometimes over the water. Generally, you will want to dress light and wear natural fibers that absorb perspiration. A heavy sweater is also a must, as are sturdy shoes.

Don't bring too much, as you'll be tempted by the great variety of inexpensive clothes available here. Most tourists find a cotton *ikat* or batik shirt more comfortable than what they brought along. If you visit a government office, men should wear long trousers, shoes and a shirt with collar. Women should wear a neat dress, covering knees and shoulders, and shoes.

For those wanting to travel light, a *sarong* bought on arrival in Indonesia ($5–$10) is one of the most versatile items you could hope for. It serves as a wrap to get to the *mandi*, a beach towel, required dress for Balinese temples, pajamas, bed sheet, fast drying towel, etc.

Indonesians are renowned for their ability to sleep anytime, anywhere; so they are not likely to understand your desire for peace and quiet at night. Sponge rubber **earplugs**, available from pharmacies in the West, are great for aiding sleep on noisy journeys.

Tiny **padlocks** for use on luggage zippers are a handy deterrent to pilfering hands.

Also bring along some **pre-packaged alcohol towelettes** (swabs). These are handy for disinfecting your hands before eating, or after a trip to the *kamar kecil* (lavatory).

In most Indonesian department stores and supermarkets you can find western **toiletries**. **Contact lens** supplies for hard and soft lenses are available in major cities. Gas permeable lens wearers should come well-stocked.

Dental floss and **tampons** are available in western style grocery stores like Gelael that are fast becoming common in Indonesian cities. **Sanitary napkins** are widely available. *Kondom* (**condoms**) are available at all *apotik* (pharmacies).

On your travels you will meet people who are kind and helpful, yet you may feel too embarrassed to give money. In this kind of situation a small gift (*oleh-oleh*) is appropriate. Fake designer watches from Singapore or Hongkong selling for $5–$10 are a good idea (do tell them it's fake!). Chocolates, cookies and pens or stationery from your hotel are also appreciated.

WHEN TO TRAVEL

The height of the tourist season in Sulawesi is July and August. Particularly if you are going to Tana Toraja or to dive around Bunaken Island, make your reservations well in advance if you plan to visit at this time. Or avoid the crush, and visit off season. Two good times, in terms of tourist traffic and weather, are April–mid-June and mid-September–mid-October.

CLIMATE

The climate in this archipelago on the equator is tropical. In the lowlands, temperatures average between 21°C and 33°C, but in the mountains it can go as low as 5°C. Humidity varies but is always high, between 60% and 100%.

In general, Indonesia experiences two yearly seasons of monsoon winds: the southeast monsoon, bringing dry weather (*musim panas*— dry season), and the northwest monsoon, bringing rain (*musim hujan*—rainy season). Often the changing seasons can bring the time of high waves (*musim ombak*).

The **rainy season** is normally November to April, with a peak around January/February, when it rains for several hours each day. The rain is predictable, however, and always stops for a time, when the sun may come out. Before it rains, the air gets very sticky. Afterwards it is refreshingly cool.

The **dry season**, May to September, is a better time to come, and especially June to August. This is the time to climb mountains or visit nature reserves. This nice, neat picture is interrupted in Maluku province, where local effects alter weather patterns, and in areas in the rain shadow of mountains.

The northwesterly winds that bring on the rainy season generally arrive in Sulawesi in November or December, a bit later than usual. But because of its rugged nature, weather patterns here vary. Areas on the west coast tend to be wettest in December; those on the east coast, in May. Some areas are very dry: the sheltered Palu Valley, and the tip of the southwest peninsula.

Tides in Indonesia average between one and three meters. The only place in the country with really big tidal fluctuations is the south coast of Irian Jaya, where the shallow Arafura Sea rises and falls 5 meters or more.

TIME ZONES

Sulawesi is on Central Indonesian Standard Time, the middle of Indonesia's three time zones, which is Greenwich mean time + 8 hours. This puts Sulawesi on the same time as Singapore, Hong Kong and western Australia.

MONEY AND BANKING

Prices quoted in this book are intended as a general indication. They are quoted in US dollars because the rupiah is being allowed to devalue slowly, so prices stated in US dollars are more likely to remain accurate.

Standard **currency** is the Indonesian rupiah: Notes come in 50,000, 20,000, 10,000, 5,000, 1,000, 500 and 100 denominations. Coins come in denominations of 1,000, 500, 100, 50, 25, 10 and 5 rupiah. Unfortunately, the new coins are very similar in size, so look carefully.

Money changers and banks accepting foreign currency are found in most cities and towns. Banks are generally open 8:30 am to 1 pm, Monday to Friday and 8:30 am to 11 am on Saturdays. Some banks however, open until 2 pm on weekdays and close on Saturdays. Gold shops usually bunch together in a specific area of town and change money at competitive rates during hours when banks are closed.

Money changers offer very similar rates and are open longer hours. The bank counters at major airports offer competitive rates. Bank lines in town can be long and slow; the best way around it is to arrive promptly at opening time.

Get a supply of Rp 1,000 and Rp 500 notes when you change money, as taxi drivers and vendors often claim to have no change for big bills. When traveling in the countryside, Rp 100 notes are also useful.

Carrying **cash** (US$) can be a handy safety precaution as it is still exchangeable should you lose your passport, but it must be carefully stored and not crumpled: Indonesian banks only accept foreign currency that is crisp and clean.

Major **credit cards** are accepted in a wide variety of shops and hotels. But they often add a 3% surcharge for the privilege. Most cities have at least one bank at which cash advances can be made—look for Bank Duta, BCA and Danamon. Visa and MasterCard are the most frequently accepted foreign credit cards in Java.

There are no exchange controls and excess rupiahs can be freely reconverted at the airport on departure.

TAX, SERVICE AND TIPPING

Most larger hotels charge 21% tax and service on top of your bill. The same applies in big restaurants. Tipping is not a custom here, but it is of course appreciated for special services. Rp 500 per bag is considered a good tip for roomboys and porters. Taxi drivers will want to round up to the nearest Rp 500 or Rp 1,000.

When tipping the driver of your rental car or a *pembantu* (housekeeper) of the house in which you've been a guest, fold the money and give it with the right hand only.

OFFICE HOURS

Government offices are officially open 8 am to 3 pm, but if you want to get anything done, be there by 11 am. On Fridays they close at 11:30 am and on Saturdays at 2 pm. In large cities most offices are open 9 am to 5 pm, and shops from 9 am to 9 pm. In smaller towns shops close for a siesta at 1 pm and re-open at 6 pm.

MAIL

Indonesia's postal service is reliable, if not terribly fast. Post Offices (*kantor pos*) are usually busy and it is tedious lining up at one window for weighing, another window for stamps, etc. Hotels normally sell stamps and can post letters for you, or you can use private postal agents (*warpostel*), or freelancers set up outside the bigger offices, to avoid the aggravation.

Kilat express service is only slightly more expensive and much faster than normal mail. International *kilat* service gets postcards and letters to North America or Europe in 7 to 14 days from most cities. *Kilat khusus* (domestic special delivery) will get there overnight.

TELEPHONE AND FAX

Long distance phone calls, both within Indonesia and international, are handled by satellite. Domestic long distance calls can be dialed from most phones. To dial your own international calls, find an IDD phone, otherwise you must go via the operator which is far more expensive.

Smaller hotels often don't allow you to make long distance calls, so you have to go to the main telephone office (*kantor telepon*) or use a private postal and telephone service (*warpostel*). It can be difficult to get through during peak hours but the service in Indonesia now is quite good.

Approximate cost of a direct-dialed, one-minute call from a *warpostel*: $3.50 to Europe, $2.50 to the United States, Mexico or Australia.

International calls via MCI, Sprint, ATT, and the like can be made from IDD phones using the code for your calling card company. Recently, special telephones have been installed in airports with pre-programmed buttons to connect you via these companies to various countries.

Faxes have become common, and can also be sent (or received) at *warpostel* offices.

According to legend, the forefathers of the Toraja people descended directly from heaven to create in these ruggedly beautiful mountains, the Land of the Heavenly Kings. Even today, the Toraja live in houses whose richly carved and decorated roofs soar upwards in imitation of the prows of the ships in which the divine beings arrived.

In their isolation the Toraja kept alive a fascinating culture of unique architecture and elaborate ceremonies, which until recent years, were seen only by the most intrepid travellers.

The 4-Star MARANTE HIGHLAND RESORT is in the heart of this extraordinary travel experience, offering visitors warm hospitality and comfort in the Land of the Heavenly Kings.

*E*veryday Indonesian

ISBN: 0-945971-58-3 and ISBN: 0-8442-9913-8

Knowing a few simple phrases of Indonesian opens up an entirely new, more fulfilling travel experience. Indonesians love it if you can communicate in their language, and in only a few short hours this book allows you to do just that!

Everyday Indonesian is designed specifically with the visitor in mind, and contains everything you need to begin communicating effectively from the very first day. Vocabulary and phrases are given in order of importance, so you learn the essentials first. A bilingual dictionary at the back contains 2,000 of the most commonly-used Indonesian words. Also included are extensive notes on grammar, etiquette, body language and cultural dos and don'ts that will make your visit go a lot more smoothly.

Ordering Everyday Indonesian

If you cannot find *Everyday Indonesian* where you live, please write to us and order direct from us. The book costs US$14.95. Please add 25% for air-mail postage and packing. Payment can be made by US$ draft or major credit card.

Outside the U.S.A
Periplus Editions
2A Paterson Hill, Singapore 0923. Telephone: 65 - 734 8842 Fax: 65 - 734 8127

In the U.S.A
NTC Publishing Group
4255 W. Touhy Ave., Lincolnwood (Chicago), IL 60646, U.S.A.
Telephone: (708) 679 5500 Fax: (708) 679 2494

PERIPLUS TRAVEL MAPS

*P*eriplus Travel Maps represent a new concept in cartography. Designed specifically for travelers, each map contains insets of all major towns and areas at scales that provide exactly the detail which travelers need. The emphasis is on cities and sightseeing areas.

INDONESIA

Indonesia	ISBN 962-593-042-6
Bali	ISBN 0-945971-49-4
Bandung/West Java	ISBN 0-945971-43-5
Batam/Bintan	ISBN 0-945971-69-9
Jakarta	ISBN 0-945971-62-1
Java	ISBN 962-593-040-X
Lombak	ISBN 0-945971-46-X
Surabaya/East Java	ISBN 0-945971-48-6
Yogyakarta/Central Java	ISBN 0-945971-42-7

MALAYSIA

Malaysia	ISBN 962-593-043-4
Johor	ISBN 0-945971-98-2
Kuala Lumpur	ISBN 0-945971-75-3
Malacca	ISBN 0-945971-77-X
Penang	ISBN 0-945971-76-1
Sabah	ISBN 0-945971-78-8
Sarawak	ISBN 0-945971-79-6

THAILAND

Thailand	ISBN 962-593-044-2
Bangkok	ISBN 0-945971-81-8
Chiangmai	ISBN 0-945971-88-5
Ko Samui	ISBN 962-539-036-1
Phuket	ISBN 0-945971-82-6

CHINA

Beijing	ISBN 962-593-031-0
Shanghai	ISBN 962-593-032-9

OTHER DESTINATIONS

Cambodia	ISBN 0-945971-87-7
Hong Kong	ISBN 0-945971-74-5
Laos	ISBN 962-593-069-8
Myanmar (Burma)	ISBN 962-593-070-1
Singapore	ISBN 0-945971-41-9
Vietnam	ISBN 0-945971-72-9

Ordering Periplus Travel Maps

If you cannot find Periplus Travel Maps where you live, please write to us and order books and maps directly from us. The Maps cost US$7.95. Please add 25% for air mail postage and packing. Payment can be made by US$ draft or major credit card.

The Marketing Director,
Periplus Editions
2A Paterson Hill,
Singapore 0923,
Telephone: 65 - 734 8842
Fax: 65 - 734 8127

Telephone Codes

From outside Indonesia, reach these cities by dialing 62 (Indonesia's country code) then the city code, then the number. Within Indonesia, the city code must be preceded by a 0 (zero).

Ambon	911	Medan	61
Bajawa	384	Merauke	971
Balikpapan	542	Metro	725
Bandar Lampung	721	Mojokerto	321
Bandung	22	Nusa Dua	361
Banjarmasin	511	Padang	751
Banyuwangi	333	Palangkaraya	514
Batam	778	Palembang	711
Baubau	402	Palopo	471
Belawan	61	Palu	451
Bengkulu	736	Parapat	625
Biak	961	Parepare	421
Bima	374	Pasuruan	343
Blitar	342	Pekalongan	285
Bogor	251	Pekanbaru	761
Bojonegoro	353	Ponorogo	352
Bondowoso	332	Pontianak	561
Bukittinggi	752	Poso	452
Cilacap	282	Probolinggo	335
Cirebon	231	Rantepao	423
Denpasar	361	Ruteng	385
Dili	390	Sabang	652
Donggala	457	Salatiga	298
Ende	381	Samarinda	541
Gorontalo	435	Semarang	24
Gresik	31	Serang	254
Jakarta	21	Sibolga	631
Jambi	741	Sidoarjo	31
Jayapura	967	Sigli	653
Jember	331	Situbondo	338
Jombang	321	Solo	271
Kabanjahe	628	Sorong	951
Kalabahi	397	Sukabumi	266
Kebumen	287	Sumbawa Besar	371
Kediri	354	Sumedang	261
Kendari	401	Surabaya	31
Klaten	272	Tangerang	21
Kolaka	405	Tapak Tuan	656
Kota Pinang	624	Tarakan	551
Kotabaru	518	Tasikmalaya	265
Kudus	291	Tentena	458
Kupang	391	Ternate	921
Kuta	361	Tolitoli	453
Lahat	731	Tulung Agung	355
Larantuka	383	Ujung Pandang	411
Lumajang	334	Waikabubak	387
Luwuk	461	Waingapu	386
Madiun	351	Wamena	969
Magelang	293	Watampone	481
Malang	341	Watansoppeng	484
Manado	431	Yogyakarta	274
Manokwari	962		
Mataram	364		
Maumere	382		

ELECTRICITY

Most of Indonesia has converted to 220 volts and 50 cycles, though a few places are still on the old 110 lines. Ask before you plug in if your are uncertain. Power failures are common in smaller cities and towns. Voltage can fluctuate considerably so use a stabilizer for computers and similar equipment. Plugs are of the European two-pronged variety.

TOURIST INFORMATION

The **Directorate General of Tourism** in Jakarta has brochures and maps on all Indonesian provinces: Jl. Kramat Raya 81, Jakarta 10450. ☎ (21) 310 3117; Fax: (21) 310 1146.

Local government tourism offices, Dinas Pariwisata, are generally only good for basic information. More useful assistance is often available from privately run (but government approved) Tourist Information Services. Be aware that many offices calling themselves "Tourist Information" are simply travel agents.

Overseas, you can contact the Indonesian embassy or consulate, or one of the following Indonesia Tourist Promotion Board offices:

North America 3457 Wilshire Boulevard, Los Angeles, CA 90010-2203. ☎ (213) 3872078; Fax: (213) 3804876.

Australia Level 10, 5 Elizabeth Street Sydney, NSW 2000. ☎ (61) 2 2333630; Fax: (61) 2 2333629.

UK, Ireland, Benelux and Scandinavia Indonesia Tourist Office, 3–4 Hanover Street, London W1R 9HH, UK. ☎ (44) 71 4930030; Fax: (44) 71 4931747.

The rest of Europe Indonesia Tourist Office, Wiesenhuttenstrasse 17, D-6000 Frankfurt/Main, Germany. ☎ (069) 233677; Fax: (069) 230840.

Southeast Asia 10 Collyer Quay #15–07, Ocean Building, Singapore 0104. ☎ (65) 5342837, 5341795; Fax: (65) 5334287.

ETIQUETTE

In the areas of Indonesia most frequented by Europeans, many are familiar with the strange ways of westerners. But it is best to be aware of how certain aspects of your behavior will be viewed. You will not be able to count on an Indonesian to set you straight when you commit a *faux pas*. They are much too polite. They will stay silent or even reply *tidak apa apa* (no problem) if you ask if you did something wrong. So here are some points to keep in mind:

☛ The left hand is considered unclean as it is used for cleaning oneself in the bathroom. It is inappropriate to use the left hand to pass food into your mouth, or to give or receive anything with it. When you do accidentally use your left hand it is appropriate to say *"ma'af, tangan kiri"* (please excuse my left hand).

☛ Don't cross your legs exposing the bottom of your foot to anyone.

☛ Don't pat people on the back or head. Go for the elbow instead.

☛ Pointing with the index finger is impolite. Indonesians use their thumbs instead.

☛ If you are having a cigarette, offer one to all the men around you.

☛ Alcohol is frowned upon in Islam, so take a look around you and consider taking it easy.

☛ Hands on hips is a sign of superiority or anger.

☛ It is appropriate to drop your right hand and shoulder when passing closely in front of others.

☛ Blowing your nose in public is likely to disgust everyone within hearing distance.

☛ Take off your shoes when you enter someone's house. Often the host will stop you, but you should go through the motions until he does.

☛ Don't drink or eat until invited to, even after food and drinks have been placed in front of you. Sip your drink and don't finish it completely. Never take the last morsels from a common plate.

☛ You will often be invited to eat with the words *makan, makan* ("eat, eat") if you pass somebody who is eating. This is not really an invitation, but simply means "Excuse me as I eat."

☛ If someone prepares a meal or drink for you it is most impolite to refuse.

Some things from the west filter through to Indonesia more effectively than others and stories of "*free sek*" (free sex) made a deep and lasting impression in Indonesia. Expect this topic to appear in lists of questions you will be asked in your cultural exchanges. It is best to explain how things have changed since the 1960s and how we now are stuck with "*saf sek.*"

Also remember that Indonesia is predominantly Muslim and it can be startling for Indonesians to see women dress immodestly. Depending on where you are, exposed backs, thighs and shoulders can cause quite a stir.

SECURITY

Indonesia is a relatively safe place to travel and violent crime is almost unheard of, but pay close attention to your belongings, especially in big cities. Be sure that the door and windows of your hotel room are locked at night.

Use a small backpack or moneybelt for valuables: shoulderbags can be snatched. In Kuta, bags have been snatched from tourists by thieves on motorbikes, so be vigilant.

Big hotels have **safety boxes** for valuables. If your hotel does not have such a facility, it is better to carry all the documents along with you. Make sure you have a photocopy of your passport, return plane ticket and travelers' check numbers and keep them separate from the originals.

Be especially wary on crowded buses and trains; this is where **pick-pockets** lurk and they are very clever at slitting bags and extracting valuables without your noticing anything.

HEALTH

Before You Go

Check with your physician for the latest news on the need for malaria prophylaxis and recommended **vaccinations** before leaving home. Frequently considered vaccines are: Diphtheria, Pertussis and Tetanus (DPT); Measles, Mumps and Rubella (MMR); and oral Polio vaccine. Gamma Globulin every four months for Hepatitis A is recommended. For longer stays many doctors recommend vaccination against Hepatitis B, which requires a 7-month series of shots. Vaccinations for smallpox and cholera are no longer required, except for visitors coming from infected areas. A cholera vaccination may be recommended, but it is only 50% effective. **Malaria** is a problem in parts of Indonesia (see below) and you should take prophylactic pills.

Find out the generic names for whatever prescription medications you are likely to need as most are available in Indonesia but not under the same brand names as they are known at home. Get copies of doctors' prescriptions for the medications you bring into Indonesia to avoid questions at the customs desk. Those who wear spectacles should bring along prescriptions.

Check your health insurance before coming, to make sure you are covered. Travel agents should be able to help you with this.

Hygiene

This can be a problem. Very few places in Indonesia have running water or good sewers. Most water comes from wells, and raw sewage goes right into the ground or into the rivers. Even treated tap water in the big cities is not potable.

Most cases of stomach complaints are attributable to your system not being used to the strange foods and stray bacteria. To make sure you do not get something more serious, take the following precautions:

☛ Don't drink unboiled water from a well, tap or *mandi* (bath tub). Brush your teeth with boiled or bottled water, not water from a tap or *mandi*.

☛ Plates, glasses and silverware are washed in unboiled water, and need to be completely dry before use.

☛ Ice is not made from boiled water. It comes from water frozen in government regulated factories. Locals who are adamant about drinking only boiled water are, in general, not fearful of the purity of ice. However we advise against it.

☛ Fruits and vegetables without skins pose a higher risk of contamination. To avoid contamination by food handlers, buy fruits in the market and peel them yourself.

☛ To *mandi* (bathe) two to three times a day is a great way to stay cool and fresh. But be sure to dry yourself off well and you may wish to apply a medicated body powder such as Purol to avoid the nastiness of skin fungus.

Diarrhea

A likely traveling companion. In addition to the strange food and unfamiliar micro-fauna, diarrhea is often the result of attempting to accomplish too much in one day. Taking it easy can be an effective prevention. Ask around before leaving about what the latest and greatest of the many remedies are and bring some along. Imodium is locally available as are activated carbon tablets that will absorb the toxins giving you grief.

When it hits, it is usually self-limiting to two or three days. Relax, take it easy and drink lots of fluids, perhaps accompanied by rehydration salts such as Servidrat. Especially helpful is young coconut milk (*air kelapa mudah*) or tea. The former is especially pure and full of nutrients to keep up your strength until you can get back to a regular diet. Get it straight from the coconut without sugar, ice and color added. When you are ready, plain rice or *bubur* (rice porridge) is a good way to start. Avoid fried, spicy or heavy foods and dairy products for a while. After three days without relief, see a doctor.

Intestinal Parasites

It is estimated that 80 to 90 percent of Indonesians have intestinal parasites and these are easily passed on by food handlers. Prevention is difficult, short of fasting, when away from luxury hotel restaurants and even these are no guarantee. It's best to take care of parasites sooner rather than later, by routinely taking a dose of anti-parasite medicine such as Kombatrin (available at all *apotik*) once a month during your stay and again when you get on the plane home.

If you still have problems when you get back, even if only sporadically, have stool and blood tests. Left untreated, parasites can cause serious damage.

Cuts and Scrapes

Your skin will come into contact with more dirt and bacteria than it did back home, so wash your face and hands more often. Untreated bites or cuts can fester very quickly in the tropics, and staph infection is common. Cuts should be taken seriously and cleaned with an antiseptic such as Betadine solution available from any pharmacy (*apotik*). Once clean, antibiotic ointment (also available locally) should be applied and the cut kept covered. Repeat this ritual often. Areas of redness around the cut indicate infection and a doctor should be consulted. At the first sign

of swelling it is advisable to take broad spectrum antibiotics to prevent a really nasty infection.

Malaria

Malaria is a problem in parts of Indonesia and is nothing to be irresponsible about. Sulawesi is not the worst part of Indonesia for Malaria, but there is somewhat of a risk particularly along the South Coast, and in the Southeast.

Malaria is caused by a protozoan, *Plasmodium,* which affects the blood and liver. The vector for the *Plasmodium* parasite is the *Anopheles* mosquito. After you contract malaria, it takes a minimum of six days — and up to several weeks — before symptoms appear.

If you are visiting the above sites you should take malaria pills. Do not think that pills offer complete protection, however, as they don't.

Chloroquine phosphate is the traditional malaria prophylactic, but in the past 10–15 years, the effectiveness of the drug has deteriorated. Deciding on an appropriate anti-malarial is now more complicated. There are actually two forms of malaria: *Plasmodium vivax,* which is unpleasant, but rarely fatal to healthy adults; and *P. falciparum,* which can be quickly fatal. (*P. falciparum* has recently become dominant in parts of Nusa Tenggara and Irian Jaya.)

Malaria pills As a prophylactic for travel in the malarial areas of Indonesia, take two tablets of Chloroquine (both on the same day) once a week, and one tablet of Maloprim (pyrimethamine) once a week. Maloprim is a strong drug, and not everybody can tolerate it. If you are planning on taking Maloprim for more than two months, it is recommended that you take a folic acid supplement, 6 mg a day, to guard against anemia. Note: The anti-malarial drugs only work once the protozoan has emerged from the liver, which can be weeks after your return. You should continue on the above regimen for one month after returning.

Another recent drug that has been shown effective against both forms of the parasite is Mefloquine (Larium), although unpleasant side effects have been demonstrated for it as well. Mefloquine is also very expensive, about $3 a tablet. However, it can be a lifesaver in cases of resistant *falciparum* infection.

These drugs are not available over-the-counter in most western countries (nor, indeed, do most pharmacists stock them), and if you visit a doctor, you may have trouble convincing him of what you need. Doctors in the temperate zones are not usually familiar with tropical diseases, and may even downplay the need to guard against them. Do not be persuaded. Try to find a doctor who has had experience in these matters.

You can also buy Chloroquine and Maloprim over-the-counter in Indonesia, for very little (a few dollars for a month's supply). Maloprim, however, may still be difficult to find. [Note: there is a non–chloroquine based drug sold in Indonesia called Fansidar. This drug is not effective against resistant strains of *P. falciparum.]*

Treatment Malaria in the early stages is very hard to distinguish from a common cold or flu. A person infected may just suffer from headache and nausea, perhaps accompanied by a slight fever and achiness, for as long as a week until the disease takes hold. When it does, the classic symptoms begin:

1) Feeling of intense cold, sometimes accompanied by shaking. This stage lasts from 30 minutes to two hours.

2) High fever begins, and victim feels hot and dry, and may vomit or even become delirious. This lasts 4–5 hours.

3) Sweating stage begins, during which the victim perspires very heavily, and his body temperature begins to drop.

If you think you have malaria, you should immediately call on professional medical help. A good medical professional is your best first aid. Only if you cannot get help, initiate the following treatment:

1) Take 4 Chloroquine tablets immediately.

2) Six hours later, take 2 more Chloroquine tablets.

3) The next day, take 2 more.

4) The following day, take 2 more.

Note: If the Chloroquine treatment does not make the fever break within 24 hours, assume the infection is the very dangerous *P. falciparum* and begin the following treatment immediately:

1) Take 3 tablets (750 mg) of Mefloquine (Larium)

2) Six hours later, take 2 more tablets (500 mg) of Mefloquine.

3) After 12 hours—and only if you weigh 60 kg (130 lbs) or more—take one more tablet (250 mg) of Mefloquine.

Prevention The primary rule: if you don't get bit, you don't get malaria.

☛ While walking around, use a good quality mosquito repellent, and be very generous with it, particularly around your ankles. Wear light-colored, long-sleeved shirts or blouses and long pants.

☛ While eating or relaxing in one spot, burn mosquito coils. These are those green, slightly brittle coils of incense doped with pyrethrin that were banned in the United States some years ago. They are quite effective and you will get used to the smell. (If you are worried about inhaling some of the poison they contain, re-read the classic symptoms of malaria above.) In Indonesia, the ubiquitous coils are called *obat nyamuk bakar.* In places where there is electricity, a repellent with a similar ingredient is inserted into a unit plugged into the wall.

☛ While sleeping, burn *obat nyamuk* and use a mosquito net. Some hotels in affected areas have nets, but not many, and you should bring your own. The *obat nyamuk* coils last 6–8 hours and if you set a couple going when you go to sleep you will be protected. Remember that

mosquitoes like damp bathrooms—where few people bother to light a mosquito coil.

Other Mosquito-borne Diseases

The other mosquito concern is **dengue fever**, spread by the afternoon-biting *Aedes aegypti,* especially at the beginning of the rainy season in November. The most effective prevention is not getting bitten (there is no prophylaxis for dengue). Dengue fever symptoms are headache, pain behind the eyes, high fever, muscle and joint pains and rash.

AIDS & Hepatitis B

Surprise! **Safe sex** is also a good idea in Indonesia. AIDS is just beginning to surface with a number of documented HIV positive cases recently. Another consideration is Hepatitis B virus, which affects liver function, and is only sometimes curable and can be deadly. The prevalence of Hepatitis B in Indonesia is the basis for international concern over the ominous possibilities for the spread of HIV virus, which is spread in the same ways.

Medical Treatment

If you have to get sick while you are in Sulawesi, try to do so in Manado or, failing that, in Ujung Pandang. These two cities have the best hospitals and English-speaking doctors.

The Indonesian name for pharmacy is *apotik*; and a hospital is called *rumah sakit.* In smaller villages they only have government clinics, called *Puskesmas,* which are not equipped to deal with anything serious.

Fancier hotels often have doctors on call or can recommend one. Misuse of antibiotics is still a concern in Indonesia. They should only be used for bacterial diseases and then for at least 10 to 14 days to prevent developing antibiotic resistant strains of your affliction. Indonesians don't feel they've had their money's worth from a doctor ($5) without getting an injection or antibiotics. Be sure it's necessary. Ensure syringes have never been used before.

Even in the big cities (outside of Jakarta), emergency care leaves much to be desired. Your best bet in the event of a life-threatening emergency or accident is to get on the first plane to Jakarta or Singapore. Contact your embassy or consulate by phone for assistance (see below). Medevac airlifts are very expensive ($26,000) and most embassies will recommend that you buy insurance to cover the cost of this when traveling extensively in Indonesia.

Emergency Medical Assistance

AEA International 331 North Bridge Road, 17th Floor, Odeon Towers, Singapore 0718. ☎ (65) 338 2311, Fax: (65) 338 7611, Telex: RS23535

ASIAAS. Asia Emergency Assistance offers insurance packages for expatriates living in Indonesia and elsewhere in Asia, and individual travelers. This is a well-respected outfit, and they are considered to have the best response time and operation in Indonesia. In addition to Jakarta, AEA maintains alarm centers in Singapore, Hong Kong, Seoul, Beijing, and Ho Chi Minh City. Yearly premiums vary, depending individual conditions, but generally range from $115–$275/year, for a package covering emergency care and Medevac. **International SOS Assistance** Asia Pacific Regional Head Office: 10 Anson Road, #21-08/A International Plaza, Singapore 0207. ☎ (65) 221 3981, Fax: (65) 226 3937, Telex: 24422 SOSAFE. Offers a range of emergency services worldwide. Numerous large corporate clients. Contact them for rates and types of coverage

ACCOMMODATIONS

Indonesia has an extraordinary range of accommodations, much of it good value for money. Most cities have a number of hotels offering air-conditioned rooms with TV, minibar, hot water, swimming pool and the like costing $100 a night and up. While at the other end of the scale, you can stay in a $2-a-night *losmen* room with communal squat toilet (buy your own toilet paper), a tub of water with ladle for a bath, and a bunk with no towel or clean linen (bring your own). And there's just about everything in between: from decrepit colonial hill stations to luxurious new thatched-roof huts in the rice fields.

A whole hierarchy of lodgings and official terminology have been established by government decree. Theoretically, a "hotel" is an upmarket establishment catering for businessmen, middle to upper class travelers and tourists. A star-rating (one to five stars) is applied according to the range of facilities. Smaller places with no stars and basic facilities are not referred to as hotels but as "*losmen*" (from the French "*logement*"), "*wisma*" ("guesthouse") or "*penginapan*" ("accommodations") and cater to the masses or to budget tourists.

Prices and quality vary enormously. In the major cities that don't have many tourists, such as Jakarta, Surabaya and Medan, there is little choice in the middle ranges and you have to either pay a lot or settle for a room in a *losmen*. In areas where there are a lot of tourists, such as Bali and Yogya, you can get very comfortable and clean rooms with fan or air-conditioning for less than $20 a night. In small towns and remote areas, you don't have much choice and all accommodations tends to be very basic.

It's common to ask to see the room before checking in. Shop around before deciding, particularly if the hotel offers different rooms at different rates. Avoid carpeted rooms, especially without air-conditioning, as usually they are damp and this makes the room smell.

Advance bookings are necessary during peak tourist seasons (July to August and around Christmas and New Year). Popular resorts near big cities are always packed on weekends, and prices often double, so go during the week when it's cheaper and quieter.

In many hotels, discounts of 10%–30% from published rates are to be had for the asking, particularly if you have a business card. Booking in advance through travel agencies can also result in a much lower rate. Larger hotels always add 21% tax and service to the bill.

Bathroom Etiquette

When staying in *losmen,* particularly when using communal facilities, don't climb in or drop your soap into the tub of water (*bak mandi*). This is for storing clean water. Scoop water over yourself with the ladle in your right hand and clean with your left.

If you wish to use the native paper-free cleaning method, after using the toilet, scoop water with your right hand and clean with the left.

This is the reason one only eats with the right hand—the left is regarded as unclean, for obvious reasons. Use soap and a fingernail brush (locals use a rock) for cleaning hands. Pre-packaged alcohol towelettes from home may make you feel happier about this method.

Bring along your own towel and soap (although some places provide these if you ask).

Staying in Villages

Officially, the Indonesian government requires that foreign visitors spending the night report to the local police. This is routinely handled by *losmen* and hotels, who send in a copy of the registration form you fill out when you check in.

Where there are no commercial lodgings, you can often rely on local hospitality. But when staying in a private home, keep in mind the need to inform the local authorities. One popular solution is to stay in the *home* of the local authority, the village head or *kepala desa*.

Carry photocopies of your passport, visa stamp and embarkation card to give to officials when venturing beyond conventional tourist areas. This saves time, and potential hassles, for you and your host.

Villagers in rural Indonesia do not routinely maintain guest rooms. If a cash arrangement has not been prearranged, you should leave a gift appropriate to local needs—tinned food, clothing, cigarettes or D-cell batteries for radios in remote villages. Note down their address and send prints of the photos you took of them.

FINDING YOUR WAY

Westerners are used to finding things using

telephone directories, addresses, maps, etc. But in Indonesia, phone books are out-of-date and incomplete, addresses can be confusing and maps little understood. The way to find something, whether you have a specific destination in mind, or want to try to find a good place for *nasi goreng*, is to ask.

To ask for directions, it's better to have the name of a person and the name of the *kampung*. Thus "Bu Herlan, Mertadranan" is a better address for asking directions even though "Jalan Kaliwidas 14" is the mailing address. Knowing the language helps here but is not essential. Immediately clear answers are not common and you should be patient. You are likely to get a simple indication of direction without distance or specific instructions. The assumption is that you will be asking lots of people along the way.

Maps are useful tools for you, but introducing them into discussions with Indonesians will often confuse rather than clarify. Nevertheless, Indonesians seem to have built-in compasses and can always tell you where north is. If you introduce a map into your discussion, they are likely to insist that the north arrow on the map be oriented to the north before beginning.

FOOD AND DRINK

Pay attention to the quantity of fluids you consume in a day (drinks with alcohol or caffeine count as a minus). Tap water in Indonesia is not potable and it should be brought to a full boil for ten minutes before being considered safe. Use boiled or bottled water to brush your teeth.

Indonesians are themselves fussy about drinking water, so if you're offered a drink it is almost certainly safe.

Most Indonesians do not feel they have eaten until they have eaten rice. This is accompanied by side dishes, often just a little piece of meat and some vegetables with a spicy sauce. Other common items include *tahu* (tofu), *tempe* (soybean cake) and salted fish. Crispy fried tapioca crackers flavored with prawns and spices (*krupuk*) usually accompany a meal.

No meal is complete without *sambal*—a fiery paste of ground chili peppers with garlic, shallots, sugar, and various other ingredients.

Cooking styles vary greatly from one region to another. The Sundanese of West Java are fond of raw vegetables, eaten with chili and fermented prawn paste (*lalab/sambal trasi*). Minahasan food in North Sulawesi is very spicy, and includes some interesting specialties: fruit bat wings in coconut milk, *sambal* rat, and dog. In the more isolated parts of the archipelago, the food can be quite plain, and frankly, quite dull.

By western standards, food in Indonesia is cheap. For $1, in most places, you can get a meal with bottled drink. On the other hand, Indonesia does not have a banquet tradition and

people normally eat in restaurants only out of necessity (when they cannot eat at home). The major exception to this is the Indonesian Chinese, who are fond of restaurant banquets. Most Indonesians eat better at home than outside, and the range of dishes in restaurants is not great.

In most Indonesian restaurants you will find a standard menu consisting of *sate* (skewered barbequed meat), *gado-gado* or *pecel* (boiled vegetables with spicy peanut sauce) or *soto* (vegetable soup with or without meat). Also found are some Chinese dishes like *bakmie goreng* (fried noodles), *bakmie kuah* (noodle soup) and *cap cay* (stir-fried vegetables).

In most larger towns you can also find a number of Chinese restaurants on the main street. Some have menus with Chinese writing, but usually the cuisine is very much assimilated to local tastes. Standard dishes, in addition to the *bakmie* and *cap cay* mentioned above, are sweet and sour whole fish (*gurame asem manis*), beef with Chinese greens (*kailan/caisim ca sapi*), and prawns sauteed in butter (*udang goreng mentega*). Any one of these with a plate of vegetables (*cap cay*) and rice makes a delightful meal.

Indonesian fried chicken (*ayam goreng*) is common and usually very tasty—although the chicken can be a bit more stringy than westerners are used to. Then there is the ubiquitous *nasi goreng* (fried rice), which is often eaten for breakfast with an egg on top.

There are restaurants everywhere in Indonesia that specialize in Padang food, from this region of West Sumatra. This spicy, and very tasty cuisine has a distinctive way of being served. The glass case in front of the restaurant displays as many as 15–20 different dishes, all on little plates. You tell the waiter what you want, and he brings a whole stack of the little things and sets it in front of you. At the end of the meal, you are charged for what you have eaten, and any untouched plates are put back in the case.

The beers available in Indonesia are Bintang and Anker, both brewed under Dutch supervision and rather light (perhaps appropriately for the tropics). With electricity such a precious commodity, however, in out-of-the-way places the only way to quaff it cold is to pour it over ice.

Warung (Street Stalls)

Restaurant kitchens do not necessarily have healthier food preparation procedures than roadside *warung*. The important thing at a *warung* is to see what's going on and make a judgement as to whether or not the cooks inspire confidence. *Warung* rarely have a running water supply, so always beware.

The food is laid out on the table and you point to what you want to eat. Your first portion probably won't fill you up, so a second portion is ordered by saying *"Tambah separuh"* (I'll have another half portion, please). But only the price is halved. The amount of food is more like three-quarters. Finish off with a banana and say *"Sudah"* (I've had plenty and would like to pay now please). At this point the seller will total up the prices of what she served you and ask you how many *krupuk* and *tempe,* etc. you added; so keep track. The total will come to between Rp500 and Rp2,500 (30¢ to $1.25).

Vegetarianism

Say *"saya tidak makan daging"* (I don't eat meat) or alter menu items by saying something like *tidak pakai ayam* (without chicken) or *tidak pakai daging* (without meat). Dietary restrictions are very acceptable and common here due to the various religious and spiritual practices involving food. However, finding food that truly has no animal products is a problem. Often meals which appear to be made exclusively of vegetables will have a chunk of beef in them to add that certain oomph.

POLITICAL ORGANIZATION

Sulawesi includes four of Indonesia's 27 *propinsi,* or provinces:
1. Sulawesi Utara (Sulut) "North Sulawesi." The capital of this province is Manado.
2. Sulawesi Tengah (Sulteng) "Central Sulawesi." Its capital is Palu.
3. Sulawesi Selatan (Sulsel) "South Sulawesi." Its capital is Ujung Pandang.
4. Sulawesi Tenggara (Sultra) "Southeast Sulawesi." Its capital is Kendari.

Each of these *propinsi,* headed by a *gubernur* ("governor") is further divided into *kabupaten* (districts), headed by a *bupati* (district head); *kecamatan* (subdistricts), headed by a *camat*; villages (*desa*) headed by a *kepala desa* (mayor); and *kampung* (hamlets).

It is not quite this simple, of course, as in parts of Indonesia where there are large cities (*kota*), there are also *kotamadya,* ("municipalities"), whose "mayor" has the status of a *bupati,* and *kota administrasi* ("administrative cities") whose "mayor" falls somewhere between a *bupati* and a *camat.* But the basic progression is: *propinsi, kabupaten, kecamatan, desa, kampung.*

As an example, take Paputungan, a small village on the northern point of North Sulawesi:

Paputungan

Propinsi	Sulawesi Utara
Kabupaten	Minahasa
Kecamatan	Likupang
Desa	Paputungan

SPELLING

The Indonesian spelling of geographical features and villages varies considerably as there is no form of standardization that meets with both popular and official approval. We have seen village names spelled three different ways, all on signboards in front of various government offices. In this guide, we have tried to use the most common spellings.

CALENDAR

The Indonesian government sets a certain number of legal holidays every year, both fixed and moveable dates. Most of these holidays are for the major religions practiced in Indonesia. Both the Christian Easter and all the Muslim holidays are based on the moon, so confusion results in attempting to extrapolate several years ahead.

The fixed national holidays on the Gregorian calendar are the Christian New Year, Jan. 1; Independence Day, Aug. 17; and Christmas, Dec. 25. Easter Day, Good Friday and Ascension Day are honored in Indonesia. The Balinese new year, Nyepi, and the Buddhist Waisak New Year are also legal holidays.

Official Muslim holidays in Indonesia (the dates are for 1995):
Idul Fitri March 3 and 4. The end of the Muslim fasting month of Ramadan; this holiday is also called Lebaran. It is very difficult to travel just before and just after Idul Fitri as just about everyone wants to return to his or her home village to celebrate, then get back to their places of work in the cities.
Idul Adha May 10. The day of Abraham's sacrifice and the day that the haji pilgrims circle the Kaaba in Mecca.
Hijryah May 31. The Islamic New Year, beginning the month of Muharram, when Muhammad traveled from Mecca to Medina.
Maulud Nabi Muhammad SAW August 9. Muhammad's birthday.
Isra Mi'raj Nabi Muhammad SAW. December. 20. When Muhammad ascended on his steed Bouraq.

The 12 lunar months of the Muslim calendar are, in order:

Muharram
Safar
Rabiul Awal
Rabiul Ahir
Jumadil Awal
Jumadil Ahir
Rajab
Sa'ban
Ramadan (the fasting month)
Sawal
Kaidah
Zulhijja

Note: The Muslim calendar begins with the Hejira, Muhammad's flight to Medina, in A.D. 622 according to the Gregorian calendar. Early A.D. 1995 corresponds to A.H. 1415. The Muslim calendar is a lunar calendar, and gains 10 or 11 days on the Gregorian calendar each year. Islamic holidays will thus regress 10–11 days a year against to the Gregorian calendar.

SHOPPING

Be extremely cautious when buying antiques, works of art or other expensive objects, especially in the tourist areas. Most are reproductions, (though often very good ones, and cheap to boot!)

Handicrafts are produced all over Indonesia, and even if a good selection is available in hotels and tourist areas, it can be fun to seek out craftsmen in the villages (though often it's not cheaper unless you are very good at bargaining).

Bargaining

The secret here is not to care, or at least appear not to care. Some merchants are very upfront about giving prices that are about the minimum of what they want to sell an item for (*harga pas:* fixed price), but the trader who expects the buyer to bargain is more commonplace. A general rule of thumb is to aim for half the asking price by opening with an offer lower than that. The 50% rule is by no means universal and many sellers will only come down by 20%. On the other hand, in tourist areas, vendors will often ask 10 times or more the reasonable selling price, so don't feel shy about offering them 10% of the asking price.

More often than not the deal is closed in a ritual in which you cheerfully thank the purveyor for their time and take steps towards the next stall or the door as the case may be. At this point keep your ears pricked for the *real* final offer of the seller and either thank them again and move on or return and claim your prize. If your final price is accepted it is a major breach of etiquette not to consummate the purchase.

In any event, staying cheerful and good humored will not only be more fun but can make a huge difference in the price you finally pay (and the success of any important interaction with an Indonesian). This isn't just about money and, yes, you should pay a bit more than an Indonesian would. That's the way it works.

Souvenirs

The best place for souvenir shopping in Sulawesi is probably Ujung Pandang. Here you can find silk cloths, old cotton weavings, decorated bamboo containers, earthenware pottery, local silverwork, and old colonial coins and other artifacts.The traveler's problem is how to lug around what is brought for the rest of the trip. While the most common souvenir items, traditional cloths, are relatively light, they take up a great deal of space. One option, shipping goods home, can be a bit of a problem.

LTH International (pronounced El-Tay-Hah), on Jl. Baumesepe 5 in downtown Ujung Pandang, will airfreight goods (6–45 kilos) to any address in the United States for $17/kilo, to the Sydney airport for $6/kilo, or to Amsterdam for $11/kilo.

P.T. Jakarta Loyd (the manager of which speaks excellent English)—Jl. Sawerigading 16A, Ujung Pandang—can ship an entire container by sea to the United States or Europe for about $1,300. If you don't need 26 cubic meters, it may be possible to ship smaller amounts for about $180/cubic meter.

PHOTOGRAPHY

Some 35mm Fuji and Kodak film is available in Indonesia, including color print film from ASA 100 to 400 and Ektachrome and Fujichrome 100 ASA daylight transparency film. In larger towns you can buy Fuji Neopan 100 ASA black-and-white negative film as well. You can't buy Kodachrome in Indonesia, although Fuji Velvia is available in the larger cities. Medium- and large-format emulsions are basically unavailable. It's best to bring plenty of film from home. Avoid local processing if you value your negatives or transparencies. Bad processing has ruined more film than airport x-ray machines.

Indonesians generally enjoy being photographed. But if you are in doubt, or the situation seems awkward, it is polite to ask. Some religious activities, cockfighting (which is officially banned) and eating (which is considered a private activity) could be sensitive.

If you are from a temperate region, beware the strong shadows from the equatorial sun. Late afternoon and, especially, early morning, provide the most pleasing light and the richest colors.

TOURS AND GUIDES

All provincial capitals and tourist areas in Indonesia have travel agencies that can set up local tours. The best agencies in Ujung Pandang can set up Sulawesi-wide tours.

Guides vary widely in their English (and other language) speaking ability, as well as in their knowledge of the area. There are both official, licensed guides, and free-lance guides. Except for those provided by an agency, guide rates are usually very negotiable, especially if you want to use the guide's services for an extended period. Be clear beforehand about who covers the guide's personal expenses, and the cost of his return to home base. (See relevant practicalities sections for more specific information.)

In Tana Toraja you can find guides speaking German, French, Italian, Japanese or Spanish, but elsewhere in Sulawesi it's English-only (if you can find that!). In most areas, the hotel or *losmen* staff can recommend a guide.

Indonesian Language Primer

Personal pronouns
I   *saya*
we   *kita* (inclusive), *kami* (exclusive)
you   *anda* (formal), *saudara* (brother, sister),
kamu (for friends and children only)
he/she   *dia*   they   *mereka*

Forms of address
Father/Mr   *Bapak* ("*Pak*")
Mother/Mrs   *Ibu* ("*Bu*")
Elder brother   *Abang* ("*Bang*" or "*Bung*")
    Mas (in Java only)
Elder sister   *Mbak*
Younger brother/sister   *Adik* ("*Dik*")
Note: These terms are used not just within the family, but generally in polite speech.

Basic questions
How?   *Bagaimana?*
How much/many?   *Berapa?*
What?   *Apa?*
What's this?   *Apa ini?*
Who?   *Siapa?*
Who's that?   *Siapa itu?*
What is your name?   *Siapa namanya?*
(Literally: Who is your name?)
When?   *Kapan?*
Where?   *Mana?*
Which?   *Yang mana?*
Why?   *Kenapa?*

Useful words
yes   *ya*   no, not   *tidak, bukan*
Note: *Tidak* is used with verbs or adverbs; *bukan* with nouns.

and   *dan*
with   *dengan*
for   *untuk*
good   *bagus*
fine   *baik*
more   *lebih*
less   *kurang*
better   *lebih baik*
worse   *kurang baik*
this/these   *ini*
that/those   *itu*
same   *sama*
different   *lain*
here   *di sini*
there   *di sana*

Civilities
Welcome   *Selamat datang*
Good morning (7–11am)   *Selamat pagi*
Good midday (11am–3pm)   *Selamat siang*
Good afternoon (3–7pm)   *Selamat sore*
Goodnight (after dark)   *Selamat malam*
Goodbye (to one leaving)   *Selamat jalan*
Goodbye (to one staying)   *Selamat tinggal*
Note: *Selamat* is a word from Arabic meaning "May your time (or action) be blessed."
How are you?   *Apa kabar?*
I am fine.   *Kabar baik.*
Thank you.   *Terima kasih.*
You're welcome.   *Kembali.*
Same to you.   *Sama sama.*
Pardon me   *Ma'af*
Excuse me   *Permisi*
(when leaving a conversation, etc).

Numbers

1	*satu*		6	*enam*
2	*dua*		7	*tujuh*
3	*tiga*		8	*delapan*
4	*empat*		9	*sembilan*
5	*lima*		10	*sepuluh*

Pronunciation and Grammar

Vowels
a   As in f**a**ther
e   Three forms:
    1) Schwa, like th**e**
    2) Like **é** in touch**é**
    3) Short **è**; as in b**e**t
i   Usually like long **e** (as in Bal**i**); when bounded by consonants, like short **i** (h**i**t).
o   Long **o**, like g**o**
u   Long **u**, like y**ou**
ai   Long **i**, like cr**i**me
au   Like **ow** in **ow**l

Consonants
c   Always like **ch** in **ch**urch
g   Always hard, like **g**uard
h   Usually soft, almost unpronounced. It is hard between like vowels, e.g. *ma**h**al* (expensive).
k   Like **k** in **k**ind; at end of word, unvoiced stop.
kh   Like **k**ind, but harder
r   Rolled, like Spanish **r**
ng   Soft, like fli**ng**
ngg   Hard, like ti**ng**le
ny   Like **ny** in So**ny**a

Grammar
Grammatically, Indonesian is in many ways far simpler than English. There are no articles (a, an, the).
The verb form "to be" is usually not used. There is no ending for plurals; sometimes the word is doubled, but often number comes from context. And Indonesian verbs are not conjugated. Tense is communicated by context or with specific words for time.

11	*seblas*	100	*seratus*
12	*dua belas*	600	*enam ratus*
13	*tiga belas*	1,000	*seribu*
20	*dua puluh*	3,000	*tiga ribu*
50	*lima puluh*	10,000	*sepuluh ribu*
73	*tujuh puluh tiga*		

1,000,000   *satu juta*
2,000,000   *dua juta*
half   *setengah*

first	*pertama*	third	*ketiga*
second	*kedua*	fourth	*ke'empat*

Time

minute	*menit*	Sunday	*Hari Minggu*
hour	*jam*	Monday	*Hari Senin*
(also clock/watch)		Tuesday	*Hari Selasa*
day	*hari*	Wednesday	*Hari Rabu*
week	*minggu*	Thursday	*Hari Kamis*
month	*bulan*	Friday	*Hari Jum'at*
year	*tahun*	Saturday	*Hari Sabtu*
today	*hari ini*	later	*nanti*
tomorrow	*besok*	yesterday	*kemarin*

What time is it?   *Jam berapa?*
(It is) eight thirty.   *Jam setengah sembilan*
(Literally: "half nine")
How many hours?   *Berapa jam?*
When did you arrive?   *Kapan datang?*
Four days ago.   *Empat hari yang lalu.*
When are you leaving?
Kapan berangkat?
In a short while.   *Sebentar lagi.*

Basic vocabulary

to be, have	*ada*	correct	*betul*
to be able, can	*bisa*	wrong	*salah*
to buy	*beli*	big	*besar*
to know	*tahu*	small	*kecil*
to get	*dapat*	pretty	*cantik*
to need	*perlu*	slow	*pelan*
to want	*mau*	fast	*cepat*
to go	*pergi*	stop	*berhenti*
to wait	*tunggu*	old	*tua, lama*
at	*di*	new	*baru*
to	*ke*	then	*lalu, kemudian*
if	*kalau*	only	*hanya, saja*
near	*dekat*	crowded, noisy	*ramai*
far	*jauh*		
empty	*kosong*		

Small talk

Where are you from?   *Dari mana?*
I'm from the US.   *Saya dari Amerika.*
How old are you?   *Umurnya berapa?*
I'm 31 years old.
Umur saya tiga pulu satu tahun.
Are you married?   *Sudah kawin belum?*
Yes, I am.   *Yah, sudah.*   Not yet.   *Belum.*
Do you have children?   *Sudah punya anak?*
What is your religion?   *Agama apa?*
Where are you going?   *Mau ke mana?*
I'm just taking a walk.   *Jalan-jalan saja.*
Please come in.   *Silahkan masuk.*
This food is delicious.
Makanan ini enak sekali.

You are very hospitable.
Anda sangat ramah tamah.

Hotels

Where's a losmen?   *Di mana ada losmen?*
cheap losmen   *losmen yang murah*
average losmen   *losmen biasa*
very good hotel   *hotel cukup baik*
Please take me to...   *Tolong antar saya ke...*
Are there any empty rooms?
Ada kamar kosong?
Sorry there aren't any.   *Ma'af, tidak ada.*
How much for one night?
Berapa untuk satu malam?
One room for two of us.
Dua orang, satu kamar.
I'd like to stay for 3 days.
Saya mau tinggal tiga hari.
hot water   *air panas*
Here's the key to your room.
Ini kunci kamar.
Please call a taxi.   *Tolong panggil taksi.*
Please wash these clothes.
Tolong cucikan pakaian ini.

Restaurants

Where's a good restaurant?
Di mana ada rumah makan yang baik?
Let's have lunch.   *Mari kita makan siang.*
I want Indonesian food.
Saya mau makanan Indonesia.
I want coffee, not tea.
Saya mau kopi, bukan teh.
May I see the menu?
Boleh saya lihat daftar makanan?
I want to wash my hands.
Saya mau cuci tangan.
Where is the toilet?   *Di mana kamar kecil?*
fish, squid, goat, beef
ikan, cumi, kambing, sapi
salty, sour, sweet, spicy
asin, asam, manis, pedas

Shopping

I don't understand.   *Saya tidak mengerti.*
I can't speak Indonesian.
Saya tidak bisa bicara Bahasa Indonesia.
Please, speak slowly.
Tolong, berbicara lebih pelan.
I want to buy...   *Saya mau beli...*
Where can I buy...   *Di mana saya bisa beli...*
How much does this cost?   *Berapa harga ini?*
2,500 Rupiah.   *Dua ribu, lima ratus rupiah.*
That cannot be true!   *Masa!*
That's still a bit expensive.   *Masih agak mahal.*

Directions

north	*utara*	west	*barat*
south	*selatan*	east	*timur*
right	*kanan*	left	*kiri*
near	*dekat*	far	*jauh*
inside	*di dalam*	outside	*di luar*

I am looking for this address.
Saya cari alamat ini.
How far is it?   *Berapa jauh dari sini?*

Transportation

GETTING AROUND IN INDONESIA

This advisory gives you an overview of the wide range of travel options available during your stay in Indonesia. A comprehensive run-down of travel services enables you to plan your way around the island according to time and budget. More specific details for each area you will be visiting can be found in the relevant Practicalities sections. Prices are in US dollars, unless otherwise stated. Prices and schedules are given as an indication only, as they change frequently according to the season. Check with a travel agent prior to departure for the most up-to-date information.

In many ways, Indonesia is an easy place to get around. Indonesians are as a rule hospitable and good-humored, and will always help a lost or confused traveler. The weather is warm, the pace of life relaxed, and the air is rich with the smells of clove cigarettes, the blessed durian fruit and countless other wonders.

On the other hand, the nation's transportation infrastructure does not move with the kind of speed and efficiency that western travelers expect, which often leads to frustration. It is best to adjust your pace to local conditions. There is nothing more pathetic than a tourist who has traveled halfway around the world just to shout at some poor clerk at the airport counter.

The golden rule is: things will sort themselves out. Eventually. Be persistent, of course, but relax and keep your sense of humor. Before you explode, have a *kretek* cigarette, a cup of sweet coffee, or a cool glass of *kelapa muda* (young coconut water). Things might look different.

GETTING TO INDONESIA

You can fly to Indonesia from just about anywhere. Most people traveling from Europe and the US arrive on direct flights to Jakarta, while those coming from Australia generally first go to Bali. The main international entry points are Sukarno-Hatta airport in Jakarta, Ngurah Rai airport in Bali, and Polonia airport in Medan, North Sumatra. There are now also flights between Singapore and Surabaya, in East Java, on Singapore Airlines (direct) and Garuda (via Jakarta). SilkAir, also based in Singapore, flies direct from Singapore to Manado, in North Sulawesi.

Sukarno-Hatta airport is served by many international airlines, with over a dozen flights a day from Singapore alone. A cut-price alternative from Europe or the US may be to get a cheap flight to Singapore, and buy an onward discount ticket to Jakarta from there: the cost of these can be as low as $90 single, $155 return. A return ticket from Singapore to Bali with stops in Jakarta and Yogyakarta, good for a month, is available in Singapore for around $450. Buy through travel agents—check the *Straits Times* for details. Note: you need a return or onward ticket to get a tourist visa on arrival.

Direct flights also connect Jakarta with many major cities in Asia and Europe. Air fares vary depending on the carrier, the season and the type of ticket purchased. A discount RT fare from the US or Europe costs from $850: about half that from Australia or East Asian capitals.

Air tickets from **Batam** and **Bintan** are less expensive, and these Indonesian islands just off the coast of Singapore can be reached via short ferry hops from Singapore's World Trade Centre. Tickets to Batam cost $12 single, $18 return, and to Bintan $35 single, $55 return.

There are several daily jet flights from Batam as well as Tanjung Pinang, Bintan, to Jakarta via Merpati/Garuda and Sempati: $130 single and $180 return. **Merpati/Garuda** office in Batam ☎ (778) 45820. **Sempati** in Batam ☎ (778) 411612, 453050. **Sempati** in Tanjung Pinang, Bintan ☎ (771) 21612, 25283.

Airport tax for departing passengers is Rp 17,000 for international routes and between Rp 1,500 and Rp 6,000 for domestic flights.

Having arrived in Indonesia, your choices for onward travel depend, as always, on time and money. Possibilities range from boats, trains, cars—chauffeur driven, and in some places, rented—to both slow and fast buses. Hiring a car or minibus with a driver is one of the most rewarding ways of getting around, if you can afford it.

Visas

Nationals of the following 36 countries do not need visas, and are granted visa-free entry for 60 days upon arrival (this is non-renewable). For other nationals, visas are required and must be obtained in advance from an Indonesian embassy or consulate.

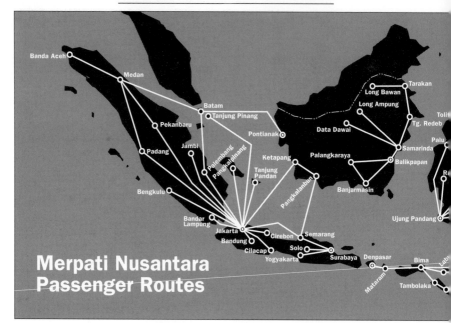

Merpati Nusantara Passenger Routes

Argentina	Iceland	Norway
Australia	Ireland	Philippines
Austria	Italy	Singapore
Belgium	Japan	South Korea
Brazil	Liechtenstein	Spain
Canada	Luxemburg	Sweden
Chile	Malaysia	Switzerland
Denmark	Malta	Thailand
Finland	Mexico	United Kingdom
France	Morocco	United States
Germany	Netherlands	Venezuela
Greece	New Zealand	Yugoslavia

Be sure to check your passport before leaving for Indonesia. You must have at least one empty page to be stamped on arrival, and the passport must be valid for at least six months after the date of arrival. For visa-free entry, you must also have proof of onward journey, either a return or through ticket. Employment is strictly forbidden on tourist visas or visa-free entry.

Visa-free entry to Indonesia cannot be extended beyond two months (60 days) and is only given to passengers arriving at the following airports: Ambon, Bali, Batam, Biak, Jakarta, Manado, Medan, Padang, Pontianak, Surabaya. Or at the following seaports: Bali, Balikpapan, Batam, Tanjung Pinang (Bintan), Jakarta, Kupang, Pontianak, Semarang.

OTHER VISAS

The 2-month, non-extendable **tourist pass** is the only entry permit that comes without a great deal of paperwork.

A **visitor's visa**, usually valid for 4–5 weeks, can be extended for up to 6 months, but is difficult to get. You must have a good reason for spending time in Indonesia (research, relatives, religious study) and you must have a sponsor and lots of supporting letters. Even with a sponsor and the best of reasons, however, you might still be denied. The process can take days or even weeks, and extensions are at the discretion of the immigration office where you apply.

A **business visa**, valid for 30 days and extendable to 3 months requires a letter from a company stating that you are performing a needed service for a company in Indonesia. This is not intended as an employment visa, but is for investors, consultants, or other business purposes.

Two other types of passes are available: the temporary residence pass (KIM-S) and permanent residence pass (KIM). Both are hard to get.

Customs

Narcotics, firearms and ammunition are strictly prohibited. The standard duty-free allowance is: 2 liters of alcoholic beverages, 200 cigarettes, 50 cigars or 100 grams of tobacco. There is no restriction on import and export of foreign currencies in cash or travelers checks, but there is an export limit of 50,000 Indonesian rupiah.

All narcotics are illegal in Indonesia. The use, sale or purchase of narcotics results in long prison terms and huge fines. Once caught, you are immediately placed in detention until trial, and the sentences are stiff, as demonstrated by westerners currently serving sentences as long as 30 years for possession of marijuana.

Keeping Your Cool

At government offices like immigration or police, talking loudly and forcefully doesn't make things

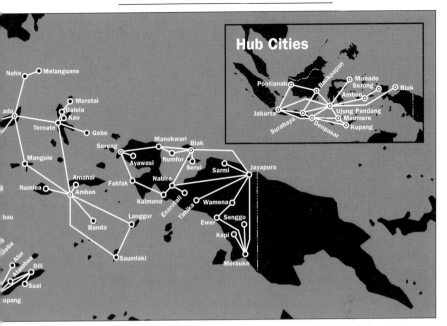

easier. Patience and politeness are virtues that open many doors in Indonesia. Good manners and dress are also to your advantage.

TRAVELING IN INDONESIA

Getting around in Indonesia is not—to those used to efficient and punctual transportation—effortless. Bookings are often difficult to make; flights and reservations are sometimes mysteriously canceled.

What seems like nerve-wracking inefficiency is really so only if one is in a hurry. If you have to be somewhere at a particular time, allow plenty of time to get there. Check and double-check your bookings. Otherwise just go with the flow. You can't just turn off the archipelago's famous *jam karet*—"rubber time"—when it's time to take an airplane and turn it on again when you want to relax. You will get there eventually.

Peak periods around holidays and during the August tourist season are the most difficult. It is imperative to book well in advance and reconfirm your bookings at every step along the way. Travel anywhere in Indonesia during the week of the Islamic Lebaran (Ramadan) holiday (usually around 14 or 15 March) is practically impossible. Find a nice spot and sit it out.

Getting Around in Sulawesi

Ujung Pandang is the best connected city in Sulawesi, and is the communications gateway for all of eastern Indonesia. This city receives flights from all over the archipelago. Manado also receives direct flights from major Indonesian

hubs, and Silk Air flies directly from Singapore.

From Ujung Pandang or Manado to the provincial capitals and Toraja—to Palu, to Rantetayo, to Kendari—air travel is the most efficient way to go, but for shorter hops airplanes are not necessarily the fastest way to travel. Although there are many smaller airstrips in Sulawesi, flight delays, schedule changes, over-bookings and cancelled flights are common. You must wait until you arrive, and there you might find that your onward flight is woefully over-committed.

In many cases, bus travel is much easier (and even faster!) than air travel, particularly as major roads in the region have improved tremendously over the past few years. Buses are frequent, cheap and fast— albeit crowded. You can usually get your hotel or *losmen* to arrange for your tickets, and alert the driver to pick you up. But be prepared—once you board, there could still be as much as another hour used up rounding up passengers in town. Use your judgement: if you get on early, when the bus is still almost empty, you get a good seat, but have to drive around town for an hour; if you get on late, when the bus is crowded, you get a lousy seat, but it cuts an hour off your travel time.

There are ferry connections between "mainland" Sulawesi and the islands of the Bonerate group, the Banggai group, the Togians and the Sangihe-Talaud islands to the north. On some of these, space is at a premium and the overnight rides are no fun at all.

Aside from the scheduled Pelni boats (see below), you have to take unscheduled ships to move around Sulawesi by sea. But for those with time, native boat travel around Sulawesi's is-

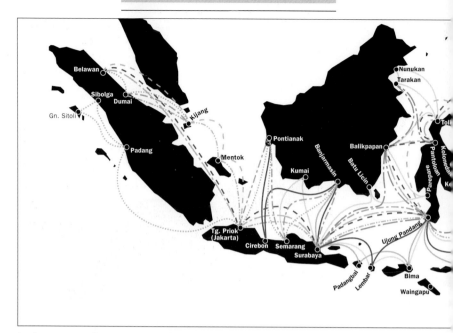

land groups can be a great experience. Bring food, drinks, a hat and enjoy the sea.

AIR TRAVEL

The cardinal rule is book early, confirm and reconfirm often. If you are told a flight is fully booked, go to the airport anyway and stand in line. While Garuda's booking system is computerized, the other airlines' are not, and bookings evaporate at the last minute all the time. However it is rare that flights are completely full. Always keep the following points in mind:

✈ It's practically impossible to get a confirmed booking out of a city other than the one you're in. You can buy a ticket and it may say you have a booking, but don't believe it until you reconfirm with the airline in the city of departure.

✈ Reconfirm bookings directly with the airline office in the city of departure between 24 and 72 hours before your flight, particularly during peak tourist seasons and Indonesian holidays. Your seat may be given away if you reconfirm either too early or too late (or not at all).

✈ Make bookings in person, not by phone. (Reconfirmations only can be done by phone.)

✈ Get written evidence of bookings. Note the name of the person who gives it to you so you can hold them responsible if you're later told you don't have one.

✈ Note the computer booking code. Names have a tendency to go astray or be misspelled. Concrete proof of your booking is essential.

✈ If your name isn't on the computer try looking under your first or middle names as these are frequently mistaken for surnames.

✈ If you are told a flight is full, go to the airport about two hours before departure and ask that your name be put on the waiting list. See that it is. Hang around the desk and be friendly to the staff and you will probably get on the flight. A tip will sometimes, but not always, help.

✈ There are usually alternate ways of getting from point A to B. For example, from Yogyakarta to Bali, if there is no space left on the flights, take a bus to Surakarta (Solo) and fly from there.

Garuda Indonesia's flagship airline has been in business for 45 years. It serves all major cities in Indonesia and at least 28 international destinations. They fly only jets, mainly wide-bodies, and the service is reasonably good. Head office is at Jl. Merdeka Selatan 13, ☎ (021) 2311801; fax: (021) 365986 with convenient sales counters in Hotel Indonesia, Hotel Borobudur and BDN Bldg., Jl. Thamrin 5. After normal office hours, tickets can be purchased in a small Garuda office on the 3rd floor of Wisma Dharmala Sakti, Jl. Sudirman 32 (open 24 hours).

Merpati A Garuda subsidiary, with a domestic network serving more than 160 airports throughout Indonesia. Merpati (literally "pigeon") flies smaller jets and turboprops (DC-9s, F-28s, and F-27s) as well as various propeller planes (DHC Twin-Otters, Casa CN-212s and CN-235s).

Merpati is not known for its punctuality or its service, but the airline does at least connect towns and villages all across Indonesia, in some cases landing on a grass airstrip in a highland village of only 100 people that would take days to reach by any other means. Consider yourself lucky that you can even fly to these places.

Merpati's standard baggage allowance is 20

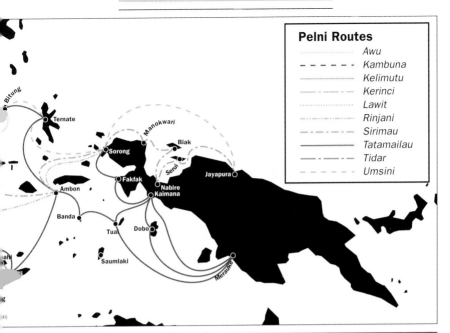

Pelni Routes

············· *Awu*
– – – – – – *Kambuna*
——————— *Kelimutu*
—·—·—·— *Kerinci*
················ *Lawit*
—··—··—··— *Rinjani*
—··—··—··— *Sirimau*
——————— *Tatamailau*
—·—·—·— *Tidar*
– – – – – *Umsini*

kilos for economy class, but some of the smaller aircraft permit only 10 kilos (after which excess baggage charges of $1 per kilo apply).

Students (12–26 years old) receive a discount of 25% (show an international student ID card), and children between the ages of 2 and 10 pay 50% of the regular fare. Infants not occupying a seat pay 10% of the regular fare.

Main office: Jl. Angkasa 2, Jakarta. ☎ (21) 424 3608; Fax: (21) 424 6616.

Sempati A new, privately-owned competitor on the scene, with quality service and a growing network inside and outside of Indonesia. Sempati flies new F-100s to several cities in Asia, such as Singapore, Kuala Lumpur, Bangkok, Hong Kong and Taipei.

Domestically they fly between major cities such as Jakarta, Yogya, Surabaya and Denpasar. Head office: Ground floor terminal building, Halim Perdana Kusuma Airport, Jakarta. ☎ (21) 809 4407; Fax: (21) 809 4420.

Bouraq A small, private company, flying mainly older planes linking cities in Sulawesi, as well as Bali, secondary cities in Java, Kalimantan, Nusa Tenggara, and other destinations. Main office: Jl. Angkasa 1–3, Jakarta. ☎ (21) 659 5364; Fax: 600 8729.

Mandala Operates a few prop planes to out-of-the-way airstrips in Sulawesi, Kalimantan and Sumatra. Main office: Jl. Garuda 76, Jakarta. ☎ (21) 424 9360; Fax: 424 9491.

NOTE: Travel agents often give cheaper fares than airline offices and are easily found. The best for ticketing are **Pacto** Jl. Surabaya 8, Menteng, Jakarta ☎ (21) 348 7447 and **Vayatour** Chase Plaza, Jl. Sudirman, Jakarta ☎ (21) 570 4119.

SEA TRAVEL

There is four times as much sea in Indonesia as land, and for many centuries transportation among the islands has been principally by boat. Tiny ports are scattered all over the archipelago, and the only way to reach many areas is by sea.

To travel by boat, you need plenty of time. Most ships are small, and are at the mercy of the sea and the seasons. Think of it as a romantic journey, and don't be in a hurry.

Pelni (Pelayaran Nasional Indonesia) the national passenger line, has 10 large ships (some 70 ships total) criss-crossing the archipelago carrying up to 1,500 passengers each. These boats travel on fixed schedules and the first and second class cabins are comfortable. Several Pelni boats ply routes that include ports in Sulawesi. Check the route map above and contact Pelni's main office for a current schedule.

Many of the older vessels look like floating trash cans, but the new German-built passenger ships are modern and comfortable. Fares are fixed, and there are up to 5 classes, with different numbers of people sharing each cabin, and different service.

Head office: 5th floor, Jl. Gajah Mada 14, Jakarta 10130. ☎ (21) 384 4342, 384 4366; Fax: (21) 385 4130. Main ticket office: Jl. Angkasa 18, Kemayoran ☎ 421 1921. Open in the mornings.

There are a myriad of other options. Rusty old **coastal steamers** ply the eastern islands, stopping at tiny ports to pick up copra, seaweed and other cash crops and deliver commodities like metal wares, fuel and the occasional outboard motor. You can book deck passage on one of these ships in just about any harbor, for very little money. If you do, stock up on food—you will quickly tire of the rice and salt fish that the crew eat. Bring a waterproof tarpaulin and a bag to protect your gear. You can often rent bunks from the crew, to get a comfortable night's sleep. Crowded **overnight ferries** connect smaller islands. Use your luggage to stake out a spot early, and bring a straw mat to lie on. It is usually best to stay on deck, where the fresh sea breezes keep your spirits up. Below deck tends to be noisy, verminous and smelly.

Small *perahu* can be rented in many areas for day trips upriver, around the coast, or to neighboring islands. These can be hired by the hour or by the trip, to take you snorkeling, sightseeing or birdwatching. Outboard motors are expensive in Indonesia, and tend to be small. Inspect any boat carefully before hiring it, as some craft are only marginally seaworthy. See if the boatman can rig up a canopy to block the blazing sun or the occasional cloudburst.

You could even book passage on a **luxury catamaran**. P&O Travel runs several boats through Indonesia, sometimes stopping at points in Sulawesi. There are either one- or two- week packages. Sample fares: 7 days. 6 nights: $1,983 based on double occupancy. 14 days, 13 nights, $3,655. Add 30% for suite. Add 50% for single occupancy. P&O representatives: **Abercrombie and Kent International Inc.** 1420 Kensington Road, Oak Brook, Illinois 60521-2106. ☎ (708) 954-2944, (800) 323-7308; fax: (708) 954-3324. Representative in UK: **Swan Hellenic Ltd.** 77 New Oxford Street, London WC1A 1PP. ☎ (071) 8311234; fax: (071) 8311280. Representative in Singapore: **P&O Travel(S) Pte. Ltd.** 80 Anson Road, IBM Towers Suite 31-01, Singapore 0207. ☎ 2247433; Fax: 2227925.

TRAVEL OVERLAND

Road conditions in Indonesia have improved dramatically over the past years, but traffic has also increased and driving is a slow and hazardous affair.

Trucks and buses, minivans, swarms of motorcycles piled with goods or carrying a family of four, ox-drawn carts, bicycles and pedicabs (*becak*) and pedestrians of all ages, compete in what is at times a crazy battle for tarmac, where the biggest and fastest rule.

Rental cars and motorcycles are available in many major cities, and a number of different types of buses run cheap and regular services.

Planning an Itinerary

The first thing to realize is that you can never cover the entire island even if you were to spend months here. Don't give yourself an impossibly tight schedule. Be aware that things happen slowly here, and adjust yourself to the pace. Better to spend more time in a few places and see them in a leisurely way, than to end up hot and bothered. You'll see *more* this way, not less.

Wherever you are, keep in mind that the tropical heat takes its toll and you should avoid the midday sun. Get an early start, before the rays become punishing (the tropical light is beautiful at dawn). Retreat to a cool place after lunch and go out again in the afternoon and early evening, when it's much more pleasant.

The Trans-Sulawesi Highway

The Trans-Sulawesi Highway (Transul), stretches over 1,800 km in a sweeping arc from Ujung Pandang in the south to Manado in the northeast. While much of this highway was, until recently, fit only for Camel Trophy rallies, the final sectin was completed just last year and now it is possible to make the whole run without ending up in an orthopedic ward; although it's still no smooth ride. (See map on the front endpapers.)

Big air-conditioned buses, previously used only between Gorontalo and Manado, now make extended runs, providing an inexpensive alternative to flying between the major cities of Ujung Pandang, Poso, Palu, Gorontalo and Manado.

The bus companies claim it's possible to cover Transul end-to-end in 60 hours (30 hours from Ujung Pandang to Palu; 30 more from there to Manado) but about 100 hours is much more likely, with half of the travel time at night. However, only a punishment freak would make the run straight through—the idea is to use parts of the road to get to interesting areas and then make side trips.

Some worthwhile sidetrips from the Transul: Kolonodale and the Morowali Reserve; Lake Poso and the Bada Valley megaliths; the central peninsula from Poso to the east; Palu and Donggala; the Gorontalo area along with Kotamobagu; and the Dumoga-Bone National Park. **Geography lesson** Throughout the length of the Transul Highway, the view from the bus window provides a continuous lesson in the geography, economics and daily life of Sulawesi. The terrain ranges from bone dry mountainous areas, where there are no settlements, to rich alluvial plains with an abundance of river water. These expanses of irrigated rice fields are worked by Javanese and Balinese transmigrants.

Heavily laden ox-drawn carts creak along the highway, past neatly uniformed children, who seem to spend most of their time walking to or from school. Weekly markets, which start at dawn and peter out around noon, are traffic-stopping beehives of activity, milling with brisk trade.

The sweet scent of cloves drifts into the bus as you pass plantations of this important cash crop. Lines of coconut palms flank the roadsides in many areas. The fallen nuts are split open to expose the meat, which is dried in the sun to become copra. This is then shipped to oil-extracting plants and processed into soap and cooking oil.

In the dusk's fading light, you may glimpse roadside volleyball games played by girls dressed in long skirts and *kerundung*, (Muslim headgear which covers the shoulders and has an oval opening for the face), or young men playing *sepak takraw* with a hollow rattan ball kicked or headed over a chest-high string.

North on the Transul The southern stretch of the Transul heads north out of Ujung Pandang, follows the east coast as far as Parepare, heads east to Pangkajene and Anabanua, and then up the east coast to Palopo. As most people begin their visit of Sulawesi from the Tator Toraja area, we will also start from there, on the side road which runs some 60 km east from Rantepao to join the Transul at Palopo. Try and get a seat in front or on the left side for the best views along this stretch.

The first 15 km out of Rantepao passes through scenery dotted with pine trees, rice fields, clumps of bamboo and some *tongkonan*. You may see miniature versions of these traditional Toraja houses on the roadside: these are temporary resting places for the deceased awaiting a proper funeral.

After passing the village of Nanggala, the road climbs to reach 1,100 m at the base of a telecoms building, 25 km from Rantepao. Here a huge valley opens to the sea, with thick vegetation covering near vertical mountainsides. The narrow road, hacked out of the cliff, has recently being widened and resurfaced.

Primary tropical rain forest clings to these mountains. Ferns grow in abundance near the summits, along with pandanus trees which stand out from the rest of the vegetation, on top of their complex root systems. Pandanus leaves are used to make rough mats.

Lower down, the clove trees are easy to spot. These bushy, pine cone shaped trees are related to the myrtle and have a solid mass of leaves from ground level up, with lighter colored leaves near the top. The lower valley vegetation includes cacao, banana and coconut trees.

Early morning fog often obscures the view of this valley. It's worth waiting it out in one of the roadside restaurants which face the gorge, about 35 km out of Rantepao. The fog usually dissipates between 9 and 10 am and there are plenty of *bemos* on to Palopo.

From Palopo, it's a flat 140-km stretch to Mangkutana, which lies east of Mount Balease (3,016 m). This is as good a time as any to catch up on some sleep. Leaving Palopo, the road passes through coastal rice fields, then swings inland to skirt the low deltas of the Rongkong and Balease rivers.

This section passes through coastal rice fields, then swings inland past coconut and oil palm plantations, and plenty of kapok trees. In Mangkutana there are several *losmen* offering rudimentary accommodations. Early morning markets are held twice a week, on Thursdays and Sundays.

The run from Mangkutana and Pendolo, on the southern shore of Lake Poso, was formerly the worst section of the highway by far, and the rough road was often washed out or blocked by boulders. The stretch is still prone to landslides after heavy rains, fallen trees, or oncoming trucks at blind switchbacks.

The road heads out of Mangkutana over hills and across a plain with lots of oil palms, hybrid coconut trees and large kapoks. Sit to the left of the bus for the best views. It's a steep climb until the road tickles the 1,250 m mark, where perpendicular valleys fall away below and mountain tops tower above. As you cross the border between South and Central Sulawesi, at Sulteng, a roadside marker indicates 586 km to Ujung Pandang and 385 km to Palu.

This new road provides the region's more remote areas with access to markets and you can see land at high elevations which has recently been cleared for agriculture. After a steep descent, Lake Poso appears across a wide, flat plain in the distance.

From Pendolo (515 m), the highway runs through the hills to the east, with the lake remaining out of sight all the way to Tentena. About half way there, a side road from Taripa leads to Kolonodale and the Morowali Reserve.

Tentena, about 5 km off the highway on the northern tip of the lake, is becoming popular with travelers as a base for visiting Lake Poso, and as the most convenient starting point for treks to the Bada Valley. From the Tentena turnoff, the highway gradually descends to the seaside town of Poso, which has an airstrip and harbour. You can take a passenger ship to Gorontalo from here, via Ampana and the Togian Islands, or travel east over a long (388 km) road to Luwuk in 18 to 24 hrs by bus. You can also fly to Palu if you're in a hurry.

Detour to Palu From Poso, it's a flat 190 km to Toboli, a village which has the only turn-off west to Palu, the capital of Sulteng (Central Sulawesi). This 70 km side road via Tawaeli to Palu offers some spectacular scenery and is worth a detour. West of Toboli the road cuts across rice fields and then, looming in the distance, are the mountains marking the end of the rich coastal plain. Many Balinese farmers have settled here, and the roadside is lined with house temples, often in garish colors never seen in Bali.

Beyond the rice fields, the road rises steeply into the mountains. Gouged out of jungle and rock, it climbs to 850 m then plunges down again to sea level at Palu Bay, less than 50 km away. Like the Mangkutana–Pendolo stretch, here again there is the possibility of landslides, and close calls at blind curves.

The steep mountainous ascent, with views down vertiginous valleys, is empty of human occupants—but you may catch a glimpse of the magnificent hornbills which frequent the region. The road reaches its highest point in the highland area known as Kebun Kopi, (coffee garden or estate) from colonial times. There are clusters of small villages here. Cloves and vegetables are the principal crops today, and road stalls piled with cabbage, carrots, and lettuce.

On the Palu side, the steep descent through increasingly drier countryside is also devoid of settlements until the bayside town of Tawaeli. From here, a long road heads north to Tolitoli while the main road continues to Palu through a hot and arid coastal plain.

Toboli to Gorontalo This leg is a long one, covering just over 600 km. The early start required for this section is amply rewarded by dawn breaking over Tomini Bay. This can be spectacular, with the blood red sunrise reflected in the calm water and silhouettes of fishermen.

Some 90 km north of Toboli, just before Sigenti, the highway crosses the equator, marked by a tall stand topped by a metal sculpture in the shape of Central Sulawesi. From here the landscape is flat until the road heads inland and rises to 300 m to cut through a clove growing area before dropping down again to the sea at Moutong, just before the border with North Sulawesi province.

The highway wanders from the sea as it nears Marisa, which is on the coast surrounded by the Randangan-Panua Reserve, then wanders inland again crossing dry country. Small wooden carts are used here to haul plastic containers of water, a precious commodity. After long stretches of parched land, lush green sugar cane plantations (recently planted to supply a new sugar mill) come as a relief. At Isimu, a 30-km side road heads east for the city of Gorontalo and a well-deserved rest.

You don't have to tough it out this far if you don't want to—there are losmen in at least three places along the way: Tinombo, Moutong and Marisa. There may not be electricity after 10 or 11 am, but who cares?

Gorontalo to Manado Unfortunately, the big, comfortable buses which make the 12-hour (420km) trip from Gorontalo to Manado run only at night—when Indonesians like to travel. This may change in the future, but for now the only way to see the beautiful coastal scenery along this route is to take a local bus from Gorontalo to Bintauna, spend the night in a very basic penginapan called Safari, and take another local bus to Manado the next day. The best views are from the left side of the bus.

Once you finally get started from Gorontalo (usually an hour or two after you expect to), the road backtracks west via Isimu and traverses the low and rather drab limestone hills at the narrowest part of the long peninsula. A monu-ment to a Dutchman perches on a high rock before Molinggapoto. Locals say he died on the spot where this road begins its 150-m switchback drop to the sea.

The road passes Kwandang village, then rises over low hills and finally drops down to the sea, where it hugs the coast for some 100 km. On sunny days there are stunning vistas of light turquoise waters blending into the deep blue ocean, with the occasional island coming into view then receding as you speed onwards.

Boroko, set in an almost circular harbor, was a port in Dutch times but has now lost much of its maritime importance. Further on, past Bintauna village, the road crosses the wide Sangkup River, 250 km southwest of Manado. The Safari restaurant and penginapan, a couple of hundred meters beyond, marks the end of the bus run. This place is very basic, but cheap: $1 for a full meal; another $1 for a bed.

The next day starts with more beautiful coastline, sweeping around the bays of this hilly peninsula. The biggest of these, Uki Bay, is dotted with fishing platforms, with Baturapa village nestles on its edge. The best of the coastal scenery stops around Lolak village, shortly before the turnoff to Kotamobagu.

The rest of the run to Manado runs flat along the seaside, rising only as the road heads inland before the final descent into Manado. As the road drops, the islands off Manado spring into view, and the province's capital lies sprawling around the head of the bay.

—Kal Muller

Night Express Buses—*Bis Malam*

The preferred mode of transportation for Indonesians, these buses operate only at night. Available in a wide variety of classes: from the public *patas* air-conditioned with reclining seats (crowded, run by the army) to the ultra-luxurious "Big Top" buses that run from Jakarta (these have seats like business class airline seats).

The better buses have a bathroom and arctic air-conditioning: the other reason you brought a sweater. The key to successful *bis malam* trips is sleep. Choose the best bus available as the price difference is usually not very great, and justifiable in that a good sleep is saving you a night's accommodations.

Most buses are fitted with televisions and show movies whether you want them or not, often followed by music. You are likely to be the only one who is annoyed by the volume, but a cheerful suggestion that the music be turned off (*dimatikan*) will at least get it turned down to the point where earplugs can block out the rest. The seats to avoid are in the very front and the very back. The back seats are raised up over the engine and don't recline, while front row seats give you too intimate a view of what the driver is doing.

There are also karaoke "sing-along" buses—

for masochists and anthropologists only.
These buses leave in late afternoon and go
all night, and often well into the next day. When
bis malam cross from island to island, they go
on the ferry. Tickets are sold at the bus terminal, or by agents, and there are usually a number of different buses going your way. Shop
around, to see what you are getting.
You can also buy two seats, which will make
sure you don't get squashed. The price is cheap
enough that most budgets can handle two fares.
If possible, get the two front seats next to the
driver, as you get the best view from there. Or
at least get a window seat. On many buses, you
can reserve one day ahead. Always see if your
hotel or *losmen* can make the bookings for
you; this is a common practice, particularly in
Sumbawa and Flores.

Local Buses

The major advantages of these rattling buses
is that they are extremely cheap, run every few
minutes between major towns, and can be
picked up at the terminals or any point along their
routes. This is also their biggest disadvantage:
they stop constantly.
If you depart from a terminal, find a seat near
a window that opens. Try not to share this
breeze with passengers behind you; they are
likely to have a strong aversion to wind for fear
of *masuk angin* (the wind which enters the body
and causes a cold).
The seats are very small, both in terms of leg
room and width. You and your bag may take up
(and be charged for) two seats. This is fair. But
be sure you're not being overcharged for not
knowing any better. The key is to know better.
Ask someone what the proper fare is to your destination before getting on. A few words of Indonesian are indispensable to be able to ask
for directions. People are generally very eager
to help you.
Larger towns have city buses charging nominal fares, usually Rp300 (15¢). Flag them down
wherever you see them. The catch is knowing which
one to take as there are no maps or guides.

Express Minibuses —*Mikrolet*

These come in two varieties: old and hot (sit by
a window and keep it open) and the newer, much
revered, L300 van with air-conditioning. Even the
L300 gets a lot of engine heat, and at midday
can still be sauna-like: especially if the air-
conditioning is broken and the windows shut.
These 8 to 11 passenger vans connect major
cities and deliver you right to your destination.
They sometimes also pick you up. They usually
travel during the day, though on longer routes
they travel at night like the *bis malam*. Express
minibuses are slightly more expensive than *bis
malam* but more convenient.

Local Minibuses —*Bemo*

These non–air-conditioned vans ("*bemo*") are the
real workhorses of the transport network, going
up and down even relatively impassable mountain tracks to deliver villagers and produce all
over the island. Regular seats are supplemented
by wooden benches, boosting the capacity of
these sardine cans to 25. And there is *always*
room for more. Take a seat up front with the driver whenever possible.
There are standard fares but these are flexible to account for how much room you and your
bag are taking up. Ask someone before flagging
one down if you are concerned by the potential
Rp100 price gouging. Flag one down on any roadside. You can also charter one to most destinations. Just say "charter" and where you want to
go, then bargain for the fare in advance.

Car Rentals

At first glance the unwritten driving rules of
Indonesia seem like a maniacal free-for-all. It is
only later that the subtle hierarchy (truck vs. car:
you lose) and finesse (2-centimeter tolerances)
become evident. This is as good a reason as
any that self-drive car rentals are rare. Sedans
are available in Jakarta but are very expensive.
In Bali, various companies offer self-drive cars,
for reasonable rates. In Sulawesi, self-drive
cars (usually Toyota Landcruisers) are quite expensive, if you can even find one. To drive in Indonesia you need a valid international license.
Traffic here moves on the left, British style.

Chartering a Car or Minibus

This can be the best way to handle a land tour as
you have the freedom to stop whenever things look
interesting and the flexibility to try out some less
traveled routes. This can also be an economical
alternative if you can fill up a van. The minibus can
take up to 7, but you need extra space if you are
to be in it for a few days, so 5 passengers is generally maximum.
Some asking around will quickly give you an
idea of where to hire a driver and what the local
going rates are for a specific excursion or longer
itinerary. A full day of driving one-way will cost
from $50 to $80 and a five-day trip around
$300. Much of this is for fuel, so distance is a
major factor. Most of the rest goes to the owner
of the vehicle, and only a tiny percentage left
for the driver. It is understood that you will pay
for the driver's meals and accommodations
both while he is with you and on his journey back
home. A tip of Rp5,000 per day is also appreciated if the driver is good.
The quality of both the driver and the vehicle
will figure heavily in the enjoyability of your trip
so don't be shy about checking both out before
striking a deal.

1 Ujung Pandang PRACTICALITIES

Most visitors to South Sulawesi simply pass through Ujung Pandang on their way to Tana Toraja, perhaps staying overnight in order to catch the morning bus or plane. But the city—for almost five hundred years the gateway to the fabled "Spice Islands" of the eastern archipelago—has much to offer the interested visitor: Shopping, historical sites, and a bustling urban setting.

Prices in US dollars. S = Single; D = Double; T = Triple; AC = Air-conditioning. Telephone code for Ujung Pandang is 411 (0411 within Indonesia).

Ujung Pandang is the capital and administrative center of the province of South Sulawesi, a city where development experts and international bankers gather to plan the island's future. Yet the city still maintains a relaxed, unhurried atmosphere. Many of the large grassy areas have been preserved from the Dutch period, but traffic is thick all day. (See color map pg. 69.)

GETTING THERE

Ujung Pandang's Hasanuddin (International) Airport, the gateway to eastern Indonesia, is well connected to the rest of the archipelago.

By Air

The airport is 25 km (16 mi) north of town on the road to Maros, half an hour's drive. The information counter at the airport keeps a list of hotels and telephone numbers, but you will have to ask for this. Certain hotels are strongly promoted. The Makassar Golden Hotel and the Marannu City Hotel have offices at the airport. There is a telegraph and telephone office (open 8 am–6 pm) and a coin-operated phone booth, as well as a money changer, restaurant and snack bar. Pay at the airport for an irresponsibly fast half-hour taxi ride into town ($6 or $8 AC), or walk 500 meters to the main road and catch a *bemo* for $1 including luggage.

Garuda Jl. Slamet Rijadi 6, ☎ 317350, 322705, 322804. Three daily flights to Jakarta $150, one daily to Bali, $60, two weekly midnight flights to Jayapura $270.

Mandala Komp. Latanette Plaza D7, Jl. Sungai Saddang ☎ 324288. Two weekly flights to Surabaya ($75), Jakarta ($120) and Ambon ($75).

Bouraq Jl. Veteran Selatan #1, ☎ 851906. Daily flights to Palu ($49), Gorontalo ($112), Balikpapan ($64).

Sempati at the Makassar Golden Hotel ☎ 311-612. With three daily flights to Surabaya ($92); daily to Palu ($65) and twice daily to Jakarta

($145). Daily flights to Ambon ($162) and Jayapura ($250), and twice weekly to Kendari ($76).

Merpati Jl. Gn Bawakaraeng 109, ☎ 234114, 324118, 323086. With four flights daily to Surabaya ($96) and Jakarta ($150); three daily to Ambon ($105); twice daily to Jayapura ($245); daily to Balikpapan ($80), Biak ($185), Bali ($75), Palu ($65) and Tana Toraja ($40); if enough passengers, two flights a week to Buton ($82) and Pomalaa ($55). Although it is improving, Merpati efficiency leaves much to be desired, especially in the more out-of-the-way places where they have no competition.

By Sea

Ships to and from many Indonesian ports stop at the Sukarno-Hatta harbor in the center of Ujung Pandang. Twelve of the national Pelni line's large ships stop at Ujung Pandang (see "Transportation" pg. 237), and if you speak Indonesian, you can catch a *perahu* to just about anywhere in Indonesia. Travel is slow: most of your time will be spent waiting for the boat to leave.

PELNI

Twelve Pelni ships call at Ujung Pandang. Seven of these can hold 2,000 passengers each; each of the other five carry 1,000. These ships were designed to move people around the archipelago economically, and are not luxury "love-boats." Fares depend on distances traveled, and are considerably cheaper than flying. For example, first class passage from Ujung Pandang to Jakarta runs $102, second class $75, third class $56, fourth class $43 and economy class $26. A flight between the cities costs $150. First class cabins, quite small, hold two passengers. The number of people per cabin increases as the fare and class decreases, until you reach the sprawling dormitories of economy class.

While it's cheap and leisurely, Pelni-travel can be inconvenient: the ships' schedules seldom coincide with yours. Plan ahead if you expect to travel by ship. The larger boats are on fixed schedules of 14 days while it's 14 or 28 days for the smaller ones. These smaller ships have only first and second class, plus economy. Also, the routes are not always convenient. For example, on its Ujung Pandang–Bali run, the 1,000-passenger *Awu* first calls at Bima, Sumbawa, which jacks up the first-class fare to the price of a flight: $75 (second class $48; economy $18).

Pelni Just off the harbor at Jl. Martadinata 38. With the port expansion hogging land, the office will probably have to move. If it proves impossible to obtain your ticket, try one of the many re-seller shops around the Pelni office. They charge a premium of about 25%, but save you lots of frustration.

By Land

There is daily bus service to and from all the major towns in South Sulawesi. Getting out of Ujung Pandang, however, can be a hassle.

Coaches and minibuses to other towns leave from terminal Pasar Daya at km 15. Allow at least a half hour for the journey. First take a *bemo* (Rp150) or *becak* (Rp500–Rp1,000) to Sentral (the central *bemo* terminus) and from there a second *bemo* to Panaikan. From here, buses leave regularly throughout the day for major towns in South Sulawesi, leaving as late as 7 pm.

If you want a good seat on a comfortable coach, it is better to book tickets at the bus companies' offices in town, but if you simply turn up at Panaikan you are almost certain to get a seat. Minibuses are faster, but rather cramped.

Fares are very reasonable: to Soppeng and Bone $2, to Singkang $2.50. The journeys take four and five hours respectively. Buses for Toraja leave at 7 am, 9:30 am, 1 pm and 5 pm: the fare is $4 and the journey takes 8 hours.

Liman Express (Jl. Laiya 25), and **Litha & Co.** (Jl. Gunung Merapi 160) are two of the better bus companies.

TRANSPORTATION IN TOWN

Self-drive cars and Toyota Land Cruisers are difficult to find, and expensive to rent. Taxis can be hired through most hotels for about $40/day.

Bemo The best way to get around is by *bemo* ("pete-pete" in local slang). The drivers are usually helpful and will tell you which *bemo* to stop, and where to get off. It helps to know a few words of Indonesian. The fare in town is Rp300 for any distance. The station is on Jl. Cokroaminoto.

Becak For Rp500–Rp1,000, you can travel by *becak* to almost any part of the city. Ignore the coaches and lorries bearing down on you as your driver executes a sudden turn across a two-lane highway; the best policy is not to look. Arrange the price before you set off, and check that the driver knows where you want to go to, which is hardly ever the case. Many of the dri-

vers are from the impoverished south and their knowledge of Ujung Pandang is hazy.

Taxi services are provided by Bosowa ☎ 311311 (blue cars), Amal ☎ 313131 (white cars), Mallomo ☎ 442200 and Mankasara.

ACCOMMODATIONS

Lodging in Ujung Pandang is expensive by Indonesian standards. At the lower end of the scale there are many cheap *penginapan* around the port area, but these are not recommended. Most of the larger hotels add 21% service and tax; smaller ones may add 10%. Location is important: Ujung Pandang can be trouble to get around if you have to walk long distances in the heat, or bargain constantly with non–English-speaking *becak* drivers.

Budget (below $20)

Afiat Jl. Bandar Udara Hasanuddin 1, Mandai (Right at the entrance to the airport on the road to Ujung Pandang), ☎ 510724. 20 rms. Restaurant, Chinese-Indonesian menu. A convenient and reasonably priced hotel from which to make forays into town. $12–$16S, $21–$25D, AC.

Kenari Pantai Jl. Somba Opu 289, ☎ 872183, 852352. 15 rms. Good location on the beachfront boulevard, opposite the Taman Sari which serves passable seafood. Excellent staff, some English. Good (free) snacks, breakfast included. Recommended. $15–$20S, $19–$24D.

Legend Hostel Jl. Jampea 5G (Jampea Plaza), ☎ 328203. 4 rms ($6) and 12 dormitory style bunk beds ($2.50). A place low-budget travelers can call their own. Clean, and the best value in town. Helpful staff who can arrange everything from trips to Toraja to sailing in a cargo *pinisi*. Great T-shirts, cheap laundry, book exchange. They take care of some orphan street kids—you can help by donating old clothes, anything. Sunday all-day snorkeling trip with kids to Samalona Island costs $4, including lunch.

Makassar Cottage Jl. Dangko 50–52, ☎ 873-559. 16 Bugis-style cottages or rooms. Inconveniently far from town center, but close to Sombaopu for history buffs. Frequented by local Chinese businessmen seeking R & R. Restaurant serves inexpensive dishes. $13–$19, S or D.

Pulau Samalona Island Resort (12 rooms/cottages), a 25 minute boat ride from the city for those who want to get away from it all. Contact the Aksa Utama Samalona Travel Agency, Artis Building, Jl. Lompobattang 3, ☎ 312838. Call them from the airport for a free ride into town if you are going to stay at Samalona. They were also planning to open a dormitory-style hostel on the island, $3 per person. Cottages: $4–$15S, $6–$20D. Meals $1.50–$5, rental of snorkeling gear $3, boat rental $3–6 per hour.

Ramayana Satrya Jl. Gn. Bawakaraeng 121.

☎ 442478; fax: 442479. 65 rms. This hotel offers direct bus service to the Wisma Maria in Rantepao. $6–$14 S; $10–$16 D, some AC.

Virgo Jl. Sumba 109, ☎ 321451, 322244. 40 rms. Fairly centrally located. No restaurant, but you can eat at the budget Samalona or Lumayan restaurants nearby on Jl. Samalona. $10–$15 S, $12–$16 D.

Wisata Inn Jl. Hasanuddin 36–38, ☎ 324344; fax: 312783. Quiet with pleasant staff. Price inclusive of breakfast. $15–$20 S, $17–$26 D.

Wisma Tiatira House Jl. Dr Sutomo 25, ☎ 318-948. 15 rms. A pleasant little hotel just ten minutes from the center of town on a quiet street. $12–$15 S, $15–$20 D.

Intermediate ($20–$50)

Delia Orchid Park Km 6, Jl. Urip Sumohardjo. ☎ 442325. 22 rms. Contact in Ujung Pandang: Delia Florist and catering, Jl. Bawakaraeng 57, ☎ 318219, 323967. Inconveniently located off the main road north out of Ujung Pandang (it's closer to the airport than to the harbor: make sure your driver knows the location!), but this place is a haven for orchid lovers. Also many other plants on the premises. Beautifully built and landscaped, all modern indoor facilities, very clean. $20–$40 S or D.

Losari Beach Jl. Penghibur 10, ☎ 326062; fax: 319611; telex: 71306 ARIES IA. 60 rms. The most expensive rooms look out to sea, across busy Jl. Penghibur. TVs with satellite reception in all rooms. Lobby bar with piano music 7:30–10:30 pm except Sunday. Travel agency on the premises. Free airport transfer on request. All rooms AC: $33–$68 S, $43–$78 D.

Losari also has a guesthouse half a block away on the same street, located just above two restaurants with live music/karaoke. Rooms here go for $10–$38 S or D.

Makassar City (65 rooms), Jl. Chairil Anwar 28. ☎ 317055; fax: 311818; telex: 71526 MCHUP IA. 65 rms. Coffee shop, bar and restaurant. A cozy hotel located in the commercial center of Ujung Pandang offering a useful range of services, including a drug store. Pleasant staff. $10–$45 S, $48 D; $63–$68 suite.

Pasanggarahan Makassar Jl. Somba Opu 297. ☎ 872616, 854218. 40 rms. A real seaside hotel, with a restaurant serving Chinese-Indonesian food. Breezy and clean, with pleasant and helpful staff. All AC, $25 S, $35 D.

Pondok Suada Indah Jl. Sultan Hasanuddin 12. ☎ 317179; fax: 312856. 12 rms. A cavernous hotel, centrally located but overpriced. Breakfast is included; service is decidedly unimpressive. All AC, $20–$25 S, $25–$30 D. The Marannu City Hotel is directly opposite.

Widhana Jl. Botolempangan 53, ☎ 321393. 25 rms. Bar and restaurant, Western, Chinese and Indonesian menu. A modern, clean, and dark hotel ten minutes south of the city center. All

AC. $15–$25 S, $20–$30 D.

Luxury ($50 and up)

There are two international-standard hotels in Ujung Pandang. The Makassar Golden is well located, but the Victoria is quieter and offers excellent service.

Kenari Jl. Yosep Latumahina 30. ☎ 874250, 852353; fax: 872126. Set lunch $8, set dinner $10. Lounge with soft piano music, business centre, limousine service and karaoke. $75 S or D, $150 suite.

Makassar Golden Jl. Pasar Ikan 50–52. ☎ 314-408; fax: 320951; telex: 71290 MGHUP IA. Spectacularly situated on the waterfront in the center of town, with views of the offshore islands. Coffee shop, bar and restaurants, swimming pool. Magnificent sunsets from the Toraja-style terrace restaurant. Free transport to the airport (with reservation). Major credit cards. $66–$95 S, $85–$110 D, $150–$390 suite.

Marannu City Jl. Sultan Hasanuddin 3–5, ☎ 315087, and **Marannu Tower** Jl. Kajaolalido 16, ☎ 327051. Fax for both: 319934; telex for both: 71303 MARANU IA. 400 rms between both hotels. These two hotels are adjacent, and share facilities. Centrally located, just 10 mins walk from the harbor, fort and main post office. Three restaurants serving Chinese and Indonesian food (set lunch $9.50; dinner, $12), coffee shop and bars. Disco and billiard room. Small swimming pool. (Non-guests can use the pool for $2, including towel). Major credit cards. Free airport transfers. All AC. $65–$85 S, $80–$95 D, $140–$600 suite.

Victoria Panghegar Jl. Jendral Sudirman 24. ☎ 311863; fax: 312468. 115 rms. Bar and restaurant, coffee shop, swimming pool. This luxurious, privately owned hotel offers a range of services, from safety deposit boxes to chauffeur-driven cars. Free transport from airport and seaport upon request. Major credit cards accepted. $50–$80 S, $70–$90 D.

DINING

The main attraction of eating out in Ujung Pandang is the seafood: huge shrimps and lobsters, dark-skinned fish with delicate white flesh, and giant, juicy crabs. The best cooking is usually the simplest. The true local specialty is *ikan bakar*, fresh fish lightly cooked over a charcoal brazier. The fresh-water crab and the local fish are a bargain. Strangely, tea and coffee are usually quite awful: although some of the best coffee in the world is grown in the mountains behind Palopo, little ever reaches Ujung Pandang. Really cold beer (ask to feel the bottle) is the perfect accompaniment to seafood: Bir Bintang is streets ahead of its cheaper rivals Anker and San Miguel. Or try refreshing *jeruk nipis*, freshly squeezed lime juice with sugar and ice.

Seafood

Aroma Mattoangin Jl. Gunung Latimojong. Standard Indonesian menu of chicken and *ikan bakar* at reasonable prices. There are several similar restaurants on Jl. Gunung Latimojong, popular with budget travelers.
Asia Baru Jl. Salahutu. Grilled prawns and fish.
Rumah Makan Pacific Jl. Kerungkerung 5A. Grilled fish $1.50–$4 (according to type and size), prawns $2–$2.50, lobster (when available) $3.50–$7.50, crab $2–$3, and Indonesian and Chinese dishes $1.50–$2.
Bamboo Den Jl. Gunung Latimojong. Coldest beer in town. Ask for a bottle from the green refrigerator—the jacket of ice melts while you drink. Wide range of saccharin-sweet seafood dishes in a dark, AC room, accompanied by loud music and *karaoke*. Expensive at $20–$30 for two. Better to sit outside with your drink and sample their ice creams. Pleasant, efficient service.
Restaurant Ujung Pandang Jl. Irian 42. Live singing. Expatriate residents rate the *saus kepiting* (freshwater crab in sauce) even more highly than Surya's. Prices are similar: $10 per head including drinks. Try the grilled *baronang* (rabbitfish), at $3.25 enough for two; adding veggies, rice and Aqua, two can eat for $7. Other dishes include crab ($5), shrimp ($2–$4), squid ($2.50). Non–seafood dishes include chicken, goat or water–buffalo *sate* at $2–$3 per 10 brochettes, as well as Chinese dishes, including frog, at $2–$4. Many local Chinese eat here; the best kind of recommendation.
Rumah Makan Aroma Labbakang Jl. Chairil Anwar. Delicious *udang kukus* (steamed shrimps with lime) for just $3. Also worth trying are the *ikan baronang* ($3) and the *ikan bandeng* ($4). Strongly recommended.
Surya Super Crab Jl. Nusakambangan 16. The best-known crab restaurant in Ujung Pandang. The Super Crab ($4) comes in a gluey sweet sauce, but the crab is delicious, and one serving is enough for two people. The *cumi-cumi mentega* (squid in margarine) is enough to induce diabetes. Refuse the bottled *sambal* and ask for some freshly chopped chili in soy sauce. Try the garlic shrimps ($4), the shark's-fin and crab soup ($12.50) and the squid in batter ($3). The *kangkong* (water spinach) is delicious. Pork, chicken and vegetable dishes are available.

Local Food

At night the food stalls on the waterfront along Jl. Penghibur stretch for more than a kilometer. This is where the ordinary people of Ujung Pandang eat: *bakso, mi goreng, mi kuah, gado-gado* and freshly-grilled *ikan bakar*, served with the minimum of fuss and eaten sitting cross-legged along the sea front wall.

Most famous is *coto Makassar*, a spicy soup made from bits of water buffalo: lungs, intestines, liver and tripe. Located at Jl. Ranggong, devotees go a long way for the most renowned stalls. For dessert, try delicious *pisang epe*, grilled honeyed banana, an Ujung Pandang specialty, or saunter up to the ice cream and cake shop outside the Golden Makassar Hotel for real ice cream at just 60 cents a cone. Flavors include durian, *salak* and *lychee* as well as the more familiar mocha, chocolate and strawberry. Good *murtabak*, a delicious Indian folded omelet, can be found near the mosque. Alternatively, eat in one of the inexpensive restaurants facing the food stalls on the other side of Jl. Penghibur.

Japanese Restaurant

Shogun Jl. Penghibur 2, ☎ 324102. The first authentic Japanese restaurant in Sulawesi, run by owner-chef Kiyosumi Nishikawa. Some ingredients from Japan, but mostly very fresh local fish. Excellent quality and authentic, reasonably priced dishes. Try their sushi and anything else on their menu. Cold beer or real sake. Expect to pay about $10–$15 per person.

Western Food

Donald Bakery and Ice Cream Jl. Karunrun (at the southern end of Jl. Sutomo). A wide range of rolls and cakes and good tea and coffee. The perfect place for breakfast if you are staying at the nearby Wisma Tiatira House.
Golden Ice Cream and Pastry Shop In front of the Golden Makassar Hotel. Sells a variety of delicious ice cream at 60¢ a cone, inside apple pie and good, sticky Danish pastries.
Kantin Murah Dan Baik ("The Good and Cheap Canteen") on the same floor as KFC, above the Gelael Supermarket on Jl. Sultan Hasanuddin. Tasty Indonesian food at very reasonable prices.
Kentucky Fried Chicken has a large AC restaurant over the Gelael Supermarket on Jl. Sultan Hasanuddin, close to the Marannu Hotel. Rival **California Fried Chicken** is on the floor above Gloria Supermarket, Jl. Panakkukang Mas Boulevard, far from the city center.
Modern Bakery (formerly Holland Modern Bakery) On the corner of Jl. Bawakaraeng and Jl. Gunung Latimojong. Breakfast of sweet rolls with raisins and chocolate rice topping, with bad tea and coffee. $2–$3.

NIGHTLIFE

Nightlife in Ujung Pandang is surprisingly good. Apart from the usual establishments for sailors, there are many respectable bars and places of entertainment. Many feature "beer girls" who will fetch and pour your beer, making sure to keep your glass full. These girls are not hostesses, but are employed by the beer companies and receive a small commission from every bottle sold. Unlike the ordinary staff, these girls know where the coldest bottles are. Just ask for the girl selling your favorite brand.

An excellent place to begin a night tour of Ujung Pandang is the **Kios Semarang** on Jl. Penghibur, a favorite watering hole for the Western expat community. Go to the top floor for the best view of the sea and the mile-long row of foodstalls below, or try the quieter **Kios Makassar** next door.

After dinner at a good seafood restaurant, stroll along the stalls along the seafront, or play a game of billiards with the locals in the **Marannu City Hotel**, or **Blue Ocean**, Jl. Nusantara. There are several discos; the best is probably the Marannu's. The Makassar Golden Hotel has live music on the terrace.

Film fans will enjoy the newly opened **Studio 21 complex** on Jl. Ratulangi, which has several theaters and shows Western and Asian Films for $3. Bring a sweater: the air-conditioning is powerful. The soft padded chairs will leave you sore for a week, and the reels may not shown in the order you remember, but none of this seems to bother the locals.

But the real Ujung Pandang action is in the *karaoke* lounges. If you have never sung in public before, this is the place to start. The largely Japanese expatriate audience will applaud your most hesitant performance and even pay for your songs (a small charge is levied). If you completely flub it, your beer girl will hum the tune. The top *karaoke* spot is the **Irani** (5th floor) at the south end of Jl. Somba Opu.

At night it is a regular disco, but during the day visitors with kids might try the **Jumbo Roller Disco** on Jl. Timur, a roller skating disco with western music. Skates can be rented.

SHOPPING

Some of the things you will find in the shops along Jl. Pasar Ikan, Jl. Somba Opu and Jl. Pasar Baru: gaudy silks from Soppeng, old cotton weavings from the remote mountains of Rongkong, smoke-blackened Toraja bamboo *tuak* containers (some perhaps a century old), decorated black earthenware pots from Barombong, fake Dutch and real Spanish silver coins (dozens dated 1759), elaborately carved wooden Toraja trays and engraved bamboo containers, antique porcelain and 14th-century *celadon* stoneware—looted by grave robbers and prohibited from export.

Somba Opu is the street of the gold and silver workers; the delicate filigree jewelry is called Kendari silver, although today it is mostly made in Ujung Pandang. Filigree silver haircombs sell for $15 and elegant earrings for $5. The silver is about 80% pure and will darken over time, but the work is exquisite. Antique silver can still be picked up in some of the shops; if you are fortunate, you may find an antique silver *cache-sexe*;

all that the young daughters of the Makassar nobility wore until puberty. Try the **Kanebo Art Shop**, at the head of Jl. Somba Opu. Here and elsewhere, bargain like mad. At the **Pertenunan Sutera Alam** you can buy silk men's shirts for $40, silk ties for $7.50; matching *sarong* and *selendang* for $40–$60 and cuts of solid-colored silk at $10–$15 per meter. Open every day except Sunday 8 am to 8 pm.

MEDICAL

The **Rumah Sakit Akademis** and the **Rumah Sakit Stella Maris** are the best hospitals in Ujung Pandang; hospitals outside the capital offer only basic medical attention.

Should you require emergency treatment, **Dr Louis Rajawane** at the Rumah Sakit Akademis is a highly-regarded surgeon. **Dr Santa Jota** on Jl. Baumasepe is a Dutch-trained cardiologist and internist. His hours are 4–7 pm daily. **Dr Sedjawidada** (who works at the Rumah Sakit Stella Maris) is an ear, nose and throat specialist. If you need a good orthopedist who speaks English, contact **Dr Chaeruddin Rasyad** (Jl. Lanto Dg Pasewang 32, ☎ 854739).

The largest pharmacy in Ujung Pandang is **Kimia Firma** (Jl. Ahmad Yani) which is open 24 hrs; generally a prescription is not required.

TRAVELERS' SERVICES

The money changer **Haji La Tunrung** on Jl. Monginsidi 42, just north of the fort, offers a similar rate to the banks, no service charge.

Jameson's Supermarket and Restaurant, Jl. Irian 147–9 and **Gelael Supermarket** in Jl. Sultan Hasanuddin stock a wide range of Western products and food. Jameson's restaurant on the second floor serves Western and dishes; it also has a salad bar.

The **Tourist Information Office** is inconveniently located on Jl. Panggeran Petta Rani. Unless you stop in on your way in from the airport it is hardly worth the journey to collect the odd hotel brochure and inaccurate street map of Ujung Pandang.

The **General Post office** is at Jl. Slamet Riyadi 10. The **Telephone** and **Telex** are at Jl. Balaikota 2 and Jl. Jend. Sudirman.

TRAVEL AGENCIES

There are many travel agencies in Ujung Pandang catering to local needs, and a fair number concentrating on foreign visitors. All specialize in tours to Tana Toraja, offering roughly similar prices for the same number of days and similar standards of accommodations. Aside from Tanah Toraja, agencies offer city tours and trips of varying lengths around South Sulawesi.

The bigger outfits can arrange tours to most

parts of Indonesia with an English-speaking guide, but this can get very expensive for one or two persons as the tours were designed for groups. Some Ujung Pandang–based agencies have their own field offices in eastern Indonesia, while others work with local agencies.
Ceria Nugraha Jl. Usmar Jafar 9, ☎ 311846; fax: 311848. Conveniently located behind the Marannu Hotel. Owned by a Toraja aristocrat and with pleasant staff. Tours within Sulawesi as well as other parts of Indonesia.
Iramasuka Tours Jl. Amanagappa 3. ☎ 316643; fax: 31777. With Toraja and south Sulawesi tours as well as to Buton and Raha.
Limbunan Tours Jl. Gunung Bawakaraeng 40–42 (Mailing address: P.O. Box 97). ☎ 323333, 316350; fax: 314344, 314567. Cable LIMCO, telex: 71185 LIMTOUUP IA. This is the only outfit with an on-line computer system linked with Garuda and Merpati: if it's humanly possible to book or confirm a flight, they can do it. Offices in Jayapura and Labuhanbajo, with plans to open one in Ambon. They concentrate on eastern Indonesia, offering tours of varying length to Tana Toraja, Manado, Ambon, Banda, Irian, the Mahakam River in Kalimantan, Flores and Komodo, along with a short tour of Ujung Pandang and vicinity. Their 18 permanent and 9 freelance guides can handle English, German, Dutch, French, Spanish and Italian.
Mattappa Jl. Patimura 38. ☎ 323932; fax: 312804. Specializing in tours of the Bugis and Makassarese areas.
Nitour Jl. Lamadukelleng 2. ☎ /fax: 317723. Local branch of a large national agency.
Pacto Jl. Jendral Sudirman 52. ☎ 873208; fax: 853906. This is the local office of Indonesia's largest, and widest-ranging in-bound travel agency. From their Ujung Pandang office, they run tours to Tana Toraja (including trekking), to Central Sulawesi and the Bada Valley megaliths, to Southeast Sulawesi for the traditional horsefighting, and to Selayar Island. Their Bali office also handles regular cruises to Selayar, with some 15 departures per year.
Ramayana Satrya Tours Jl. Bulukunyi 9A (PO Box 107). ☎ 853665; fax: 853665/853676; telex: 71496 RAINT IA. A large, efficient agency owned by a personable Torajan. Branch offices in Maumere and Irian. Many tours to various parts of eastern Indonesia, including trekking in Torajaland, Ikat tours, bird-watching and other nature tours along with dive instructor–led scuba diving in Manado, Banda, Flores and Seram. With 16 guides speaking English, Spanish, German, Dutch, French, and Japanese.
Rantenusa Tours Jl. Kakatua 38. ☎ /fax: 854678. Trips to Torajaland, Central and North Sulawesi.
Tunas Indonesia Jl. Martadinata 66. ☎ /fax: 314040. Tours to Toraja and south Sulawesi.

VISITING NEARBY ISLANDS

For boat trips to nearby islands, go to the dock called Tumba Kayu Bangkoa (literally "stacked mangrove wood," which you will see), just north of the Makassar Golden Hotel, opposite Jl. Wahab Tarru. Here you can charter outrigger boats with roofs to about 20 islands, with the cost depending on distance and waiting time.

The most popular islands are **Samalona** (30 min, $15 rt), **Kudingareng Keke** or **Barang Lompo** or **Barang Caddi** (1 hr away, $25 rt), **Bone Tambung** (1.5 hrs, $30 rt). Six people fit comfortably in the boats, powered by 25–40 hp engines.

Just across the street from Fort Rotterdam, frequent boats take mostly locals (foreigners are welcome) to **Pulau Kayangan** (15 min, $1 on weekdays, $1.25 on Saturdays, $1.75 Sundays). This island features beaches, swimming, karaoke singing, cheap eating. Lots of rooms for overnighting, $9–$11. Crowded on weekends.

VISITING HISTORICAL SITES

Gowa Gowa's Sungguminasa palace is on the main road south from Ujung Pandang. Its entrance facing away from the highway. It now goes under the name Museum Balla Lompoa (literally "big house") and is open daily 8 am–5 pm. If you want to try for the *bupati*'s permission to visit the treasure room, dress properly and think of a good reason beforehand—this is not for casual tourists. The room is usually open only once a year on Idul Adha (in 1995, May 10). The ceremony of the yearly cleansing of the mystical treasures lasts a week.
Sombaopu Take a car to visit these 17th century ruins. As we went to press, public transportation stopped well short of the toll bridge crossing the northern branch of the Jeneberang River, although there was talk of extending it. The big, yearly South Sulawesi Cultural Festival takes place here during the third week of July.
Tallo Tallo is only for the most fanatic south Sulawesi history buffs. The royal graves are just off Jl. Tallo Lama, recently renamed Tallo Umar. Public transportation seldom swings this way.

SCUBA DIVING

Makassar Diving Center Jl. Ujung Pandang 3, opposite Fort Rotterdam. ☎ 326056; fax: (c/o Shogun Restaurant) 319842. Offering day trip diving on nearby islands. $50 for boat, weights, two tanks and a guide, minimum two divers. The 3-dive overnight trip to Kapoposang runs $150 per person, with a minimum party of four. Their well-maintained dive gear includes, per day: mask, snorkel, fins $5; BC, $7; regulator $7. Director Pak Wim can get along in English.
—*Ian Caldwell, Kal Muller & Bert W. Hoeksema*

South PRACTICALITIES

2

Travel in South Sulawesi is remarkably easy. Coaches and minibuses cover the entire province, leaving throughout the day from terminals in every major town. It is not necessary to book (except for Toraja in the peak season), though you should be prepared to wait an hour or two until there are enough passengers. Accommodations in this area are generally quite basic.

Prices in US dollars. S = Single; D = Double; T = Triple; AC = Air-conditioning. Telephone codes as noted.

In South Sulawesi—outside Ujung Pandang and Toraja—tourist facilities are limited. There are clean and comfortable hotels in Parepare, Watansoppeng (Soppeng), Pinrang, Watampone (Bone) and Palopo, though food is sometimes a problem. A basic command of Indonesian is useful, but someone who speaks a few words of English can usually be found. Bring some essentials: a *sarung* for sleeping in, a pair of rubber flip-flops and your own toilet paper. Mosquito repellent is a must.

The major roads are now well paved and maintained. Vestiges of the old colonial roads are the gracious roadside tamarind trees, and stone markers showing the distance from "Makassar" and the nearest *kabupaten* capital.

One way of visiting the extremities of the province would be to take a Merpati flight to Soroako from Ujung Pandang and a bus back. The reverse procedure involves risks of being stranded, since local flights do not always run according to the timetable.

Taxis and minibuses with an English-speaking driver/guide can be hired at good hotels in Ujung Pandang. Rates are about $3 per hour (two hours minimum) or $30–$40 per day, a bit more for air-conditioning, newer vehicles and longer journeys. A private mini-bus with driver runs $30–$60 per day plus fuel.

Parepare

Telephone code 0421
Parepare was formerly part of the kingdom of Suppa and an important coastal port for the inland kingdoms of Sidenreng and Rappang, near the central lakes. Today it is a busy port and a stopover between Ujung Pandang and Toraja.

FACILITIES

The most interesting place to stay is the **Hotel Gandaria** at Jl. Bau Massepe 171 (rooms w/bath $6). Haji Zainuddin, the proprietor, has a valu-

able collection of ritual objects, ornaments, and wedding costumes which were once used by royal families, some of which he rents for marriages. He is happy to show these to his guests.

Restaurant Sempurna, also Jl. Bau Massepe, serves reasonably priced seafood. The newer **Restaurant Asia** serves decent Chinese-Indonesian food in clean surroundings.

Majene

Telephone code 0422
Majene, like the rest of Mandar district, is not equipped for tourists. The most attractive alternative is to stay at the pleasant, centrally located harbor home of **Ibu Darmi Masud** at Jl. Amanna Wewang 12. Inquiries must first be made in Ujung Pandang with Dr Darmawan Masud (Jl. Usman Jafarno 9, ☎ 22482). Nice rooms with delicious meals at reasonable prices.

For breakfast, as you watch the *bago* fleet return, you can drink rich Mandar coffee and eat fried sweet bananas, and sticky rice with palm sugar and fresh coconut. Dinner may be fresh scad, or sauteed tuna in green mango sauce.

Walk around the corner to the *warung* on Jl. Syukur Rahim, for an excellent lunch of *soto ayam* (chicken soup), crisp fried chicken, fried rice, or stir-fried vegetables.

Southeastern Peninsula

Telephone code 0413 (Bulukumba)
There are a few accommodations in the boat-building area of the southeast, at Bulukumba, Tana Beru and Bira.

FACILITIES

Bulukumba

Accommodations in Bulukumba is very basic. Try **Penginapan Sinar Jaya**, Jl. Sawerigading 4,

☎ 129. 4 rooms with toilet/*mandi* and fan, $4.50. Dormitory upstairs $1.50. Grubby.

Tana Beru

Homestay Anda $2.50 S per night.

Bira

Anda Bungalows 100 meters from the beach. 7 bungalows with private shower and toilet and veranda. Restaurant. $5 D, $4 S, w/breakfast. **Bira Beach** 16 bungalows. $15. **Makassar Cottages** 8 rooms, 16 more planned. $15 S or D. **Riswan Guest House** In Tanateng, near the beach. 10 rms. Shared toilet/*mandi*. $4, including tea, coffee and 3 meals. **Yaya Homestay** In the village, a couple of kilometers from the beach. 6 rms. Two *mandi*/toilets. $5 including 3 meals.

North of Bira, those visiting the Tamatoa can stay at the **Losmen Sisilorong**. The Tamatoa put on cultural performances here for tour groups.

FOOD

In addition to the restaurant at Anda Bungalows, there is a *warung* near the ferry.

Selayar Island

The ferry from Bira (southeasternmost tip of South Sulawesi) to Pamatata harbor on Selayar leaves daily at 2 pm. The return ferry leaves Selayar at 10 am the following day. There is a direct bus from Ujung Pandang's Panaikan terminal at 7 am which connects up with the ferry.

There are two hotels in Benteng, the largest town on the island. **Hotel Berlian** ($4 S, $6 D) is the newest and best. Pacto Tours conducts regular cruises to Selayar from Bali (See "Ujung Pandang Practicalities, pg. 247).

Watampone (Bone)

Telephone code 0481
This is a sleepy, spacious town with several old wooden buildings from the Dutch period set in grassy, overgrown gardens. The main attractions are the museum and the great wooden palace built in the 1930s to house the reinstated Raja of Bone. Alongside is the *rumah adat*, where the *hadat* (council of seven) used to meet.

The museum is on the corner of the main square. Its knowledgeable and enthusiastic director is named Andi Mappassissi. Among the sacred objects in the museum, held essential to validity of a Bone ruler, are a Javanese *keris* called La Makawa, with a massive golden handle, and a lavish sword named La Teariduni, which got its name because it refused to be buried with its original owner, the ruler of Alitta (a small kingdom near Parepare), leaving the tomb on its own. The ruler's gold necklace,

given to him by the Dutch in recognition of his military services, also forms part of the regalia.

The museum contains ceremonial umbrellas, traditional clothing, and the ritual gear used by the *bissu* (transvestite priests).

Watampone is small enough to cover on foot. Bemos will take you any distance for Rp150, and *becak* can be hired for Rp2,500. **To other cities** Coaches and minibuses to Ujung Pandang, Sengkang, Sinjai and as far away as Palopo depart from the central terminal. The fare to Ujung Pandang is $2. **To the Mampu Caves** Take a mini-bus north to Uloe (35 km), then a *bemo* to Gua Mampu. **To Southeast Sulawesi** Travelers to Sultra can catch a *bemo* to the port at Bajoe, 6 km (3.5 mi) east of Bone. The fare is 30¢. The daily ferry here departs at 11 pm and arrives in Kolaka at dawn. The first-class fare is $5 with AC and comfortable, fully reclining seats. Alternatively, pay a little less for second class and sleep out under the stars on a mat on the bow of the ship.

There are several small, reasonably priced hotels in Watampone; the price generally includes breakfast of bread, eggs and tea or coffee. **Wisma Watampone** Jl. Biru 14, ☎ 21362. the best hotel in Bone. All rooms AC; coffee shop, drugstore and swimming pool. Modern, clean, good service, but somewhat characterless. 21% tax and service. $15–$30 S, $20–$40 D. **Wisma Bola Ridie**, Jl. Merdeka 6, ☎ 412. 5 minutes from the town center. 6 rms. A rambling Dutch building straight out of the 1930s; the cool, spacious rooms have 4-meter-high ceilings and decorated tile floors. The name translates as "the yellow house": yellow was the color of South Sulawesi nobility and the hotel is owned by a descendant of the last Rajah of Bone. $4–$8, including tea and a simple breakfast. **Wisma Rio Rita**, Jl. Kawerang 4, ☎ 253. 10 rms. A small, pleasant hotel with white tiled walls and floors and a cool, open lounge. It is set on a quiet street. Some AC rms, each w/bathroom, $9–$14 with a simple breakfast. **Mario Pulama Hotel** Jl. Kawerang 16. Less attractive than the Rio Rita. Breakfast, some rooms AC. $6–9 S, $9–15 D. **Wisma Amarah**, Jl. Jendral Ahmad Yani 2A, ☎ 569. 7 rms. Small, but clean. Set on the main road near the center of town, it might be a little noisy. Breakfast. $6. **Wisma Cempaka**, Jl. Biru 36, ☎ 414. 18 rms. $4–$10, including breakfast. **Penginapan Ramayana** *Losmen*-style hotel in the center of town, above a car-repair shop. 18 rms. $4–$6.

Losmen National Jl. Mesjid 86. More spacious than the Ramayana. $3.

DINING

Not one of Bone's major attractions. There are several restaurants along Jalan Mesjid. The **Ramayana** is a clean restaurant serving Chinese-Indonesian food. But their *gadogado* is a cold, coagulated mess. Nor do the **Padang Raya** and the **Victoria's** flyblown window displays of Padang style fried chicken wings inspire confidence. Much better to eat *murtabak* from the roadside stalls outside for 30¢ a portion.

The only decent place to eat in Bone is the **Restaurant Pondok Selera**, Jl. Biru 28. This spacious, clean restaurant serves a good range of Chinese and Indonesian dishes and seafood. Service is prompt; the food is fresh and tasty. A half-serving of steamed shrimp, *cap cai*, rice and fresh lime juice will set you back $3. At the back of the restaurant is a rock garden and pool.

SHOPPING

Local crafts include spinning and weaving in silk, gold-threaded *songkok* (Muslim hats) of fine white straw, and mats. These are in the market and at **Usaha Rakyat Bone** ("Handicrafts of Bone") at Jl. Makmur 37.

Watansoppeng (Soppeng)

Telephone code 0484
This is a small town set amid rolling hills on the western edge of the fertile Walanae Valley, which runs north to Lake Tempe. Kab. Soppeng (pop. 240,000), of which Watansoppeng is the capital, is primarily a rice-producing area.

Watansoppeng is known for its silkworm factories which produce the raw silk used by weavers in Enrekang, Rappang and Singkang, while on the eastern hills farmers grow *kemiri* (candle nuts), palm sugar, peanuts and tobacco. The tobacco is cured with palm sugar in bamboo tubes and exported as far as Sumatra. *Bemos* are Rp 100 for any distance; horse-drawn carts called *dokar,* Rp 200–300.

ACCOMMODATIONS

Wisma Munasko Jl. Kemakmuran 12. Spartan but reasonably clean rooms, $4 w/bathroom and $3 w/o. The more up-market **Hotel Makmur** at Jl. Kemakmuran 104 has rooms from $4 to $8 w/bathroom. Breakfast, lunch and dinner can be ordered in advance. The **Hotel Aman**, near the royal graves at Jera Lomopoe, is an old Dutch house with large, cool rooms.

The government rest house, **Villa Julianna**, is an extraordinary neo-Gothic house built in 1911. It was formerly the residence of the Dutch *Controleur* or Commissioner.

DINING

There are very few eating places in Soppeng. **Rumah Makan Ompo** and **Rumah Makan Sedap** at 27 and 33 Jl. Attang Benteng serve grilled squid, *ikan bakar* and fried chicken, plus the usual Chinese-Indonesian dishes. Be sure to ask for the small, tasty bananas called *pisang berangen*, grown only in Bone and Soppeng.

Singkang

Singkang is a pleasant, medium-sized town nestling in the foothills overlooking Lake Tempe. There are many attractive walks in the region and good views of the lake, which is only 2 meters deep and varies in size according to the season. Silk *sarung*s and cloths are woven in town and in outlying villages. Singkang is a town for early risers: the extraordinarily powerful loudspeaker system in the large central mosque is guaranteed to wake the soundest sleeper.

TRANSPORTATION

*Bemo*s are Rp 100 for any distance; *becak*s can be hired for Rp 500 for anywhere in town. Coaches and mini-buses leave regularly from the terminal in the center of town. Fares to Palopo $1.50, Ujung Pandang $2, Cabenge 30¢ and Bone $1. From here you can also catch a *bemo* to Tosora, on the edge of Lake Tempe, for Rp 500. Allow half a day for the return journey.

ACCOMMODATIONS

Singkang offers a wide range of medium to cheap accommodations. The **Hotel Apada** on Jl. Durian has clean, comfortable rooms with green and pleasant surroundings for $8–$11. This is *the* place to stay, though the cultural atmosphere can be overpowering. The owner is a local aristocrat keen to recreate Bugis civilization for his visitors. Eating here is expensive. In the evenings, a traditional Bugis meal is served to guests sitting cross-legged on mats, waited on by girls dressed in traditional costumes. There is a 10% tax and a service charge.

For a hotel with a view contact the Regional Office (*Kantor Daerah*) next to the central mosque, for permission to stay at the government-owned **Pasanggrahan Hirawati**, atop a hill overlooking Lake Tempe. Alternatively, the **Wisma Bukit Nusa Indah** on Jl. Lamungkace Toaddamang, halfway up the hill, has quiet rooms (with bathroom) for $4. The **Wisma Pondok Eka** on Jl. Maluku is a traditional raised wooden house owned by a friendly Bugis family on a quiet street, close to the center of town. At the budget end, **Wisma Ayuni** on Jl.

Puang Ri Maggalatung is an old Dutch house with huge, high-ceilinged rooms for $2 a person. The rooms are clean, with shower and toilet.

DINING

There are a number of very presentable little restaurants in Singkang, and the food is surprisingly good. The **Restaurant Tomudi** on Jl. Andi Oddang offers a wide range of chicken dishes; portions are small but satisfying. **Rumah Makan Melati**, Jl. Kartini 54, serves ten sticks of good beef *satay*, rice and soup for under $1. The cool and breezy **Rumah Makan Romantis** on Jl. AP Petta Rani 2 looks up-market, but prices here are very reasonable. The *nasi campur* is good, as are the chicken dishes, and the beer is cold. A restaurant specializing in *ayam kampung* (farmyard chicken) is the **Warung Singkang** on Jl. Mesjid Raya: next door is the **Rumah Makan Mini Indah,** which serves *ikan bakar.*

SHOPPING

Singkang is an excellent place to buy traditional silk *sarungs* and woven silk cloth, though it is getting harder and harder to find high-quality hand-made pieces. (The best place to look is along the road south of Rappang.) Factory produced cloth is attractive, if not of the same quality as, say, Thai factory silk. A 10–15 meter piece takes about a week to complete. Quality and prices are fairly standard, except on the home-woven pieces. Patterned lengths from 10–20 meters sell for $12–$14 per meter; plain lengths for $10–$12. Heavier plain cloth for jackets goes for $17–$20, and 2-meter *sarung* and *selendang* sets (*sarung* plus shoulder scarves) sell for $30. Traditional *sarungs* in check patterns sell for $20–$50, depending on quality. When sewn in a tube, the *sarung*s measure 110 x 200 cm.

The best place to start is the **Mustaquiem** factory, on Jl. A. Panggaru I, southwest of the market. Here you can see the thread being processed and dyed before being woven into *kain* lengths.

A small range of silk *sarung* and *kain* are sold in **Toko Akbar**, Jl. Kartini 16B. **Griya Sutera** on Jl. Hasanuddin 5, on the outskirts of town, has decent modern and traditional pieces, as well as a loom which you can inspect.

Pinrang

A pleasant town along a tree-lined street, in the heart of a rice-growing district. The **Penginapan Sinapati** on Jl. Jend. Sudirman is clean and pleasant. The **Penginapan Purnama** on Jl. Sultan Hasanuddin is cheaper and more spartan: the adjoining restaurant serves decent Chinese-Indonesian food.

Palopo

Telephone code 0471
This slow-moving town is dominated by the cloud-covered mountain ranges which tower imperiously behind it. The journey down to Palopo from Tana Toraja is worth it for the ride alone. This spectacular pass was for centuries the major east coast trade exit. Down the pass came gold, resins, rare woods, fine coffee and slaves. Up went iron swords and weapons from Luwu's coastal armories, salt and dried fish.

The **Museum Barara Guru**, Jl. Andi Jemma diagonally opposite the old mosque, is well worth a visit. The former palace of the ruler of Luwu, the old Dutch-style house contains a collection of Chinese and Southeast Asian ceramics, ritual *bissu* equipment and other strange objects. Admission $1.

TRANSPORTATION

*Becak*s will take you any distance in town for Rp 200–300. Buses bound for major destinations in South Sulawesi depart from the main terminal: Ujung Pandang (8 hrs, $5); Rantepao (2 hrs, $1.25); Malili (4 hrs, $2.50). Also : Palu (12 hrs, $15–18); Tentena (8 hrs, $8–$10).

There are ferries leaving nightly for Malili from the pier. There are also boats to Kolaka.

ACCOMMODATIONS

The **Wisma Kumda Indah** on Jl. Opu Tosapaille, opposite the police station, is by far the best hotel to stay in. Spotlessly clean. The lounge has tropical fish tanks and a friendly, talkative parrot. $6–$9; $9–$11 w/AC. The **Palopo Hotel** opposite the bus terminal has large, grimy rooms for $3–$9. The **Hotel Buana** on Jl. KH Ahmad Dahlan is cleaner, $4 non-AC and $11 AC. **Pondok Risma** on Jl. A Jemma is clean but the rooms are small and box-like.

The **Victoria** on Jl. Diponegoro, near the Apollo Theatre, is a large, clean Chinese restaurant serving decent shrimp and crab dishes for $3, as well as the usual Chinese-Indonesian menu. (The *bistik* is *not* recommended.) Most visitors to Palopo eat here. The **Pondok Mantili** opposite serves *nasi campur*, as does the **Kios Mimi-Indah** a few doors down. Long-term residents eat at the **Segar** on Jl. Sawerigading for a change from the Victoria.

East of Palopo

Accommodations east of Palopo is basic. Malili is the next big town: **Setia II** is marginally preferable to **Setia I**; neither is recommended. There is an expensive guest house owned by PT Inco at Soroako, a *losmen* and several restaurants.

—Ian Caldwell and Kal Muller

3 Tana Toraja PRACTICALITIES

INCLUDES RANTEPAO, TREKKING IN TORAJA, AND MAMASA

Rantepao is an unprepossessing, dusty little town of four main roads which converge at a *tongkonan* raised over the road. The town is developing fast; the number of visitors is increasing rapidly, and new hotels and restaurants are opening monthly. Street names are in a state of confusion; many have been renamed but even residents have yet to learn what they are. Most journeys into Tana Toraja begin and end at Rantepao.

Prices in US dollars. S = Single; D = Double; T = Triple; AC = Air-conditioning.

Telephone code for Rantepao is 423. (0423 within Indonesia.)

Rantepao

Peak season in Rantepao, the "capital" of Tana Toraja, is July through August, and although accommodations and services are expanding, there are shortages of rooms, cars and just about everything else around this time. Better to schedule your visit off-season. If you must go in mid-summer, make sure you have confirmed reservations with a reputable agency. Note: Listed here are the "published" off-season prices. In high season they go up as much as 20%.

GETTING THERE

By Air

The airport serving Rantepao is at Rantetayo, near Makale, 24 km south of Rantepao. Merpati runs a bus service to town ($2.50).

Merpati flies here from Ujung Pandang daily ($40 one-way), and twice on Monday, Thursday and Sunday. Planes leave Ujung Pandang at 9 am and arrive at 9:55 am. The return flight leaves at 10:15 am, and arrives in Ujung Pandang at 11:15 am. The second flight leaves Ujung Pandang at 11:30 am, arriving at 12:25 pm. It leaves at 12:45 pm, arriving at 1:45 pm.

Due to the short runway at Rantetayo, flights in carry 22 passengers, but flights out carry only 14. (Plans to extend the runway are still afoot). Flights are sometimes cancelled without notice due to weather or lack of passengers. During high season these flights are heavily booked. **Merpati** At the Rantepao Lodge. ☎ 21248; fax: 21485 (it actually works, sometimes). Hours 8 am–4 pm weekdays, 8 am–2 pm Sundays.

By Land

From Ujung Pandang. Buses to Rantepao leave daily from Ujung Pandang. The journey takes 8 hours and includes a meal stop ($4–$5). Tickets should be bought in town (see "Ujung Pandang Practicalities" pg. 243) but coaches actually leave from Panaikan bus terminal, 20 minutes out of town by *bemo*. Coaches typically leave at 7 am, 1 pm and 7 pm. We suggest **Liman Express** and **Litho & Co.**

Several companies in Rantepao run buses back to Ujung Pandang (departure times and prices are the same as above). The number of buses each day depends on the number of passengers. Get your ticket early. For the most legroom, we suggest **Liman Express, Falitah** and **Alam Indah**. All their offices are on Jl. Mappanyuki, just north of the traffic circle.

TO OTHER DESTINATIONS

Two companies, **Segeri Indah** and **Bina Wisata Sulteng**, make the run north along the Trans-Sulawesi Highway to Tentena (10 hrs, $10), Poso (12 hrs, $11) and Palu (20 hrs, $12.50), in central Sulawesi. Again, the number of buses depends on traffic but you can count on at least with two a week. Bima Wisata leaves Rantepao on Mondays and Fridays; Segeri Indah's departures depend on market days.

You can also break up the trip into segments by taking short-run buses. To start, there are frequent minibuses to Palopo (2 hrs, $1).

LOCAL TRANSPORTATION

Public transportation. *Bemo*s into town terminate in the field behind the old market. *Bemo*s to any place out of Rantepao can be picked up around the traffic island in the center of town; passing ones can be flagged down along any road. Fares start at Rp200 with a maximum of about Rp 2,500 to the furthest villages from Rantepao. They are always crowded, leave only when full, and have no legroom, but it's the best way to get to know the locals.

Chartered vehicles. Kijang (Indonesian manufactured jeeps) and minibuses can be hired at the better hotels from $30/day including driver. *Bemo* drivers can be persuaded to take you to almost any destination for $5/hour.

Self-drive Toyota Land Cruisers—when available—cost $50/day or more (international driver's license required). Motorcycle rentals are not yet very popular—if you can find one, figure $10–$12 per day.

ACCOMMODATIONS

In July and August most hotels are full, prices go up as much as 20%, and advance booking is advisable. The rest of the year hotels are often empty. All hotels in the luxury and intermediate classes have private bathrooms with hot showers. The better hotels add 8% government tax and 8% service charge. The climate is cool and pleasant and only the luxury hotels have AC.

Budget (under $10)

Wisma Maria II Just off the road to Makale, about 2 km south of Rantepao, ☎ 21288. 17 rms. Set in lush greenery and above traditional Toraja houses and rice barns. Plants and paraphernalia everywhere. The best views are from the five top floor rooms. Restaurant prepares traditional Toraja food for groups. $8–$12 S, $10–$16 D. **Wisma Monika** Jl. Ratulangi 36, ☎ 21216. 20 rms. Restaurant and small bar. $7.50 S or D with cold water; $12.50 S or D with hot water; two VIP rooms $20 S or D.

Pison Jl. Pong Tiku 8, ☎ 21344. 16 rms, with more planned. Very pleasant hotel set in a quiet lane, close to town. The rooms are spacious and spotlessly clean with verandah and private bathroom, some with a view across backyards and onto the western mountains. All rooms with hot water. Small restaurant serves Chinese, Indonesian and Torajan (order 2 hrs in advance) food. The owner, Luther Pongrekun, a Toraja of noble descent, is an exceptionally personable man. Highly recommended. $7.50 S, $12.50 D, extra bed $2.50; (During high season add $2–$2.50).

Pia's Poppies Jl. Pong Tiku 27A (separated from the Pison by a church) ☎ 21121. 12 rms. Great views across rice fields and onto the mountains. All rooms with hot water. The owner, Pak Yus Paulus, is also cook and chief bottle-washer, with 13 years experience at the Bali Beach. Healthy breakfasts of yogurt, juices, homemade croissants; excellent main menu with seafood and Toraja dishes with humorous English explanations—$3.50 per dish. Specialty: crêpes suzette with Grand Mariner, $4. Recommended by discriminating gastronomes. $7.50 S, $10 D.

Wisma Tebass Jl. Mangadir 14, ☎ 21415, 5 rms. No hot water. $7.50 S or D.

Wisma Rosa Jl. Sa'dan (formerly Jl. Pahlawan) just past the bridge on the road to Sa'dan, ☎ 21075. 15 rms. The oldest *wisma* in Rantepao; recently renovated. Quiet, with verandah, trees and a small garden. The more expensive rooms have hot water. $6–$12 S, $7–$20 D.

Indra City Jl. Ratulangi 26 (same as Indra II, see below). ☎ 21163. 12 rms. Set lunch $5, dinner $6 at the Indra Restaurant (see below). $6–$10 S, $9–$12 D.

Wisma Maria I Jl. Ratulangi 23, ☎ 21165. 17 rms. One of the older *wismas* in Rantepao, ageing gracefully. Traditional rice barn, small yard, glass showcase with fine Toraja antique heirlooms (not for sale). Restaurant: breakfast $1.50, lunch and dinner $4. $5–$8 S, $10–$14 D.

Wisma Rantepao Jl. Landorundun 35, ☎ 21397. 14 rms. Good deal for the price, central location. Restaurant with Indonesian, Chinese dishes $1.25–$2; watch your head going up or down the stairs! $5–$7.50 S or D.

Wisma Indo Grace Jl. Mappanyuki 72, ☎ 21291. 7 rms. Above a restaurant, clean, prices very flexible. $5 S or D.

Wisma Wisata Jl. Mongonsidi 36. 5 rms. Clean and next to the river. $4 S, $6.50 D.

Wisma Lindai Jl. Abdul Gani 2, ☎ 21113. 6 rms. Fairly clean, on a quiet street close to downtown. *Mandi* ladle baths. $4 S or D.

Wisma Nirmala Jl. Mappanyuki 118, ☎ 21319. 12 rms. Good value. $4 S, $6.50 D.

Wisma Nanggala Jl. A Yani 81, ☎ 21269. 10 rms. All rooms with private facilities, just off the main drag. $3.25 S, $4 D.

Marlin Inn Jl. Mappanyuki 75, ☎ 21215. 16 rms. Above a restaurant of the same name on the main street. Front rooms noisy, but bright, other rooms quieter, but dark. $3 S, $4 D.

Wisma Palawa, Jl. Mappanyuki 81. 5 rms, but only one w/attached toilet/bath. Planned renovation includes addition of 8 rooms with attached facilities. $3/room.

Wisma Surya Jl. Mongonsidi 36, ☎ 21312. 8 rms. Quiet place next to a ferry river crossing, which can be seen from the back rooms. Run by Mrs. Rosboby who speaks some English and works at the Tourist Information Office. Breakfast $2.50 for two. $7.50 S or D.

Wisma Martini Jl. Ratulangi 62, ☎ 21240. 9 rms. Run down. Some of the rooms are very dark—take a good look first before settling in. Cheaper rooms share toilet/bath facilities. Simple meals available. $2.50–$4 S, $5–$6.50 D.

Victoria Jl. Mappanyuki 48, ☎ 21308. 12 rms. Excellent value, but there's a noisy mosque nearby. Each room with own toilet/bath. Varying number of beds in each room. $2.50/person.

Wisma Flora Jl. Emi Saelan, ☎ 21586. 8 rms. Noisy; close to main mosque and *bemo* traffic. Some rooms w/attached toilets. $2.50/head.

Wisma Sederhana Jl. Sulora 110 ☎ 21011. 5 rms. Located about 2 km out of town on the road to Tikala, opposite a handicrafts workshop and showroom. $2.50/person.

Wisma Batutumonga Jl. Mappanyuki 65. 11 rms. Noisy and dark, but attached toilets. Varying number of beds in each room. $1.50 / head.

Intermediate ($10–$40)

Most hotels in this category are family homes with added guestrooms. They are almost always clean and quiet. They differ in location, view of the surrounding valley, and the warmth of the family in whose compound you stay.

Most *wisma* provide food if you order in advance. If a *wisma* does not have transportation, a car and perhaps an invitation to a death feast can be arranged with the owner's relatives.

It is worth asking whether tax or service is added to the bill; some places add 21%. Prices are flexible in the off-season, and if you are staying for more than a couple of days, you may be able to get a 10–20% discount.

Indra II Jl. Ratulangi 26, ☎ 31583, fax: 21547. 19 rms. Overlooking a flower-filled central patio. The back of the hotel—and its Marendang restaurant—overlooks the Sa'dan River. Excellent set lunch $7, dinner $9, with Toraja dances and bamboo flute music on Saturday nights (8 pm). Highly recommended. $32 S, $40 D (including taxes and surcharges).

Pondok Torsina Jl. Pao Rura, 1.5 km (1 mi) just off the main road south to Makale. 24 rms. In an oversize imitation of a Toraja house with modern rooms. Swimming pool, panoramic view over rice fields backed by steep hills. Restaurant with Indonesian, Chinese dishes $2.50, Toraja dishes (order 2 hrs in advance) $2–$4. $30 S, $36 D.

Hebron Inn Jl. Pembangunan 27, ☎ 21519. 12 rms. New and clean. All rooms have hot water. $25 S, $28 D.

Rantepao Lodge Jl. Pao Rura, just behind the Pondok Torsima 1.5 km south on the road to Makale, ☎ 21248; fax: 21485. 29 rms. A bit run down and the hot water often isn't. $24 S, $32 D.

Wisma Tanabua Jl. Diponegoro 43, ☎ 21072. 22 rms. Meals (only at night) at $5 per person. $17 S, $20 D.

Indra I Jl. Landorundun 63, ☎ 21060. 17 rms. $12.50–$15 S or D.

Wisma Tikala Indah Out of town about 8 km on the road to Tikala, at the junction with the road to Bori. 22 rms. Restaurant serves Indonesian food. $12.50 S or D.

Wisma Drama Jl. Gain 16, ☎ 21371. 21 rms, half with hot water. Breakfast $2, lunch and dinner $3.50. $10–$20, S or D.

Pondok Wisata Jl. Pembangunan 23, ☎ 21-595. 8 rms. New and clean. Cheaper rooms w/o hot water. $10–$20 S or D.

Pondok Pelangi Jl. Pembangunan 11A, ☎ 21753. 5 rms. New and sparkling clean. $10–$17 S or D.

Wisma Monition, Jl. Gain 14A, 75 m off the street, ☎ 21675. 4 rms, more under construction. New. The owners work at Merpati and the Tourist Information office. Rooms with hot water

$15 S or D; cold water only, $10 S or D.

Luxury ($40–$125)

The best hotels are a short way out of town, either south off the road to Makale or northeast, next to the road to Palopo.

Toraja Prince Just across the road from the Toraja Cottages, ☎ 21458; fax: 21304. 45 rms (another 55 planned). Two restaurants, one Japanese, the other western and Indonesian/Chinese, both $13 for set meal. Mountain bikes for rent, satellite TV including CNN. If you missed a big funeral, they have it on videotape. $60 S, $67 D.

Toraja Cottages Jalan Pakubalasalu, 4 km northeast of town, on the road to Palopo, ☎ 210892; fax: 21369. 62 rms. Attractive complex of bungalows spread out on the side of a landscaped hill. Swimming pool. Bar and two restaurants, excellent western and Chinese/Indonesian menu. Bar is the focus of the (wealthy) nightlife in Rantepao. $57 S, $63 D, $125 suite. *Note: The above hotels are near the new Pasar Bolu market held every six days.*

Toraja Misiliana and **Misiliana Hotel**, 3 km south of town, ☎ 21212, fax: 21512. Reservations can also be made at their counter at the Hassanudin airport in Ujung Pandang, or, in Rantepao, at their office on Jl. Anuang 24, ☎ 85-4181; fax: 27812. These two adjacent hotels, with a combined 120 rms, are managed jointly. All rooms—in Toraja style decor—with terrace, taped music, mini-bar, fridge, TV. There's also a swimming pool, souvenir shops and a money changer. Very good meals: breakfast $9, lunch $11, dinner $13. Misiliana Hotel: $53 S, $60 D, $123 suite. Toraja Misiliana: $31 S, $39 D.

DINING

The specialty of the region is *piong*, food cooked in bamboo sections. Most restaurants serve *piong*, but you have to order at least two hours in advance and specify the kind of meat you want, usually chicken or pork. *Ikan bakar* (charcoal-grilled fish), *bistik kerbau* (fried buffalo steak), and black rice are definitely worth trying. Nothing is too spicy for the western palate, but if you want to make your meal more authentic, ask for the various condiments (*sambal tomat, sambal asli, sambal lombok*) that traditionally accompany a meal.

The menu at most restaurants is a combination of western, Torajan and Chinese dishes. Most will provide a packed lunch of sandwiches, eggs, chicken, fruit and drinks if you are going walking. Some of the smaller restaurants do not have a refrigerator; meat is best avoided unless you know it is fresh.

Chez Dodeng At the corner of Jl. Mongonsidi and Emi Saelan. One of the oldest cafés in town. Classic *warung*-style Chinese/Indonesian/Torajan food. Inexpensive at $1–$2 for most non-Torajan dishes. The open sewer outside the front door does not inspire confidence. Chess players gather here in the late afternoon.

Dodeng Jl. Pembangunan 30. Clean, *warung*-style with nice bamboo chairs, facing what was the old market in the center of town.

Indra Marendeng Restaurant (At the Hotel Indra, Jl. Landorundun 63). Good food and excellent service from friendly staff. One of the best places to sample a Torajan meal; try the *papiong ayam*, black rice and *sayur paku* (cooked fern tips). One order is enough for two persons; total cost $7. Staff will even go out and fetch *tuak* for you; better still, go to the road circle and sample it yourself (bring your own *tuak* container).

Mart's Coffee House and Restaurant Jl. Ratulangi 44A. Clean and pleasant. Indonesian and Chinese dishes $1–$3; seafood from Palopo $2.50–$4; juices 50¢. Torajan dishes need one day advance notice.

Marurua Jl. Pasar. Neat little café that serves good charcoal-grilled fish and freshly fried potatoes. Steer clear of meat dishes. Attracts younger travelers. When the rock music is off you can dine to the sound of the *muezzin*'s call to prayer from the mosque opposite.

Pia's Poppies (See above under "Accommodations"). The menu recommends giant *masapi* eel from the depths of the Sa'dan river. Small but elegant portions of delicious fruit salad and crêpes suzette with Grand Marnier. Service may be slow, but everything is freshly prepared.

Pison Restaurant (at Hotel Pison, Jl. Pong Tiku 8). Clean white table linen and pleasant, attentive service. The grilled fish is fresh from their own pond and the enormous fruit salads are attractively presented. Excellent pancakes; one of the few places where you can get chilled Bir Bintang in small bottles. (Refuse all other brands!) Chinese/Indonesian menu, western breakfast, juices. Torajan specialties on request.

Rahmat Restaurant Centrally located facing the traffic island, this restaurant caters to tourist groups. This high-ceiling, huge (for Torajaland) restaurant serves an indifferent Indonesian/Chinese/Torajan menu, $3–$5 for most dishes.

Restaurant Mambo Jl. Ratulangi. Huge menu of Indonesian, Chinese and Torajan dishes. Water buffalo meat prepared three different ways, lots of juices. Steak $3, fish $2–$3.

Rima Jl. Mappanyuki 115. Nice decor with woven, cracked bamboo walls and decorated Toraja panels. Indonesian and Chinese dishes about $1, Toraja cuisine, $3–$5.

Salota Jl. Mappanyuki 109. Usual dishes, 75¢–$1.75, Torajan dishes (with some explanation on the menu) $2–$5. Super Kijang (utility vehicle) for rent, $30 per day, driver and gas included. Ask about river rafting here.

Takumande Opa Restaurant At the Misiliana Hotel, 3 km out of town on the road to Makale. Tourist-style European, Chinese and Indonesian cuisines and traditional Torajan food.

Toraja Cottages Restaurant Good food and service at reasonable prices (about $4–$6 for a main dish) in a nice atmosphere. A drink in the bar and a meal here will set you back $10–$15 and make a very pleasant evening out.

NIGHTLIFE

The government of South Sulawesi is resisting attempts to turn Rantepao into another Kuta. There is only one disco in town, the **Tongkonan Pub** on Jl. Mappanyuki, next to the Wisma Indo Grace. Open from 7:30 pm until whenever. No door fee. Whiskey, vodka, beer, $2. Live band, playing reggae, rock, jazz, blues. Flashing lights, intimate spaces with pillows, small dance floor. Also, **Toraja Cottages** has a bar and resident band; a noisy, gregarious crowd hangs out here.

Karaoke fans have to leave town, to the **Rama Restaurant** and the **Delta Garden Restaurant**, both about 4 km south of Rantepao on the road to Makale, past the Misiliana Hotel.

The **Misiliana Hotel** stages traditional dance performances, including the *Paranding* war dance. Every Saturday night at 8 pm, if there are enough guests, the **Marendang Restaurant** at the Indra II also features traditional Toraja dances and bamboo flute music in a most pleasant atmosphere. The show is free if you are staying at one of their hotels, if not it's $1.

All restaurants serve alcohol, mainly beer (Bintang, Anker, Becks, Carlsberg). *Tuak* sellers gather in the town center after dark. Cup your hand and ask for a sample; the taste ranges from a sweetness that makes your teeth sing to a sourness that makes your ears ring. The sour is more alcoholic—drink it with caution.

SHOPPING

Antique baskets, ancient bamboo *tuak* containers, old weavings, stringed musical instruments and ceremonial food containers all still make it from the mountain villages to Rantepao, where they are sold at reasonable prices. Weavings are expensive, but you may pick up an old Torajan house panel for as little as $25.

Modern handicrafts include carved Toraja trays, boxes and mirrors, and various-sized models of *tongkonan*. Long knives with carved buffalo-horn handles hang in shop windows. Bead necklaces and attractive bamboo containers of Torajan coffee make ideal presents.

Most of the antique and souvenir shops are in the shopping center area around the traffic circle. New weavings, as well as weavings from other parts of Indonesia, are sold in the villages of **Sa'dan Sangkombong** and **Sa'dan Tobarana**. You can expect to pay $30 and upwards for hand-woven *kain kipris*, colorful striped local cloth, 8 meters in length, woven on a backstrap loom.

It will cost $120 for a weaving from Rongkong, an isolated mountain region northwest of Palopo.

TRAVELERS' SERVICES

Information

Finding out where funeral feasts and other ceremonies are being held can be difficult, unless you are willing to hire a guide. Keep asking: if you've heard the same story several times it is probably correct. Avoid asking a question that can be answered with a simple yes. When asking about distances, it is better to ask "how long" rather than "how far." Most people have only a hazy idea about distances, but know how long it takes to walk or drive.

Tourist Information Center, 62 Jl. Ahmad Yani. Pleasant, helpful staff. Open 7 am–1 pm. They can help with car/minibus rental, or an English-speaking guide ($12.50/day; $15/day if for trekking). Sketch maps of the area can be obtained here or from most hotels.

Travel Agencies

Most tourists arrive in Tana Toraja on packages run by Ujung Pandang–based agencies. Only one—but highly recommended—agency maintains an office in Rantepao.

Ramayana Satrya Jl. Pong Tiku, south of town, just before the turnoff to Ke'te Kesu. ☎ 21615, 21248; fax: 21485. Run by Pak Palidan, who speaks excellent English. They are very knowledgeable about Toraja Land, and give out free information in several languages. They can also help with transportation, and arrange tailormade long or short tours for individuals or groups. A very efficient outfit.

Money Changing

Close to the center of town, on Jl. Ahmad Yani, are two money changers and two banks.

Communications

The **Post Office** (Jl. Ahmad Yani 111) is on the left just before the town center. There is a Poste Restante service here. Next door is the Telegraph and **Telephone Office**, open 24 hours.

Necessities and Sundries

The **Hotel Indra** runs a well-stocked little supermarket where you can buy stamps, guide books, canned and bottled drinks, blankets, towels and chocolates. **Toko Remaja** (Jl. Ahmad Yani 181), is the largest department store in Rantepao. Second-hand paperbacks and travelers' books can be bought from the **bookshop** up the lane to the right off the Makale-Rantepao road, just before you reach the *tongkonan*. You

can get film at **Toko Foto Duta Wisata** on the corner of Jl. Ahmad Yani and Jl. Landorundun; prices are higher than in Ujung Pandang. There are several pharmacies in Rantepao; the **Apotik Delta** (48 Ahmad Yani) is open 8 am–8:30 pm, Mon–Sat. If it's closed, knock.

RAFTING

Sobek Expeditions, a very experienced rafting outfit (☎ 22143), runs an easy one-day trip for $50 per person (minimum of three) and a much tougher but far more exciting three-day white water rafting of the Sa'dan River canyon for $225 per person (minimum of three clients).

Trekking in Toraja

Treks in Tana Toraja can be divided into two types: Day treks out of Rantepao or Mamasa (which you can usually do on your own) and longer, 3–8 day treks for which a guide is extremely useful, unless you speak Indonesian and do not mind getting lost occasionally.

Trekking is much more pleasant in dry weather, and in the middle of the rainy season the trails are often impassable and leeches become a real nuisance. Ten years ago, the dry and wet seasons came regularly (April and November, respectively) but today no one is willing to predict the weather. Basically, March–May and mid-July–mid-October are the best times for trekking. The rainy season is October/November to February, with December the worst.

On any longer trek, bring a knapsack, sleeping bag or blanket, rain gear, sunscreen, hat, shorts, T-shirts, long pants, long-sleeved shirt. As there are strategically placed homes for overnighting (mattresses and meals) there is no need to bring food or a sleeping mat.

At most of the traditional houses, someone will whip out a guest book for you to sign. A payment is then expected: 25¢–50¢ is about right. Electricity available only in Mamasa, 6 pm–6 am.

GUIDES

The standard rate for a guide is $15 per day for short treks. Like most things in Indonesia, this rate is negotiable, depending on season and the number of people in the group. The better guides charge $25–$40/day for the longer treks, whether they lead one or many. Porters run $5–$10/day, well worth it: when not laboring under a load, the scenery is more enjoyable and it's easier to take advantage of photo opportunities. On top of guide and porter fees, you will have to pay for food and lodging for yourself and your guide and porters. This will average $4–$6/person per day. If you are traveling without a guide, ask for the village head (*kepala desa*) who will help arrange food and accommodations.

TRAILSIDE ACCOMMODATIONS

Pasangtau

One homestay—no name, no fixed price.

Belau

Pa'aru Three double beds, $4 per person, including evening meal and light breakfast.

Ponding

One homestay—no name, one double bed with mosquito netting: $1/person, plus $1 per meal.

Mawai

Pak Teofilus Meals available—if there are a few of you, it's worth splitting a chicken, $2.50–$5 according to size. $1/person on mattress.

Timbaan

Pak Amri Four rooms, each with a mattress on the floor. An attached store sells cans of beer at $1 and bottles at $2.25. $3.50/person including two meals and coffee.
Timbaan Home Stay Four rooms, each with a real bed. (At both of these places, meals usually include rice, chicken, vegetables and eggs.) $3/person, including two meals, tea, coffee.

Pakassasan

Two homestays, no names, negotiable prices.

Mamasa

In the Polmas (Polewali–Mamasa) district, four of the subdistricts are home to the Toraja people: Mamasa (pop. 37,000, 3% Muslim, 92% Christian, 5% animist), Mambi (pop. 37,000, 40% Muslim, 60% Christian, animists not counted), Pana (pop. 16,000, 2% Muslim, 5% animist, 93% Christian) and Sumarorong (pop. 18,000, 30% Muslim, 10% animist, 60% Christian). Mamasa town itself has a population of approximately 2,500.

The Mamasa subdistrict grows vegetables and rice (enough to export a surplus), and coffee is the main cash crop. Damar and rattan are brought out of the woods. Hunting in the mountains is for wild pigs and *anoa* (dwarf buffalo).

There are lots of hot water springs for soaking weary bodies around Mamasa, some of which are too hot for comfort. Nine of the springs have facilities, geared for locals, but foreigners are welcomed.

TRANSPORTATION

The best way to get around Mamasa is by trekking (free) or motorcycle ($12.50–$15/day). A horse goes for $7.50/day, and a jeep with driver, $20/day.

Inexpensive public minibuses run between Mamasa and the roadside villages on the way to Polewali. Minibuses also go as far as Pakassasan and Tawalian on a daily basis, more frequently on Mondays, Mamasa's market day. There are several buses a day to Polewali (92 km, 4 hrs) $1.50 out, $1.75 back to Mamasa.

Three times a week—Mon, Tue, Thurs—buses make the 340-km run from Mamasa to Ujung Pandang ($5). There's also a weekly bus to Rantepao, (10 hrs, $5).

ACCOMMODATIONS

Guest House Mamasa Located a bit out of the way, quiet but on a short road, muddy after rains. 4 rms. Meals can be ordered. $5 S or D, all w/attached facilities.
Losmen Marapan Centrally located. 10 rms. Restaurant. $3, $4.50 w/attached facilities.
Losmen Mini Centrally located. 15 rms. Restaurant, but no menu—they let you know what's available, $2.50–$4/meal. $4; $5 w/facilities.
Wisma Gereja 6 rms. Meals can be ordered. One room w/attached facilities, $4 S or D; others $2.50 S or D.
Note: At the time of writing, construction had begun an a new hotel, aiming for 3-star rating.

GUIDES

There are four guides in Mamasa speaking English at various levels. They can be contacted at any of the *losmen*. The standard fee is $15/day around Mamasa; to Bittuang, $25/day. For the 3-day trek to Bittuang, it's $25 for a pack horse. We recommend **Daniel**. He is pleasant, and knowledgeable about places and traditions.

SOUVENIRS

Marapan Souvenir Next to the *losmen* of the same name. Good selection, cheaper than Rantepao. Carved wooden statues ($7.75); new but good quality woven cloth with natural colors ($17–$75); boars' tusk necklaces ($20). Some bargaining possible. If interested, see the owner Pak Markus Bongasao's collection of antiques from the region, kept in a room at the very top of his *losmen*.

—Ian Caldwell, Nancy Caldwell, Kal Muller

Central PRACTICALITIES

4

INCLUDES BADA VALLEY MEGALITHS

Central Sulawesi is a vast, mountainous province of virgin forests and rugged scenery. Until recently, few westerners visited the area, which is cut off from the south by a natural wall of jungle and mountain. But recent improvements in the Trans-Sulawesi Highway now bring in some 200 visitors a month. Still, the province is so large that for several months of the year you can travel for days without meeting another foreigner.

Prices in US dollars. S = Single; D = Double; T = Triple; AC = Air-conditioning. Telephone code for Palu is 451. (0451 within Indonesia.)

Central Sulawesi's main attractions are the Lore Lindu National Park, which offers magnificent trekking across wild savannahs and deep river gorges, Lake Poso, and the megaliths of the Bada, Besoa and Napu valleys.

The easiest way to reach this area is by flying into the provincial capital of Palu (or you can take the Trans-Sulawesi Highway from Ujung Pandang or Manado) and then making your way to the sites by a combination of public or chartered vehicles and trekking.

Also interesting, but rarely visited, are the Togian Islands, in Tomini Bay, and the Banggai Islands, in Tolo Bay. You can reach these by flying into Poso or Luwuk, and overlanding to the point of ferry and boat departure.

Central Sulawesi offers the most potential for adventure travel on this island. Even the relatively accessible "tourist" attractions—the megaliths of the Bada Valley, Tentena and Lake Poso—require a modicum of initiative, except for those "packaged" by a travel agency. While MAF can fly you in and out of these places in a small Cessna, it's almost impossible to reserve a place ahead. It takes hours of road travel to reach even these areas and some walking is required to see the megaliths.

For those who really want to get away from the tourist scene, there are isolated villages in the mountains, coastal settlements and remote islands. But there are always trails: even remote mountain people need kerosene, matches and clothing.

Look at the maps and our texts: there is very little information available for most of the mountainous areas. Ditto for the west coast from Mamaju to Donggala and the east coast from Kendari to Kolonodale. These are the areas for those who seek something very different. Creature comforts will be few, food very basic and you will need to speak at least some Indonesian. If you travel to any of these areas, let us know what you found: and if you survived.

Palu

Palu is set on the innermost point of a deep bay ringed by high, grassy hills, and criss-crossed by small trails. The city has a pleasant, relaxed atmosphere. (See map pg. 154.)

TRANSPORTATION

By Air

Merpati flies daily to Palu from Ujung Pandang. There are also flights to Palu from Jakarta, Bandung, Denpasar and Surabaya, calling first at Ujung Pandang. Taxis to and from the airport cost $2.50; you can also catch a *bemo* for the 7-km ride into town.

Bouraq Jl. Juanda 87, ☎ 22995. Daily flights to Balikpapan, Kalimantan ($51) and Manado ($82), thrice weekly to Gorontalo ($49).

Merpati Jl. Mongonsidi 71, ☎ 21172. Daily flights to Ujung Pandang ($65), Luwuk ($62), Jakarta ($212), and Toli-Toli ($53). Four flights weekly to Denpasar ($183, via Surabaya); three per week to Poso ($28) and to Buol ($64).

Sempati At the Central Hotel, ☎ 23833; fax: 23256. Five flights weekly to: Denpasar ($132); Jakarta ($211, with continuation to Singapore); and Ujung Pandang ($65).

By Land

Several buses run daily from **Terminal Masomba** on Jl. Mongonsidi: to Ujung Pandang (30 hrs, $15); to Toli-Toli (18 hrs, $10); to Gorontalo (16–24 hrs, $17). Another bus station, called **Terminal Inpres** or Manonda, handles traffic to Donggala.

By Sea

Shipping traffic to and from Palu comes out of

Pantaloan Harbor, about 22 km north of town, beyond Tawaeli on the east coast of Palu Bay. Cargo boats stop at the port, built in 1978, on their runs between Pare-Pare and Mamuju to the south, and Toli-Toli in the north. There are several departures each week in each direction. Example: to Toli Toli (17 hrs, $9 for deck passage).

During much of the 1980s, Pantaloan was an important port for the export of logs, rattan and ebony, but it declined somewhat after restrictions were placed on the export of these items. With the recent lifting of the ban, this port might soon see more activity.

Pantaloan Harbor ☎ 23815, 91027

PELNI

Pelni lines' *Kambuna* calls four times a month on its back-and-forth between Ujung Pandang, Balikpapan (Kalimantan), Toli-Toli and Bitung. On a similar schedule, the *Tidar* also calls at Pantaloan on its route, which includes Tarakan (Kalimantan), Balikpapan (Kalimantan) and Ujung Pandang (but not Toli-Toli and Bitung). **Pelni** Jl. RA Kartini, ☎ 21696.

SMALL BOATS

The small port of Wani, just north of Pantaloan, is the place to find passage on small boats to local destinations north as far as Toli-Toli, and south to Mamaju. Smaller *pinisi* (two masted adaptations of traditional sailboats) call at Donggala, while shuttling copra to Surabaya.

Local Transportation

Bemos (also called "Mitsubishi") take you anywhere in town for Rp300. After dark, more leisurely *dokar* cost Rp300–500, or you can hail passing motorbikes for Rp500.

ACCOMMODATIONS

Palu Golden Jl. Raden Saleh 1, ☎ 21126; fax: 23230. 55 rms. Located next to the bay. Dirty beach, but good view from some rooms. This formerly decrepit hotel is slowly getting back into shape, but is still overpriced (bargaining is possible). The swimming pool might actually function one of these years. Nice lobby, restaurant, disco of sorts. Usually frequented by expense accounts. $43–$54 S, $54–$66 D.
Hotel Wisata, Jl. Letjen Sultan Parman 39, ☎ 21175. AC rooms from $14.
Buni Nyiur City Jl. Sultan Parman 28, ☎ 21076. Restaurant, AC rooms. $14 on up.
Central Hotel Jl. Kartini 6, ☎ 21738; fax: 23256. 50 rms. Good central location, attentive service, best value in town. Swimming pool, tennis court, restaurant serving Chinese, Indonesian, European cooking plus seafood. Airline tickets and *Jakarta Post* delivered to your room. In-town car rental $2.50/hour or $38/day, including driver and fuel. Located next to a supermarket and Wartel (mail, phone, fax). $12.50–$28 S or D.

All taxes, service included.
New Dely Hotel, Jl. Tadulaho 17. Clean and efficient. $7–$9 w/o AC; $12.50–$30 w/AC.
Hotel Taurus, Jl. Hasanuddin. Small, but clean rooms. $3.50–$5.

Cheaper accommodations include **Losmen Arafah** on Jl. Sultan Lewara, **Angkasa Raya** on Jl. Danau Poso, **Bukit Indah** on Jl. Maluku, **Losmen Pasific** and **Penginapan Latimojong** on Jl. Gajah Madah. Rooms $2–$5.

DINING

The **Milano** (on the shopping alley running parallel to Jl. Hassanudin) serves European, Indonesian and Chinese food, and Italian style ice cream. Pleasant, and very clean. Prices reasonable. You can reserve accommodations at Prinz John's Dive Resort here, and make arrangements for scuba diving. (See "Scuba Diving" under Donggala below.) Also information on trekking tours. Ask for Peter Meroniak who's German and also speaks English.

For seafood, especially grilled fish, try the **Oriental** (near the Milano) or the **Citra** (Jl. Hasanudin). Out of town, the best are **Pondok Selera** (at Mambro, 10 km towards Tawaeli) and **Buluri Indah** (8 km toward Donggala), which also serves *kaledo*, a local specialty made of manioc and beef leg marrow. Both restaurants are built out over the bay.

There are several restaurants along Jl. Yos Sudarso, north of Palu Beach Hotel. **Restaurant Meranu Setia Budi** (Jl. Setia Budi 44) serves perhaps the best Chinese-Indonesian food in Palu. The seafood is cheap and delicious. The **Kembang Joyo** is said to be best for chicken dishes. **Padang Raya** on Jl. Iman Bonjol serves spicy Sumatran meat and fish dishes. The **Palu Beach Hotel Restaurant** has a lovely view of the bay and is a good place to linger over a cold beer, though is not noted for its cooking. At night the **foodstalls** near the central bridge on Jl. Hasanuddin sell delicious *murtabak* (Rp250). Small evening **foodstalls** also line Jl. Gajah Madah.

HANDICRAFTS

The **Museum of Central Sulawesi** (Jl. Sapiri, west of the river) houses a large collection of prehistoric stone axes and mortars, pottery burial jars and a wide range of wooden artifacts and basketry. Open 8 am–5 pm, Tue–Fri; 9 am to 2 pm, Sat and Sun. Closed Mon. Rp200.

Kain Donggala, the famous *ikat* cloth of Central Sulawesi, is difficult to find in Palu; as yet there are few tourists and the majority of pieces are exported to Jakarta. **Ibu Fauzia Hassan** (Jl. Jambu 11, ☎ 22940) has the widest selection of pieces. Prices: man's silk *sarung* ($50 on up); woman's *kain* and *selendang* ($80 on up).

TRAVELER'S SERVICES

Telephone From Wartel offices, direct dialed, about $3.50/min to Europe, $2.50/min to USA, Mexico, Australia, all taxes included.

Travel Agency Wisata Gautama Putra Tour and Travel, Jl. Sis Al Jufri 10A, Komplex Palu Plaza, ☎ 52334 and 51797. Trekking in Lore Lindu and elsewhere in the area.

Donggala

Telephone code 0457
Taxis depart for Donggala when full (4 passengers) from Palu's Manonda terminal, near the Pasar Inpres market. It's 60¢/head, or rent the whole taxi for $2.50 for yourself. Chartered taxi to the Prinz, $4, capacity of four.

LOCAL TRANSPORTATION

Horse-drawn *dokar* go anywhere in town for 15¢. Minibus-taxis leave from the market next to the Wisma Rame, to Towale, 20¢/ a head. Or charter one for immediate departure, $2 one-way. Same for Boneage, about 7 km away.

ACCOMMODATIONS

Prinz John's (See below under "Scuba Diving.") **Wisma Rame** Run by Haji Umar, this is a small, clean place. Meals can be arranged, $1–$2. Haji Umar can help you get a local guide (usually one of his relations) as well as a canoe for snorkeling or touring the harbor. Guide $3–$4/day; canoe w/paddler $3/half day. $3/night for a room w/attached facilities.

Penginapan Anda is cheap at $1.50. There are also the **Penginapan Bruri** ($1.50) and the **Wisma Bakti** ($1.75–$2.50).

SCUBA DIVING

There is a little-known piece of tropical paradise at Tanjung Karang near Donggala—Prinz John's Dive Resort. The setting is idyllic: well-built wood-and-thatch cottages, excellent meals, no electricity or TV, white sand beach, and year-round water sports, including scuba diving. Expert divers can explore the wrecks just off Donggala Harbor. The best one, recently discovered and completely unmolested since it sank, lies on her side at 32–50 meters.

Prinz John's Dive Resort Just before the end of the road to Tanjung Karang, off a right turn. Booking via the Hotel Central in Palu (see above). 3 bungalows plus 10 rooms. Owner Peter Meroniak is almost always there on weekends. $8–$12.50 S, $15–$17.50 D, meals included.

All inclusive dive package, $50 per day. Wind surfing, $2.50 per hour; sailing local traditional boat, $3 for half day, including free fishing with local gear—good chance for tuna. Mask and snorkel rental, $2 per day, fins $2 per day.

Poso

Telephone code 0452
Poso is a small port town on the shores of Tomini Bay, and the gateway to the rarely visited eastern regions of Central Sulawesi. There is little to see or do in Poso; for most travelers it is simply a stopoff point. The large market on the western side of the Poso River is worth an early morning visit by *sampan* (a small wooden boat) and there is a reasonable beach at Kanawo, 8 km to the west.

TRANSPORTATION

By Air

Merpati flies small Casa 212s from Palu to Poso 3 times a week ($28). The airline also flies back 3 times a week. The airline flies from Poso to Luwuk ($34) 3 times a week as well. Public transport to the airport is difficult, and Merpati will collect you at your hotel for $1.80.
Merpati Jl. Pulau Sumatra 69A, ☎ 94619.

By Land

Bina Wisata Jl. Pulau Sumatra 69A, ☎ 94619. (Same office as Merpati.) The Bina Wisata bus company runs coaches to Palu leaving at 1 pm, 2 pm and 10 pm (6 hrs, $4 AC; $3 non-AC). There are also buses east to Ampana (6 hrs, $3), and on to Luwuk (18–24 hrs, $7.50).

By Sea

Boats for Gorontalo in North Sulawesi leave Poso every few days. The journey takes two days, calling at Dolong in the Togian Islands.

Local Transportation

Bemos will take you anywhere in Poso for Rp200, though you can easily walk most places.

ACCOMMODATIONS

Hotel Bambu Jaya Jl. Agus Salim 105, right on the seashore. The perfect place to recover from an overland journey. There is little competition at the price. Clean and breezy. Next door is the Bambu Jaya restaurant: the only possible drawback is the proposed Karaoke lounge. $7 w/o AC; $11–$22 w/AC, all w/attached facilities. **Hotel Wisata** Jl. Patimura 19 on the waterfront. Large, gloomy rooms with mosquitoes.

$6–$12, depending on whether the AC is working.

Hotel Nels $4.50–$8.50 w/attached facilities. **Anugrah Inn** Jl. Pulau Samosir. Decent, but away from the beach. $4 w/o AC; $8 w/AC and breakfast.

Cheaper, *penginapan* style accommodations include the **Penginapan Poso** and the **Penginapan Beringin** ($2–$3), both on Jl. Pulau Sumatera, and **Penginapan Sulawesi** on the corner Jl. Imam Bonjol and Jl. Agus Salim.

DINING

The **Bambu Jaya Restaurant** serves decent Chinese-Indonesian food, but the **Rumah Makan Jawa Timur** (Jl. Pulau Sumatra) is cheaper and better. Further along the same road is **Padang Raya**, serving spicy Sumatran cuisine. The **Mekar** (Jl. Imam Bonjol) and **Warung Lumayan** (Jl. Teluk Umar) offer cheaper Indonesian food.

MONEY CHANGING

Bank Negara Indonesia 1946 Jl. Yos Sudarso.

Tentena

Telephone code 0458
Tentena is a little Christian town set on the northeastern edge of Lake Poso, with white sand beaches and high, forested mountains. The two halves of the town are connected by a covered bridge. The town is the headquarters of the Central Sulawesi Christian Church, which operates a twice-weekly flight into the Bada Valley and Lore Lindu National Park.

The weather here is cool—the lake is at 515 m—and coffee, cloves and vegetables grow on the surrounding hills. The rainy season starts mid to late November and continues until April, with shorter, lighter rains during August and September, but don't trust the weatherman.

The Pamona people who live around Lake Poso are distantly related to the Bare'e or southern Toraja, but all Central Sulawesi culture is now extinct. Dutch missionaries arrived in the 1890s, and conversion was more rapid and complete than in Toraja.

If you are here from Aug 24 to 31, you can witness the Festival Danau Poso, an annual event featuring raft and small boat races as well as traditional dances.

TRANSPORTATION

With the recent improvements in the Trans-Sulawesi highway, which passes right through Tentena, the easiest way to reach the town is overland on a variety of public buses. (See map pg. 169.) From Palu (7–8 hrs, via Poso, $5); from Poso ($1, 58 km, 1.5 hrs). From South Sulawesi and Tana Toraja, take public buses north on the Transul—via Wotu and Mangkutana—to Pendolo, at the southern edge of the lake, and continue for another 74 km on the Transul to Tentena. Or take the boat (3–4 hrs, $1).

From Tentena, in addition to traveling north and south on the Transul, you can also travel east by public minibus on a good road to Kolonodale (8 hrs, 180 km, $2.50). From Kolonodale you can catch a boat to the Morowali Nature Reserve. There is daily public transportation from Tentena to Taipa (75¢), on the western shore of Lake Poso. The road south to Bancea should also be open by the time you read this, and public transport will then continue to Pendolo down the west side of the lake.

Local Vehicle Rental

At the **Pamona Indah**, bicycles rent for $2.25/day; motorcycles $7.50/day. A car to nearby places runs $15, plus food and smokes for the driver.

Regional Air Travel

Mission Aviation Fellowship, a support service for the Protestant missions in the area, runs public flights on small Cessna aircraft from from Tentena to other small airstrips in the region. Aside from nearby Bada and Besoa ($15), MAF runs weekly flights to Uentango, just north of the Morowali area, near the Protestant Church and school located at Uebone. There are also weekly flights to Rampi, Seko and Kantewu in the mountains south and west of Tentena. Fly in and trek out. Check schedules and flight availability with MAF at the Tentena airstrip.

Boats on Lake Poso

From Pendolo to Tentena, public boats depart at 6 am, arrive at 9 am; the other way, 4 pm to 10 pm ($1 each way).

Charter prices for jaunts around the lake are highly variable, subject to bargaining, and depend on the size of the boat and its engine. The "official" base price is $10/hr, but you can arrange for a round trip to the Bancea Orchid Reserve (see below) for about $30 in a boat big enough for 2 or 3 large westerners.

The owner of the Pamona Hotel, Pak Yavet Satigi, has a 40 HP speedboat (seats 4–5), and charges $42 for a 5–8 hr tour of the lake.

ACCOMMODATIONS

Wasantara Hotel The best view in town is from the VIP rooms on the second floor of this hotel. The second-floor balcony also overlooks the Poso River. No restaurant, but meals can be arranged. 2 VIP rms, $22; 2 bungalows, $11; 6 standard rms $9; 2 economy rms $2/person. **Pamona Indah** Another good view, right on the lakeshore where the larger boats start and stop their run to Pendolo. 26 rms. Restaurant serves genuine cold beer, and has a fair variety of Chinese and Indonesian dishes, 75¢–$2.50. Try the *sugili,* a local specialty: chunks of large eel either fried or prepared in a hot sauce. Bicycles, motorcycles, car and a boat for rent. $7–$17, all w/attached facilities.

Penginapan Wisata Remaja 7 rms. Close to the boat landing. Clean and convenient place to stay. $4–$5, S or D.

Victory. Just off the main street in the dock/bus area. 10 rms. New *losmen*, very clean. $6.50–$10 S or D, all w/attached facilities.

Penginapan Rio Next to the bus station. 12 rms. Small boat landing. 2 toilets, 1 bath. $2/head.

Wisata Tiberias Church-run. 2 VIP rms w/attached facilities, $7.50; 6 rms w/shared, $6.

Panorama Hotel Inconveniently located, but has a good view of rice fields, town and a small corner of the lake. 5 rms. Meals can be arranged if requested at least a couple of hours ahead. $1.50/person. (Note: the VIP rm, for up to three, $9, is not worth it; the only difference is a tiled floor.)

GUIDES

There are at least 10 licensed guides in Tentena. They maintain a sort of information booth across from the Litha bus "station." You don't have to look for them. They will find you and latch on. Fees negotiable. For the Bada megaliths, it's about $10/day, plus their expenses. Individuals' levels of English, experience and knowledge vary considerably.

Guides often hustle hard to take you to the Lore Lindu National Park from Tentena. It's not really necessary to take a guide for the first section, and guides in the village of Gintu, some 85 km west, are certainly cheaper and may be much more informative, as many speak the local language. These local guides often have difficulty contacting tourists, as the Tentena hustlers often beat them to it.

A Tentena guide also will have a deal with a particular homestay, and inevitably take you there. Others worth checking out (which don't appear to be part of the Tentena cartel): **The Merry Homestay** in Gintu and the **Bomba Homestay** in Bomba.

Pendolo

Pendolo, on the south shore of Lake Poso, is a good spot to break up overland journeys. The **Jawa Indah** bus agent, next to the Masamba *los-*

men, offers tickets to Poso, Palu, Ampana and Kolonodale. The bus to Tentena takes 2 hrs and costs $1.25; to Poso 5 hrs, $2.50. The only regular boat to Tentena, the **Wisata**, (now that most people go overland), departs from in front of the Victoria *losmen* at 8 am (3 hrs w/stops, $1).

ACCOMMODATIONS

Danau Poso Hotel 300 meters from the lake. 12 rms. Meals $1.25. $1.25/person w/o attached facilities, $1.75 w/attached facilities.

Losmen Victoria On the shore of the lake. 8 rms, 6 w/attached facilities. Meals $1–$2. Has two Kijangs that run to Mangkutana (3 hrs, $2.50). $3.50 w/attached facilities; $2.50 w/o.

Masamba Lakeside, near Victoria. 6 rms, 4 with attached facilities. Meals $1.25. $2.50 w/facilities; $2 w/o.

BANCEA ORCHID RESERVE

From Pendolo, a paved road cuts west across rice fields along the lake's southwestern shore. After 13 km the hard surface ends but the road continues another 6 km to peter out after passing through Bancea village. (At the time of this writing, this road was scheduled for improvement.) From here it's an easy, if steep, 1.5 km walk from the bridge to the orchid reserve.

There you find a half dozen completed but empty cabins and a steep path down to the orchids which leads to wonderfully picturesque lakeside setting in a bay at the base of steep, vegetation-covered headlands.

Public transportation does not often run to Bancea village as traffic to and from Pendolo is usually by boat. From Pendolo, a boat can be chartered for a round-trip to the orchid reserve for about $20. (From Tentena, about $30.)

Bada Valley

You can see the principal megaliths of the Bada Valley in one tough day of hiking, or two more leisurely ones. Expect mud and river crossings, during which sand will fill your boots. Wear long pants for the thorns, and bring along a hat, long-sleeved apparel and a canteen.

You should be careful of a common parasite infestation in the Bada Valley (also in Lore Lindu) called schistosomiasis, which is about as bad as it sounds. This is a parasitic trematode worm that damages the kidneys, liver and other organs. The fluke is passed through the skin, so you should never walk barefoot in the area, and if you want to be really careful, wear rubber boots.

Unless you have an English-speaking guide

from Palu or elsewhere, it's essential to know at least some basic Indonesian to get to and around the Bada Valley. You can hire a guide from the valley if you speak Indonesian (none speaks English) for about $3/day. It's almost impossible to find the megaliths alone.

You are expected to report with your passport to the main police station at Gintu, and, perhaps, to a policeman at the office of the *camat*.

GETTING THERE

It is easiest to fly into Bada from Tentana on a Mission Aviation Fellowship (MAF) flight, scheduled Tuesdays and Fridays ($15). The flight continues to Besoa, same price. You can also get on at Bada, and fly to Besoa ($10). On all flights you get a free baggage allowance of 15 kilos. These are small planes, however, and you might have to wait for a seat. Or the plane might be in Tarakan for an overhaul. Or the pilot might be sick. Or he might be out of fuel. Generally, though, it's reliable. If you know your date of arrival, telegram ahead to book: MAF Pilot, Airfield, Tentena, Kabupaten Poso, Sulawesi Tengah.

There are frequent buses from Tentana to Tonusu, 19 km away. At Tonusu the fun begins. During the rainy season (mid-November–April) the 53-km journey on this dirt road could be a five-day nightmare, with the jeeps (they travel in convoys of three or more) getting continuously stuck in the mud. Bring food. During the dry season, June to August, it could be as little as 8 hrs. The jeeps which make the Tonusu–Bada passenger run (once or twice a week) charge $8.50/head, or $85 for a one-way charter. Jeeps seat 6 or 7 in relative comfort along with gear. On the normal run, 10 or more passengers are somehow squeezed in, somehow. If the jeep gets stuck in the mud, you are expected to help push, knee-deep in the ooze.

During the rainy season, it's probably faster to walk, sleeping under any of the six bridges. Some 20 km out, there's a great view back over Lake Poso. You will need about two days of steady trekking to cover the 53 hilly kilometers to Bomba, the first village in the Bada Valley. A porter/guide, if you can find one, will charge $5–$7.50/day to accompany you on this trip. If you backpack, it's possible to do it alone, as there is only one road and you will not get lost. Bring food. (See map pg. 161.)

Note: This road is scheduled for paving. If and when that's done, public transportation and charters will be cheaper and much easier. MAF will probably stop its flights then.

The other way to get to the Bada Valley is by trail from Gimpu, located 99 km south of Palu along a surfaced road ($3 by public minibus). From here it's an easier two days for the 50 km to Gintu. Porter/guides for this trip, same price. If you want a horse, it's $15 for the two days.

No muddy feet, but slower.

A good, level footpath connects Gimpu to Gintu. The 2-day hike is relieved with an overnight stay at Moa village, a bit more than halfway along. Mostly forest trekking with a few panoramic views. Several long suspension bridges cross the Lariang River, which the trail follows. Possible sightings of *anoa,* the rare dwarf buffalo.

FOOD/ACCOMMODATIONS

There are no villages between Tonusu and Bomba, the first Bada village. On the trail from GImpu, you spend the first and only night on the road with the *kepala desa* of Moa. Overnight and meals for yourself and porters, $5–$10 negotiable. At GIntu there is an unregistered little hotel with no name, 6 rms, 1 bath, 4 toilets, $5.50 w/meals. Or ask the *kepala desa* (village head) of any village for a place to stay and pay about $5/person for room and board.

THE MEGALITHS

The origin and age of the works of stone that dot the valleys of Bada, Besoa and Napu remain a mystery. Recent excavations of some of the stone cisterns or vats indicate that they probably date back to the first millennium AD (they could be of a later date, but are not likely to be much older, as some have speculated).

In many areas where they are found, large upright stones (menhirs) are often associated with human sacrifice and with worship of the ancestors. A Swiss explorer named Kaudern, who visited the region in 1918–1919, inquired into the 2-meter (6.5 ft) menhir outside the house temple at Kantewu, southeast of Gimpu.

"When questioned about the stone," writes Kaudern, "the natives always gave an evasive answer, but for certain reasons I believe it to have been used as a torture pole, to which in olden times, on certain occasions the victims who were to be killed, were fettered."

Following are the major megaliths found in the Bada Valley (the numbers are keyed to the map on page 264):

1. Palindo ("the entertainer") Also known as Raksasa Sepe ("the Sepe giant") or the "Bada Man." 4.5 meters. Near Sepe, 1.5 km from Bewa. Almost 15 ft in height, this statue is the largest of the subdistrict and certainly the most celebrated of the region. It can be reached by rafting across the Lariang River near Bewa. It is perhaps a representation of Sepe's first mythological inhabitant, Tosaloge.

According to local tradition, the Raja of Luwu once ordered 1800 subjects to carry this statue to Palopo as a demonstration that Bada should be considered subject to him, but the effort failed. The statue is said originally to have faced Luwu in the south, but the Bada people turned it

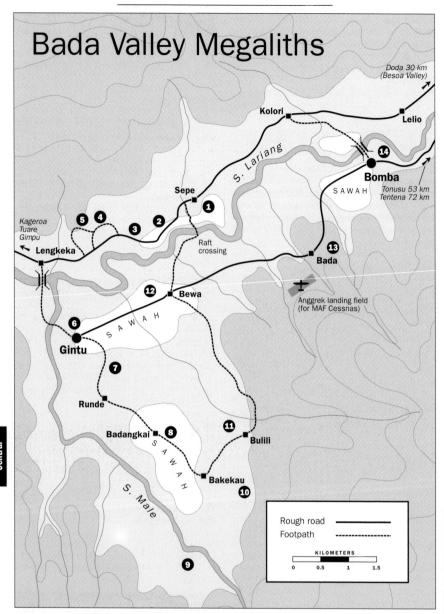

Bada Valley Megaliths

Doda 30 km
(Besoa Valley)

Kolori

Lelio

S. Lariang

Sepe

14

Bomba

1

SAWAH

Tonusu 53 km
Tentena 72 km

Kageroa
Tuare
Gimpu

5 **4**

3 **2**

← Lengkeka

Raft
crossing

13

Bada

12 **Bewa**

SAWAH

Anggrek landing field
(for MAF Cessnas)

6

SAWAH

Gintu

7

Runde

11

Badangkai **8**

SAWAH

Bulili

10 **Bakekau**

S. Male

9

Rough road ──────

Footpath ┈┈┈┈┈┈┈

KILOMETERS

0   0.5   1   1.5

around (it now faces west) to assert their autonomy. When the Raja of Luwu's followers tried to turn it back, it fell on its side, killing 200 of them. In the past, offerings were brought to this figure before embarking on any new enterprise such as opening up a new garden.

2. Mesinga ("Wearing a scarf") Southwest of Sepe. A small, fallen statue with faded features. It wears a barkcloth headdress. Nearby are 13 stone vats.

3. Maturu ("Sleeping") 3.5 meters. Northeast of Lengkeka. Statue lies on its back.

4. Oba ("Monkey") Northeast of Lengkeka. A nice, smallish statue in a rice paddy.

5. Mpeime Northeast of Lengkeka. A large statue, lying down. Plans are afoot to right it.

6. Tarai Roe ("Banyan Tree") or Pombekadoi. Small. Near Gintu. Faded features. Found in the backyard of the former district head of Bada. This statue presumably was erected above a buried mass of gold. Its presence symbolized Gintu's pre-eminence among the villages of south Lore.

7. Maturu ("Sleeping") Between Gintu and Runde. Large statue lying down.

8. Dula Boe or **Baulu** ("Water buffalo") At Badangkai. Face like the other megaliths, but the body, lying down, looks like a water buffalo. According to local lore, this statue now rests askew because its owner, irate at having lost a pig, kicked it over.

9. Torumpana (Place name meaning, perhaps, "noble arrow") 1 m. South of Bakekau. Faded features, hard to get to. For masochists and archaeologists only.

10. Tinoe (Place name meaning, perhaps, "late woman") 1.5 m. About 1 km from Bakekau. Nice features. Bearing the likeness of a woman and child, this statue may once have represented a fertility deity. In the past, farmers offered water buffalo to her to insure a good harvest. Even hunters were supposed to request her permission, and after the hunt to hang the skin of their prey upon her head.

11. Oboka In Bulili. Missing its head, which lies face-down nearby. In a fenced-off area with some stone jars. This statue was once the protector of the local inhabitants, who gathered around it with fires blazing. In the past it was used as a sacred place to which people brought offerings in order to reach particular goals or fulfill personal desires.

12. Ari Impohi ("Main house pillar") In Bewa. Small statue, good features. This name suggests the megalith was once the central post of a now vanished ritual meeting house.

13. Loga ("Relieved heart") In Bada. 1.5 m. Female. Nice view, and easy to reach. Standing askew on a hill out in the fields, she is said to be gazing emptily at her husband, now a statue placed some distance away, who was sentenced to death for committing adultery.

14. Langke Bulawa ("Gold anklet") In Bomba. 2 m. Female. Tough mud and thorn path, and the locals charge a $1.25 fee (no charge at any of the others.) Not really worth it, except for the masochists and anthropologists. Langke Bulawa was perhaps a patroness of the local *haute coûtume*, through whom the upper-class ladies justified their exclusion from labor in the fields.

There are a number of other works to be seen in the valley, including a stone carved with the motif of banyan tree leaves; the four judgment stones where the raja formerly held court (including the Tohemu stone said to have been Sawerigading's umbrella left behind on his visit to Bada); and the mortar stone where the first fruits of the harvest were hulled.

Vast stone cisterns, called *kalamba*, which may have been used as baths or as burial chambers for aristocrats, are found scattered throughout the region. Interestingly—and mysteriously—all of the objects in the area are made from a type of grey stone of which there are no deposits in the near vicinity.

—Greg Acciaoli and Kal Muller

MEGALITH HIKES

You can see all the major megaliths in either a rather tough, one-day hike, or in a more leisurely two-day hike.

One day hike Starting from Gintu, first visit the statue known as Tinoe, near the village of Bakekau (See map opposite). This statue faces north, the only one of the major megaliths that does not gaze west. (Note: This means afternoon is the best time to photograph the other stone carvings, if there is sunshine.) From Tinoe, walk back along the main road to Badangkai, then through rice fields to nearby Baula, the "water buffalo."

Although it may look faster on the map to proceed directly to Ari Impohi in Bewa village, walking through rice fields is a time-consuming business. It's faster to return the main road, then trek through Runde and Gintu to Bewa. From there, head past the landing field to Bada village and the Loga statue, close to the road on a hill with a good view of the valley. Then backtrack to Bewa, walk north to the Lariang River, cross it on a poled bamboo raft, and follow the clean, sandy creek to a short climb and the path to Palindo, the largest and best statue, located at a former village site called Sepe.

Two day hike First day, from Gintu, walk to the suspension bridge near Lenkela village, then head up the valley to the Oba or "monkey" statue, proceed to Sepe and Palindo, raft across the river, walk to Bada and back to Gintu. On the second day, start as on the suggested one-day walk, but after the Loga megalith, go through Bomba village and on to Langke Bulawe.

—Kal Muller

Ampana

Telephone code 0464
This little coast town is the access point for Tanjung Api ("Fire Cape") and the Togian Islands in Tomini Bay to the north.

TRANSPORTATION

The bus from Poso to Ampana (5–7 hrs, $3.50) follows the road along the coast. The fare includes a simple meal of fish and rice taken at a roadside restaurant, at the tiny fishing village of Padapu. The road is decent, but washes out frequently. For the foreseeable future, the minibus crosses the Bangka River on a raft of lashed together canoes (impossible for a day or two after a heavy rain). Three different contractors have built bridges; each has collapsed.

Horse-drawn carriages or *bendi* will take you around town for 5¢–10¢.

Passenger boats leave a couple of times a week from Poso (8 hrs, $4, including meal). Check at the Poso harbor for departure days.

TO TANJUNG API

To get to Tanjung Api just stroll around the Ampana docks, and you will be besieged by offers. No official price, so bargain. An outriggered canoe with a 15 hp engine should cost $8–$14 round-trip. Bring water and a hat.

ACCOMMODATIONS

There are 4 small 10-room hotels in town, charging similar prices: $2 w/shared facilities; $5.50 w/attached facilities and meals. The **Mekar** and the **Irama** are both on Jalan Kartini, conveniently close to the dock, bus depot and market. The **Plaza** is a half kilometer inland; the **Rejeki** an inconvenient kilometer away. Try to get rooms away from the afternoon sun, or you are in for sweat-soaked siestas.

Togian Islands

Boats of 60 to 100 tons frequently ply the Tomini Gulf among these islands. The most convenient places to board are Poso or Gorontalo in North Sulawesi. Passage, which includes basic rice-and-fish meals and a foam sleeping mat, is cheap: $11 for the 3-day trip between Poso and Gorontalo.

You might be able to negotiate one of the crewmembers' bunk ($2–$5) if your Indonesian bargaining skills are up to it, but they tend to be too short. Unless the boats are crowded, it's best to sleep in the large passenger compartments, piling up two mattresses for extra cushioning. By all means have your valuables locked in one of the ship's officers' cabins.

It helps to be friendly with the crew. They will invite you to join them for meals, their fare being somewhat better than the passengers'. Bottled water is usually sold on board while boiled drinking water is freely dispensed. Unless you can survive on a rice-and-fish diet (hard-boiled eggs might be sold by an enterprising youth), bring your own victuals, or purchase them in little stores near the dock. Food prepared on board is spiced for Indonesian palates.

Toilet facilities are few and basic. There are no sit-downs: it's the squat, water-and-left-hand universal variety, so bring toilet paper unless used to the Indonesian way of doing things.

The boat's roof is the best spot for sightseeing and photography. Bring sunscreen. If you want to get off the ship for a couple of days and wait for the next boat, the villages where you stop have simple accommodations called *penginapan*. About $4 for room and board. Don't expect too much.

Kolonodale

Kolonodale is nestled at the tip of one of the fingers of Tomori Bay, at the crook of Sulawesi's eastern and southeastern peninsulas. This small town is the jumping off point for treks to the Ranu Lakes and other sites in the Morowali Nature Reserve.

TRANSPORTATION

The usual route to Kolonodale is from Poso, on one of the 2–3 buses a day (8 hrs, $3.50). You can also get on the bus at Tentena (although they don't stop in town, rather at a point on the Trans-Sulawesi Highway about 4 km away). There may not be any seats available at Tentena, but extra bodies can usually be squeezed in, as this means more profit for the driver and his helper. This is not a fun trip, although the surfacing is due to be improved soon. There are also regular direct buses from Palu (14 hrs, $6.50) and twice a week from Ujung Pandang, (about 20 hrs, $15). From Luwuk there's bus service to Pandaoke ($2.50) continuing, road conditions permitting, to Baturube, where you can catch boats to Kolonodale (6 hrs, $2.50).

You can also fly to Soroako, take a boat across Lake Matano to Nuha, and then travel overland by bus (5 hrs) to Beteleme, where there are regular buses and trucks to Kolonodale. Pelni's *Awu* calls at Kolonodale twice a month on its Iong run which includes Kendari and Luwuk (see "Transportation" pg. 237).

TO KENDARI

There's also a weekly wooden passenger boat from Kolonodale to Kendari (about 24 hrs, $7.50).

ACCOMMODATIONS

Both *losmen* are close to each other, and easy to find in this small town.
Losmen Lestari 20 rms. The best in town. Clean and with a view of the bay. Meals, $1.25. $2.50 per person, w/attached facilities; $1.75 per person w/shared facilities.
Losmen Sederhana 9 rms. No enclosed toilets (two shared ones). A tourist information center and a shop selling Wana handicrafts was planning to open across the street. $1.75 per person, meals 75¢.

GUIDES

There is fierce competition between the 8 guides in Kolonodale and the ones from Tentena. The latter get first crack at latching on to the foreign bodies, as most tourists first go to Tentena. Levels of English and competence vary greatly, but in general we suggest a guide from Kolonodale, even if they do not have an official license (as do those in Tentena). The usual guide fee is $20 per day, sometimes negotiable. Add about $2.50 per person per day for food. Local porters charge $7.50–$10 a day.

TREKKING IN MOROWALI

The one way boat ride across Tomori Bay to where the trekking begins costs $20 for a boat big enough for 4 people. Check at the harbormaster's office (Kantor Perhubungan Laut) at the entrance to the dock area to find out which of the boats are safe.

Given the effort getting to Kolonodale, and into the reserve, trekking here is hardly worth it for less than about 3 days. If you're really ambitious, take the 16-day jaunt—which ends at Ampana! You will need good footwear, obviously, a light sleeping bag, canteen, hat and basic first aid kit.

If you want to leave by another route, have your guide drop you off at Tambaiyoli, at the northwest tip of Tomori Bay. From there, it's a 1-day trek to reach Uwekuli, on the north coast of the peninsula, on the road to Poso. If you walk to Malino—about half way to Poso—you will likely be able to find a ride for the rest of the way.

Luwuk and Banggai

Telephone code for Luwuk 0461
Luwuk, on the south coast of Sulawesi's eastern peninsula, is the access point for the Banggai Islands. Few tourists visit this area. Perhaps because of this, you have to report personally to the police with your passport, which they will keep until the electricity comes on at night and they can photocopy it. (They've got nothing better to do.) The weather here is tough to predict. Locals provide the following, but we offer no guarantees: It rains most from April until September, especially in the early part of this season; the highest waves are in December and January; the calmest seas, from April to August.

TRANSPORTATION

Merpati flies daily to Luwuk from Palu ($62), 3 times a week from Poso ($34), and twice a week from Manado ($55). All flights are Casa 212s.

By Land

Several buses a day run from Poso (20 hrs, $8). Traveling time will drop considerably as bridges are completed and the rest of the road paved (perhaps even by the time you read this). Buses also run from Pandaoke (6 hrs, $2.50).

By Sea

The large Pelni ship *Awu* calls at Luwuk twice a month on its round-trip between Semarang (Java) and Tahuna (Sangihe-Talaud).

TO THE BANGGAI ISLANDS
There are one or two daily boats from Luwuk shuttling back and forth between three ports on Peleng Island (e.g.: Tataba, 4–5 hrs, $2.)

The boats to Banggai Island (8–9 hours, $3–$4) leave Luwuk at night and arrive at 6 am–8 am. For an additional $2.50 you can get a very short bunk in a cabin; reserve the bunk early or sleep with the masses.

In Banggai, take a *becak* to the *losmen* (25¢) or a short walk. The return boat to Luwuk leaves in the late morning.

ACCOMMODATIONS

In Luwuk

Ramayana 32 rms. The best in town. Restaurant, large verandah over the sea with a view of the harbor entrance. Fan-cooled $8.50 S, $14 D; AC $11–$27 S, $16–$33 D

Safari Beach Short ride from downtown. 10 rms. The back of the hotel is on a sand beach with swimming possible. Fan-cooled $8/person; AC $11 S, $20 D w/meals.

Hotel Kota Near the market and the Poso bus station. 12 rms. $3/person.

There are three places for the down-and-out, all in the downtown area and noisy:
Rahmat (6 rms, $2.50/person); **Senang Hati** (32 rms, $2/person); **Sadar** (10 rms, $1.75).

In Banggai

Don Mery 9 rms. Pak Fenny, the owner of the Don Mery, works at the harbormaster's office and can help with boat passage and charters. A boat with outboard, big enough for 3–4 western bodies, can be chartered for $15–$20/day. Pak Fenny's wife can prepare picnic lunches, free if you stay at their *losmen*. Bring your own mask, snorkel and fins. $5.50/person w/meals.
Padang Laya 4 rms. Roomier than Don Mery, $7.50 w/meals.

PULAU TIKUS / MAKAILU ISLAND

Take the regular night passenger boat to Tataba on Peleng Island (4–5 hours, $2) which arrives at dawn. The *camat* (sub district official) can help arrange a boat to Makailu, about 45 min away; count on $15–$20 for a round-trip for up to 6 passengers, but more if you plan to spend the night or stay for a couple of days. Your boatman can help prepare meals.

—*Ian Caldwell and Kal Muller*

5 North PRACTICALITIES

INCLUDES MANADO, SANGIHE, BITUNG, AND MINAHASA

North Sulawesi is a rugged, forested place with beautiful vistas of still-active volcanoes and clove trees. Manado, the provincial capital and largest city in the area, has an international airport and many services. The area offers world-famous scuba diving, volcano climbing, peaceful mountain resorts, national parks, and the unique Minihasan culture and hospitality.

Prices in US dollars. S = Single; D = Double; T = Triple; AC = Air-conditioning. Telephone codes as noted.

Manado

Telephone code 0431
Manado is a thriving city of some 300,000, on a bay of the same name near the tip of Sulawesi's northern peninsula. Just offshore is an island group that offers some of the world's best drop-off diving. Unlike most major cities in Indonesia, Manado is an overwhelmingly Christian town, a legacy of colonial times. The Manadonese are famous for their ebullience and hospitality, and you will hear singing every night.

TRANSPORTATION

By Air

Because of the Garuda/Merpati monopoly on flights, in the past it was a long and expensive proposition to get to Manado. But this is now changing. First Bouraq opened its flight to Manado, followed by Sempati. But still no international flights were allowed to land, except for a short-lived and mysteriously ended series of flights from Guam.

Then Manado began to open its skies to international flights, with Bouraq's flights to Davao City (Philippines), being the first step. Now there is a direct, twice a week, 3.5-hour run from/to Singapore by Silk Air, the daughter airline of Singapore Airlines. There were also rumors of flights from Taiwan, Japan, and Korea. If these come to pass, the attractions of North Sulawesi will be appreciated by many more visitors.

Dr Sam Ratulangi Airport is 7km outside of town, and taxi coupons to just about anywhere in Manado cost $3–$4. You can also walk to the main road and hop on an *oplet* or minibus for Rp 250. Airport info: ☎ 52117 and 60865.
Bouraq Jl. Sarapung 27B, ☎ 62757, 62675. Daily flights to Balikpapan ($119), Banjarmasin ($160), Jakarta ($245), and Palu ($82); four

times weekly to Gorontalo ($42) and Tarakan ($185); three times a week to Ujung Pandang ($109); twice weekly to Ternate ($44); and twice weekly to Davao City, ($200 one-way, $400 RT; or $150 one-way, $262 RT with advance purchase).
Garuda Jl. Diponegoro 15, ☎ 52154, 51544. Open 8 am–4 pm weekdays, Sat. 7:30 am–12:30 pm, Sun. 8 am–12 noon. Airbus flights daily to Ujung Pandang ($109), Jakarta ($246).
Merpati Jl. Sudirman 132, ☎ 64027, 64028. Same hours as Garuda. Ambon, 4 weekly flights ($106); Bali, daily ($170) continuing to Jakarta ($246); also daily to Gorontalo, ($42) and Ternate ($44); four flights weekly to Naha, near Tahuna, Sagihe Besar ($46); twice weekly to Sorong ($93); twice weekly to Mangole ($75); twice weekly to Melanguane on Karakelong Island in the Talaud group ($63); once weekly to Palu ($83); and once weekly to Poso ($93).
Sempati At the Kawanus City Hotel. Open 8 am to 6 pm, Sun. 9 am to 4 pm. Six weekly flights to Surabaya ($186) continuing to Jakarta ($245) and Singapore ($355).
Silk Air 77 Robinson Rd, #10–03 SIA Building, Singapore 0106. Reservations: ☎ (65) 221-2221. (No Manado office at the time of writing.) The 3.5 hr flight to Manado runs about $400.

By Land

Buses run to and from Malalayang Terminal, 7–8 km south of Manado. Night buses to and from Gorontalo (12 hrs; $6 non-AC, $7.50 AC); Palu (48 hrs; non–AC $16, non-AC $22 AC). All are getting faster as road surfaces improve.

By Sea

From Manado harbor boats frequently depart (always at night) to the Sangihe–Talaud archipelago to the north. Often crowded, but inexpensive. To Tahuna, for example, takes 14 hours and costs $9. Bargain with crew for cabin space.

There are also departures to Ternate and

Ambon a couple of times a week. The Ambon run takes about 3-and-a-half days, with several stops along the way and costs $27, including very simple meals.

PELNI

Several of the large Pelni boats stop at Bitung, just across the peninsula from Manado. For information, contact the Manado office: **Pelni Lines**, Jl. Sam Ratulangi 7, ☎ 62884.

Local Transportation

Oplet and *Mikrolet* The ubiquitous *oplet*—a tiny minivan you enter through the rear—has a Rp 250 (12¢) flat rate fare which is paid at the end of your journey; have correct change ready. These shuttle back and forth between downtown and the city outskirts, usually to places where there are markets. Destinations are marked on the roof or on a plaque dangling inside the front window, and they will pick you up anywhere along the route: just raise your arm slightly. To signal a stop, ring the bell on the ceiling. If the bell is broken (which it usually is) tap the window behind the driver.

The *mikrolet* operates on the same principle, but carries more passengers and is entered at the side. Two passengers can sit beside the driver. For short city journeys the fare is Rp 250. Some are fitted with internal bells as in *oplets*, but you can also alert the driver by shouting "stop," which he will do with alarming alacrity. All manner of things are carried on board, so be prepared to step over live, trussed chickens and sacks of coconuts.

Most routes converge at the terminal at Pasar 45, outside Jumbo Supermarket. Transfer to onward destinations from the endpoints of the *oplet/mikrolet* routes: Tuminting for Molas (dive centers); Paal Dua for Bitung and points east and northeast; Malalayang for points south, including connections with buses on the Transul Highway; Wanea for Tomohon and Lake Tondano.

Oplet and *mikrolet* are not allowed to stop near main traffic junctions or directly in front of the Kawanua City Hotel. People will ask the driver to make short diversions to their destination, so don't be alarmed if the *oplet* suddenly leaves the main road down a narrow side street; enjoy the change of scenery. It is also possible to charter an empty *oplet* for around $2/hour (no minimum) which makes a cheap alternative to a taxi.

Taxis There are two types of taxi operating in Manado. One looks like an ordinary car or minibus and has no meter. These will take you anywhere in the city, but you have to negotiate a price. Or you can hire them by the hour at $3/hour with a three-hour minimum. You can get one at the Kawanua City Hotel, the Garden Hotel, or on the south side of the city center square (Taman Kesatuan Bangsa). You can also telephone:

Indra Kelana Taxi Company ☎ 52033.

The other—recently introduced—taxis are metered white sedans with a large sign on the roof. These are run by a company called **Dian Taksi** (☎ 62421), which currently has 20 cars that tour the city looking for customers. The first km is Rp 700 (30¢) and every subsequent km Rp 600 plus a time charge. There are no car rentals in Manado yet.

ACCOMMODATIONS

Manado has a wide range of accommodations, from luxury hotels to budget *losmen*. Credit cards are generally accepted at the best hotels.

Luxury $40–$90

Manado Beach Hotel At Tasik Ria, 20 km south of the city, ☎ 67001, 67005; fax: 67007. 200 rms. Got off a shaky start, but now living up to its 4–star rating. Coffee shop, restaurant—breakfast $5–$7, lunch $10, dinner $16—bar, disco, two swimming pools, fitness center, tennis, badminton, squash. Passable beach. All rooms with AC, phone, color TV (satellite reception). $70–$80 S, $80–90 D plus $17.5% for tax and service.

Kawanua City Hotel Jl. Sam Ratulangi 1, ☎ 522-22, fax: 65220. 100 rms. Swimming pool, two bars, cafeteria, restaurant, swimming pool, travel agent in lobby. Conveniently located near downtown area and considerably upgraded recently. Part of the Sahid Group. $60–65 S, $70–75 D plus 21% tax and service charge.

Note: Several 4–5 star hotels with golf courses are scheduled to open 1995 on the northernmost part of the peninsula. One is already under construction.

Intermediate ($10–$40)

Prices include tax & service. Higher priced rooms have AC.

New Queen Hotel Jl. Wakeke 12–14, ☎ 65979, 64440, fax: 65748. 35 rms. Pleasant and rated the cleanest hotel in town. Satellite TV with CNN, bar, coffee shop. $27–$46 S, $36–$54 D.

Manado Plaza Hotel Jl. W Maramis 110, ☎ 62940, 63808; fax: 62940. 50 rms. In the heart of downtown. Has the city's biggest restaurant, a health center, karaoke, and the Ebony Disco. Cinema next door, and taxi stand nearby. Tours organized. $25 S, $30 D.

Sahid Manado Hotel Jl. Babe Palar 1, ☎ 51688, 52688, fax: 63326. 60 rms. Bar and restaurant. Away from the downtown area, some rooms have good views. $21–$54 S, $24–$64 D.

Yuta Jl. Santu Joseph, ☎ 52153, fax: 63857. 14 rms. Very clean and efficient, recommended. Restaurant and, next door, the Helista travel agency. $15 S, $18.50 D; Suites $45 S or D.

Malalayang Indah 5 km south of the city on the

Transul Highway, next to the Tarsius restaurant, ☎ 65538. Cottages and rooms $15–$40.

Manado Inn Jl. 14 Pebruari, ☎ 51129. 12 rms. Dark, but well furnished, good restaurant serving grilled fish, seafood. $15 S, $18 D.

Arison Jl. Sam Ratulangi-Titiwungen, ☎ 64739, 64748. 15 rms. On a quiet side street, just off the main drag. $14–$19 S, $16–$21 D, breakfast included.

Kolongan Beach Near km 8 marker south, ☎ 51001. 14 rms. Restaurant serves seafood, and Chinese, Japanese, Indonesian and Minahasan dishes. $13.50 S, $15.50 D with fan; $17.50 S, $19 D with AC.

Manado Seaside Cottages In Melalayang, near the km 8 marker south of town, ☎ 61197. 2 cottages. These belong to a large seafood restaurant, specializing in grilled fish. $12.50 S, $15 D with breakfast.

Jepindra Jl. Sam Ratulangi 33, ☎ 64049. 11 rms, all AC. Nice lobby and eating area, drab rooms, noisy street just outside. $10.50 S, $12.50 D, breakfast included.

Angkasa Raya Jl. Soegiono 12A, ☎ 62039. 30 rms. Just outside the downtown area. Lunch $4, dinner $5. $10–$20 S or D.

Jawa Timur Jl. Kartini 5, ☎ 51970. 11 rms. Clean and quiet, satellite TV. $10–$17 S or D.

Panorama Jl. Winangun III/70, ☎ 51158. 22 rms. On the far outskirts of town, just off the road to Tomohon. Fantastic view of the bay, lousy staff. Breakfast $2, lunch/dinner $4. $10–$14 S, $11.50–$16 D.

Budget (under $10)

Mini Cakalele Jl. Korengkeng 40, ☎ 52942. 19 rms. $9–$22 S or D.

Minahasa Jl. Sam Ratulangi 199, ☎ 62059, 62559. 11 rms. Family run hotel in an old Dutch house, friendly, homely atmosphere, highly recommended. Breakfast $1.50, lunch $3, dinner $3. $9–$16.50 S, $11–$20 D.

Toutemboan Hotel Jl. Sam Ratulangi 110, ☎ 51117, 51228. 18 rms. Located on the extension of this street, (not the section near downtown). Lobby and eating area are pleasant, but rooms are dingy. Breakfast $1, Indonesian lunch/dinner, $2. $9–$15 S, $11–$18 D.

Crown, Jl. Hasanudin 28A, ☎ 66277, 66288. 20 rms above a restaurant. Close to the Singkil Bridge. Clean, but a bit noisy but. Cold beer can be ordered in advance. Good views of Manado Tua, Mahawu and Lokon. Some rooms, $3 S; the rest $5–$10 S or D. Best value are those on second and third floors for $7.50 S or D.

Pingkan Satu, Jl. TNI 42, (near Lapangan Tikala), ☎ 64411. 17 rms, all with fans and attached facilities. $7–$9 S, $8–$10 D.

Wisma Tokambene JL. Sam Ratulangi VII 12/A, ☎ 63753. 6 rms. Good location. Charming, small, well-run. Recommended. $6.50 S, $10 D.

Mitisylna Jl. Sarapung 11, ☎ 63445. 12 rms.

Basic but clean, on a street choked with non-stop traffic near downtown. $6–$8 S, $8–$10 D.

Pingkan Dua Jl. A Yani 16/1, on a side street, ☎ 63375. 10 rms. $6–$9 S or D.

Penginapan Anda Jl. Dr Sutomo 42, behind the Chinese temple, ☎ 62882. 11 rms, all with fans. Close to downtown, restaurant, laundry, help with taxis, ticketing. $6–$7.50 S or D.

Kawanua Jl. Jend. Sudirman 40, ☎ 63842, 51923; fax; 61974. 32 rms. Quiet, but close to downtown. Great value for the money, highly recommended. $4.50–$12.50 S, $7.50–$12.50 D, including breakfast.

Jakarta Jaya Jl. Hasanudin 25, across the street from the Crown, ☎ 64330. 16 rms, all with fans. Muslim run: no alcoholic drinks or men with non–wives. $2/head.

There are many restaurants in Manado, serving most of the popular Indonesian cuisines from Padang to Javanese. Particular effort should be made to enjoy at least one meal at a restaurant specializing in the hot and spicy Minahasan dishes. It is served like Padang food, wherein a large selection is brought to your table and you pay only for what you eat.

Two such restaurants, highly recommended if you can get to them are **Inspirasi** (15 minutes out of town in Tinoor), and **Kasuang Indah** (45-minutes on the road to Remboken). In town, try **Tinoor Jaya** (Jl. Sam Ratulangi near the Minahasa Hotel), or the **Selera**, rather unprepossessing, but conveniently located in the city center.

If you wish to sample, or avoid sampling, some of the more exotic local dishes, you will need to know the following words: *tikus* (field rat), *paniki* (fruitbat) and of course, *RW*, pronounced "airway," (Man's Best Friend).

Because seafood is plentiful and cheap, it is eaten daily in the home but is not usually considered worthy of being served at parties or in restaurants. However, the **Manado Seaside Cottages Restaurant** (10 minutes out of town in Malalayang) specializes in seafood that is consistently delicious, although a little expensive. **Klabat Indah** is a good second choice. Large shrimp (*udang besar*) and squid (*cumi-cumi*) are also available in many of the carp (*ikan mas*) restaurants. The nicest of these in Manado is the **New Bamboo Den**. Other carp restaurants are found outside the city, on the road to the airport and elsewhere.

Your best choices for Javanese fare are the **Surabaya** or **Kalasan**. For Chinese food try the popular **Dua Raya**, **Fiesta Ria** or the **Manado Hilltop Restaurant**, which also offers a spectacular view of the city. Padang cooking can be sampled at **Singgalang Sago**.

The following list of dining establishments

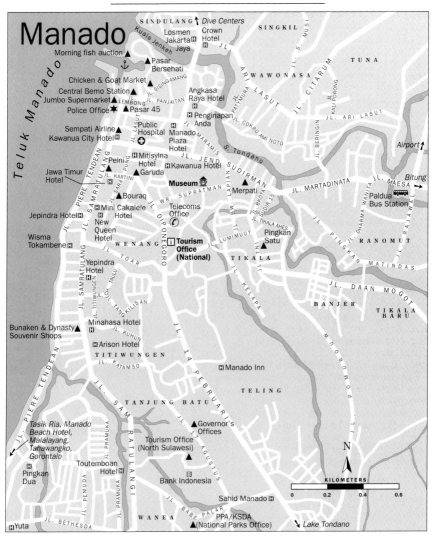

Manado

includes some of the more popular eateries, but is by no means exhaustive. Ask for advice at your hotel or *losmen* and it's unlikely that you'll be disappointed. The Manadonese love to eat.

Restaurants in Town

Cakalang Kawanua City Hotel, Jl. Sam Ratulangi 1, ☎ 52222. Indonesian, Chinese, American and European dishes. Food is good but expensive.
California Spicy Chicken One floor above Jumbo Supermarket, Jl. Let. Jend. Soeprapto No. 1, ☎ 51465, 51455. Fried chicken, burgers, chips, etc. An American-style fast-food joint in town along with Kentucky Fried Chicken at the Gelael Supermarket, Jl. Sudirman.
Dua Raya Jl. Walanda Maramis 84, ☎ 62236. Good Chinese food; nice interior. Popular with the local Chinese community. Sit upstairs on the second floor where it is quieter if a wedding reception isn't in progress.
Fiesta Ria Jl. Sam Ratulangi. Next door to Fiesta Ria Supermarket. Chinese and some European food available in a pleasant interior. Try the shrimp hotplate (*udang besi panas*). Expensive.
Jawa Timur Jl. Diponegoro No. 73, ☎ 51085. Good Javanese food. There is a branch on Jl. Sarapung, but the interior of this one is nicer.
Kalasan Jl. Sudirman 9, ☎ 63253. Javanese fried chicken. Fixed menu of flavorful chicken (Kalasan-style), good *sate*, vegetables in a spicy broth (*sayur asam*) and rice. Very good, cheap food.
Klabat Indah Jl. Sam Ratulangi 211, ☎ 62405. Serves seafood including *baronang*, *oci* (a small fish, good barbequed), *cumi-cumi* and *ikan mas*.
Manado Inn Jl. 14 Februari, ☎ 51129. Cheap and tasty Indonesian food.

Manado Hilltop Restaurant Up the hill from the Tourist Office, located on a sidestreet off Jl. 17 Agustus; watch for the large sign. Average Chinese food but the view is great.

Mentari Jl. Sam Ratulangi. Carp, squid, and prawns (*udang*) available with rice and water spinach (*kangkung*) to go with it. Interior is basic, but you can sit outside to eat. The food is good and cheap.

Minahasa Hotel Jl. Sam Ratulangi 199. Good, fresh European and Indonesian food. It's better to order in advance. Cheap.

New Bamboo Den Jl. Tumatenden 5, ☎ 52459. The best *ikan mas* restaurant in the city; basically the same menu as the Mentari.

Pondok Mutiara Bambu, Jl. Sudirman near the Gelael Supermarket. One of the very best seafood restaurants around. Dishes are well presented and delicious, but stay away from the Minahasa–style cooking unless you enjoy *very* spicy food. Reasonably priced.

Selera Minahasa Jl. Dotu Lolong Lasut on the main square—center of town, a convenient place to try Minahasan food. Cafeteria style. A popular place for business lunches. Cheap.

Singgalang Sago Jl. Sam Ratulangi 164, ☎ 52573. Cheap Padang food. You can buy good box lunches to go. Inside is spartan. Closes early.

RM Serimpih, Jl. Dr. Sutomo 25, behind the Chinese Temple. Honest Chinese cooking, cold beer. $1 for an evening meal.

Surabaya Jl. M Hatta, ☎ 52317. A large selection of Javanese dishes. Good food served in a pleasant interior.

Tinoor Jaya Jl. Sam Ratulangi. Minahasan cuisine. Clean and bright inside.

Turin Italian Restaurant and Bakery Jl. Sam Ratulangi 50, ☎ 51611. A very limited selection of Indonesian dishes, but this place does have decent ice cream. A new branch has opened opposite Fiesta Ria Supermarket.

In addition to the above, there is an endless range of small **warungs** which usually provide good value for the money. There are also many night food stalls which offer food-to-go including fried bananas, noodle dishes, *murtabak* and *malabar* (omelette-like concoctions; the former savory, the latter sweet) and fried, filled *tahu* (tofu). These can be found on the road to Kalabat Stadium or on Jl. Sudirman near the city center.

Restaurants Outside of Town

There are also a number of good restaurants within a half-hour of Manado. These might be good stops on sightseeing trips. A few in the immediate vicinity of Manado are:

Inspirasi On the road to Tomohon in Tinoor. A lovely interior, combined with a spectacular view of coconut and clove plantations, with Manado and the ocean in the background, make this place a must. Excellent, spicy food, at

reasonable prices.

Kelapa Gading On the road to Tomohon in Pineleng. A nice, spacious interior. Serves *ikan mas*. Food is good, but expensive.

Manado Seaside Cottages On the road to Tasik Ria in Malalayang. This open-air restaurant, built in the traditional Minahasan style, absolutely should not be missed. Best to go before sunset, as it is located just across the street from the ocean, and has a beautiful sea view. Before dark order coconut punch (a delicious combination of young coconut, coconut water and palm sugar) and watch a man climb a nearby palm tree to gather the ingredients. Excellent fresh seafood.

Pondok Bambu On the road to the airport in Paniki Bawah. *Ikan mas* and fried chicken served in a nice, peaceful setting.

Pongkor Just before Airmadidi in Suwaan. *Ikan mas* is available as you prefer—baked, fried or in a tangy soup. On Saturday evenings you can listen to a live *kolintang* band while you eat.

Tarsius Jl. Raya Malalayang, next door to the Malalayang Indah Hotel, on the main road south of the city at km 5, ☎ 61525. Chinese, European, Japanese dishes, all reasonably priced. French wine, $50 per bottle: not reasonably priced, but try to find it somewhere else in Manado. Open evenings only.

Tinoor Indah On the road to Tomohon in Tinoor. The menu and prices are the same as Inspirasi.

Tinoor Jaya Also on the road to Tomohon in Tinoor. Menu and prices the same as Inspirasi. Has a branch in Manado.

HEALTH

The best hospital in Manado is the **Pancaran Kasih**, Jl. Sam Ratulangi. It is a branch of the Rumah Sakit Betesda, the province's best, run by the Protestant Church in Tomohon. The **Rumah Sakit Gunung Maria**, run by the Roman Catholic Church, has similar standards. Manado's government hospital, **Rumah Sakit Umum**, Jl. Yos Sudarso, is cheap but time consuming.

Dr. Batuna, who operates the Murex dive resort (and speaks excellent English), has an office across from the Rumah Sakit Umum, open in the late afternoon and evening. (Batuna's brother is the region's top opthalmologist.) Next to Dr. Batuna is a very good English-speaking dentist, **Dr. Liman**, with modern equipment.

Drugstores are plentiful and cheap; prescriptions are not usually necessary.

TOURS

Arrange tours of the area through either a travel agency or the fancier hotels. Tours include the popular day trip through the Minahasa area ($25), the crater lake of the Mahawu volcano ($15) and the less common trip, with a 4-wheel-drive vehicle, through a section of the Tangkoko–Batuangus–Dua Saudara Nature Reserve ($45). All prices are based on a minimum of two clients.

Information

Available either from travel agencies and hotels or the following offices:

North Sulawesi Tourism Office Hard to find, on a side street just off Jl. 17 Augustus, ☎ 64299. Open Mon.–Thurs. 7 am–2 pm, Fri. to 11 am, Sat. to 12:30 pm.

Tourist Information and Booking Center At Bunaken Souvenir Shop on Jl. Sam Ratulangi 178. More conveniently located than the provincial office. Open every day except Sunday, from 8 am to 10 pm.

Nature Conservation Office (PPA, PHPA, KSDA) Jl. Babe Palar 67, ☎ 62688.

Agencies

Pandu Express Jl. Sam Ratulangi 91, ☎ 51188; fax: 61487.

Pola Pelita Jl. Sam Ratulangi 113, ☎ 52231; fax: 64520.

Manado Land and Sea Jl. Diponegoro 5, ☎ /fax: 64476.

Helista Tour and Travel Jl. Bethesda 75, ☎ 628-80, fax: 63857. Runs its own dive operation.

TRAVELERS' SERVICES

Communications

Post office (Kantor Pos.) Jl. Sam Ratulangi 23, 5 minutes walk south of Kawanua City Hotel: 8 am–8 pm, Mon.–Fri.; to 6 pm, Sat. and Sun.

Perum Tel (Telephone office.) Jl. Sam Ratulangi between the Kawanua Hotel and the post office (across the street). Open 24 hrs.

Banks and Money Changing

All of the national banks have Manado branches, most in the city center. Hours: Mon–Sat 7 am–12:30 pm, 2:30 pm–5 pm. There is very little difference between their exchange rates.

Bank Negara Indonesia (BNI) 1946, Jl. MT Haryono, ☎ 62977.

Bank Bumi Daya (BBD), Jl. Dotu Lolong Lasut, ☎ 61017.

Bank Ekspor Impor (Bank EXIM), Jl. Yos. Sudarso, ☎ 64177.

Bank Central Asia (BCA), Jl. Dotu Lolong Lasut, ☎ 52778.

Bank Dagang Negara (BDN), Jl. Dotu Lolong Lasut, ☎ 63278.

Books & Magazines

President Located in the Shopping Complex. Has several dictionaries, a few books in English, chil-dren's stories based on Indonesian myths or history, and postcards. An unattractive place.

Toko Buku Borobudur A bit further from downtown, but the best for English language materials. We saw English-, German- and French-Indonesian dictionaries, English language Indonesia travel books, and a good selection of postcards.

The Kawanua City Hotel receives *Time* magazine a bit late—it arrives earlier at the **Jumbo Supermarket**, along with the Jakarta Post, sometimes the same day. The **Fiesta Supermarket** (Jl. Sam Ratulangi 331) gets *Time* magazine once every two weeks.

Photo Supplies

There are many photo shops of all kinds throughout the city but two are highly recommended for their reliable, fast service.

P.T. Modern Photo Film Co Fuji Color Plaza, Jl. M.T. Haryono, between Jumbo Supermarket and the central square. ☎ 51556.

Angkasa Color Photo Service Jl. Yos Sudarso 20, ☎ 62467. One-day slide service.

LOCAL ACTIVITIES

There is a 9-hole **golf** course 7 km from Manado on the way to the airport. Fees are $5. Two sets of clubs are available for rental.

Tennis is quite popular in Manado and there are several courts. Those at Sario Sports Complex on Jl. Ahmad Yani in the south part of the city are modern and well-maintained.

Horse and bull races are held on major holidays at the **Maesa Race Track** east of town.

There are four **movie theaters** which often show fairly recent North American movies.

SCUBA DIVING

Scuba diving off the islands in the Bunaken group just off Manado is one of North Sulawesi's prime attractions. The water is clear and there is a profusion of underwater life. Almost all the dive sites are drop-off reefs, steep walls of coral. There is an interesting wreck nearby, although it is fairly deep. Some of the operators take clients to Bangka Island to the north, and to rich and very little explored Sangihe–Talaud archipelago (see "Murex" below, and "*Cehili*" in the Bitung section).

There is also a new dive operator just north of Bitung, taking clients to sites in the Lembeh Strait (See "Kungkungan Bay Resort" in the Bitung section below.) This area is richer in marine life than the Manado side, has been little dived, and has a pristine, just-discovered wreck. All the sites in the Strait are quite shallow, although the water clarity is not as good as at the Bunaken group, and there are no drop-offs.

Manado Area Dive Operators

There are currently three dive operators taking divers to the Bunaken group. If you come to Manado to dive—or even as a serious snorkeler—there is no reason to stay anywhere except at one of the three dive resorts.

The only exception is for casual snorkelers, who might want to sleep in one of the dozen or so simple rooms on Bunaken Island. Room and board costs $5–$7.50 per day. Small local passenger boats motor to Bunaken, usually in the early morning or late afternoon, with passage costing about $1.50. These boats leave from Kuala Jenkey, between the bridge and the mouth of the Tondano River and occasionally from the harbor area near the fish-auction market.

Each of the three established diving clubs has a slightly different atmosphere, but all can be recommended.

Barracuda Located in Molas (just beyond NDC), about 10 kilometers north of Manado. Office in Manado: Jl. Sam Ratulangi 61 (Babe Palar), ☎ 62033, 66249, Fax: 64848. European representative: Michael Smith, Geibelstr. 43, 3000 Hannover 1, Germany. ☎ (0511) 888-8836 and 647-6129, Fax: 647-6120.

Barracuda, established in 1989, offers chalet-type accommodations on a small hill, the only one of the three resorts that has a view. It has the same quiet charm as Murex; so much so, perhaps, that the place seems a bit dead when there are few guests around. They also have the only glass-bottom boat around, on-boat dive profiles, the larger craft equipped with radio. They also carry oxygen onboard during their longer trips or for the shipwreck dives. Their boats are new, and in good shape: three large dive boats, and 6 outriggered dive boats, each with a 40hp engine. They also have a glass-bottom sight-seeing and dive boat—which carries up to 28—with two 80hp engines.

Day rate—(2 dives, tanks, weights, boat, lunch)—$65, min. 2 persons. Sightseeing, $20; snorkeling, $35. Package rate, including full room and board and two dives, $80/day. Night dive, $10 extra. One dive master and three guides (no dive instructor). 56 tanks, 30 BCs ($10/day), 25 regulators ($5/day), and 8 UW lights ($2.50/day). Barracuda offers dives off Bangka Island, at no extra charge. They take you there by catamaran (2.5 hrs) and bring you back overland from Likupang (1.5 hrs.).

Accommodations: The resort has 12 double rooms, more under construction. Good seafood restaurant. $20S, $30D. Food, $2.50 for breakfast, $3.50 lunch, and $4 supper.

Murex Jl. Sudirman 28, (or P.O. Box 236), Manado 95123. ☎ 66280, Fax/phone: 52116. About 10 kilometers (25 minutes) south of Manado.

This is the smallest, quietest and most "intimate" of the resorts, with very nice landscaping featuring lotus pools. It has the best boats, and the only dive guides to use computers and safe second stages. It is also located furthest from the dive sites. Murex is run by a personal medical doctor and dive instructor, who divides his time between several occupations. Dr Hanny Batuna, the owner, pioneered diving off Bangka Island and has the only live-aboard, the *Serenade,* which runs regular cruises to the Sangihe–Talaud Islands.

Quite good, wide diving boats. The ride from here to Bunaken is a bit longer than that from the Molas-based clubs, and the boats cut through more open water (thus waves and spray). Good use of space on boats for tank and equipment storage and suiting up.

Accommodations: 14 rooms in both old-fashioned and modern cottages $20–$30 S, $27.50 D, $12/day for board.

Day rate—(2 dives, tanks, weights, boat, lunch)—$65/ head, minimum 3 in group. Package rate—double occupancy room, meals, diving—$80/person. Dives to the Lembeh Strait or Bangka Island, $20 extra, as it's a lot further from this site. 60 tanks, 6 BCs ($5–$15/day), 12 regulators ($10/day). Medical doctor and NAUI instructor Hanny Batuna offers a 40-hour dive course leading to NAUI certification ($250). Three other dive guides in addition to Hanny.

Serenade The 25-meter (5 meter in beam) *Serenade* has 4 double air-conditioned cabins, and two fan-cooled cabins with a shared bathroom. It has regular departures—about once a month—to sites in the Sangihe–Talaud group, north of Manado. The *Serenade* has a depth sounder and radar, carries 35–40 tanks, and has two Bauer compressors. She is good for 8–10 knots.

Week-long dive cruises to the Sangihe islands run $170/person a day. The boat can be chartered (8 persons) for $1,000/day.

Nusantara Diving Centre (NDC). P.O. Box 15, Molas Beach, Manado 95001. ☎ 63988 and 60638, Fax: 60368 and 63688, Telex: 74293 Sutras and 74100 BCA.

NDC is the largest and liveliest of the three dive centers near Manado. It is run by Loky Herlambang, who pioneered diving here. Young, devoted staff, some of whom have been working for NDC for 15 years. This place has the best ambiance, with night-time singing, guitar playing and xylophones during supper and afterwards. CNN available 24 hours a day in a corner of the large lobby. Very open, friendly staff. New rental equipment, BCs and regulators, plus trained personnel to service there. The only place with draft beer (cold too!). Located close to the sea, but the beach is mangrove and mud. NDC has 11 boats, 12 outboards (40hp), 25 guides, and 140 tanks.

Accommodations: 25 fan-cooled rooms in several cottages. Rooms $7.50–$35 S, $10–$40 D. Meals $10/day.

Day rate—(2 dives, tanks, weights, boat, lunch)—min. two persons, $60. Package rates— 2 dives, room, meals— run $70–$90, depending on room. 6 BCs available for rent ($7.50/ day), and 6 regulators ($7.50/day). Night dive (after two day dives) $15 extra. Snorkeling or sightseeing (land or sea) available. Dive courses $250 for those who can already snorkel,. No pool, all beginning underwater instruction takes place on a shallow reef.

Reservations recommended, especially for July and August. Major travelers' checks accepted as well as Mastercard, Visa and American Express, with at least one day's notice before checkout.

Heliste Tour and Travel Jl. Bethesda 5, ☎ 62880, Fax: 63857. This is a travel agency that began running its own dive operation in 1992. They offer prices and services similar to the three established operators, but charge higher prices for some rentals: mask/snorkel fins $10/day, BC $10/day.

SHOPPING

Minahasa has a limited range of native arts and crafts, but it is possible to buy *krawang*, the fine embroidery from Gorontolo, and carved ebony wood from the Sangihe-Talaud Islands in several Manado stores. There are a number of local specialties, especially sweets. These include candied nutmeg fruit (*pala manis*), an unusual candy made from candle nuts cooked in brown sugar (*halua kenari*), coconut cookies (*kue kelapa*) and a cookie made from sago flower baked in leaves (*bagea*). You can find these at the following shops:

Bunaken Souvenir Shop Jl. Sam Ratulangi 178. Has a good selection of souvenirs as well as a tourist information service.

Dynasty Art Shop, Jl. Sam Ratulangi 187 has a good selection of antiques. Flexible prices.

Krawang Jl. Walanda Maramis. Large selection of *krawang* goods.

U.D. Kawanua, Jl. BW Lapian 41, ☎ 66659. *Krawang*; reputed to sell the best cloth for the lowest prices. Lampshades made of shells and miniature canoes carved of ebony.

Warung Ventje I Jl. Panjaitan 65 (near the Chinese temple) ☎ 65105. This shop and Ventje II are the hot spots to buy cookies.

Warung Ventje II Jl. Sam Ratulangi 184. Larger and newer than Ventje I.

For western style baked goods, try **President Bakery**, President Shopping Center, 2nd floor. Good cakes, pastries and ice cream. Nice place for a snack with fresh fruit juice or coffee.

Clothing

The **Ramayana** and the **Makmur** department stores, both on Jl. Walanda Maramis, sell mainly clothing, very cheap and usually of good qual-

ity. Another place to stroll around, either to buy or just to enjoy the variety, is **Pasar 45**, across from Jumbo Supermarket. A maze of small shops that sell clothing and many other goods.

Tailoring in Manado is quick and inexpensive. Bring a picture or a garment to be copied and have yourself measured. Fabric is between $1.75–$3.50 per meter. There are many shops selling textiles along Jl. Dotu Lolong Lasut near the President Shopping Center. North down this street and left around the corner at Jl. Lembong 11. is **Toko Esa Genangku**, a fabric store with a large selection of good-quality material. Throughout the city there are numerous tailors and seamstresses. Some of the better ones are:

Kalvin Tailor, President Shopping Center, 3rd floor, Jl. Dotu Lolong Lasut.

Paris Menswear Tailoring, Jl. Babe Palar 7 ☎ 52183. Good quality, priced accordingly.

Aneka Darma, Jl. Walanda Maramis. Women's clothing only.

Bitung

Telephone code 0438

Bitung is set spectacularly beneath the mountains of the northern peninsula's tip, on the western shore of the Lembeh Strait. Lembeh Island to the east shelters the town's natural harbor from the full force of the weather, making it a perfect hub for the region's commercial fishing industry.

The town itself is neatly laid out with wide boulevards, and boasts a bizarre replica of the Eiffel Tower (with an anchor on top, marking the way to the port) as well as an odd pseudo–rococo church.

Bitung has five hotels (Dynasty is the best) and some good restaurants, but everything is set up for foreign fishermen (read: sailors with money to burn).

Rather than staying in town, head north about 5 km along the coast to the Kunkungan Bay Resort. The resort is a bit pricey, but the setting is splendid and the diving is excellent—for divers interested in unusual marine life, better than Bunaken. On the way, there's a tuna processing plant at Aer Tembaga, a fisheries school and wooden boat construction at Tanda Rusa.

TRANSPORTATION

The port of Bitung handles the large Pelni ships with scheduled runs to both east and west Indonesia. Smaller passenger boats to the Sangihe-Talaud Islands and to Ternate also leave from Bitung, but less frequently than those from Manado. For a trip far away from the tourist circuit, take one of the small boats to the

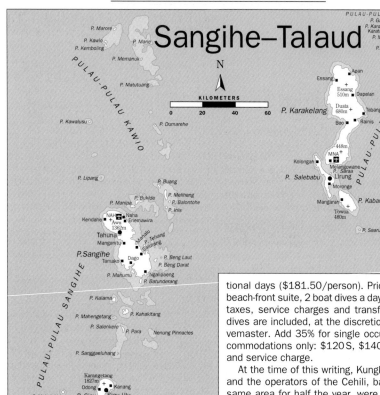

Sangihe–Talaud

Batang Dua Islands (6–7 hrs, $2) halfway to Ternate—tell us what you find there.

For ship schedules (Indonesian only), call the harbormaster: ☎ 21617, 31342.

DIVING/ACCOMMODATIONS

Kungkungan Bay Resort On a bay of the same name in the village of Tanduk Rusa, about 5 kilometers north of Bitung. Mailing address: P.O. Box 16, Bitung, Sulawesi Utara, Indonesia. ☎ (438) 30300; Fax: (438) 31400. Make reservations through the U.S. office: Staples Ecenbarger, Inc., P.O. Box 5577, Concord, CA 94524. ☎ (510) 825-1939; Fax: (510) 825-0105.

This quiet, beautifully designed resort sits on the site of an old coconut plantation, facing a small bay north of Bitung, in the protected waters of the Lembeh Strait. The suites are spacious, all face the water, and have comfortable porches. A large lobby/restaurant, built out over the water, is the center of activities. The operation, just beginning, has one dive boat, several dozen tanks and a new Bauer compressor. Note: This resort does not offer rental equipment.

Packages: 7 nights/6 days ($1,210/person); 3 nights/4 days ($484/person); additional days ($181.50/person). Prices include beach-front suite, 2 boat dives a day, all meals, taxes, service charges and transfers. Beach dives are included, at the discretion of the divemaster. Add 35% for single occupancy. Accommodations only: $120 S, $140 D plus tax and service charge.

At the time of this writing, Kungkungan Bay and the operators of the Cehili, based in the same area for half the year, were working on packages that combine trips on the live-aboard with stays at Kungkungan. Contact the Cehili or Kungkungan Bay if you are interested.

THE CEHILI

The live-aboard Cehili, owned by a Norwegian outfit, is stationed half the year in Bitung, when it runs north to the Sangihe and Talaud Islands, and south to the Banggai Islands. The other half of the year it is stationed in Ambon.

MV Cehili SeaRoads Group A/S, Ovre Tverrstredet 1, 4890 Grimstad, Norway. Tel: 47 (370) 44611; Fax: 47 (370) 44915. As we went to press with this edition, the live-aboard Cehili had just come back from a refurbishment in Singapore, with a new operator/marketing agent. Divemaster Larry Smith and the crew are the same.

The vessel has been redesigned slightly, and now limits its number of passengers to 20. There are 5 deluxe cabins, and 5 suites. The length of the boat is 45 meters, and the beam 9 meters. Gross tonnage is 377.

The standard 7 nights/8 days package costs from $1,960 (per person in shared 4-pax cabin) to $2,538 a head for the largest suite.

A variety of rental gear is available, and there is an onboard shop with both general and non-diving essentials, including batteries. Other extras are alcoholic beverages and soft drinks, laundry, E-6 processing ($10 roll) and international telephone calls ($18/minute). No extra charge

for water-skiing or sea kayaking.
Agent in Manado:
Tarsius Cruises ☎ 62 (431) 61764; Fax: 55716.
Contact: Billy Matindas.

Sangihe-Talaud

These two island groups stretch north of Sulawesi up to the Philippines. They are quite isolated, and few tourists make the journey, although dedicated scuba divers are exploring the waters here on the *Cehili* and the *Serenade*. (See above.) If you need an English–speaking guide, arrange for one to accompany you from Manado.

TRANSPORTATION

By Air Merpati flies from Manado four times weekly to Naha on Sangihe Besar Island in the Sangihe group ($47), and twice weekly to Melanguane on Karakelang Island in the Talaud group ($63, via Naha). Note: These flights are canceled regularly.
By Boat Regular boats run from Manado, one a day or more, to the major ports of the Sangihe Talaud archipelago. They're often crowded, especially during school holidays. The sea is roughest in November and December but just before and after this period could also be unpleasant. One way fares: Siau ($5), Tahuna ($8), Beo and Lirung ($11).
Local boat charter Depending on distance, size of boat and engine. From Mahoro to Siau, boat big enough for a half dozen, $40/day.

ACCOMMODATIONS

SIAU
Home Stay Mohede (2 rms). $5; $10 w/meals.
Penginapan Serui (4 rms). $3; $7.50 w/meals.

TAHUNA
The are around half a dozen *losmen* here. The higher priced and better **Nasional** and **Victoria Tangaroa** cost $10–$20. The **John Merry**, the **White House** and the **Anugerah**, $3–$5.

Minahasa

Area Code is 0436
The Minahasa region south of Manado, including the cool and salubrious highlands around Tomohon and Lake Tondano, the area around Kotamobagu, and the coastal area around Inobonto and Lolak, provides relaxing retreats from Manado. (See maps pgs. 180–181, 193.)

ACCOMMODATIONS

TOMOHON
Gardenia Home Stay Kakaskasen II, ☎ 51333, 51282; fax: 51363. 5 rms. Homestay in name only: facilities and price of star–ranked hotel. Recommended. Beautiful place, nice views. Restaurant features fresh carp from their own ponds and Korean dishes. Tours to see local crafts and farms. $40 S, $50 D, breakfast and laundry included.
Lokon Resting Resort Just off the main road from Manado, about 5 km before Tomohon, ☎ 51203. 8 rms. Great view of the Lokon Volcano. Meals available. $17.50–$22 per room.
Indraloka Just before Tomohon, at Desa Kimilow on the main road. 12 rms. Run down, but still functioning. $10–$12.50.

TONDANO
Alam Raya Near the Ranuposo hot springs. 5 rms. $10–$17.
New Astra 20 rms. $10–$15.
Ranuposu 3 km from Tondano, amid rice fields and hot water springs. 12 cottages. The inexpensive restaurant serves Indonesian-Chinese dishes. Large heated swimming pool. Two bicycles free for guests, motorcycles $7.50/day. Crowded with locals on weekends, deserted weekdays. English-speaking owner. $8–$22.
Tamaska Hijau Near Tondano. 6 rms. $8–$12.50.
Nusantara 7 rms. $3–$5.
Wengkol Indah 5 rms. $3–$5.

REMBOKEN
Sumaruendo 7 cottages. Large park–on–lake complex. Several restaurants. Boats for hire for up to 20 passengers, around $8/hour. Fishing possible. $17–$30.

SONDER
Toar–Lumimuut Tourist Resort 8 rms. Swimming pool and large park. $14–$20 with breakfast.

KWANGKOAN
Pinanglimbalian 5 rms. $3–$7.

KOTAMOBAGU
New Plaza Jl. Suprapto. 30 rms. $13–$20.
Kota Mas Jaya Jl. Suprapto. 15 rms Considered the best in town. $5–$20.
Ramayana Jl. Adampe Dolot. 12 rms. $4–$7.
Tentram Jl. Adampe Dolot. 12 rms. $4–$7.
Sarinah Jl. Suprapto. 6 rms. $3–$5.
Widuri Jl. Adampe Dolot. 6 rms. $3–$5.

INOBONTO
Tepi Laut and **Totambuan**. 8 rms each. $1.50–$3.

LOLAK
Mololosing Beach Motel and Cottages. 18 rms and cottages, on the mainland and on Mololosing Island, a 30-min boat trip. $12–$30.

North 5

Gorontalo

Telephone code is 0435
Gorontalo, a port city on the south coast of Sulawesi's northern peninsula, is the access point for Lake Limboto, and the Togian Islands.

TRANSPORTATION

BY AIR
Gorontalo's airport is 30 km from town, $1.75 in a collective taxi.
Bouraq Jl. A Yani, ☎ 21070. Daily flights to Manado ($36); three times weekly to Palu ($36).
Merpati Jl. 23 Januari 19 (at the Hotel Wisata), ☎ 21736. Daily flights to Manado ($36).

BY SEA
Pelni's passenger ship *Awu* stops in Gorontalo twice a month, once heading toward Bitung, once on the return, heading towards Luwuk. About $7 in economy class to both places.
At least three times a week, 100-ton wooden ships make the 3-day run between Gorontalo and Poso, calling at the Togian Islands, Pagimana and Ampana on the way. Passage (mattress provided) $10. A berth in a crewmember's cabin, subject to supply and your bargaining ability, $20. Crowded during school holidays.

BY LAND
Buses arrive and leave from the Terminal Luar Kota, about 4 km from the main *bemo* terminal (15¢ to get from one to the other). Buses to Manado (night only, 10 hrs; $6.50, $9 w/AC). To Kotamobagu (7–8 hrs; $4, $5.50 w/AC). To Palu (24 hrs until the road improves, $12.50, no AC).

ACCOMMODATIONS

Krawang City Jl. Basuki Rahmat, ☎ 22437. 18 rms. New hotel, away from downtown. Double beds, hot water, fridge, phone, satellite reception, restaurant. $20–$35/room, all with AC.
Indah Ria, Jl. A Yani 29, ☎ 21296. 14 rms. Basic but comfortable. Price includes all meals. Good value. $10 w/shared facilities, $11 w/attached facilities, $14 w/AC.
Mini Saronde Jl. Walanda Maramis 17, ☎ 21735; fax: 22677. 34 rms. Best hotel in town and centrally located. Restaurant on premises. Range of prices. All rooms with attached facilities. $6 S, $9 D fan-cooled; $10 S, $14 D w/AC; $27 S or D with the works: hot water, bathtub, fridge, color TV with satellite reception.
Wisata Jl. 23 Januari 19, ☎ 21736 (this is also the Merpati office). 14 rms. The cheaper rooms have shared facilities. $4.50–$8 S; $7–$15 D; $12.50–$16 S, $18–$25 D meals included.
Melati Jl. Gajah Mada 33, ☎ 21853. 7 rooms in an old colonial house. Excellent value for budget travelers. Large verandah, and next door to

a good, inexpensive restaurant and well-stocked store. The owner, Pak Alex, speaks Dutch and English and can provide all kinds of information. Bring your own mosquito coils, earplugs and fans. $3.25/head.

DINING

For good, inexpensive Chinese meals, try **Agung Baru** (Jl. 23 Januari) or **Milado**, also downtown. **Brantas**, opposite the central mosque, is good but a bit pricey. For the best *sate kambing*, **Dirgahayu** (Jl. Lombongo). For local food, try the **Pasar Jajan** market stalls, open only at night.

National Parks

GUNUNG AMBANG

The KSDA/PPA headquarters for this park is about 20 km east of Kotamobagu, on a good road near Mooat village, overlooking a highland lake of the same name. You can overnight at the park headquarters. Entrance to the park is from Mongkudai Baru, about 1.5 km away.

DUMOGA BONE

Take the express bus from either Manado or Gorontalo to Kotamobagu, then local transportation to park headquarters, near Doloduo, 50 km away. It's possible to stay at Toraut for about $5 per person per day.

TANGKOKO-BATUANGUS

Permits are available from the KSDA/PPA office in Manado (25¢) or at the park ($1.25, same permit). To reach the park, go to Manado's Paal Dua *bemo* terminal, then take the minibus towards Bitung, but get off before, at Girian (50¢). Several crowded jeeps a day leave Girian to Batu Putih (75¢; 23 km, partially paved).
There's a friendly *losmen*, known as either Mama Ros or Tangkoko, just outside the park headquarters, across a hanging bridge over a small river. $11–$12 for a double room and meals for two. Prices negotiable. The in-park guest houses charge $5/person, but they are very basic. Two more *losmen* are being built just outside the park to handle the summer crowds.
You must hire a guide to visit the park ($5–$6/day). They are invaluable for directions and spotting animals, and will even carry your pack, but you should tip for this.
—*Sheridan Angerilli, Kal Muller and Mary Thorne*

6 Southeast PRACTICALITIES

INCLUDES KENDARI, KOLAKA, BUTON AND MUNA

The main attraction of Southeast Sulawesi is its grand scenery, and the fact that it is so remote. Very few tourists visit, and you should expect to be the center of attention. This is "Hello Mister!" country, but people are friendly and helpful. A smile and a "Hello Mister" in return work wonders, as do a few words of Indonesian. The provincial capital and main entry point to the region is Kendari.

Prices in US dollars. S = Single; D = Double; T = Triple; AC = Air-conditioning.
Telephone code for Kendari is 401. (0401 within Indonesia.)

Kendari

It is impossible to get lost in Kendari. The town is a single main road 8 kilometers long (its name changes several times along the way. The hotels, restaurants and offices are on this road. Money-changing is difficult here, bring rupiah.

TRANSPORTATION

BY AIR

Kendari's airport is 35 km southwest of town. Merpati runs a taxi service ($2.50). You can also hop on one of the crowded minibuses at the airport ($2, 30 min to anywhere in town).
Merpati Jl. Konggoasa 29, ☎ 21729. Daily morning flights and four afternoon flights a week from Ujung Pandang ($45). The morning flight, by Fokker F28, begins in Palu.

BY SEA

A passenger ship, makes the following run twice a month: Surabaya—Ujung Pandang—Kendari— Kolonodale—Poso—Gorontolo—Bitung—Tahuna. Check at any of these ports.

LOCAL TRANSPORTATION

Bemos run constantly along the main road from Wawotobi to the shipping offices at the mouth of the bay (Rp150, any distance). Minibuses, or *mikrolet*, zip all over town (Rp200 to anywhere). There are four bus stations: (1) Sentral Kota, for in-town minibuses; (2) Powatu, for minibuses to Kolaka; (3) Madonga, to waterfalls and villages near Kendari and (4) Wawa, to Tampo (2 hrs), the ferry terminal opposite Muna Island.

ACCOMMODATIONS

Kendari Beach Hotel Jl. Sultan Hasanuddin 44, ☎ 21988. The only really good hotel in town, with the town's only good restaurant. On a hill a few minutes from the town center, of-

fering a sweeping view of the bay. At the rear is a landscaped garden and tennis court. $30–$80 S, $35–$85 D.
Arnis Hotel Jl. Diponegoro 75. Second-best hotel in town. (Note: Do not confuse this with the old Armins at Jl. Diponegoro 55, with small, dim, hot rooms.) Some rooms w/AC. $8–$12 S, $10–$15 D.
Sultra Hotel Jl. Sultan Hasanuddin 94. Nothing special. $8–$20.
Resik Hotel Jl.Sultan Hasanuddin 90. $8–$20.
Wisma Dua Jl. Drs. Abdullah Silondae (just off the main road). Set on a hill with a view.
Wisma Nirmala Jl. Ir. Sukarno 115. A rambling wooden building up on a small hill close to the Merpati offices. Family owned, and worth a try for budget travelers. Inexpensive.

DINING

Eating in Kendari is more a challenge than a pleasure. Only the **Kendari Beach Hotel** can be positively recommended. Its restaurant serves a wide range of Chinese seafood for around $3 a dish, plus ice-cold beer and fresh lime juice. At the back of the menu are cheaper, but tasty, Indonesian dishes: *nasi cap cai* (rice with vegetables and meat) and *nasi udang* (rice with shrimp) for just $1.50. The kitchen is spotless.

The dingy, dimly-lit **Restaurant Hilman** and the marginally more inspiring **Restaurant Royal**, opposite the old Arnis Hotel, offer little competition, although the food at **RM Pekalongan** on Jl. Sultan Hasanuddin is said to be tasty. At night, the food stalls outside the cinema serve *bakso*, *mie* and other cheap dishes.

TOURS AND SIGHTSEEING

To see the wild and lovely scenery around Kendari it is best to hire a car or minibus. Check with the BPU (listed below).

The month before Ramadan, the Muslim

month of fasting, is the usual time for marriages, which you may observe if you are decently dressed. Bring a small gift.

Muslim circumcisions (*sunat*) are frequent occurrences. These are festive occasions to which many guests may be invited, depending on the family's resources.

Badan Pekerjaan Umum (BPU) (Department of Public Works) Jl. Konggoasa 48, ☎ 21019. The public works department functions as a sort of travel agent, and is delighted to show visitors around the area. The BPU (pronounced Bay-Pay-Ooo) has its own boats and vehicles and its rates are reasonable (minibus: $25/day). Basic diving equipment and water skis are available, and the BPU has a glass-bottomed boat.

Kantor Parawisata Diparda (Tourism Office) On the hill just behind the harbor, ☎ 21764. The head of this office, Pak Abdul Galib, speaks some English. His home phone is ☎ 21421.

PT Alam Jaya Jl. Kongoasa 50, ☎ 21729, 21019; telex: 71447. The owner, Pak Suroso, and some of his staff, speak English. 5–7 day all-inclusive tours of Kendari and vicinity, Raha and Baubau, about $270 per person for 2, slightly less for larger groups.

HANDICRAFTS

Handicraft Exhibition Center Jl. Abdullah Silonda (across from the BPU). Run by the Association of Government Wives, this is good place to buy silver jewelry, carved ironwood and other items.

Pusat Kerajinan Jl. A Yani, about 5 min from the center of town, towards the airport. The government-run craft center is worth a visit. There are usually a half dozen men making jewelry or carving, while the women dye and weave *ikat*. A shop sells silver jewelry, scale model sailing ships (fine quality, $75–$800), woven cloths ($20), and beautiful (but heavy) teak tables ($50–$500). Hours: 8 am–1:30 pm, except Sun.

Kolaka

Telephone code 0405
Kolaka is on the other side of the peninsula from Kendari, facing the Gulf of Bone. There are more than a dozen *losmen*, but as yet no hotel. Few visitors stay here. The main attraction is the hot springs 15 km north of town. Kolaka is small enough to walk around by foot.

A well-paved road connects Kolaka to Kendari, and you can catch a minibus to Kolaka (4hrs, $2) at Kendari's Powatu bus terminal. Also, Merpati flies to Pomalaa ($55), north of Kolaka, twice a week from Ujung Pandang. Numerous paved roads connect Kolaka with the north and south of the peninsula. The ferry across the Gulf to Bajowe (near Watampone) leaves 9 pm nightly.

The best places to stay are the **Losmen Rahmat** (Jl. Kadue 6, 10 rms w/attached bath, $4/person) and the **Losmen Alkaosar** (Jl. Jendral Sudirman 20, $3–$5/room).

Cheaper *wisma* include the spacious and clean **Losmen Aloha** (Jl. Kewanangan 19, $3.50 per person); **Losmen Pelita** (Jl. Repelita 56, $3/room); **Losmen Family** (Jl. Jendral Sudirman 6, $3/room); and **Wisma Mustika** ($3/room). Ten minutes from town in the countryside is **Losmen Monalisa** (9 rms w/bathroom, $4/person).

There are few good eating places in Kolaka. The **RM Santana** (Jl. Kadue 17) and the **Cita Rasa** (Jl. Repelita) are okay. There are several more places alongside the bus terminal, the appearances of which do not inspire confidence. There are a **pharmacy** and **doctor** on Jl. Rahma Farma: doctor's hours are 4 pm–7 pm.

Buton Island

Telephone code for Baubau 0402
Baubau, on Buton Island, is an attractive little town stretching along the foot of steep hills. The commercial district is around the river mouth; to the north are pleasant suburbs with old, Dutch-style bungalows and leafy gardens. The Post Office is to the right of the harbor entrance. Further into town there is a bank some well-stocked shops, some even selling film.

TRANSPORTATION

By Air

Merpati flies to Baubau twice a week from Ujung Pandang ($82). See "Ujung Pandang Practicalities," above, for more information.

By Sea

Baubau is on the route of Pelni's *Rinjani,* which stops in Ujung Pandang and all the way west to Jakarta. First-class ticket, on the Baubau to Ujung Pandang leg, sharing a private cabin with AC and shower, TV and meals, costs just $30 (versus $82 for the Merpati flight). The Rinjani sails once a month—any Pelni office may have the schedule. (See "Sea Travel" pg. 237.) Book in Ujung Pandang or in Baubau (the agent in Kendari deals only with freight and has little useful information). The Pelni office is up the hill a bit—the local kids will lead you there for a fee.

KENDARI-MUNA-BUTON FERRY

From Kendari, the only way to get to Muna and Buton is on the ferry. (Note: purchase your return ticket as soon as you disembark in Raha or Baubau—the ticket offices get crowded around departure times.)

While some of the trip takes place at night, there is enough scenery in the daytime to make the trip memorable. The best views are in the late afternoon leaving Kendari. You pass several idyllic islands on the left, and you will get a close-up view of Pulau Hari. On the right, steep vegetation-clad mountains tumble directly into the sea, with an occasional sliver of deserted white sand beach. You will pass the odd sailing craft, as well as Campada, a Bajau village located on an island of the same name. Night falls much too soon for the rest of the ride.

During the east monsoon, from June through August, the seas can get quite rough between Kendari and Raha, before reaching the shelter provided by Buton Island.

On the way back about 45 minutes out of Baubau, naked kids in canoes line the ferry's passage, begging for coins to be thrown into the water. Their eager expressions and shouts will force you to part with any spare change. A bit further, more canoes wait in "ambush."

We recommend one of the ferries with the two-passenger VIP cabins, where you can safely lock away your gear while wandering around the ferry, or even for a half-day looking around Baubau before the ship returns to Raha.

FERRY SCHEDULE

Departs		Arrives	
Kendari	(2 pm)	Raha	(9 pm)
Raha	(10 pm)	Baubau	(5 am)
Baubau	(1 pm)	Raha	(5 pm)
Raha	(11 pm)	Kendari	(5 am)

Local Transportation

Baubau is small enough to walk around. When you get in at the harbor entrance, take a *becak* to the Pasar Sentral minibus terminal. There you can catch a *bemo* to anywhere in the city for around Rp150. For example, to get to the old fort (called the *kraton*), catch a *bemo* going up the hill, or wait for the *mikrolet* marked "Kraton," although this will usually be crowded. You can charter a *bemo* for a half-day for $2.50–$4, depending on your Indonesian.

ACCOMMODATIONS AND FOOD

Lodgings in Baubau are neither good nor cheap. The **Losmen Debora** (Jl. Kartini) has dingy, box-like rooms for $6–$10; $25 w/AC. Across the street, the older but more spacious **Losmen Liliyana** has rooms for $6–$10, plus a lounge and TV. **Losmen Pelangi** down at the waterfront has rooms for $1.50. There are several small restaurants; if you are there during *puasa* (the fasting month) many will be closed. The small, unnamed restaurant on the corner of Jl. Mohd. Husni Thamrin and Jl. Jos Sudarso serves decent, if overpriced Chinese-Indonesian food.

Muna Island

Telephone code for Raha 0403

Muna is a little-visited and still rather traditional island. Most famous here are the stallion fights ($140 to organize one), and there are also traditional dances ($100, with full costumes). Ask if there are *sunats* or weddings on.

There is excellent swimming and snorkeling on an island called Pasi Kuta ("Squid Reef" in Bajau) off southwest Muna. Another island, Tapitapi, offers probably the best snorkeling anywhere in the vicinity. Bajau/Bugis villages on stilts are located at Pulau Bangko and Pulau Renda islands, along with Lakarama village.

TRANSPORTATION

You can get to Raha on the ferry from Kendari (see "Kendari-Raha-Baubau Ferry" under Baubau section above). You can also take the bis Artur from Kendari to Raha—2 hours by bus to the village of Torobuku; 2 hours by ferry to Tampo, Muna; 1 hour by bus to Raha. $3.25 for the trip (buy 2 seats, as things get mighty crowded). Not much to see, the ferry ride is much better.

If you arrive on the ferry, eager hands will carry your luggage about 50 meters to waiting *becaks*. The peddlers know all the hotels (Rp200). Public minibuses charge 20¢–$2, depending on distance. They leave when fully crowded. The Andalas Hotel has an AC minibus for charter, $30/day.

FOOD/ACCOMMODATIONS

There are 8 hotels/*losmen* on Muna Island, all in Raha. The **Andalas Hotel** ($8S, $14D) is the best—you even get toilet paper with the attached, sit-down toilets. Three others are more or less suitable: the **Rauda**, the **Alia** and the **Uham** ($7 S, $12 D). The **Berlian**, **Wuna**, **Tani**, and **Karmia** ($3S, $6D) have shared facilities.

The hotels provide a light breakfast, and other meals can be ordered ($1.75). The Andalas Hotel provides western style meals ($3). There are 3 restaurants: the **Pacific**, the **Hawaii** and the **Nikmat**, all serving Chinese and Indonesian dishes, $1.50–$2.50/meal, plus drinks.

GUIDES

Have your hotel contact Pak Siddo Thamin ($20 a half-day, $30 full day). His English is quite good and he knows heaps about Muna's history and culture. You can also get a guide through the *bupati*'s office (cheaper but not as good as Pak Siddo). Contact Pak Suarnadi there. Indonesian-speaking guides, who also carry gear, will take you to the cave paintings ($3–$4).

—*Ian Caldwell and Kal Muller*

Further Readings

Andaya, Leonard Y. *The Heritage of Arung Palakka: A History of South Sulawesi (Celebes) in the Seventeenth Century*. Martinus Nijhoff, The Hague, 1981. Dull but solidly researched study of the 17th-century Bugis warlord who allied himself with Admiral Speelman to overthrow the kingdom of Gowa.

Blok, R. *History of the Island of Celebes*. Calcutta, 1817. Written in Dutch in 1759, Blok's history is a valuable source on 15th- and 16th-century South Sulawesi.

Errington, Shelly. *Meaning and Power in a Southeast Asian Realm*. Princeton University Press, 1989. A rather speculative reconstruction of state and society in pre-colonial Luwu.

Gervaise, Nicolas. *An Historical Description of the Kingdom of Makasar*. London, 1701. Recently republished in facsimile, this is an absorbing and entertaining account of the customs and manners of 17th-century Makasar.

Holt, Claire. *Dance quest in Celebes*. Paris; Archives Internationales de la Danse, 1939. Standard work on the subject, recently reprinted.

Horridge, Adrian G. *The Konjo Boat Builders and the Bugis prahus of South Sulawesi*. London, National Maritime Museum, 1979. Detailed, well-illustrated account of the construction and launching of a Konjo *prahu*, describing the various types of Bugis *prahus*. A simpler and very readable account of Bugis ships is found in the same author's book *The Prahu: Traditional Sailing Boat of Indonesia*. Singapore, OUP, 1985.

Kaudern, Walter. *Megalithic Finds in Central Celebes*. Göteborg, Elanders Boktryckeri Aktiebolag, 1938. The standard work in English on the megalithic culture of Central Sulawesi by a Swiss scientist who visited the region in 1918-19. Illustrated with drawings, maps and photographs.

Macknight, C.C. *The Voyage to Marege*. Melbourne, Melbourne University Press, 1976. An informative, readable account of the Makassar traders who sailed to the north coast of Australia to collect *trepang* (sea cucumber) for the Chinese market—bringing with them smallpox.

Millar, Susan B. *Bugis Weddings; Rituals of Social Location in Modern Indonesia*. Berkeley, Center for South and Southeast Asian Studies, University of California, 1989. The best study of the Bugis yet published.

Mundy, R. *Narrative of Events in Borneo and Celebes Down to the Occupation of Labuan. From the Journals of James Brooke, Esq. Rajah of Sarawak*. London, 1848. Before becoming Raja of Sarawak, Brooke visited South Sulawesi.

Nooy-Palm, C.H.M. *The Sa'dan Toraja; A Study of Their Social Life and Religion*. 2 vols., Dordrecht, Foris Publications, 1979, 1986. The standard work on the subject in English.

Robinson, Kathryn M. *Stepchildren of Progress: The Political Economy of Development in an Indonesian Mining Town*. Albany, State University of New York Press, 1986. On the impact of PT Inco's nickel mine on the village of Soroako, Luwu.

Stavorinus, Jan Splinter. *Voyages to the East. Indies* 2 vols., London; 1798, facsimile reprint 1969.

Volkman, Toby Alice. *Feasts of Honor; Ritual and Change in the Toraja Highlands*. Urbana; University of Illinois Press, 1985. Based on the author's Ph.D. thesis, with the intriguing title: *The Pig Has Eaten the Vegetables*. A good introduction to modern Torajan society.

Wallace, Alfred Russel. *The Malay Archipelago*. London, 1869; reprint New York 1962. A 19th-century classic; one of the greatest books written on Indonesia.

Waterson, Roxana. *The Living House: An Anthropology of Architecture in Southeast Asia*. Singapore, OUP, 1990. A fascinating and beautifully illustrated study with many examples from Tana Toraja.

Westerling, Raymond 'Turk'. *Challenge to Terror*. London, Kimber, 1952. The notorious Captain Westerling's account of his suppression of 'terrorists' during the Indonesian revolution.

Whitten, Anthony J., Muslimin Mustafa, and Gregory S. Henderson. *The Ecology of Sulawesi*. Penerbit Periplus c/o C.V Java Books, 1988. (P.O. Box 55 JKCP, Jakarta 10510, Indonesia). A thorough, clearly written study of the flora and fauna of Sulawesi. Copiously illustrated.

Wilcox, Harry. *White Stranger: Six Moons in Celebes*. London, Collins, 1949. Toraja before the tourists: "Like millions of others I wanted to escape for a while from the postwar world and the twentieth century; unlike those others, I did escape." Recently reprinted in paperback by OUP, Singapore.

About the Authors

Greg Acciaioli is a Lecturer at the University of Western Australia. He has spent over three years in Indonesia, and has written on ritual change in Central Sulawesi, stressing the effect of national culture on indigenous ceremonies. **Kathleen M. Adams** is an Assistant Professor of Anthropology at Beloit College in Wisconsin and a Research Associate in Asian Ethnology at the Logan Museum of Anthropology. She spent two years in Sulawesi conducting research on ethnic and artistic change in Tana Toraja.
Sheridan Angerilli spent two years exploring Manado and the surrounding area. She now lives in Jakarta.
Lorraine Aragon is a doctoral candidate in anthropology at the University of Illinois. Her dissertation concerns cosmology and social change in Christian regions of highland Central Sulawesi. She is currently working at the Smithsonian Museum of Natural History.
Tim Babcock is an anthropologist and author of the book *Religion and Culture in Kampung Jawa Tondano*. He has worked on regional development projects in Sulawesi, and has also worked in Malaysia, Sumatra and Peru. He lives in Jakarta and is a faculty member of the School of Rural Planning, University of Guelph, Canada.
Peter Bellwood is a Reader in Prehistory at the Australian National University, specializing in Southeast Asian and Pacific prehistory. His books include *Man's Conquest of the Pacific*, *Prehistory of the Indo-Malaysian Archipelago* and *The Polynesians*.
Dinah Bergink, a cultural anthropologist (Free University of Amsterdam), is a researcher at the Faculty of Social Science, University of Leiden, and works for Pelita Foundation, an organization supporting Dutch Indies victims of World War II.
Ian Caldwell was educated in London at the School of Oriental and African Studies, and holds a Ph.D. from Australian National University. He lectures at Singapore National University.
Nancy Caldwell was born in India and grew up in Singapore. She has traveled widely in Asia and Europe and worked as a freelance writer and editor. She has a degree in modern and primitive Indonesian art.
René W.R.J. Dekker is an ornithologist who worked for a year and a half in the Dumoga-Bone National Park in North Sulawesi, on the conservation of the maleo, Sulawesi's endemic megapode. He is currently employed as a biologist,

specializing in megapode biology and conservation at the Institute of Taxonomic Zoology of the University of Amsterdam.
Horst Liebner conducted research among the Ara boatbuilders and sailors of South Sulawesi from 1987 to 1989. As part of his research he and a crew from Ara circumnavigated Sulawesi on a two-masted, five-sailed *prahu*.
Kal Muller is a veteran photographer whose travels have taken him to over 80 countries. For the last 20 years he has explored, photographed and reported on the Indonesian archipelago. He has a Ph.D. in French literature, and has authored several travel guides on some of Indonesia's more remote areas.
Anthony Reid is professor of Southeast Asian history at the Australian National University in Canberra, and has published numerous articles on the history of South Sulawesi. His most recent book: *Southeast Asia in the Age of Commerce, 1450–1680: The Lands Below the Winds.*
Mary Thorne worked in Manado in 1988–90 as a senior planner in the provincial government, and has toured North Sulawesi extensively. She now works in Glasgow, Scotland.
Roger Tol is a lecturer at the State University of Leiden, where he received a doctorate for his work on Bugis-language texts. He works in Jakarta at the National Language Center for the Indonesian Linguistics Development Project.
Toby Alice Volkman, an anthropologist, is the author of *Feasts of Honor: Ritual and Change in the Toraja Highlands*, as well as several articles on Toraja cultural identity, social and religious change, and tourism. She works at the Social Science Research Council in New York.
Roxana Waterson studied anthropology at Cambridge University, and wrote her thesis on the Sa'dan Toraja people. She is the author of *The Living House: An Anthropology of Architecture in South-East Asia*, and presently lectures in anthropology at the Department of Sociology, National University of Singapore.
Tony Whitten is an ecologist who has lived in Indonesia for nearly nine years, working with the State Ministry for Population and Environment. He is the author of *The Ecology of Sulawesi* in English and Indonesian language editions.
Charles Zerner, a lawyer and environmental consultant, studied fishing and conceptions of the marine environment in Mandar in 1989. He has also studied tourism in Tana Toraja, and published numerous articles on Torajan culture.

Index

Bold numerals indicate a chapter or section on the subject. Numerals in Italic indicate an illustration.

adat/hadat 44, 114, 120, 160
Aer Tembaga 181
agama 120
Ageng, Sultan 84
agriculture 38
airline companies 236–237
Airmadidi 196
airport tax 233
Alauddin, Sultan 68
Alfalah mosque 192
Alor Island 68
aluk to dolo 63, 111, 114, **120**, 126, 131, 135
Ambuea, Kaledup I. 213
Ammusu 211
Ampana 171, *175*
—practicalities 265–266
anak Makassar cannon 88
Anca village 162
anemones 157
Anggrek Hitam (black orchid) 192
aniline dyes 54
animism 46
anoa (dwarf buffalo) 20, 21, 24, 159, 175, 199, 200–202, 256
Antarctica 16
antiseptics 225
Ara 92, 94
arabica coffee 57, 112
arajang (regalia) 86f
Arabs 184
archaeological deposits 24
architecture 50–51
Ari Impohi statue *166*
arts and crafts **54–55**, 154–5
Aru Islands 52
Aru Palakka 32, 33, 81, 101
arung 87
Arung Sengkang La Ma'dukelleng, Wajo 33

asphalt 38
Austronesians 25, 26–27, 44
Awal-ul-Islam, Sultan 82
ayam kampung 251
babirusa ("pig deer") 21, 23, 159, 172, 175, 200, 215
Bacukiki 87
Bada *152*, 153, 165
—practicalities 258
Bada megaliths 26, 28, **163–166**, 269
Bada Valley *27*, *45*, *148–149*, 159, 162, **163–166**, 167
—practicalities 262
Bagea 57, 275
bado tree 67
Bagea 57, 203
Bahasa Indonesia 42, 48, 68, 214
bajasa 154, 160
Bajau ("Sea Gypsies") 15, 45, 46, 52, 66, 101–102, 171, 174, 184, 209–210
—lingua franca 172
bajé 131
Bajoe 102
Bakiriang egg hatchery 173
Balangnipa 94
Balaniparang, waterfall 79
Balepe 140
Bali 44, 50, 155
Balinese 44, 68, 153
balolang 72
Balusu 87
Bamba Puang 131
bamboo 54, 55, 77
Ban Hian Kiong, Temple 186
bananas 154
Bancea, orchid reserve 170, 262
Banda 68
bandeng 56
Bangange 87
Banggai
Banggai archipelago 171, 174
—practicalities 267

Banggai, raja of 171
Bangka Island 189, 273
Bangkala 91, 92
banks 222
Bantaeng 32, 34, 35, 84, 92, 101
Banten 32, 80
Bantimurung, waterfall 22, 76, 77, *78*
Banua 116
banua sura 145, 145, 146, 147
Barang Caddi 75
Barang Lompo 75
Bare'e 167
bark cloth **152–153**
Barombong 32, 90
baronang 56
Barracuda Diving Center 274
basa bissu 87
Batak 68
Batam 233
Batara Guru 106
Batara Guru Museum 105
Bate 120
Batu Bangga 158
Batudaka *173*, 172
Batui 173
Batuputih 196
Batu Tumonga 140
Bau 140
Baubau 35, 212, *213*
—practicalities 280
Baulu 264
becak 72, 80, 238, 243, 249, 251
belau 257
bemo 80, 140, 142, 198, 241, 243, 249, 250, 252, 259, 260
bendi 191, 265
Bengkulu 52
Benteng 99
Benteng Panyu (turtle) 70
Besoa Valley 153, 159, 162, 164
—megaliths 258

Map Index

Bada Valley Megaliths 264
Eastern Peninsula 171
Historical Sites 81
Indonesia 218
Key map 8
Language groups 43
Lore Lindu National Park 161
Luwu 105
Manado 271

Merpati Routes 234–235
Minahasa 193
North Sulawesi 180–181
Old Gowa 80
Palu Area 156
Palu City 154
Parepare 86
Pelni Routes 236–237
Poso and Tentena 169

Rantepao 133
Sangihe-Talaud 276
Selayar Island 99
South Coast 91
Southeast Sulawesi 208
Sulawesi 2–3
Sulawesi Formation 16
Tana Toraja 141
Ujung Pandang 69

Betel nuts 68
Bewa *166*, 265
Binamu dynasty 92
Bintan 233
Bir Bintang (Heineken) 244, 255
Bira 34, 53, 84, 90, 93
—practicalities 249
birds 20, 21–22, 77, 159, 196,
  199, *200*, 200, 203
Biromaru 159
Bissapu, Waterfall 93
bissu 86, 104, 160
Bittuang 140, 142
Bitung 196
—Diving 276
—practicalities 275
boat building 96
boat ritual 90
boat trip 204, 237, 269
—Kendari-Muna-Buton 280
—Kolonodale-Kendari 266
—Togian Islands 266
Bolaang Mongondow 190, 194,
  210, 217
Bolo 227
Bone 17, 29, 32–36, 45, 46, 76,
  86, 87, 90, **100**, 101, 112,
  118, 209
—practicalities 249
Bone Tambung Island 75
Boneage 156, 157
Bonebone 104, 106
Bonerate 68
Bontobangun 98, 99
Bontoramba 92
Bora 159
Bori 139
Borneo 17, 20, 46, 156
Borobudur 50
botinu 107
Bouraq 80, 237, 242, 258, 268
"Brave People" 210
breadfruit 152, 211
Bronze Age 26–27
Brooke, James 34, 52, 93,
  101–102
buah lontara 91
bubur Manado 56
Buddha 76
Buddhists 44
buffalo 20, 56, 74, 111, 119,
  121, 138, 165, 166, 196, 209
buffalo coffin *146*, 147
Bugis 14, 33, 42, *42*, 48, 61, 63,
  68, 93, 103, 104, 112, 130,
  156, 158, 184, 209
—architecture 50, 159
—immigrants 173
—kingdoms 100
—*prahu* 52
—warriors 167
Bugis-Makassar script 28
Bukaka 100
Bukit Inspirasi 191
Bulu Saraung 100
Bulukumba 88, 90, 93, 101
—practicalities 248
Bunaken Island **196**, 216
—sea gardens 196-198
Bunaken Marine Reserve 187

Bungaro caves and springs 82
Bungaya, Treaty of 32, 68, 88,
  94
Bungku 163, 167
Bungsu, Khatib 94
Buntao, TT 137, 138, 140
Buntukalando, TT 138
Buntulengke 138
Buntupune 136
burial chamber (*waruga*) 185,
  192
burial jar (*kalamba*) 27, 163
Buton Island 18, 32, 38, 209
—palace 212
—practicalities 280
Buton, Raja of 213
butterflies 77
Butung *see* Buton
cacao 39, 61, 165, 209
caballo 183
cabe 56
cactus 19, 151
cakalang fufu 56
cakalele 185, 191
Cakke 131
camat 162
Camba 100
cambay cloth 52
Cambodia 52
Campada village 281
Campalagian language 42
Candien, nutmeg fruit 181
cannon (Wolio) *213*
canoe 260
canoers *206–207*
Cap Go Mei 186
caping 55
carp 56, 168
cashews 209, 215
cassava 38, 61, 111
Catholicism 44, 45, 111, 184
cave paintings 25, 76, 77, 214
caves 22, 74, 76, 77, 94, 168,
  195, 214; *see also* Gua
—Latea 168
—Leang-Leang 77
—Pamona 168
celadon stoneware 246
Celebes macaque *22*
cement factory 38
cengkeh 180
Central Indonesiian Time 222
Cerekang 104, 106
ceremonies 61, 88, 153, 160,
  195
chick, Maleo 203
children 8, *185*
Chinese 15, 44, 46, 52, 66, 98,
  165, 173, 184, 186, 210
—pottery 27
—temples 68, 72, 186
Christianity 44–45, 87, 112, 114,
  165, 171, 184, 186
Church of Central Sulawesi 167
church spires 45
churches 68, 186
Cikuang 91
Cilalang 88
Cina, prehistoric kingdom 28
circumcision 63, 280

cisterns, Besoa Valley 163
class structure 62
climate of Sulawesi 19, 221
clitoridectomy 63
clothing 152, 221
clothing, ceremonial 153
—traditional 152
clove cultivation 158
clove fever 38, 180, 181
clove oil 181
clove plantations 168, 205
clove trees 158, 179
cloves 38, 61, 158, 165, 168,
  171, 179, 180, 182, 194
cocoa 194
coconut 38, 61, 94, 150, 154,
  172, 173
—factory 192
—oil 88, 154, 180
—palm 151, 158, 160
coffee 34, 38, 165, 168, 180
coffin, Toraja 124
colonial government 112
colonial period 34, 154, 155
Conrad, Joseph 66
copper 38, 181
copra 37, 52, 156–158, 171,
  180
coral 17, 22, 74, 75, 157, 172,
  188, 211, 213
—reef 17, 173, *179*, 186
coto Mankasara 56
cotton 98
crab 22, 172, 188
crayfish 188
crocodile 22, 172, 190
cumi cumi 270, 271
cumi cumi mentega 82
currency 222
cuscus *20*, 21, 172
Da'a 158
dabu-dabu 56
dance 183, 185, 191, 255
dangke (buffalo milk cheese) 56
Danowudu 196
Darul Islam 37, 71, 104
Dato Karama 155
Dato Tiro, Khatib Bungsu's grave
  94
Datu ri Bandang 99
Dayak 158
deata 122
Demak 82
Deri 138, 140
dero dance 155
diarrhea 225
Diemen, Anthony van 213
Diponegoro, Prince 71, 73
diver *188*
diving 75,157, **186**, 273
dodol 191
dog 56, 191
—meat ("RW") 56, 186, 270
dokar 250, 259, 260
dolphins 172, 188
Dolo 160
Dolong 172
dokar 259, 260
Dong Son drum 50, 98, 99, 164
—Selayar *25*, 26, *98*

Donggala 34, 35, 45, **156**, *157*
—practicalities 260
Drake, Sir Francis 174
Dula Boe 166
Dumoga Valley 180, 184
Dumoga-Bone National Park 198, 199, 201
durian 57, 191
Dutch **32**, 36, 100, 101, 104, 112, 114, 156–158, 160, 183
Dutch East India Company (VOC) 32, 34, 71, 183, 212, 213
Dutch Reformed Church 45, 112, 120, 151, 162, 167, 184
Dutch rule 153
Dutch-Buginese military power 66
dynamite fishing 74
ear-piercing 63
east of Palopo
—practicalities 251
Easter Island 48
Eastern peninsula **171**
ebony 158, 168, 185, 209, 275
economy 38–39
—Central Sulawesi 151
—Southeast Sulawesi 209
education 112–113
eels, giant 168
effigies, Toraja (see tau tau)
eggs 102, 174, *203*
Eiffel Tower replica 196
embroidery, (*krawang*) 185, 275
erosion 180
"erotic mountain" 131
eskrim goreng 57
ethnic rivalry 63
ethnology museum 87
etiquette 223
eucalyptus 16
Europeans in Sulawesi 84–85
Expats 245
Export 38
farming *38*, 179, 180
fault lines 17
fauna **20**, 76, 203
ferry, Kendari-Muna-Buton 280
festival 216
filigree 54, 210, 246
fish of Sulawesi 22
fishing 179, 181
flora and fauna 20–23
flowers 191
flying fish 88, 90
forestry 38
forests 151 *see also* rainforests
Fort Amsterdam 33, 182, 183
Fort Otanaha 198
Fort Rotterdam 33, 66, 68–71, 98, 101
fossils 20
frigate bird 172, 196
fruit 57, 224
fumaroles 179
funeral ceremonies *8*, *42*, *111*, 121
funeral chant *121*
funeral debts 125
funeral ritual 121, 122–125, 135
funeral shrouds 54
Galesong 90

gas, natural 18
geography of Sulawesi 16–19
Gima (Bima on Sumbawa) 28
Gimpu 159, 162
Gintu 162, 163, 166
glass-bottomed boat 280
gold 18, 38, 165–166, 181
Gondwanaland 16, 17
Gorontalo 34–36, 42, 44, 45, 158, 167, 179, 180–182, 184, **197–198**
—practicalities 278
Golf courses 107, 157, 273, 210
Government resthouse 103, 138
Gowa 29, 32, 34, 35, 45, 66, 67, 80, 84, 101, 112, 118
—palace 81, 85, 247
Gowa Purbakala Ara 94
grave carvings 164
grave of Collipujie *101*
graves *82*, 83, 89, 137, 140
—cliffside 107, 124, 126, 131, 132, 136
—hanging 136, 137, 140
—royal 80, 81, 82, 93
graveyard, Ondongan 88, 89
Gulf of Tolo 174
Gulf of Tomini 167, 172
gravestones 131, 132
Gua Bappajeng 94
Gua Karampuang 94
Gua Mampu 102
Guan Di 72
Guan Yin 72
Guangdong 72
guava 57, 211
guides 256, 257, 262, 266, 281
Gujerati 66
Gumbasa River 160
Gunung Api Siau 18, 205
Gunung Balease 106
Gunung Bawa Karaeng 78, 79
Gunung Colo 173
Gunung Kambuno 106
Gunung Klabat 179
—climbing 195
Gunung Lokon *18*, 179, *190*
—climbing 191
Gunung Lompobatang 18, 94
Gunung Momi 160
Gunung Nokilalaki 159
Gunung Soputan 18, 179
Gunung Tangkoko 196
Gunung Tokosa 159
hadat 162
haji 156
Haji Akbar 92
Haji Hamzah 87
hand stencils 25, 27
handicraft 54
harbors 72, 249, *157*, 186, 196
Harmonie, De (Dutch society) 74
Hasanuddin, Sultan 32
Hasanuddin University 67, 76
headhunting 167
health 224
health care 180, 183
Heutsz, Governor General Van 34
hierarchy 61, 114
Hinduism 98, 122

historical sites 80–85
—practicalities 247
historical writings 49
history 24, 28, 32, 36
—North Sulawesi 182
—South Sulawesi 66, 67, 80–83, 85, 100, 102, 103
—Toraja 112–113
—Ujung Pandang 68, 70, 77
Homo erectus 24
hornbill 21
horse meat 91
horseback trek 162
horsefighting *214*, 215, 217
hospitality 57
hot springs 160, 179, 194, 195, 280
house of origin 138–139
houses, stilt 159, 172
I La Galigo 106
I La Padoma 49
Ice Ages 17, 24
ikan bakar 244, 250, 254
ikan bandeng 82
ikan barongan 82
ikan mas 56, 272
ikat cloth 54, 68, 118, 146, 155, 280
Imam Bonjol, mausoleum 191
immigrant groups 184
Inco, P.T. 18, 38, *39*, 106
Independence 35–36, 103
Indian influence 26
Indian textiles 156
Indic ritual 88
Inobonto 277
insurance, travel 227
intestinal troubles 225
Iron Age 26–27
Islam 29, 44–45, 88, 98, 112, 155, 171
Islamic rebels 113
Jakarta 37, 52
Jalan kate 57
Jalan Penghibur 66
Jalan Sudirman 67
Japanese 36, 38, 54, 70, 73, 78, 153, 113, 174, 183, 192
Java 36, 44, 48, 50, 52
—War 192
Javanese 44, 73, 162
awa Rilau 28
Jawa Ritengga 28
jeeps 263
jellyfish 22
Jeneponto 90, 91, 93
Jeneponto Lama 92
jeruk nipis 245
jeruk panas 57
jeruk siompu 57
Jumbo Roller Disco 246
Jumpandang Fort 68
Jusuf, Andi Mohammad 37
Jusuf, Edi 173
Kabaena Island 209, 210
Kabere 130
kabupaten
—Bone 94, 100
—Bulukumba 93
—Luwu 104

—Mandar 88
—Polmas 89
—Sidrap 105
—Sopeng 102
—Wajo 103
Kageroa 162
Kahumamoan 42
Kai 68
Kaidipan 44
Kakaskasan village 191
kalamba 265
kalambu 164
Kale Gowa 80, 82
Kaledupa Island 212, 213
Kaili people 42, 45, 154, 156, 158, 159, 173
kain 251
kain Donggala 155, 156, 259
kain kipris 255
Kajang 90, 94, 95
Kalimantan 33, 52, 158
Kalingsusu Island 212
Kalukubula 159
Kambira 140
Kampung Belanda 66
Kampung Jawa 192
Kampung Kaluku Badoa 83
Kampung Lere 155
Kampung Melayu 66
Kampung Wajo 67
kangkong 245
Kantewu 164
Kantor Parawisata Diparda 280
Kapopasang 75
Karaeng Bayo 81, 82
Karaeng Bontolangkasa 32, 68
Karaeng Getah 92
Karaeng Loe 86
Karaeng Matoaya, Tallo Prince 29, 44, 82, 83
Karaeng Pattingalloang 81
Karakelang 204
karaoke 246, 255
Karasik village 129
Karumenga 185
Kasuang 194
Katangka Mosque 81
Katrili 183
Katulungan 106
Kaudern, Walter 164
Kawangkoan 195
Kayamanya 168
Kayangan Island 75
Ke'te Kesu' 136, 137
kebon Kopi 158
kemeri (candle nuts) 250
Kendari 46, 209, 210, 211
—practicalities 279
—silver 246
Kendari-Muna-Buton Ferry 280
Kentewu 162
kerajinan kuningan 213
keris 82, 118
Kesu' district 117
Ketupat 172
Khalwatiah 76, 80
Khatib Tunggal Datu ri Bandang 83
kick-fighting 123
Kilo Lima beach 174

Kingdom of Buton 212
kingdoms 28, 29, 182
KNIL 36
Kolaka 104, 209, 210–211
—practicalities 280
kolami 107
kolintang orchestra 185, 191
Kolonodale 174, 175
—practicalities 266
Kompleks Makam Kuno 100
Konaweha 210
Konjo horseman 46
Kotamobagu 37, 180, 277
Kotu 131
kramat (miracle-working) site 83
kraton (fort, Buton) 281
kraton (Wolio) 213
krawang 185, 275
kretek cigarettes 38, 181
Krishna 76
Kruyt, Dr. Albert C., Dutch missionary 163, 167
Kudingarang Keke 75
Kudingareng Lompo 75
kue (type of cake) 57
Kulawi 34, 153, 159–162
Kunkungan Bay Resort 189, 275
Kumbuti River 211
Kyai Modjo mausoleum 192
La Darapung, legendary prince 94
La Galigo epic 106
La Galigo Museum 71
La Padoma, Tragedy of 49
La Pawawoi 34, 35
La Sinrang 34
Laboratory, Le Petit Soleil 162
ladang cultivation 182
lagoons 206–207, 216, 217
Lahendong 194
lakes of Sulawesi 19, 22
—Limboto 197
—Lindu 22, 159, 162
—Mahalona 22
—Matana 18, 22, 106, 107
—Poso 106, 168, 170, 261
—Tempe 17, 18, 19, 29, 100, 102, 103, 250
—Tondano 24, 32, 179, 181, 192, 196
—Towuti 19, 22, 107
—Wawontoa 22
Laki Padada, mythical ancestor 82, 118
Lakiung 81
Lalang 209, 211
lambo 72
lambo cutter 52
Lamuru 100
Langkai 75
Langke Bulawa 166
Langko 162
Langoon 182
Langsat 191
language 25, 42, 48, 68, 182, 192, 231–232
language groups 68
language, ritual 122, 124
Lanjukang 75
Lapita culture 26
Lariang 19, 163

Latea Creek (Kuala Latea) 168
Laterite soils 111
Latugo 215, 217
Lauje 42, 158
Laurasia 16
Lawada village TT 130
Le Petit Soleil research laboratory 162
Leang Buidane cave 26
Leang Jarie 77
Leang Karrasa 77
Leang Saripa 77
leather 52
leather work 68
leeches 164, 211
leg room 203
Lembeh 189, 212
Lemo 127, 134, 136
lepa lepa 72
Lepangun 100
leprosy 94
leper colony 132
Lere 155
Lesser Sunda Islands 20
Liang Kobori 216
Liang Lasabo 215
Liang Toko 216, 216
Likupang 187
Limboto Lake 197
Limbung 91
limestone 22, 24, 38, 76, 86, 100, 131
Limung cina 57
Lindu 162
—Lake 22, 159
—Plain 159, 162
Lingga Archipelago 46
literature of Sulawesi 28, 48–49
L'ko'mata 140
Lolak 277
Loli Indah recreation park 157
Lombok 20
Lompobatang, Mt. 93, 94
Londa 134, 135, 136
Long Xian Gong temple 72
lontara palm 57, 91
loom, backstrap 54
Loosdrecht, A.A. van de 120
Lore Lindu National Park 27, 49, 159–162
Luaor 88, 89
Lumimuut 182
Luwu 34, 101, 104–107, 112
—side trips 42
Luwu, Kingdom of 28, 46, 49, 55, 87, 102, 118
Luwuk 36, 173–174
—practicalities 248
ma' badang 121
Ma'kale 112
Macao 152
macaque 21, 22, 159, 172, 196
mace 181
Madagascar 48
maengket dancing 185, 191
MAF (Missionary Aviation Fellowship) 166, 258, 261, 263
magau 159
magic plow 87
Mahalona Lake 22

Mahdi Akbar uprising 98
Mahoro Island 205
maize 38, 91, 209
Majapahit 99, 212
Majene 35, 88, 89
—practicalities 248
Makale 131, 132, 140
Makassar (see also Ujung Pandang) 15, 17, 28, **32–35**, 42, 48, 61, 62, 66–67, 80, 84, 88, 98, 101, 112, 154, 184, 209, 212
Makki 106
Makula 138
Malacca 32, 52
Malakaji hill station 92
malam jum'at 45
malaria 225
Malay 34, 48
Malay bellows 55
Malay market (Makassar) *67*
Malei River 164
maleo bird 22, 174, 196, 199, **203**, *203*
Makailu Island 267
Malili 55, 104, 106, 251
Malimbong 140
Malimongan 140
Malino **78**, 79, 90, 94
Malino Conference 79
Maluccas 32, 98, 185
mammals 20–21, 172
Mamasa Toraja 42, *144*, **145–147**
Mampu caves 249
Mamuju 89, 157
Manado 19, 32, 33, 36, 37, 44, 158, 179, 182, 183, 184, **186–189**, 191
—Bay *187*, 191
—diving 274
—Malay 48, 183
—practicalities 268
—region **190**
Manado-Bitung region 181
Manado Tua Island 187, 188
Mandar 33, 54, 61, **88**
—practicalities 248
Mandarese 42, 48, 61, 62
Mandarese boatbuilder *89*
manggis 57
mango 57
mangrove swamps 158
Manila 152
manioc 57
manufacturing 38, 39
manuscript 42
mapalili ceremony 88
Mappanyuki, Andi 35, 101
marambak 185
Marante 138
Marawola 160
Marinding 140
marine reserve 187, 188
Marisa area 184
market 130, 132, 155
markisa (passion fruit) 57
maro ritual 47, 122
Maros 24, *27*, 34, 62, 67, 76
Maros points 24

marriage 63
Masamba 106
Masks 68
Massenrempulu language 48
Mata Allo 130
Matana 107
Matana lake 19, 22, *107*
Matthes Foundation 71
Maudu Lompoa 92
Maulud 92
Mausoleum of Imam Bonjol 191
Mawai 144, 257
Mawang Lake 79
Mebali village 111
me'datu 121
Megalithic Finds in Central Celebes 164
megalths 27, 102, *148–149*, 155, 162, **163**, 269
—practicalities 263–265
menhirs 89, 136, 137, 269
Menkongga Mt. 209
Meramo waterfall 210
Merpati 236, 242, 252, 258, 260, 268, 277, 278, 279, 280
Mesjid Agung 213
Mesjid Kuno Batupassi 105
Metalallong 99
metalwork 55, 137
metalworking village La'bo' 137
mica 152
microliths 24
Micronesia 50
migrants 157, 158, 184
migration 113, 114
mikrolet 241, 269
milu 57
Minahasa 18, 32–35, 42, 51, 179–181, 182, 183, 184, 185, 275, **190**
Minangkabau 44, 50, 68, 94
minerals 18, 38
Ming porcelain *15*, 28
minibus 241, 249, 250, 257
mining 38, 106, 181
missionaries 35, 45, 112, 114, 120, 162
Miu River 160
Moa 162
Moluccas 182
Moluccan Spice Islands 84
Mongondow 184
monkey, the 164
Moramo, waterfall *211*
Mori 42, 171
Morowali Nature Reserve 174, 261
—trekking 266, 267
Mowewe 211
mosquito coils 226
mother-of-pearl 209
mountain climbing
—Gunung Klabat 195–196
—Gunung Lokon 191
—Gunung Bawa Karaeng 79
mountains, *see* Gunung
Mt. Awu 18, 204
Mt. Klabat 195–196
Mt. Lokon *19*, 191
Mt. Lompobatang 93, 94

Mt. Rantemario 18
Muddaria, Princess Andi Bau 103
Muna Island 209, **214**, *206–207*
—practicalities 281
Murex Diving Centre 188, 274
Museum 136, 155, 192
—Batara Guru 251
—Jakarta 26
—of Central Sulawesi 259
—of North Sulawesi 186
music 191
Muslim women at mosque *47*
Mutiara (sunken ship) 157
Muzakkar, Kahar **36**
MV Cehili *205*, 276
myth 182
Nabokov, Vladimir 77
Nagarakertagama 98
megalths 27
Nain 188
Nanggala 138, 140
nangka 57
Napabale *206–207*, 216, 217
Napu Valley 159, 162, 263
National Geographic 122
National Parks
—Dumoga-Bone 278
—Gunung Abang 278
—Lore Lindu **159**, 262
—Tangkoko-Batuangus 278
nationalism 36
natural gas 172
nature reserves 174, 186, 196
Navarette, Domingo 152, 153
navel of the house 50
Netherlands Indian Army (KNIL) 36
"Northern neck" *157*
Nusantara Diving Center 274
nutmeg 38, 181, 204
Oba *165*
Odongan 89
Ompo springs and pool 102
oplet 269
opo-opo gods 185
opudi 107
orang Manado 184
orchid 73, 192
Orchid Reserve, Bancea 170, 262
Osena River 211
Pabaisenan 136
Pabrik Kertas Gowa 78
Pada 166
Padada, Laki 112
paddy field 154, 264
Padtbrugge, Robert 33
Pagimanan 173
Paguyaman 184
palace of the ruler of Bone *101*
Palakka, Aru 32, 33, 81, 93, 100, 101
Palatokke village 137
Palawa' 139
Pali 140
Palindo *148–149*, 164, 165, *165*
Palipu 140
Pallengu 92
pallumura 56
palm leaf map 85
palm wine (tuak) 57, 135
palmyra (lontar) fruit 57

Palolo valley 159
Palopo 28, 35, 36, *104*, 130, 132, 165
—practicalities 251
Palu 154–155, 156, 158, 159
—practicalities 258
Palu Valley 19, 151, 152, 154, 162
Pambusuang 89
Pamona 167, 171, 173
Pana 140
Panada 57
Pandang Lae-Lae 75
Pandere 153
Pangala 112
Pangkajene 34, 86
Pangleon 140
Pangli 138
pantun 216
Paotere 52, 66, 72
Papalohia 99
papaya 57
paper factory 39
Parepare 35, 44, 86, **87**, 130
—practicalities 248
Parigi 158
Parinding 139
Pasangtau 257
Pasar 154, 156, 168, 186
Pasar Bersehati 186
Pasarwajo 213
peak season 134, 221
pearls 173, 174
Peleng Island 174
Pelni 259, 269
Pendolo 167, 170
—practicalities 262
Pentecostal Church 162
peoples of Sulawesi 42–47
Permesta Proclamation 37
Permesta uprising 157
Perumtel 273
pesantren 130
peti mayat 168
petroleum 18
phalangers 16
Philippines 27, 32, 158, 182–183
Phillips, Roy 70
photography 230
Pineleng 191
Pinrang 251
Pintu Dua 66
piong 254
Pipikoro 153
Pipikoro region 162
pisang lilin 57
pisang tanduh 57
Pires, Tomé 52
plant varieties 152
Pong Maramba 136
Pong Massangka 138
Pong Tiku 34, 112
population 42–47, 61, 62, 151, 184, 209
PPA/KSDA office 162, 278
Portuguese 32, 66, 158, 183
Poso 35, 45, 51, 132, 153, **167–170**
—practicalities 260
Poso Lake 19, 22, 106, 168,

170, 261
prahu pinisi 53, 72, *73*, 92, 93
prehistory of Sulawesi **24–27**
prices 222
Protestant Church 34, 163, 184
Protestantism 34, 45, 111, 114, 164, 183, 184
P.T. Inco's nickel smelting plant, Soroako *39 see also* Inco
Pulau Hari 211, 281
Pulau Mas 200
Pulau Popaya 200
Pulau Sembilan 94
Pulau Tikus 267
Puncak Lakawan 131
Pura Giri Natha 76
Pusat Kerajinan 280
python 22, 172
Raffles, Stamford 70
rafting 256
Raha (Muna Island) 214–217
—practicalities 281
rain 180, 209
rainy season 221
rainforest 131, 168, 174, 196, *199*
Raksasa Sepe 263
rambutan 57
Ranorano 162
rante 124, 135
Rantelobe 140
Rantemario 17
Rantepao 131, 132
—practicalities 252
Rantetayo 252
Rappang village 130
rat 191
Raterate 211
rattan 38, 209
Ratulangi, Dr. Sam 36, 194, 195
rebellion, anti-government 37
regalia 82, 86, *183*, 249
religion 87, 92, 98, 111–112, 114, **120–125**, 151, 184
Remboken 194
Riau Archipelago 46
rica-rica 56
rice 38, 114, 122, 130, 136, 138, 139, 151, 158, 160, 163, *164*, 168, 179, 209
Riedel, Johan 34
ritual 46, 47
—clothing 153
—field 134, 137,139
rivers of Sulawesi 19
rupiah 222
RW (dog meat) 56, 186, 270
Sabbang 106
sacred ancestor stone 185
sacrifice, animal 121, 123, 165, 185, 216
sacrifice, human 263
Sa'dan River 130
Sa'dan Sangkombong 139, 255
Sa'dan To'barana 139, 255
Sa'dan Toraja 42, 47, 51
Sadang 131
sago 160, 171
Salabose 89
salak 57

Salayar *see* Selayar
Saluan group 173
Salubarani 131
Salumpaga 158
Saluputti 117
Salvation Army 45, 51, 151, 162
Samalona 74
sampan 260
Sandalwood 52
Sander, Lijst van 73
Sangalla 112, 132, 137, 140
Sangihe 33, 45, 184, 186, **204**
—practicalities 277
Sangihe Besar 204
Sangihe Talaud Islands 179, 183, 185, **204–205**
Sarasin, Paul and Fritz 24, 35, 164
sarcophagi *195*
Saroako 38, 106, 107, 132
Sawangan village 192
Sawerigading, Bugis hero 101
Sawitto (Pinrang) 34
schistosomiasis 162
schooner *52*
Schwartz, Johannes 34
scuba diving 158, 247, 260, 273
seafarers *62*
Segeri 86
Selayar Island 93, 98–99
—practicalities 249
Seventh Day Adventists 162
sharks 75
ship building 52–53, 72, **88–89**
Siau Island 186, 204, 277
Sigi rajadom 159
silk 54, 102, 155, 251
—cloth, *kain Donggala* 154, 156
—weaving 73, 103
silkworms 131
silversmithing 210, 246, 280
Singkang 102–103
—practicalities 250
Sinjai 94
slavery 124
Smithsonian Institute 135
snorkeling 74, 75, 157, 158, 168, 174, 189, 274–275, 281
Social Hierarchy 62
Sombaopu 83–85, 247
Sonder 194, 277
Soppeng 28, 102–103, 250
Soroako nickel plant 106
soursop 57
South Lindu 162
soybeans 38, 182
Spanish influence 182
Speelman, Admiral 32, 68, 84–85
statues, stone 159
stone tools 24, 25
Suaya, Tana Toraja 138
Suharto, President 37
Sukarno, President 37
Sulawesi Sea 27
Sungguminasa palace 81, 83, *83*
Suppa kingdom 87
table manners 57
taboos 103, 153
Tahuna 186, 204, 277
Taijo group 42, 158

Taipa village 170
Takalar 90
Takalar Lama 91
Talaud 33, 45
Talise 186
talisman 153
Tallo 29, 66, 80, 82, 83, 247
Talude 205
Tallumpoco 100
Tamalate 81
Taman Anggrek 192
Taman Purbakala Kompleks Makam Kuno Jena Lomoe 102
Taman Purbakala Leang-Leang 77
Tambusisi Mountain 175
Tamlea 106
Tampangallo 140
Tana Beru 92, **96–97**
—practicalities 249
Tana Toraja *8*, 15, 35, 45, 51, 55, **111–147**
—death feast 40, 41
—Dutch in 112–113
—funerals 47, 114, 120, 123, 124
—history 112–114
—houses of origin (*tongkonan*) 116–119
—practicalities 252
—society 114
—traditional customs 113
—weaving 55
Tanawangko 190
Tanete 63
Tangka River 94
Tangkoko-Batuangus Reserve 21, *199*, 199, 200, 278
Tanimbar 68
Tanjung Api 172, 265, 266
Tanjung Karang 156–157, *157*
Tarai Roi 164
Taranate 28
Taratara 190, 191
taro 158
tarsier 21, 159, 172, 196, 200
Tasik Ria 190, *191*
Tasmania 213
tau tau figures *125*, **126–127**, 135–139
Tawaeli 158
teak 38, 209
Tembamba 138
Temboan 194
Tempe Lake 19, 29, 100, *103*, 103
Tengganan 155
Tentena 150, **167–170**
—practicalities 281
Ternate 32, 33, 98, 182
Ternate, sultanate 171, 182–183
Ternatean language 182
textiles 54–55
Thailand 98
Tian Hou Gong temple 72
Tikala 140
Tiku, Pong 112
tikus 270
Tilanga 135
Timbaan 143, 144, 257
time 222

Tinanbung 89
Tinombo 158
Tinoor 191
tinutuan 56
Tiro 94
Tirta Ria 92
Tiworo 212
to laki 210
To Maki 51
to ri aja 112
To'duri 140
To'lamba 140
Toala 106
Toale people 24
Toar 182
Toar-Lumimuut myth 182
Toar-Lumimuut resort 195, 277
tobacco 102
Toba Batak 50
Tobaku 153
Toboli 158
Tobone 140
Togian Islands 17, 172, *173*
—practicalities 266
Toi Torengke, Kulawi leader 160
Tokala 174
tolak bala 216
Tolaki 42, 209, 210
Tolitoli 34, 36, 45, 157
Tolo, Gulf of 174
Tomado 162
Tomanurung 29
tomb 158
Tomekongga 209
Tomini 17, 158
Tomohon 179, 190, 191, *194*, 277
Tomori Bay 174
Tomoronene 209, 210
Tonasa II Cement Factory 86
Tondanese 194
Tondano Lake 24, 32, 179, 181, 192, 194, 196, 277
Tongkabu 180
tongkonan **116–119**, *131*, 132, 138, 139, 140, 252
tooth filing 63
tour and travel agents 230
tourist season 221
Towale village 156
"tractor of Asia" 166
Trans-Sulawesi Highway 167, *167*, 238
transmigration 44, 104, 106, 158, 162, 180, 184, 209, 211
transportation 39, 233
transvestite priests 86, 154, 160
"tree grave" 137
trekking 134–139, **140**, 162, 256, 262, 265
trepang (sea cucumber) 46, 52, 67, 172
tropical fruit 57
trumpet fish 188
Trunojoyo 32
tuak 55, 57, 91, *135*, 246, 255
Tuanta Salamaka 80
Tuare 162
Tuban, Java 99
Tukang Besi Islands 17, 209, 212

Tulang Didi 119
turtle, sea 22
Tuwa 160
ubi-ubi 211
ula', plant dye 152
Ujung Pandang 24, *32*, 42, 52, 54, 56, 67, **68**, *71*, 72, 74–79
—(old) **66**
—practicalities 242–247
—vicinity 68–73
Ujung Pandang, bronze flask 26
Ujunglamuru 100
Ulu Leang 24, 77
Unauna 173
United Coconut Tina Indonesia 192
United Nations 36
Ussu 28, 106
Uwae, warm springs 94
Valentyn, François 154
vanilla 181
vats, stone 159
vegetables *159*
volcanoes 18, 173, 178, 179, 188, 204, 205
Wajo 33, 46, 49, 87, 100
Wakaakaa 212
Wakai 172, 173
Walanae River 101, 103
Walanae Valley 24, 28, 250
Wallace, Alfred Russel 20, 77, 179, 196, 200
Wallace Line **20–22**, 77, 199
Wallasea 24
Wana 42, 47, 174
Wani 157, 158
waringin leaves 166
warm springs 160, 179, 194–195
Wartabone, Nani 36
waruga 27, 192
Watampone (see Bone)
water-skiing 211, 280
waterfalls 18, 77, 78, 79
—Bantimurung 76
—Hangahanga 174
—Moramo 210, 211
Watansoppeng (see Soppeng)
Watu Pinabetengan (sacred ancestor stone) 182, 185, 194
weaving 54, 139, 152, 213, 25
Westerling, Raymond "Turk" 36, 37
wet rice cultivation 29, 154
wildlife 20
winds 19
Wolio 213
—kingdom 212
—language 210
woodcarving 167
World War II 67, 70, 106, 113, 153, 174, 195
woven material 54, 139, 152, 213, 251
Xian Mu 72
Xuan Tian Shang Di 72
xylophones, wooden 185
yoni-linggam 213
Yusuf, Syech 80